AF836079

The Development of the Chinese Legal System

In recent years, the Chinese legal system has undergone many reforms, and this book brings the literature up-to-date, offering a contemporary account of the law and administration in China.

This book is the result of collective efforts in analysing the political, economic and social factors that affect the development of Chinese law. The volume contains contributions from a number of experts and scholars of Chinese law who examine some of its most important areas. The book covers constitutional law, criminal law, property law, mortgage law, intellectual property law, corporate law, securities regulation, banking regulation, civil procedural law, arbitration law, environmental law and the regulation of telecommunications services.

Whilst the book addresses a number of diverse legal areas, all the contributions look to explain the factors that led to the development of the law and the consequences of such developments, as well as the progress made by developing legal institutions and the possible obstacles to future development.

Guanghua Yu is an Associate Professor in the Faculty of Law, University of Hong Kong.

The Development of the Chinese Legal System

Change and challenges

Edited By
Guanghua Yu
BA, JD, LLM, SJD
Director, Centre for Chinese Law
Faculty of Law
The University of Hong Kong

Routledge
Taylor & Francis Group
LONDON AND NEW YORK

First published 2011
by Routledge
2 Park Square, Milton Park, Abingdon, Oxon, OX14 4RN

Simultaneously published in the USA and Canada
by Routledge
270 Madison Avenue, New York, NY 10016

Routledge is an imprint of the Taylor & Francis Group, an informa business

© 2011 editorial matter and selection: Guanghua Yu, individual chapters: the contributors.

The right of Guanghua Yu to be identified as editor of this work has been asserted by him in accordance with sections 77 and 78 of the Copyright, Designs and Patents Act 1988.

Typeset in Garamond by Glyph International Ltd.

Printed and bound in Great Britain by
CPI Antony Rowe, Chippenham, Wiltshire

All rights reserved. No part of this book may be reprinted or reproduced or utilised in any form or by any electronic, mechanical, or other means, now known or hereafter invented, including photocopying and recording, or in any information storage or retrieval system, without permission in writing from the publishers.

British Library Cataloguing in Publication Data
A catalogue record for this book is available from the British Library

Library of Congress Cataloging in Publication Data
The development of the Chinese legal system : change and challenges/ Guanghua Yu.
p. cm.
Includes index.
ISBN 978-0-415-59420-2
1. Law—China. I. Yu, Guanghua.
KNQ74.D48 2010
349.51–dc22 2010021548

ISBN13: 978-0-415-59420-2 (hbk)
ISBN13: 978-0-203-83775-7 (ebk)

Contents

List of charts

List of tables

List of contributors

Albert H. Y. Chen, Chan Professor in Constitutional Law, Faculty of Law, the University of Hong Kong.

Chao Xi, Assistant Professor, Faculty of Law, the Chinese University of Hong Kong.

Guanghua Yu, Associate Professor, Faculty of Law, the University of Hong Kong.

Hualing Fu, Professor of Law, Faculty of Law, the University of Hong Kong.

Jianfu Chen, Professor of Law, Department of Law, La Trobe University.

Jiangyu Wang, Associate Professor, Faculty of Law, the National University of Singapore.

Jolene Lin, Assistant Professor, Faculty of Law, the University of Hong Kong.

Pitman B. Potter, Professor of Law, Faculty of Law, the Institute of Asian Research, The University of British Columbia.

Roman Tomasic, Professor of Law, Department of Law, Durham University.

Weixia Gu, Assistant Professor, Faculty of Law, the University of Hong Kong.

Xianchu Zhang, Professor of Law, Faculty of Law, the University of Hong Kong.

Yahong Li, Associate Professor, Faculty of Law, the University of Hong Kong.

Yun Zhao, Associate Professor, Faculty of Law, the University of Hong Kong.

Yuwa Wei, Professor of Law, Kenneth Wang School of Law, Soochow University, China.

Preface

The year 2009 witnessed the birth of the Centre for Chinese Law (Centre) at the Faculty of Law of the University of Hong Kong. In that year, a book project was conceived before the establishment of the Centre and the project was contemplated to become the first collective academic effort of the Centre. With this objective in mind, I had already started to solicit the interest of Chinese law scholars and specialists from around the world to contribute a chapter in their respective area before I was formally appointed as the Director of the Centre. I was fortunate to be able to receive overwhelmingly positive responses from fourteen law academics to participate in this book project and I am profoundly grateful to them.

The Centre organized a conference in December 2009 to discuss all the papers to be included in the book. In this respect, I am very grateful to the commentators at the conference. These commentators include Pitman Potter, Jacques deLisle, Benjamin L. Liebman, Donald Clarke, Randall Peerenboom, Liming Wang and Jin Wang. Their comments and suggestions have greatly benefited the contributors of this book.

I am very grateful to Johannes Chan, the Dean of the Faculty of Law of the University of Hong Kong, for his strong support of the initiatives undertaken by the Centre. With his support, the Centre was able to receive partial funding for the said conference. The remaining funding for the conference came from the Constitutionalism Network Project. Funding for the research of my chapter was provided by the General Research Fund of the Research Grants Council of Hong Kong.

My sincere thanks go to Stephen D. Mau. Without his superb editing assistance, this book would not have been so smoothly born. Special thanks also go to Katherine Carpenter and Khanam Virjee at Routledge for their interest in this book project and their strong support and encouragement in bring this book to press. Finally, I would like to thank Hualing Fu, Head of the Department, and Cecilia Man, Secretary of the Centre, for their excellent management support to the Centre. Their support has made it possible for me to concentrate on this book project.

Guanghua Yu
Hong Kong
28 April 2010

Acknowledgements

Some of the chapters of this book are derived from articles published elsewhere. Chapter 5 by Guanghua Yu is based on 'The Role of Mortgages: A Case for Formal Law', *The Journal of Contract Law* (2009). Chapter 7 by Chao Xi is adapted from an article entitled 'Piercing the Corporate Veil in China: How Did We Get There', which will appear in the *Journal of Business Law*. Chapter 14 by Yun Zhao is partly based on an earlier version of an article appearing at *Journal of Chinese and Comparative Law* (2003). I thank the generous consent from the respective copyright holders to permit the contributors to include their chapters in this book.

Introduction

Guanghua Yu

China is a nation with a long history. It has been an authoritarian regime both during the feudalist period and since communist rule. It goes without saying that history matters to studies on the political, economic and legal institutions of contemporary China. In this book, the contributors are dealing with the development of the legal institutions after 1978.

The year of 1978 is important as it marks the beginning of a new era. Since then, China has moved gradually from a rigid planned economy with the public ownership of the means of production towards a socialist market economy. Related to this change of the political economy is the proliferation of legal rules. Compared with scholars and students interested in Chinese law in the 1960s, who were struggling for materials on Chinese law and politics,[1] scholars and students of contemporary Chinese law have ready access to all sorts of primary and secondary materials. It is now almost impossible to complete a book on Chinese law which covers all aspects of the Chinese legal institutions. To solve that problem, editors need to be selective. Whatever the efforts, however, a certain degree of arbitrariness is inevitable. What I attempted is to reflect a relatively good picture of the Chinese legal institutions from a historical perspective.

Similar to Lubman,[2] the contributors in this book try to examine the development of the Chinese legal institutions and analyse the constraints on the scope and further development of such institutions. In that process, we have made our effort to discover some more fundamental factors shaping the change and resistance.

As Peerenboom pointed out many years ago, legal scholars tend to emphasize the deficiencies of the legal system despite the significant change in the legal system.[3] Although some of the criticisms have a strong moral basis, most are the result of using the benchmark of the legal institutions in the developed Western countries. Pfeffer's remark written in the 1970 that 'those who compare our ideals with foreign realities engage in rhetoric rather than scholarship' is still relevant (Cohen's emphasis).[4] Rather than looking at Chinese law through the lens of Western law, most contributors in this book examine legal issues with a historical perspective.

Scholars may not like the authoritarian regime in China. They may also differ on the means of moving towards a political legal regime which provides the framework within which people can pursue a flourishing life. Drastic social transformation from a planned economy towards a market economy with fast development of the economy and urbanization does require a strong government with a clear reform agenda. A strong government is needed to solve all sorts of conflicts in society. Capability building of human agents also requires enormous resources by competing sectors or groups.[5] A strong government, however, may also create its own problems. Economists focusing on market-preserving federalism observe that a state strong enough to enforce contracts and protect property rights is also strong enough to expropriate the wealth of the people.[6] A similar question which can be raised by legal scholars is that an authoritarian government pursuing legal changes may also block changes when its interest is at stake. Many chapters in this book can be loosely organized along this theme.

Pitman Potter's selective adaptation theory explains variations in local reception of non-local standards by reference to the extent of normative consensus. With respect to the development of China's property rights regime, his theory shows dynamics and outcomes of ongoing normative tensions between globalized liberal ideology and local legal and political culture. More broadly, his theory is able to explain the difficulty of adopting more liberal political reforms in China in the areas of judicial independence and governmental constraints.

The chapter by Jianfu Chen demonstrates his main thesis that 'constitutional litigation is not dead in China; it simply has not taken off in the first place, and constitutionalism, however it is understood, remains an illusive goal in contemporary China'. Since 1978, the market has expanded enormously. It is also very obvious, however, that the Chinese government has retained considerable control of the economy. Active constitutional litigation requires a strong moral foundation and a liberal market order. Jiangyu Wang argues in his chapter that securities regulation is part of the Chinese government's political legitimacy management efforts. Political factors may also well explain why courts have difficulties with cases involving large number of investors in China. Similarly, Xianchu Zhang in his chapter also reveals that courts have a political role to play in providing the Party-state with legitimacy. Despite the progress made during the last 30 years in improving judicial efficiency and professionalism, the progress, however, is fragile. Judicial independence will be difficult to achieve in the foreseeable future. While Weixia Gu in her chapter also claims that lack of party autonomy in arbitration and ad hoc arbitration in China is mainly due to political factors, it is harder to substantiate the claim. It is not very clear why the Part-state needs to control arbitration institutions which mainly deal with individualized and decentralized business disputes. When local courts are not following the guidelines of the Supreme People's Court, empowering the courts and individual judges may also not improve judicial review of arbitration decisions.

Peerenboom has pointed out that the existing accounts of the Chinese legal institutions appeared unduly dismissive of the remarkable progress that had been achieved.[7] While acknowledging the existing problems of the lack of procedural protection of rights and of the relatively slow progress in comparison with legal reform in social and economic spheres, the chapter by Hualing Fu demonstrates the institutionalization of the criminal justice system in terms of judicial autonomy, professional competence and fairness. He also urges critics to pay attention to the dynamics of the reform process in the particular Chinese political and social context.

Lubman once observed that 'the economic bird has already escaped from its cage, the economic plan, but the legal bird remains in its own cage, although it is stirring and the dimensions of the cage may be changing'.[8] Although his remarks remain partially true, things are more promising if we pay close attention to the expansion of private rights in many different areas. Scholars and students of Chinese law familiar with the Chinese legal history know that there was a lack of development of civil and commercial law in the history of ancient and modern China. Penal provisions dominate the Tang Code and the Qing Code. Hualing Fu's chapter reveals that cases dealt with by Chinese courts in the 1950s, 1960s and 1970s were predominately criminal cases. Since 1978, however, there has been a significant development of civil and commercial law. Notable examples include the Contract Law, the Law on Property Rights, the Company Law, the Law on Negotiable Instruments and the Insurance Law. The development of private rights of individuals and legal entities will definitely reshape public governance of Chinese society in the years to come. The last 30 years or so witnessed the impressive accomplishments of the development of legal institutions. If it would take another 30 years to build a strong moral and economic foundation for a liberal political legal order, that is still a very short moment in history. While we cherish the goal of establishing a liberal political legal order in China in the future, scholars and students of Chinese law still need to pay greater attention on the means of realizing the goal. If it is really important to pay close attention to the development of China's civil and commercial law, most chapters in this book organized along the theme of assessing the progress made and the obstacles in the development of China's civil and commercial law are very meaningful. From the perspective of change and challenges, some of the chapters in this book also reveal different consequences flowing from the legal change.

Examined from the historical perspective, Yahong Li in her chapter demonstrates that the transplantation of a Western style of intellectual property law since 1978 has been, by and large, very successful. The Western-style intellectual property law, however, has adapted to the local conditions due to China's socialist ideologies, heavy reliance on administrative enforcement and the relative weak protection of private rights. Through the example of piercing the corporate veil, Chao Xi iC his chapter explains the changing dynamics of law making in China. He argues that law making in China can no longer be viewed as the intention of a strong state or merely the product of bargaining between governmental agencies. Recognizing some progress made in China in improving corporate governance rules, Roman Tomasic in his chapter calls for empirical research in closely looking at the actual workings of Chinese corporations from a wider economic and social perspective. Yuwa Wei in her chapter reviews the reform of the banking sector and its regulatory framework. She cautions that deregulation of the banking sector poses complex challenges for both the policy-makers and the banking institutions. Obviously, it will take time and effort to have a strong and liberal banking sector established in China.

Virtually all the chapters in this book are written from a historical perspective. They explain the dynamic process of legal transplantation and domestic political, economic and social factors in shaping the outcome of different institutions. While these chapters all have value for comparative law studies, it is the chapter by Albert Chen that specifically utilizes the comparative perspective. He demonstrates that the current law of property rights in China is influenced by both the Soviet law and the Continental European law. According to him, the reform in the last 30 years has also considerably enlarged the scope of private rights. As the Chinese property law is still evolving, further changes are inevitable to cope with the reform need. The chapter by Guanghua Yu deals with the issue on the role of formal law in China's economic development. Currently, the dominant position of scholars with an expertise on Chinese law or economy is that the formal law in China does not play any important role in China's economic development.[9] Guanghua Yu argues, however, that there is inadequate evidence to support such a claim. Analysis of the Chinese mortgage regime shows that there are clear limits to reliance upon informal contractual arrangements in China's fast economic development. Further research in this area is clearly needed.

The last two chapters focus on law and regulation with obvious international implications. Jolene Lin in her chapter deals with the legal and regulatory developments in China that have emerged in response to climate change. She rightly points out that governments now have to pay greater attention to environmental issues. While the Chinese government and the public in general become more conscious of sustainable development, the task of solving environmental problems is arduous.

Yun Zhao in his chapter takes telecommunications as an example to elaborate the influence of the WTO membership on China. While the Chinese government has done a great deal to establish an independent regulator and to facilitate the entry of foreign and domestic companies, the political goal of controlling the key sectors of the economy by state-owned enterprises makes liberalization of the telecommunication sector difficult.

This small group of scholars and experts on Chinese law has made an enormous effort in producing this book. There is no doubt that this book has clear contributions to the existing literature on Chinese law research. The contributors in this book have used both conventional methods and interdisciplinary means to assess the existing legal institutions in China. The considerable change of the political, economic and social institutions and the rapid proliferation of laws and regulations in China present a challenge to scholars and experts on Chinese law to develop any single ambitious project. Scholars and experts of Chinese law still face two major challenges. The first challenge is more general to comparative law studies. The ways of doing things and legal provisions in the developed Western countries are a complicated interaction of historical matters, ideology, political economy and other social factors. While it cannot be denied that some degree of borrowing of methods or legal provisions in the West by developing or transitional countries is possible so long as they fit the local conditions of the borrowing countries, large-scale transplantation is unlikely to be successful. This has significant implications for Chinese law research. The second challenge faced by Chinese law scholars and experts is the lack of intellectual foundation in Chinese law research. What is required is for China specific scholars and experts and scholars in the main stream to come together or to pay greater attention to each other. Such joint projects, so we promise ourselves, will be conscientiously carried out in the near future.

Notes

1 J. Cohen, 'Introduction' in J. Cohen (ed.) *Contemporary Chinese Law: Research Problems and Perspectives*, Massachusetts: Harvard University Press, 1970, pp. 1–19.
2 S. Lubman, *Bird in a Cage: Legal Reform in China after Mao*, Stanford, California: Stanford University Press, 1999, p. 2.
3 R. Peerenboom, *China's Long March toward Rule of Rule*, Cambridge: Cambridge University Press, 2002, p. xii.
4 R. Pfeffer, 'Crime and Punishment: China and the United States' in Cohen (ed.), *supra note* 1, pp. 261–281.
5 On capability building, *see* A. Sen, *Resources, Values, and Development*, Oxford: Basil Blackwell Publisher Ltd., 1984; M. Nussbaum, 'Capabilities and Social Justice', *International Studies Review* 4, 2002, 123–135.
6 G. Montinola, Yingyi Qian and B. R. Weingast, 'Federalism, Chinese Style: The Political Basis for Economic Success for China', World Politics 48, 1995, 50; Yingyi Qian and B. R. Weingast, 'Federalism as a Commitment to Preserving Market Incentives', *Journal of Economic Perspective* 11, 1997, 83.
7 Peerenboom, *supra note* 3, p. xii.
8 Lubman, *supra note* 2, p. 2.
9 Shuhe Li and Peng Lian, 'Decentralization and Coordination: China's Credible Commitment to Preserve the Market Under Authoritarianism', *China Economic Review* 10, 1999, 161; F. Allen, Jun Qian, and Meijun Qian, 'Law, Finance, and Economic Growth in China', *Journal of Financial Economics* 77, 2005, 57; T. Ginsburg, 'Does Law Matter for Economic Development? Evidence from East Asia', *Law & Society Review* 34, 2000, 829; D. C. Clarke, 'Economic Development and the

Rights Hypothesis: The China Problem', *American Journal of Comparative Law* 51, 2003, 89; D. Clarke, P. Murrell and S. Whiting, 'The Role of Law in China's Economic Development' in L. Brandt and T. G. Rawski, (eds) *China's Great Economic Transformation*, New York, Cambridge University Press, 2008; F. K. Upham, 'From Demsetz to Deng: Speculations on the Implications of Chinese Growth for Law and Development Theory', *New York University Journal of International Law and Politics* 41, 2009, 551.

Part I

Public law

1 Constitutional judicialization and popular constitutionalism in China

Are we there yet?

Jianfu Chen

1.1. Introduction

I have often been told by Chinese law students that constitutional law is among the most boring subjects in their four-year curriculum. What happened (and in many respects, what did not happen) since the turn of the century seems to have proven the students wrong. Indeed, and until quite recently, the constitutional scene has been both lively and interesting, sometimes with joy and other times with disappointment. However, in all cases, there has been some considerable popular participation and support. Whether encouraged or disappointed, the significance of the various events in the last several years need to be understood in context – political and constitutional.

I have earlier argued that understanding the Chinese Constitution lies in understanding what are not in the Constitution, rather than what are in it.[1] In light of the development in the last ten years or so, what occurred, what did not occur and what were meant to occur but are yet to be realized, are equally important in understanding and assessing constitutionalism in China today.

The various 'constitutional events' since 2001 have been analysed rather extensively, and in many cases, excellently.[2] This chapter does not intend to repeat those analyses. Instead, it tries to put these 'events' in a contextual perspective and thus sheds some light on their significance (or insignificance) for the development of constitutionalism in China. It will argue that constitutional litigation is not dead in China;[3] it simply has not taken off in the first place, and constitutionalism, however it is understood, remains an illusive goal in contemporary China.

1.2. The missing mechanisms

A constitution, however well-crafted, means little unless it has some practical effect in reality. Constitutionalism, however defined, must ultimately be supported by practical mechanisms for checks and balances of government powers. If a reference to the constitution or the citation of it in court would arouse excitement among scholars and the general population, it indicates more the lack of constitutionalism than its existence. Though references to the constitution may also mean the emergence of constitutionalism, it, nevertheless, means a rather sad reality in that given society. Chinese constitutional law may well fall into this category.

However one wishes to interpret the Chinese constitutional law, the Chinese Constitution, as it stands now, concerns itself more with state organizational structure than with the checks and balances of governmental powers, more with the future direction of the society than the protection of fundamental rights of citizens and more with general principles than with detailed rules capable of implementation. I am, however, not suggesting that we should simply dismiss the Chinese Constitution out of hand. Seen as the 'mother of all laws',[4] the Chinese Constitution does set parameters for social and legal developments.[5] And significantly for the purpose of discussion here, the Constitution does contain something one may call a mini Bill of Rights,[6] the provisions of which appear to be compatible with international human rights standards. Through the 2004 constitutional amendment, the protection by the state of human rights is also declared without qualification.

While there is always a gap between the law and reality in all countries, the disparity between the Chinese Constitution on paper and its reality is extraordinary in that few, in or outside China, have taken the Chinese Constitution seriously until very recently. Theoretically, the 1982 Constitution for the first time expressly declares that the Constitution has the supreme authority of law.[7] It further declares that the state upholds the uniformity and dignity of the socialist legal system and that no law or administrative or local regulation shall contravene the Constitution.[8] There are, however, no mechanisms or procedures established by the Constitution for citizens to challenge the constitutionality or legality of these laws and regulations, nor has the National People's Congress (NPC) or its Standing Committee (SCNPC) ever invalidated any such laws or regulations publicly.[9] Similarly, there neither is any mention of the right of citizens or organizations to challenge the constitutionality of government actions, nor is any mechanism established for the enforcement of a citizen's constitutional rights. The Constitution vests the power to supervise the enforcement of the Constitution with the NPC and the SCNPC,[10] but both authorities are legislative organs and, more problematically, there is, once again, no mechanism for either its enforcement or its supervision by these authorities. The SCNPC is further entrusted with the power to interpret the Constitution,[11] yet it rarely does so.[12] Finally, the Constitution reserves the power of constitutional amendment to the NPC and requires that any amendment must be proposed by the SCNPC or one-fifth of the deputies of the NPC and adopted by a majority vote of more than two-thirds of all deputies.[13] However, in reality, all amendments to the Constitution have been proposed by the Party and no suggestion to amend the Constitution proposed by the Party has ever been rejected or even modified by the NPC.

While many scholars insist that the 1982 Constitution is the 'best' among the four Constitutions adopted in the PRC, other scholars and officials do recognize the weakness in the present Constitution. As one prominent Chinese scholar concedes

> The supervision and enforcement mechanisms are still imperfect. ... The power of constitutional supervision has not been sufficiently exercised; constitutional interpretation has yet to be developed; education in the constitution is still being carried out, and special institutions are yet to be established.[14]

Not surprisingly, the question that whether the provisions of the Constitution may be directly enforced in a court of law remains a controversial issue and is yet to be settled.[15]

The various 'constitutional events' since 2001, and their significance or insignificance, can only be understood and make sense in the context of this conspicuous absence of practical mechanisms in the Constitution.

1.3. The 'constitutional events'

1.3.1. An overview

It is not just the intellectuals who have identified the deficiencies in the Constitution; Party and State authorities have also openly acknowledged the need to address the lack of mechanisms for constitutional implementation. Thus, the SCNPC in the mid-1990s decided that one of its major tasks was to strengthen the supervision of legal enforcement,[16] and some NPC deputies began a call for the making of a law on supervision.[17] Discussions and debate about various proposals for strengthening constitutional interpretation and supervision, including the establishment of a Constitutional Committee within the NPC, the establishment of a Constitutional Court or the granting of constitutional review powers to the Supreme People's Court also began in the 1990s.[18] Amid these talks and discussions on constitutional implementation, attempts were made to run 'test cases' by the more right-conscious and reform-minded lawyers.

The *Law on Law-Making* (*Law*), adopted in 2001, is the first serious constitutional effort to address the lack of constitutional mechanisms for practical purposes. Not surprisingly, serious talk and discourse on constitutional review mechanisms occurred during the draft of that *Law* and much of the actions occurred after the adoption of the *Law*. It would, however, be misleading to suggest that efforts to make the Chinese Constitution a relevant document only occurred after 2001. In fact, the rapid development of law before 2001, especially in the administrative law areas, has the effect of translating some of the general constitutional provisions into detailed practical arrangements, with some having effect on the operation of checks and balances, others on the actual realization and protection of rights and still others filling gaps in the constitution. While, on the whole, the development has been short of aspirations of scholars, the pre-2001 legal development, especially those after 1992, on the relationship between the rule of law and market economy,[19] had laid the foundation for significant changes in judicial attitudes towards the Constitution, and in forming a short-lived consensus on the need to establish mechanisms for the actual implementation of the Constitution.

Nevertheless, it is the *Law on Law-Making* that first makes any constitutional challenge possible and the need for further reforms inevitable if the *Law's* objectives are to be achieved. Changes in judicial attitude towards the Constitution are, to a certain extent, responses to the demand for further reforms.

1.3.2. Constitutional mechanisms?

The principal purpose of the *Law on Law-Making* is to establish some mechanisms to maintain consistency in law-making at central and local levels and in supervision over rule-making work of the government and judiciary (including the courts and the procuratorates). Essentially, the *Law* addresses the vertical division of central and local legislative powers and the horizontal distribution of legislative powers among legislative and administrative authorities;[20] inter-relations among 'laws' issued by various authorities; supervision over law, administrative regulations and rules; delegation of legislative powers; legislative processes; and interpretation of laws.

While many of the issues had already been codified in procedural rules issued by the NPC and its Standing Committee, the State Council and its ministries and commissions and the governments and legislatures at the provincial level, they are now regulated by a higher-level unified law, indicating efforts to address some the constitutional weaknesses. Not surprisingly, the enactment of the *Law on Law-Making* was declared by deputies of the NPC as a milestone in China's legislative history.[21]

While the significance of the *Law on Law-Making* is debatable, for the purpose of strengthening supervision over law and law-making, two mechanisms have been established by the *Law*. The first is Article 89 which systematically codifies the present practice and legal requirements on the filing of law and regulations for record, as already contained in various laws and regulations. With all laws and regulations filed, largely with central authorities, Article 88 sets out provisions governing the power of a higher authority to alter or even annul laws, regulations and rules enacted by a lower authority. The second mechanism, through Article 90, is to make the SCNPC a kind of constitutional committee responsible for review of conflicts among laws and regulations.

Although the *Law* stops short of establishing a constitutional committee, as advocated by many scholars and contained in the expert draft of the *Law on Law-Making*,[22] it is significant that some practical procedures and mechanisms have finally been instituted for the review of legislation. To implement the *Law on Law-Making*, a specialized unit within the Legislative Affairs Committee of the SCNPC was established in May 2004 which strengthen the work of the filing for record of laws and regulations and of reviewing these laws and regulations.[23] In December 2005, the Working Procedures on Filing for Record and Review of Administrative Regulations, Local Regulations and Regulations of Autonomous Regions and Special Economic Zones, initially issued in 2003, were revised and a new set of Working Procedures on Filing for Record and Review of Judicial Interpretations was issued by the SCNPC.[24] These working procedures further established some specific procedures for the constitutional review of regulations and rules.[25] Most recently, the SCNPC decided in 2007 to transfer the task of legislative planning from its General Office to the Legislative Affairs Committee.[26] Although this move is not a direct measure in the supervision of law-making, it surely has the potential to ensure the consistency of law-making. These initiatives, small steps as they might be,[27] are important in ensuring some degree of unity of law, but they are far from establishing a constitutional review mechanism in its true meaning.

While little is known about the actual work for ensuring the consistency of law-making, initial efforts, at least in terms of self-examination, have been made. Thus, the State Council decided in February 2007 to undertake a comprehensive review of all administrative regulations and rules issued before the end of 2006.[28] After ten months of intensive work, involving 24 legal experts acting upon 1,130 submissions,[29] a total of 655 sets of administrative regulations and rules were reviewed, with 92 (14 per cent of the total) of them being repealed.[30] Governments at the level of ministry and province had also undertaken self-review of ministerial and provincial rules, involving some 12,696 sets of rules, resulting in 2,173 being repealed and 395 revised.[31] In 2008, the SCNPC began its own self-review, resulting in its Decision to Amend Certain Laws,[32] under which 59 laws were amended. Apparently, some supervisory reviews have also been carried out. Thus, the Annual Report of Legal Construction in China (2008) reported that, in 2008, the State Council reviewed some 1,107 ministerial and local regulations and handled 44 'problematical' rules and regulations. Further, legal offices at the provincial level reviewed 9,925 lower-level government rules and handled 295 inconsistent rules. However, it is unclear how these 'problematical' rules were 'handled'.

There have also been efforts to establish some formal mechanisms for the exercise of the powers of constitutional supervision by the SCNPC. Under the Constitution, the supervisory power may be implemented or realized through different constitutional mechanisms and, among others, through interpreting the law, inspecting the implementation of selected laws and supervising the work of the administrative and judicial organs.[33] Although the power to interpret the law is not uncontroversial, as it clearly contravenes the basic principles of the separation of powers, such a power is solidly established by the Chinese Constitution. Until quite recently most scholars have not been overly concerned about this constitutional arrangement, and criticisms of this power have been more about the 'neglect of duty' by the NPC and its Standing

Committee in exercising the power than about its use.[34] The controversy over SCNPC's interpretation of the Basic Law of Hong Kong in relation to the right of abode in Hong Kong in 1999 led scholars, especially those outside China, to have second thoughts about this power. Clearly, the exercise of this interpretive power has the potential to interfere with judicial independence in Hong Kong.[35] The inspection of the implementation of selected laws by the NPC and the SCNPC is perhaps the least controversial part of the involvement of the legislature in the implementation of law, and its practice is generally seen as positively contributing to the establishment of a genuine rule of law in China.

The most controversial aspect of the supervisory functions of the legislature in the implementation of law is the attempt by some local legislatures to 'supervise' individual cases handled by the judiciary. Although there were some guidelines formulated by the SCNPC in 1989 for the exercise of this supervision,[36] the constitutional basis for such a power is questionable. Even though the principle of separation of powers is not formally recognized in China, the 1982 Constitution clearly stipulates that the power of adjudication may only be exercised independently by the people's courts. The involvement of the legislatures in individual cases thus raises serious questions and concerns about judicial independence in China.[37] In a widely publicized case, now often referred to as the 'Seeds Case' a judge in a local court (Luoyang Intermediate Court in Henan Province) invalidated a local regulation on the basis of its being in conflict with the national Seeds Law. This decision quickly attracted intervention from the Standing Committee of the Henan People's Congress. The intervention was extraordinary in that the local Standing Committee demanded the rectification of the decision and severe punishment for the judges even before an appeal had been dealt with by a higher court.[38] This simple contractual dispute, and especially its subsequent intervention by the local legislature, reveals a great deal (though not all) of the systemic problems in the Chinese legal system concerning implementation of law, as well as the sensitivity of constitutional issues, namely the existence of a hierarchy of law but the almost total absence of mechanisms and procedures for the judiciary to deal with conflict of laws in the hierarchy, the ambiguous constitutional and institutional division of powers, the tension between judicial independence and accountability, the focus on substantive justice at the expense of due process, the conflict of local and national interests and, of course, the constant power struggles between and among institutions and personnel. Clearly, some of these issues need to be addressed through the Constitution. In this context and after some twenty years of debate and discussion, a law – the *Law on Supervision by Standing Committees of the People's Congresses at Various Levels (Law on Supervision)* – was finally adopted in August 2006 to address some of these issues.[39]

According to the NPC, the making of the *Law on Supervision* took some twenty years.[40] The difficulties in drafting this law were well summarized by the Chairman of the Law Commission of the NPC: it is a politically sensitive law concerning the political and state system. This law needs to balance the strengthening of NPC supervisory power and the maintenance of the Party leadership. The *Law on Supervision* needs to exercise supervision over, yet support the work of, the government, the courts and the procuratorates.[41] As such it is not surprising that the Party leadership took a very direct interest in the drafting process: the Communist Party of China (CPC) itself formally recommended to the NPC the making of this law, and the Party Committee of the SCNPC reported, as a special topic, to the Politburo of the Central Committee of CPC three times in November 2003, December 2005 and May 2006.[42]

Even though the drafting work was apparently supported by the Party, the final version of the *Law on Supervision* is not an ambitious piece of legislation. As the law-makers made clear after its adoption, where experience is 'ripe' the Law provides detailed and concrete provisions, but where experience is not yet 'ripe', only certain principles are laid down for future development, and where there is no existing experience or consensus is not reached, the *Law on Supervision* is silent.[43] Consequently, the Law manages to avoid all controversial issues and only codifies the existing practice under the *Law on Law-Making* and other NPC procedures. Further, instead of an NPC supervision law, it is now a law on supervision by the Standing Committees at the various levels.[44] While the official reasoning was that the infrequency of meetings of the people's congresses (once a year for a short period of two weeks or so) makes routine supervision impractical,[45] the narrowing of the scope was perhaps to avoid the issue of the Party–state relationship by avoiding addressing the nature of 'supreme power' of the people's congresses. Finally, the *Law of Supervision* is largely procedural, thus avoiding any need to address the question of separation of powers.[46]

The end result is a major disappointment. The *Law on Supervision* codifies the powers of Standing Committees at various levels that have already been granted by the Constitution, the *Organic Law of the National People's Congress* and the *Organic Law of the Local People's Congresses and Local Governments*,[47] albeit in a unified code. Importantly, after much debate during the drafting process, the *Law on Supervision* avoids the more contentious issue of standing committees supervising specific cases handled by courts and procuratorates by opting for inspection of specific issues[48] and emphasizing the collective exercise of the supervisory power.[49] The *Law on Supervision* does not specify the meaning of 'specific issues', though law-makers insist that 'specific issues' refer to issues in the nature of common concerns, not individual cases.[50] This, it is claimed, represents a sensitive and practical compromise for allocating powers between the legislature and the judiciary,[51] but whether this is a workable compromise will entirely depend on the prevailing political environment in the future.

While the aforementioned developments represent some progress towards making the Constitution a practical document, they are far from establishing any meaningful or independent constitutional review mechanism or other mechanisms for checks and balances in China. The Constitution continues to fail aspirations for constitutionalism in China, at least in the sense of making the constitution a genuine document with practical consequences.

1.3.3. Test cases?

Constitutional review of legislation, as established by Articles 90 and 91 of the *Law on Law-Making* suffers a number of serious defects. First, Article 88(1) provides that the NPC has the power to alter or annul improper laws enacted by the SCNPC, but the SCNPC is the actual reviewing authority under Article 90. How then is the NPC to actually conduct its supervision over laws enacted by the SCNPC? Secondly, organizations and citizens are entitled to make suggestions to the SCNPC for review of administrative regulations, local regulations, autonomous regulations and specific regulations, but they do not have a right to demand this, nor can they request the SCNPC to conduct a review of laws – only the State Council, the Central Military Commission, the Supreme People's Court, the Supreme People's Procuratorate or Standing Committees of the people's congresses of provinces, autonomous regions or directly administered municipalities can do so.[52] Finally, and more importantly, the *Law* fails to define any criteria for such a review or for making requests for such a review; Article 90 and 91 only speak of 'contravening' – an important term without definition, although the need for definition had been consistently advocated by scholars.[53]

Further, as Chinese laws are mostly written in general and vague terms, their interpretation by various authorities effectively forms an important source of law. Without these interpretations, Chinese law is unusable, if not meaningless. The Constitution provides that the SCNPC exercises the power to interpret the Constitution and laws;[54] otherwise, the Constitution has little to say about statutory interpretation. Chinese jurisprudence commonly divides authoritative interpretation into three categories: legislative, administrative and judicial. Generally speaking, legislative interpretation means interpretation given by legislative authorities on laws and rules issued by themselves; administrative interpretation refers to interpretations given by administrative authorities of these rules and regulations; and judicial interpretations are those issued by the Supreme People's Court and the Supreme People's Procuratorate in their adjudicative and procuratorial work.[55] This jurisprudential division of the power of statutory interpretation is reflected in the 1981 Resolution of the Standing Committee concerning the Strengthening of Legal Interpretive Work,[56] which provides some more detailed, but still very general, provisions on dividing the power of legal interpretation.

The provisions on the interpretation of law in the *Law on Law-Making* represent one of the most disappointing aspects of this piece of legislation. Section 2.4 of Chapter 2 contains six short articles on the interpretation of law, only dealing with interpretation by the SCNPC. The *Law* is totally silent on administrative, adjudicative and procuratorial interpretations of law. The reasons for these omissions are unclear.[57]

In short, efforts to introduce constitutional mechanisms for the supervision and enforcement of the Constitution (at least in terms of maintaining unity and consistency of the legal system) have made little inroads into achieving their objectives, and the roles of the Supreme People's Court or any other courts in interpretation of law, especially the Constitution, are left as ambiguous as ever. At the same time, there has been a significant change of attitude towards the enforceability of the constitutional provisions, with increasing numbers of Chinese scholars shifting to an affirmative view on this point.[58] Thus, with or without a practical mechanism for enforcing the supreme law, attempts have been made by Chinese scholars and the Supreme People's Court to project the Constitution as a document with practical consequences. It is in this context that efforts have been made to launch 'test cases'. Among these, two are particularly relevant to our discussion here: one relates to constitutional review of legislation, and the other raises some fundamental questions about constitutional judicialization in China.

In 2003, a university graduate named Sun Zhigang was detained in a city in Guangdong Province under the then State Council Measures on Detention and Repatriation and was apparently beaten to death (hence often referred to as the 'Sun Zhigang incident'). After a public outcry and wide discussions (largely through the new media – the Internet), several scholars then petitioned the SCNPC to start a constitutional review of the Measures. There were hopes that this petition would test the practicality of the newly enacted *Law on Law-Making* and, perhaps, create a precedent for citizen-initiated constitutional review. However, the Measures were quickly repealed by the State Council before any SCNPC procedure was actually activated,[59] thus ending a potential constitutional review that had yet to start. Clearly, an opportunity was lost. Nevertheless, the repeal of the Measures caused some 'euphoria' in the Chinese media, calling it a 'milestone' in and a 'great leap forward' to establishing the rule of law in China etc.[60] What the scholars and the media did not realize at the time was that the 'euphoria' was soon to be dampened by strict control over the Internet and the media, the restrictions on and banning of further discussion and the apparent retributive punishment imposed on the more 'aggressive' reporters and lawyers.[61] Thereafter, some twenty-plus petitions on various subject matters that were submitted to the SCNPC have been disregarded, neither having been acknowledged nor formally dismissed.[62] The message seems to be clear: As far as constitutional review is concerned, it is not for the citizens to initiate bottom-up actions; the Party shall decide what actions, if any, should be taken for constitutional reform. This is so even though Chinese scholars involved in the petition have made clear that they did not have any intention to create any confrontation with the government or the Party.[63]

The second case examined here relates to a one-short-paragraph reply from the Supreme People's Court to a Shandong High Court in a 2001. The case is widely reported as the first constitutional case in China (often referred to as 'Qi Yuling' case,[64] but some went further to call it China's *Marbury v Madison*).[65] The case, however, is not a constitutional law case in a strict sense;

it is, technically, a straightforward tort case. In this case, the identity of the plaintiff/appellant, together with her vocational school entry examination scores, was appropriated by another person to enter into a Chinese vocational school. The defendant/respondent, after graduation and still using the plaintiff's identity, also took up a position in a local branch of the Bank of China. Upon discovery of this identity theft some nine years later, the plaintiff, Ms Qi filed a civil suit for compensation and civil injunction in her local intermediate court on the basis of violation of her right to name and her right to education. There is no need to devolve into the details of the case, but suffice to say that it was a civil suit between private parties for tort remedies. The central issue relevant to our discussion is whether the violation of the right to education, a right that is contained in the Constitution but not in the *General Principles of Civil Law* or other civil laws,[66] would constitute a ground for civil remedies. The Shandong High Court (the appellate court) sought advice from the Supreme People's Court, which held that the appellant's constitutional right to education was violated by the respondents by means of violating the appellant's rights to name and, because such violation had caused actual damages, civil remedies are to be granted.[67]

Apparently, the Supreme People's Court seems to suggest that the Constitution could be a legal basis for private law suit and legal remedies. However, with its extreme brevity and without any reasoning for its Reply, this Reply raised more questions than answers and led to speculations as to its actual meaning and practical significance as well as heightened excitement among many scholars and practitioners.[68] It is important to note that much of the excitement was further fuelled by an article published shortly after the issuance of the Reply by a Supreme People's Court judge, Huang Songyou.[69] Huang started his article by stating that courts in China were unsure whether the Constitution could be directly relied upon for judicial judgement and this issue must now be resolved. He then made it clear that the Party has now called for specific mechanisms for the actual implementation of the Constitution and, in his view,[70] judicialization of the Constitution was one such mechanism that the Party has called for. He further emphasized that, without introducing the Constitution to judicial processes, there would be a major gap between the Constitution and the other 'ordinary' laws, leaving much of the constitutionally guarantied rights 'sleeping'. He therefore effectively suggested that the Constitution could have a 'gap-filling' function in litigations. However, Huang's reasoning for judicialization of the Constitution was fundamentally flawed. He started his reasoning by citing the *Marbury v Madison*[71] case, which was about the constitutionality of a federal act which conflicted with the US Constitution, and relying on this, moved to discuss possibility and feasibility of judicial application of the Constitution in China. While the logical flaw in his reasoning is easy to identify, it could only be speculated whether the choice of a private civil suit for trying the implementation of the constitution was a deliberate and well-considered one by the Court as a tentative experiment for judicialization of the Constitution. Nevertheless, it is important to note that there is no hint, either in the Court Reply or in Huang's article, that the Constitution might be used against the State and/or its various authorities, or against the Party. In other words, *Marbury v Madison* might be frequently invoked in the Chinese discussion, the Qi Yuling case is no *Marbury v Madison* at all.

In short, Qi Yuling case was a private civil suit, neither meant to be nor in reality a constitutional litigation. While there were some public institutions (the government-run Middle School and the vocational school, the Bureau of Education of the local government) involved as defendants in the case, there was no argument about public liability or the violation of the Constitution by any public authorities. As such, as pointed out by Shen Kui, the Reply might be a well-meaning and well-intended attempt by the Supreme People's Court, but it was a wrong case for the Court to try its effort for judicialization of the constitution.[72]

The foregoing two cases are the most widely publicized 'events' in relation to constitutional review in China, but they are not the only ones. There have also been many more cases, some successful and other not so, in which citizens attempt to use the Constitution for the protection of their rights. These issues range from labour contracts to discrimination (on various grounds and in different areas).[73] Many of these cases probably fall under the label of 'public interest law' litigation, but none could properly be defined as constitutional litigation, even though occasionally courts made references to constitutional provisions.[74] It is, however, worth noting that, in many of these cases, scholars have urged the government to consider the establishment of practical constitutional mechanisms for the protection of constitutionally guaranteed rights, but there has been no sign of government willingness to take such a route for the development of constitutionalism in China.

Although the Supreme People's Court interpretation in the Qi Yuling case caused some considerable controversy and excitement, it was so simply because the Court had never directly dealt with issues of constitutionally guaranteed rights nor claimed to have done so until then.[75] On the other had, it has been argued for some time that the Supreme People's Court is in fact exercising certain powers to interpret and supervise the enforcement of the Constitution, though the Court has no such powers in the Constitution. This has been done through the publication of selected cases and opinions on legal issues.[76] There is no doubt that certain cases and legal opinions endorsed by the Supreme People's Court included references to the Constitution and, hence, indirect interpretation of the Constitution.[77] However, the ability of the Court to do so is a result of the lack of mechanisms and procedures for constitutional interpretation and supervision of its enforcement, rather than with any particular constitutional grounds or procedures.

The sad reality remains: there is a conspicuous absence of any intention to remedy the deficiencies in the Constitution by the real power in China – the Communist Party of China. Not surprisingly, the Court experiment was to end abruptly once the political circumstances have changed.

1.3.4. Popular constitutionalism?

There has been some considerable amount of online discussions as well as other forms of support for 'public interest law' (*Weiquan*) litigation. Are we therefore seeing some form of popular constitutionalism emerging in China?

The answer probably is negative. First, although we do not know the number of public interest law cases, we can reasonably say that the numbers are not large, at least not significant in a country of 1.3 billion residents. Second, it is clear that, with some very small exceptions, they are largely about specific rights albeit in the nature of public interests. They are also largely led by a small number of social 'elites' – lawyers, political scientists, academics, etc. – and an equally small number of social activists. Third, it is true many of these cases have aroused significant Internet interest, hence popular support and public debate and discourse, the lasting impact on constitutionalism in China must not be overstated. As Fu and Cullen correctly point out, 'People in the "cyber space" become excited by the cases, debate them with great passion, but then forget about them as quickly as they attract their attention. They move on to other attractions'.[78] If popular constitutionalism is referred to as 'a form of constitutionalism that is found not so much on formal texts and documents, but in individual sentiment of justice',[79] I doubt if there is sufficient number of individuals with a consistent sentiment of justice to proclaim such a movement.[80] As such, these *ad hoc* cyber discussions can hardly constitute a popular movement with any consistent theme, least that of constitutionalism.[81]

Perhaps the idea of popular constitutionalism does not sit well with the Chinese historical experiences. As I have discussed in some length elsewhere,[82] the movement towards constitutionalism has had a troubled history ever since its inception in China at the turn of the twentieth century. The constitutions and their practice before 1949 had had little effect on the life of ordinary people in China. While this constitutionalism movement does establish firmly the idea that the legitimacy of government, be it the warlords, the Kuomintang or the Communist Party of China (CPC), must be established by a document called a 'constitution', it was largely an 'elitist' movement. In terms of constitutions after 1949, its development has been strictly controlled by the CPC rather than any popular movement. In this age of modern technologies, it is true to say that the Party leadership and state authorities are no longer the only driving forces for reform in contemporary China, and ordinary people[83] and, especially, intellectuals[84] are also, to a certain extent, active agents that often push against the constitutional parameters for further political, legal and economic reform, it is nevertheless largely an 'elitist' rather than popular movement.

Realistically, constitutionalism – in its narrow meaning of checks and balances or power accountability – is by definition a hugely complicated issue involving the design of complicated constitutional mechanisms. The idea might be pushed, advocated and supported by the general populace, but the end product has perhaps always been designed and produced by the educated 'elites' in any country.

In any case, it is doubtful whether the current leadership of the Party, which is obsessed with the notions of stability and law-and-order, would allow any popular constitutionalism movement to develop in China. The periodical crackdown on rights movements, especially group-based movements such as the Falonggong,[85] suggest that any tolerance of such movement is temporary, and there has been no tolerance towards any movement that would challenge the leadership of the Party.[86]

In short, it is premature to suggest that there is a popular movement towards constitutionalism; much of the push was made by elitist academics and a limited number of right-conscious practitioners.

1.4. Concluding remarks

The death of constitutional litigation in China was pronounced upon the quiet abolition of the Qi Yuling Reply by the Supreme People's Court in December 2008.[87] However, the reality is that constitutional litigation or constitutional judicialization in the sense of judicial review has never started. Since the Supreme People's Court has kept silent on this matter, any analysis on the reasons for the abolition could only be speculative.[88] Chinese media reports, however, seem to suggest a fundamental reversal of policy direction. According to Sichuan News, there had been a special investigation group established upon instructions from the Party leaders on the issues relating to judicialization of the constitution and the Qi Yuling Reply. It was reported that the Reply was destined to be abolished once the Group was established.[89] Most recently, on 26 October 2009, the Supreme People's Court issued its *Provisions on the Citation in Judicial Judgements and Decisions of Laws, Regulations, Rules and Other Normative Documents*.[90] While the Provisions do not explicitly exclude citation of the Constitution in judicial decisions, the Constitution is not listed as one of the sources of law to be cited as legal grounds for judicial decisions. The master of ambiguity has clearly returned and questions on the enforceability of the Constitution continue to be as unsettled as ever.[91] It is plainly clear, however, that the Party is not going to allow any authority or anyone other than itself to control or push directions for constitutional reforms.

These latest developments suggest that, while any positive development in constitutionalism is to be welcome, one must not read too much into those 'incidents' or get too excited about them. Making direct reference to constitutional provisions may be of some symbolic significance; it is not of fundamental importance.[92] Constitutionalism would only develop in China if institutional weaknesses in the Constitution are addressed systematically.

Even if the Qi Yuling and other public interest law cases are to be seen as tentative experiments by the judiciary, the judiciary has done so without any rule to go by. Such a practice is neither sustainable nor, indeed, particularly conducive for long-term constitutionalism development. This suggests that the educated 'elites' might need a new strategy – not just arousing public interest but pushing for specific designs and mechanisms. The very productive discussions, in the 1990s, on specific constitutional review mechanisms seem to have waned, but that is precisely the kind of debate that public intellectuals should seek. Politically, such a movement is perhaps more likely to be perceived by the Party leadership as being constructive rather than confrontational and, as such, may lead to more practical and sustainable results.

Notes

1 *See*, Jianfu Chen, *Chinese Law: Context and Transformation*, Leiden/Boston: Martinus Nijhoff Publishers, 2008: 144. I am not suggesting that we look for elements that are in Western constitutions and then examine whether they are missing from the Chinese constitutional law. This approach would unduly privilege Western constitutional law and constitutionalism that have evolved in the developed countries. What I propose to do is to revisit those elements that have been identified by the Chinese scholars, government and Party officials and the general population as necessary to be incorporated into the Chinese constitutional law for constitutionalism to develop in China.

2 A most useful starting point for a comprehensive reading of these events is the edited volume by S. Balme and M. W. Dowdle, *Building Constitutionalism in China*, New York: Palgrave MacMillan (2009). I am most grateful to Professor Dowdle who kindly provided me a set of the manuscript's proof before publication.

3 *See*, T. E. Kellogg, 'The Death of Constitutional Litigation in China?', (April 2009) 9(7) China Brief, available at http://www.jamestown.org/programs/chinabrief/single/?tx_ttnews%5Btt_news%5D=34791&tx_ttnews%5BbackPid%5D=414&no_cache=1 (accessed 15 July 2009).

4 Bikun Jiang *et al.* (eds), *Constitutional Law* (*Xianfa Xue*), Beijing: China University of Political Science and Law Press, 1993: 5.

5 It is not unusual these days, when discussing specific legal reforms with Chinese scholars, to hear them arguing that certain reforms are constrained by the present constitutional arrangement.

6 *See*, Chapter Two on Fundamental Rights and Duties of Citizens of the 1982 Constitution.

7 *See*, the Preamble of the 1982 Constitution.

8 Article 5 of the 1982 Constitution.

9 *See*, Shuwen Wang, 'On the Guarantee of Constitutional Enforcement', *Legal Science in China* (*Zhongguo Faxue*) no. 6, 1992: 15, 18; Jianmiao Hu and Chunyan Gao, 'Constitutional Review of Law and Regulation in China – Problems and Solutions', in *Printed Newspaper and Journal Articles (D411 Constitutional & Administrative Law)* no. 3, 2006: 46.

10 *See*, Articles 62(2) and 67(1) of the 1982 Constitution.

11 Article 67(1) of the 1982 Constitution.

12 Jilin People's Press in 1993–1994 published a large collection of normative interpretations of laws; the collection does not contain a section on constitutional interpretation. *See*, *A Collection of Normative Interpretations of Laws in the PRC* (*Zhonghua Renmin gonghe Guo Falü Guifanxing Jieshi Jicheng*) (Changchun: Jilin

People's Press, 1990, further supplemented annually since 1993). However, some Chinese scholars have argued that certain decisions of the SCNPC on specific issues may be interpreted as constitutional interpretations by the SCNPC. *See*, Lei Wang, 'On Constitutional Interpretation Organs in Our Country', *Journal of Chinese and Foreign Legal Science* (*Zhongwai Faxue*) no. 6, 1993: 21; Wang, *supra note* 9, p. 19. If this interpretation is accepted, then, logically, all legislation by the SCNPC would have to be treated as constitutional interpretations by the SCNPC.

13 *See*, Articles 62(1) and 64 of the 1982 Constitution.

14 Jiang *et al.*, *supra note* 4, p. 43. For a similar view, *see*, Dingjian Cai, 'Constitutional Supervision and Interpretation in the People's Republic of China', *Journal of Chinese Law* 9, 1995: 219, 223.

15 Until quite recently, the established view was that they might not be directly enforced. Youyu Zhang and Shuwen Wang (eds), *Forty Years of PRC's Legal Science* (*Zhonggu Faxue Sishinian*), Shanghai: Shanghai People's Press, 1989: 160; Yunsheng Chen, 'Ruling the Country according to the Constitution is the Core of Ruling the Country by Law', in *People's Daily* (*Renmin RiBao*), 15 November 1997, at p. 4. As will be shown in the next section, these views have been questioned and challenged by many scholars of younger generations. The doubt about the enforceability of the Constitution has as much to do with Chinese constitutional practice as with the provisions of the Constitution itself. Indeed, the provision '[a]ll acts in violation of the Constitution and the law must be investigated' was only added to Article 5 of the Constitution at the NPC's Fifth Session at which the Constitution was adopted. *See*, Angran Gu, *The Construction of a Socialist Legal System and Legislative Work* (*Shehui Zhuyi Fazhi Jianshe He Lifa Gongzuo*), Beijing: China University of Political Science and Law Press, 1989: 59; Youyu Zhang, 'Strengthening the Research on Constitutional Theories', in Chinese Society of Legal Science (ed.), *A Selection of Papers on the Constitution* (*Xianfa Lunwen Xuan*), Beijing: Press of the Masses, 1983: 4.

16 *See*, Major Tasks of the Standing Committee of the 8th NPC, in *People's Daily* (*Renmin Ribao*), 3 July 1993: 4; 'Work Report of the Standing Committee', delivered by Tian Jiyun at the 1st Plenary Session of the 9th NPC on 10 March 1998, in *People's Daily* (*Renmin Ribao*), 23 March 1998, at p. 4.

17 *See*, *People's Daily* (*Renmin Ribao*), 19 March 1998, at p. 5. Such a law was indeed adopted in 2006. *See*, discussions below.

18 *See*, Cai, *supra note* 14, p. 219; 'Considerations and Proposals for Strengthening the Work of Supervision by the NPC – A Summary of Newspaper and Journal Discussions', *Legal Science in China* (*Zhonggu Faxue*) no. 6, 1990: 13; Xieying Wu, Zhiyong Li and Ruihe Wang, 'On a Constitutional Ligation System in China', *Legal Science in China* (*Zhonggu Faxue*) no. 5, 1989: 62; Wang, *supra note* 9; Wang, *supra note* 12; Weijiu Zhu, *Legal Supervision Over Government* (*Zhengfu Fazhi Jiandu Lun*), Beijing: China University of Political Science and Law Press, 1994; Chen, *supra note* 15.

19 *See*, Jianfu Chen, 'The Transformation of Chinese Law – From Formal to Substantial', *Hong Kong Law Journal* 37(2): 2007, 689.

20 Judicial law-making is, however, not addressed by the Law.

21 *See*, *People's Daily* (*Renmin Ribao*), 14 March 2000, at 5.

22 *See*, Buyun Li, 'Explanations on the Proposed Law on Law-Making of the PRC', in J. M. Otto, M. V. Polak, J. Chen and Y. Li (eds), *Law-Making in the People's Republic*

of China, The Hague/London/Boston: Kluwer Law International, 2000: 157–173; According to Chinese scholars this remained an aspirational goal among academics after the adoption of the *Law on Law-Making*. *See*, 'Constitutional Experts: a major step towards constitutional review', available at http://www1.people.com.cn/GB/14576/14528/2590424.html (accessed 24 June 2004).

23 While the establishment of the specialized unit was widely publicized, we know very little about the functions and working procedures of the unit, as some Chinese scholars have pointed out. *See*, Hu and Gao, *supra note* 9, p. 52.

24 These are seen as internal working procedures (Hu and Gao, *supra note* 9, p. 52) and none of them has been published.

25 *See*, Hu and Gao, *supra note* 9, p. 52; 'The Standing Committee of the NPC Clarifies Constitutional Review Procedures', available at http://news.xinhuanet.com/politics/2005-12/20/content_3944117.htm (accessed 20 December 2005).

26 *See*, 'Major Adjustment Made by the National Legislative Authority Regarding the Law-Making System', available at http://www.legaldaily.com.cn/misc/2007-03/01/content_547023.htm (accessed 2 March 2007).

27 *See*, 'The Establishment of the Constitutional Review and Filing for Record Unit Should Be Reported', available at http://www1.people.com.cn/GB/14576/14528/2590398.html (accessed 24 June 2004).

28 *See*, 'Person-in-charge of the State Council Legal Office Answers Journalist Questions in relation to the State Council Decision to Repeal Certain Administrative Regulations and Rules', available at http://www.chinalaw.gov.cn/article/fzjd/fggzql/200801/20080100024006.shtml (accessed 16 September 2009).

29 *Ibid.*

30 *See*, State Council Decision to Repeal Certain Administrative Regulations and Rules, State Council Order No 516, issued on 15 January 2008, available at http://www.chinalaw.gov.cn/article/fzjd/fggzql/200806/20080600017063.shtml (accessed 16 September 2009).

31 *See*, Annual Report of Legal Construction in China (2008), China Law Society, June 2009, available at http://news.xinhuanet.com/legal/2009-06/02/content_11476146.htm (accessed 16 September 2009).

32 Adopted by the Standing Committee of the NPC on 27 August 2009.

33 For a detailed discussion, *see*, Dingjian Cai, 'Functions of the People's Congress in the Process of Implementation of Law', in Jianfu Chen, Yuwen Li and J. M. Otto, *Implementation of Law in the PRC*, The Hague/London/New York: Kluwer Law International, 2002: 35–54.

34 *See*, P. Keller, 'Sources of Order in Chinese Law', *American Journal of Comparative Law* 42, 1994: 711.

35 The interpretation in 1999 of the Basic Law of Hong Kong on the right to abode is seen by a prominent Chinese scholar, Professor Cai Dingjian, as one of the positive examples of the exercise of the supervisory power by the SCNPC, but by others as the first perceived constitutional crisis in Hong Kong since the handover of sovereignty in 1997. For different views on this, *see*, Dingjian Cai, 'Functions of the People's Congress in the Process of Implementation of Law' and Albert Chen, 'Hong Kong's Legal System in the New Constitutional Order: The Experience of 1997–2000', both in Chen, Li and Otto, *supra note* 33, pp. 35–54 and 213–246, respectively.

36 Basically, such supervision may only start after a case is completed, and it may not try to influence or intervene in ongoing judicial work; secondly, the supervision

shall focus on legal procedures and interpretation; and finally, the supervisory body may request the court to retry or review the case but it must not substitute its own judgement for that of the courts. *See*, M. W. Dowdle, 'The Constitutional Development and Operations of the National People's Congress', *Columbia Journal of Asian Law* 11, 1997: 1, 110. Some local authorities have also issued their rules for implementing such supervision. *See, e.g. Working Rules for Supervision of the Judicial Organs by the Standing Committee of the Zhejiang Provincial People's Congress*, adopted and issued by the Standing Committee of the Zhejiang Provincial People's Congress on 28 December 2000 and effective on promulgation.

37 It should be pointed out that a controversial draft law on supervision of major violations of law in adjudication and prosecution work was submitted to the 12th Meeting of the Standing Committee of the NPC (October 1999), but it seems to have now been abandoned permanently.

38 Despite the controversy and major debates in legal circles, the original judgement has not been published. There were however many media reports on the case and its decision: 'Judge holds local regulation invalid: a violation of law or a support for law', *Nanfang Zhoumo* (*Southern Weekly*), Internet edition (http://www.nanfandaily.com.cn/zm/20031120/xw/fz/200311200861.asp) (accessed 20 November 2003); 'Judge sows seeds of lawmaking dispute', *China Daily*, Internet edition (http://www.chinadaily.com.cn/en/doc/2003-11/24/content_283973.htm) (accessed 24 November 2003); 'Lawyers request the National Congress to undertake legislative review over "Luoyang Seed Case"', Phoenix TV, Internet edition (http://www.phoenixtv.com/home/news/society/200311/21/151034.html) (last accessed 21 November 2003); and articles available at http://www.law-thinker.com (accessed 21 November 2003). After the intervention by the provincial legislature, the Luoyang Intermediary Court Party Committee then decided to remove Judge Zhao as Deputy Head of the Economic Chamber, Judge Li as presiding judge as well as dismissing her from the position of assistant judge, both pending formal legal procedures with the Standing Committee of the Luoyang People's Congress. However, according to follow-up reports in February 2004, the decisions to dismiss the judges were never actually submitted to the Standing Committee of the Luoyang People's Congress for deliberation and approval, apparently because of the controversy, and Judge Li, on sick leave since then, was notified to resume her work in the court. *See*, 'Conflict of law shall not be dealt with by "cool handling"', *Nanfang Doushi Bao* (*Southern Urban Daily*), Internet edition (http://www.nanfandaily.com.cn/southnews/spqy/zy/2000402070066.asp) (accessed 7 February 2004); 'Further controversy concerning Li Huijun Incident in Henan', *Zhongguo Qingnianbao*, Internet edition (http://www.cyol.com/zqb/gb/zqb/2004-02/06/content_813990.htm) (accessed 6 February 2004).

39 This law, adopted on 27 August 2006 by the 23rd Session of the Standing Committee of the Tenth NPC, took effect on 1 January 2007.

40 The idea of enacting a supervision law emerged during the sixth NPC in 1986 and it has never been off the agenda for the SCNPC since then. *See*, 'Twenty Years in the Making – An Interview with Chairman Yang Jingyu of the Law Commission of the NPC on the Supervision Law Draft', available at http://www.npc.gov.cn/zgrdw/common/zw.jsp?label=WXZLK&ID=351389&pdmc=110118 (accessed 27 August 2006); 'Twenty Years in the Making – On the Background of the Supervision Law', available at http://www.npc.gov.cn/zgrdw/common/zw.jsp?label=WXZLK&ID=352052&pdmc=1516 (accessed 19 September 2006).

41 'Twenty Years in the Making – An Interview with Chairman Yang Jingyu of the Law Commission of the NPC on the Supervision Law Draft', *supra note* 40.

42 'Twenty Years in the Making – On the Background of the Supervision Law', *supra note* 40.

43 *See*, Zeng Wu (Legislative Commission of the Standing Committee of the NPC), 'On Several Principal Issues of the Supervision Law', available at http://www.npc.gov.cn/zgrdw/common/zw.jsp?label=WXZLK&ID=352052&pdmc=110124 (accessed 31 August 2006).

44 According to the Chairman of the Law Commission of the NPC, it was in April–May 2006 that it was decided that, instead of a Law on Supervision by People's Congresses at Various Levels, the scope was narrowed down to supervision by standing committees of the people's congresses at various levels and there was a consequential change of the law's title. *See*, 'Twenty Years in the Making – An Interview with Chairman Yang Jingyu of the Law Commission of the NPC on the Supervision Law Draft' *supra note* 40.

45 *See*, 'Twenty Years in the Making – An Interview with Chairman Yang Jingyu of the Law Commission of the NPC on the Supervision Law Draft', *supra note* 40.

46 It is nevertheless emphasized that China does not practise separation of powers, and all state authorities – the people's congresses, the government, the courts and the procuratorates – are all under one leadership, that is, the Party leadership. *See*, the *People's Daily* editorial on the passage of the Law: 'Supervision Powers now Regularised and with Procedures', *People's Daily* (*Renmin Ribao*), 28 August 2006, also available at http://www.law-lib.com (accessed 28 August 2006); 'The Leader of the Law Commission of the NPC Answers Questions relating to the Supervision Law', available at http://www.law-lib.com (accessed 27 August 2006). *See also*, deliberation speeches at the 23rd Session of the Standing Committee of the NPC available at http://www.npc.gov.cn/zgrdw/common/zw.jsp?label=WXZLK&ID=352140&pdmc=1516 (accessed 19 September 2006); http://news.xinhuanet.com/politics/2006-08/27/content_5013837.htm (accessed 28 August 2006).

47 For a detailed discussion of these supervisory powers before the enactment of the *Supervision Law*, *see*, Cai, *supra note* 35, pp. 35–54.

48 *See*, Chapter 7 of the *Supervision Law*.

49 *See*, Article 4 of the *Supervision Law*.

50 *See*, Sixi Chen (Legislative Affairs Committee of the SCNPC), 'Strengthening Supervision while Maintaining Judicial Authority', available at http://www.npc.gov.cn/zgrdw/commn/zw.jsp?label=WXZLKK&id=352329&pdmc=1516 (accessed 19 September 2006); 'The Leader of the Law Commission of the NPC Answers Questions relating to the Supervision Law', *supra note* 46; Wu, *supra note* 43. *See also*, deliberation speeches at the 23rd Session of the SCNPC, *supra note* 46.

51 For further background on the need for compromise, *see*, Cai, *supra note* 35, pp. 35–54.

52 *See*, Article 42 of the *Law on Law-Making*. Article 90 of the *Law on Law-Making*, however, provides that

> [w]here … social organisations, enterprises, institutions as well as citizens are of the opinion that certain administrative regulations, local regulations, autonomous regulations and specific regulations contravene the Constitution or laws, they may submit, in writing, suggestions to the Standing Committee of

the National People's Congress for review of these. The working organ of the Standing Committee shall examine the matters and, where necessary, refer them to relevant special committees for review and opinion.

Clearly, individuals have no right to request constitutional review of laws, but only of administrative regulations and rules.

53 Both the 1995 Draft and the Expert Draft attempted to define the meaning of 'contravening' and 'inconsistency'. On scholars' advocacy for such definitions, *see*, various chapters in Buyuan Li (ed.), *Comparative Constitutional Law* (*Xianfa Bijiao Yanjiu*), Beijing: Law Press, 1998.

54 Article 67 (1) and (4) of the Constitution.

55 *See*, Zongling Shen (ed.), *Studies in Jurisprudence* (*Falixue Yanjiu*), Shanghai: Shanghai People's Press, 1990: 224; Xianming Xu (ed.), *A Textbook on Jurisprudence* (*Falixue Jiaocheng*), Beijing: China University of Political Science and Law Press, 1994: 241–243.

56 Adopted on 10 June 1981 by the 19th Meeting of the Standing Committee of the 5th NPC. The 1981 resolution is a revised version of the Resolution concerning Legal Interpretation adopted by the same Committee in 1955.

57 In all drafts since 1993, including the 1999 Draft, there were provisions which would also deal with judicial interpretation and there were also provisions to abolish the 1981 Resolution on interpretation of law.

58 Whether the Preamble has any direct legal force remains a controversial issue in China. *See*, Zhang and Wang, *supra note* 15, p. 181; Li, *supra note* 53, pp. 182–195.

59 For a summary of the petition, *see*, 'Five jurists requested the Standing Committee to activate constitutional review process on Sun Zhigang case', in www.chinalaw.gov.cn (accessed 12 January 2004). According to Cai Dingjian, the repeal of the Measures by the State Council was in fact undertaken after the leaders of the SCNPC transmitted the petition to the State Council for processing. Thus, Cai suggests that Chinese politicians attempted to avoid the establishment and use of a constitutional review mechanism. *See*, Dingjian Cai, 'Towards a Private Law Approach to the Implementation of the Chinese Constitution', originally published in *Social Science in China* (*Zhongguo Shehui Kexue*), no. 2, 2004, republished at http://www.usc.cuhk.edu.hk/wk.asp (accessed 12 November 2004). For a detailed discussion of this 'event', *see*, K. J. Hand, 'Using Law for a Righteous Purpose: The Sun Zhigang Incident and Evolving Forms of Citizen Action in the People's Republic of China', *Columbia Journal of Transnational Law* 45, 2007: 114.

60 *See*, Hand, *supra note* 59, pp. 128–129.

61 Hand, *supra note* 59, pp. 130–131. Such retributive punishment is not isolated, but rather wide spread towards the public interest lawyers and reporters, with hundreds of lawyers being jailed or otherwise deprived of personal freedoms. *See*, Xiapoing Chen, 'The Difficult Road for Rights Advocacy: An Unpredictable Future for the Development of Rule of Law in China', *Transnational Law and Contemporary Problems* 16, 2006: 221, 235–238. Recent media reports suggest that such political persecution not only continues, but is in fact intensified. *See*, D. J. Lunch, 'Retreat in China', *USA Today*, 10 August 2005, available at http://www.usatoday.com/news/opinion/editorials/2005-08-10-forum-China_x.htm (accessed 12 August 2005); J. Kahn, 'Chinese Crackdown on Rights Lawyers Signals Efforts to Deter Increasing Legal Challenges', *New York Times*, 19 August

2006, available at http://www.nytimes.com/2006/08/19/world/asia/19china.html?_r=1&oref=slogin (accessed 22 August 2006); M. Sainsbury, 'China Targets Lawyers in Rights Crackdown', *The Australian*, 7 August 2009, available at http://www.theaustralian.news.com.au/business/story (accessed 10 September 2009). A most depressing report is from John Garnaut, 'China's Human Rights Defenders Pay Heavy Price', *The Age*, 7 November 2009, 18: the 2005 Asia Week's People of Year (contains 14 photos of *Weiquan* lawyers) now looks like a 'tombstone inscription for China's 30-year struggle towards the rule of law'. More generally, *see*, M. Goldman, *From Comrade to Citizen: The Struggle for Political Rights in China*, Cambridge: Harvard University Press, 2005; E. J. Perry and M. Goldman (eds), *Grassroots Political Reform in Contemporary China*, Cambridge: Harvard University Press, 2007.

62 Hand, *supra note* 59, p. 151. *See also*, Cai, *supra note* 59. Interestingly the Legislative Affairs Committee of the SCNPC has insisted that it never received any petition from citizens for constitutional review of laws and regulations. *See*, 'The Leader of the Legislative Affairs Commission of the Standing Committee of the NPC Answers Journalist Questions concerning the Draft of a Law on Rights *in rem* and Review of Laws and Regulations Filed-for-Record', 1 March 2006, available at http://www.lawbook.com.cn/fzdt/newshtml/20/20006030292112.htm (accessed 23 March 2006). The latest petition was the one lodged by five law professors from Beijing University Law School in July 2009, requesting the SCNPC to either repeal or ask the State Council to repeal or revise its Administrative Regulations on Urban Housing Demolition and Relocation (2001) after a series of tragic incidents occurred in protests against forced demolition in China. While the SCNPC did not formally acknowledge the receipt of the petition, in mid-December 2009, the State Council nevertheless invited the five professors to attend a consultation meeting for the revision of the Regulations. *See*, 'State Council Law Office Invites Five Petitioners to Participate in Discussions for the Revision of the Demolition and Relocation Regulations', available at http://news.xinhuanet.com/legal/2009-12/15/content_12647190.htm (accessed 17 December 2009). For a recent report on the tragic incidents, *see*, Zhiling Huang and Weita Liu, 'Tragedy Reignites Debate on Forced Demolitions', *China Daily*, 8 December 2009, available at http://www.chinadaily.com.cn/china/2009-12/08/content_9137322.htm (accessed 7 January 2010).

63 Hand, *supra note* 59, p. 146.

64 The case is reported in *Gazette of the Supreme People's Court of the PRC* 5, 2001: 158–161.

65 *See*, Kui Shen, 'The Beginning of the Age of Constitutionalism – Questions Regarding the First Constitutional Case', published at the Beijing University Law Web site: www.law-dimension.com/details.asp?id=758 (accessed 12 November 2004) (an expanded version of this article is published in English: Kui Shen, 'Is It the Beginning of the Era of the Rule of the Constitution? Reinterpreting China's "First Constitutional Case"', *Pacific Rim Law and Policy Journal* 12, 2003, 199; Huawei Li, 'A New Light in Constitutional Review in Mainland China?' available at the China Constitutionalism Web site: www.calaw.cn/include/shownews.asp?newsid=2001 (last accessed 12 November 2004). For a summary of the case, *see*, *Nanfang Zhoumo* (*Nanfang Weekend*), Internet edition, 17 August 2001; *Renmin Ribao*, 5 September 2001. The Supreme People's Court reply was issued on 24 July 2001, as Interpretation [2001] No. 25, containing merely one

short paragraph. An official version of this Reply is contained in *Gazette of the Supreme People's Court* 5, 2001: 152. Also available at special collection of papers on Constitutional judicialization: http://www.gongfa.com/xianfasifahuazhuanti.htm (accessed 30 November 2008). It must be pointed out that this Reply was abolished in December 2008: *see*, further discussion below.

66 While the right to education and civil remedies for such a violation are contained in the *Law on Education*, the torts occurred well before the *Law on Education* was enacted in March 1995 (and became effective in September 1995). Thus, the *Law on Education* was unlikely to be applicable, though this issue was not debated either in the first instance or on appeal.

67 Full English text of this Reply from the Supreme People's Court is available in Shen, *supra note* 65, p. 204.

68 Technically, it is also questionable whether the Supreme People's Court has a proper constitutional power to undertake such implementation through interpretation and, if so, whether there are any procedures that the Court must follow. For detailed academic analysis of the two cases, *see*, Shen, *supra note* 65; Li, *supra note* 65. It is also questioned whether the people's court should instead apply the *Law on Education* (for a right to education) and the *General Principles of Civil Law* (for remedies). *See*, Cai, *supra note* 59; M. C. Dorf, 'What a Chinese Height Discrimination Case Says about Chinese (and American) Constitutional Law, FindLaw's Legal Documentary, 26 May 2004, available at http://writ.findlaw.com/dorf/20040526.html (accessed 29 May 2004).

69 Judge Huang was the Chief of the First Civil Chamber of the Court, and soon was promoted to Vice President of the Court, but more recently disgraced for alleged corruption. His article, entitled 'Constitutional Judicialisation and Its Significance', was published on the *People's Court Daily* on 13 August 2001, the same day when the Supreme People's Court formally issued its Reply (although the Reply was adopted by the Judicial Committee of the Court on 28 June 2001). A copy of his article is currently available at http://www.gongfa.com/shenkuixianfasifahua.dwt (accessed 2 October 2009). According to Shen Kui, Huang was closely involved in the drafting of the Court Reply: Shen, *supra note* 65, p. 209.

70 In light of Huang's position in the Supreme People's Court and his involvement in the drafting of the Reply, it could also be speculated that Huang's view reflected that of the Court, or at least had the approval of the Court. *See*, Shen, *supra note* 65, pp. 209–211.

71 [1803] 5 *U.S.* 137.

72 Shen, *supra note* 65, p. 230.

73 Many articles have been published on these issues. A most updated and comprehensive coverage of these issues is Balme and Dowdle, *supra note* 2, Chapters 11–14. Another updated analysis is T. E. Kellogg, 'Constitutionalism with Chinse Characteristics? Constitutional Development and Civil Litigation in China', (16 March 2009) *International Journal of Constitutional Law*, (advance access) available at http://icon.oxfordjournals.org/cgi/reprint/mop001vl (accessed 18 July 2009).

74 It is difficult to determine how many courts in these cases that actually made references to constitutional provisions. *The Democracy and Legal System* reported that the reference to constitutional freedom of residence by Huangpu (Guangzhou) Court as the 'first case on constitutional freedom'. *See*, 'China's first case on

constitutional freedom', *Democracy and Legal System* (*Minzhu yu Fazhi*) no.9, 2008: 14–16. This clearly is not the first case in which reference was made to constitutional freedom. *See*, Kellogg, *supra note* 73, p. 2. According to Kellogg (*ibid*, p. 17), in 2003 alone, over thirty cases made such a reference to constitutional provisions.

75 Indeed, in the *Complete Collection of Judicial Interpretation*, the court has avoided completely the issue of constitutional law. *See*, Supreme People's Court of the PRC, *A Complete Collection of Judicial Interpretation* (*Sifa Jieshi Quanji*), Beijing: Press of the People's Court, 1994.

76 *See*, Nanping Liu, '"Judicial Review" in China: A Comparative Perspective', *Review.of Socialis. Law* 14, 1988: 241.

77 According to Kellogg's research, as early as 1988 some Chinese courts had already made reference to constitutional provisions in their judgements. *See*, Kollogg, *supra note* 73, p. 14.

78 *See*, Hualing Fu and R. Cullen, 'Weiquan (Right Protection) Lawyering in an Authoritarian State: Towards Critical Lawyering', available at http://papers.ssrn.com/sol3/papers.cfm?abstract_id=1083925 (accessed 15 October 2009), p. 21.

79 S. Balme, 'Ordinary Justice and Popular Constitutionalism in China', in Balme and Dowdle, *supra note* 2, p. 189.

80 In fact, in terms of cyber discourse, I have seen much more display of blind patriotism and narrow-minded nationalism than demands for fair and equitable justice.

81 I am not suggesting that Weiquan cases or their Internet discourses are not important. Indeed, as Fu and Cullen point out, they serve an educational function and play the role in 'identifying, highlighting and problematising social issues'. *See* Fu and Cullen, *supra note* 78.

82 Chen, *supra note* 1, Chapter 3.

83 For instance, barely two weeks after the adoption of the 2004 constitutional revision, an elderly resident in Beijing had already tried to use the revised constitutional provisions on the protection of private property to stop the demolition of his old house that was built more than a hundred years ago. *See*, Xinhuanet: http://news.xinhuanet.com/comments/2004-04/07/content_1405016.htm (accessed 28 August 2006).

84 Almost immediately after the 2004 revision of the Constitution a group of 30 prominent scholars produced some 18 suggestions for constitutional reforms to implement human rights protection as now enshrined in the Constitution. *See*, Weifang He, *et al*., 'Suggestions for the Improvement of the Constitutional Protection of Human Rights in Our Country', available at http://www.law-thinker.com/details.asp?id=2078 (accessed 28 August 2006). Even though these suggestions are unlikely to be implemented any time soon by the government, such academic activities keep constitutional reform alive and on the agenda of national debate and discussion.

85 *See*, *supra note* 61.

86 In any case, supporting the Party leadership is often taken as a constitutional duty.

87 *See*, Kellogg, *supra note* 3. The Supreme People's Court issued its Interpretation (*fasi*) (2008) No. 15 through a Public Notice on 18 December 2008. This Document No. 15 abolishes a total of 27 sets of Interpretations issued before the end of 2007 and the Qi Yuling Reply is listed among the 27, as one of those

'whose application has ceased'; no further explanations were given for this sudden yet quiet abolition.

88 For Academic debate on the abolition of the Qi Yuling Reply, *see*, special forum, *Jurisprudence* (*Faxue*), no. 3, 2009: 3–35.

89 *See*, 'The Abolition of the First Judicial Interpretation on the Judicialisation of Constitution in Our Country', available at http://www.law-thinker.com/news.php?id=297 (accessed 28 March 2009).

90 *Fasi* (2009) No. 14, adopted 13 July 2009 by the 1470 Judicial Committee of the Supreme People's Court, issued 26 October 2009, and effective from 4 November 2009.

91 Whether the term 'law' includes the Constitution has been a controversial issue debated ever since the first Constitution (1954) was enacted in the PRC. It has never been a settled issue. *See*, Han Dayuan, 'The Abolition of Qi Yuling Reply and Its Relevance to Applicability of the Constitution', *Jurisprudence* (*Faxue*), no. 3, 2009: 3, 4.

92 Shigong Qiang, 'Who Is to Interpret the Constitution?', available at http://www.usc.cuhk.edu.hk/wk.asp (accessed 9 July 2009).

2 Institutionalizing criminal process in China

Hualing Fu

2.1. Introduction

After 30 years of reform, China's criminal justice system remains significantly defective and notorious for its lack of procedural protection of rights. Commentators are particularly harsh on China's record, highlighting torture during police interrogation, unlawful detention, lack of effective criminal defence, lack of judicial independence, wide use of the death penalty, corruption and many other forms of abuse. While largely agreeing with the criticisms, this chapter explores an often-neglected dimension of the criminal justice system – the institutionalization of criminal courts in China in the past 30 years. This chapter contextualizes criminal trial reform in China's socio-economic, legal and political conditions and assesses China's criminal court in the context of its own historical development.

This chapter assesses the criminal court reform in four China-specific contexts. First, socially, China is a country in transition towards a socialist market economy. The vibrant economic growth has undermined not only the economic planning but also the associated social organizations of the planned economy. High social mobility, urbanization, stratification and inequality provide ample opportunities and incentives for crime. The crime rate has been on the rise, and the increase has been steady in the past 30 years. The trial reform addresses the conflicting needs of a fair trial for an accused and controlling the increase in street crimes.

Second, politically, China is a one-party authoritarian state seeking rule of law reform. Law increasingly provides formal legal rights, including rights in the criminal process, with suspects, defendants and their legal representatives mobilizing these rights to protect their interests. But authoritarian at its core, the Party–state relies in part on social stability to compensate for its democracy-deficit and to enhance this performance-based legitimacy. The Party has a keen interest in reducing crime and being responsive to societal need. The imperative of law reform demands more procedural protection of rights to defendants before the court, while the logic of crime control necessitates control, speedy process and harsh penalties. The trial reform takes place under this particular political system.

Third, economically, China is a lower-middle-income economy with limited financial resource and institutional capacity. Given the large number of criminal cases each year and the limited judicial resources available, judges tend to see themselves as factory workers on an assembly line without paying close attention to quality control. To put it simply, public trial is not possible without a proper courtroom; aggressive defence is unlikely without sufficient legal aid funding; and poorly paid judges tend to spend more time on alternative income than challenging the prosecution's case. The trial reform is constrained by limited judicial resources.

Finally, China's criminal justice reform takes place in its civil law tradition which relies on extensive and intensive pre-trial investigation by multiple organizations and active judicial fact-finding. The trial not only is a judge-led event with lawyers playing a minor role, but also relies extensively on documents, rendering it virtually a 'trial by affidavits'. The trial reform is path-dependent on this inquisitorial legacy.

The principal argument of this chapter is that the criminal justice system has been undergoing a process of institutionalization for the past 30 years. Due to the depoliticization of crime and criminal justice, the re-emergence of street crime as a serious social problem and the political and legal reform in which China's one-party authoritarian state is actively seeking the rule of law, the criminal court is developing a professional identity and its institutional interest. This process of institutionalization includes

- An autonomy component: the ability of the court to resist external interference/intervention into the judicial process;
- A competence component: the ability of the court to develop standard rules on evidence and procedures, and, more importantly, to force the other institutions, the prosecution in particular, to comply with the established rules; and
- A fairness component: the ability of criminal courts to act against the interest of the government and to better protect the rights of the defendants.

China's criminal justice started to develop some breathing space for its own institutional growth and professional development. With the depoliticalization of crime and criminal justice, the court is able to function in a relatively stable political and social environment. As a result, criminal trial becomes routine and normalized, hence the institutionalization of the criminal process.

2.2. Depoliticizing criminal trials

Chinese courts throughout the 1950s, 1960s and 1970s were predominately criminal courts both in terms of nature and the number of criminal cases processed, although civil cases had been growing over the decades. Before 1979, criminal cases generally accounted for approximately half of the caseload of the courts, and in a number of years, criminal cases exceeded civil cases.

The gap between civil and criminal cases started to widen in favour of civil cases from the early 1980s, and this trend has continued (Chart 2.1).

Criminal cases, in earlier times, were not only large in number but also regarded as politically and socially more significant. The defining characteristics of criminal justice were the politicization of crime and the instrumental use of courts to maximize the political control of the Chinese Communist Party (CCP). The Maoist 'two contradictions theory' had long provided the principal guideline for handling social conflict in China. The People's Republic of China (PRC) was a democratic dictatorship, often interpreted as 'democracy for the people and dictatorship for the enemies'. The repealed 1975 Constitution provided that

> Socialist society covers a considerably long historical period. Throughout this historical period, there are classes, class contradictions and class struggle, there is the struggle between the socialist road and the capitalist road, there is the danger of capitalist restoration and there is the threat of subversion and aggression by imperialism and social-imperialism. These contradictions can be resolved only by depending on the theory of continued revolution under the dictatorship of the proletariat and on practice under its guidance.[1]

The Maoist theory divides social conflict into two types of contradictions: the antagonistic contradictions between the enemies and the people, and, the non-antagonistic contradictions among the people. Like other revolutionary states,[2] the PRC is characterized by a dual system of justice: one for the people who are supportive of the regime; the other for the people who are hostile to the regime, i.e. the enemies. Criminal law had long been an instrument used by 'the people' against their enemies.

Crime, in general, was also more than a violation of the criminal law; it was regarded as a manifestation of class struggles between the proletariat and the bourgeoisie and a challenge to the political order. Courts, as 'places of dictatorship' and as 'instruments of dictatorship', were used to fulfil the function of class struggle and class repression. Punishing counter-revolutionaries, real or imagined, was the core judicial function. As the government stated, courts, as 'organs of dictatorship, should not be concerned with contradiction among the people'. Otherwise, the proletarian dictatorship would be diluted and diminished.[3]

As Chart 2.2 clearly shows, counter-revolutionary cases accounted for a large proportion of criminal cases received by the courts between 1950s and early 1970s. The most visible change in criminal law in China in the past 60 years since the establishment of the PRC is the sudden drop in political offences towards the end of the 1970s. In December 1978, the CCP called the historical Third Plenary Session of the Eleventh Central Committee in which the Party initiated an open door policy, shifting the national agenda from revolution to economic development. That depoliticization process reshaped the whole criminal justice system. At the ideological level, the CCP announced the end of class struggle which was the defining characteristic of criminal justice in the previous decades. To reflect this political change, the 1979 Criminal Law redefined counter-revolutionary offences from merely thought and status-based offences to more action-based offences. Most of the status political offenders were rehabilitated and most of the thoughts and expressions that were treated as criminal were simply tolerated.

There was a rethinking about the legal status of convicted persons. In a bold article published in the *People's Daily*, Professor Li Buyun questioned the doctrine which regarded convicted criminals as class enemies and famously announced that criminals are also citizens of the country and enjoy rights as such. The concepts of citizenship and legal rights diluted an otherwise sharp contrast between the people and their enemies and brought forward a more neutral definition of crime as a violation of statutes.

The changing ideological make-up may have only reflected a demographic change. By the late 1970s and early 1980s, the proportion of juveniles and youths in the convicted population started to increase (Charts 2.3 and 2.4). To the government's alarm, prisons were filled no longer with counter-revolutionaries or other class enemies, but children of their own, i.e. people from a working class background.

A direct result of depoliticization is a degree of stability in criminal caseloads. Criminal cases have been increasing since the early 1980s, but the increase is steady and largely predictable given the social and economic development in China. High volatility that was characteristic of the criminal courts between the 1950s and 1970s became less visible, and even the strike-hard campaigns did not have significant impact on the routine operation of the criminal courts since the late 1980s, with the exception of 1983 (Chart 2.5).

The declining status of criminal courts in the judiciary largely reflects the changing profile of criminal cases (Charts 2.6 and 2.7). Criminal cases are becoming less important, because they are no longer political. The bread-and-butter cases for courts are crimes against property, theft in particular, inter-personal violence and crimes against public order. Criminal cases are also small in percentage in the total number of cases tried in courts. While the actual number of criminal cases may have increased steadily, they consistently account for about 10 per cent of the total number of cases handled by the courts.

The percentage of criminal judges among the total number of judges also declined over the decades, especially after 2002, while the actual number of criminal judges may have grown slightly. In 2006, it was reported that there were 19,207 criminal court judges in China;[4] and in 2008, the number increased to near 20,000.[5] This figure represents slightly over 10 per cent of the judges in China, roughly proportional to the percentage of criminal cases in the overall number of court cases.[6]

How has the relationship between the CCP and the criminal justice system developed over the decades in a depoliticizing context? At the policy level, the CCP maintains a keen interest in criminal law matters and is deeply concerned with the law and order situation in the country, social stability has significant bearing on the political legitimacy of the one-party state. To a government with a democratic deficit, the ruling party relies on performance-based legitimacy, a low crime rate and a high sense of safety are key components in establishing regime legitimacy. Crime generally attracts serious political attention, and political control is an integral part of the judicial process in any case that is perceived to be sensitive. Courts ultimately lacked institutional autonomy in the process.

Reform in the criminal process in China should be seen in the light of a conflict between the political need for stability and the pressures for reform and liberalization. This tension has created a dual criminal justice system in China. On the one hand, there is the routine and institutionalized process in which legal institutions process criminal cases according to legal procedures. This routine system, despite of the drawbacks and abuses, is characterized by increasing professionalism and relative institutional autonomy. On the other hand, there is the arbitrary criminal justice system which is periodically superimposed by the CCP on the routine criminal process. When that occurs, the criminal justice institutions lose their institutional autonomy, rules are suspended and professional identity is swept away. The institutional mandate gives way to political expediency, hence resulting in a political takeover of the criminal justice system.

Over the decades, the politically-oriented arbitrary criminal process has been diluted and *ad hoc* campaigns against crime have become smaller in scale, less aggressive in style and are contained largely within the legal framework. Campaign-driven criminal justice policy remains active, but its impact on the criminal justice institutions has been reduced. Courts in particular keep a degree of distance from the politics of crime, and in their institutional and procedural design, the courts are able to factor-in, internalize and absorb the arbitrariness of the political process. Because of the ability to capture the political intrusions, criminal trial is much less volatile and more predictable.

From time to time, the control over the criminal process was exercised directly by the CCP, with the local Party Secretary personally making decisions on the disposal of cases. Judges continue to be subjected to CCP control in a variety of sensitive cases as defined by the CCP itself, ranging from the dissident trials in the aftermath of 1989, the prosecution of the China Democracy Party and the Falun Gong followers in the late 1990s, to *weiquan* cases in more recent years.

By and large, the CCP has lost interest in a hands-on approach on criminal justice matters, and generally in a hands-on approach on law. Unless a case is regarded as politically significant or involving a high-ranking member within the CCP, the CCP is content to leave the matter to the criminal justice institutions. Instead of approving individual cases, the CCP has shifted its focus to the macro-control over the criminal justice system, mainly to settle disputes between the different institutions within the system – a principal function of the CCP's political and legal committee. At the same time, criminal courts have developed their own ways to internalize political demands from outside agencies within the criminal justice system.

2.3. Judicial autonomy

It is well-known that Chinese courts are subject to supervision of multiple external institutions, especially by the local people's congresses and the procuracy. There are multiple entry-points in which the outside agencies may interfere with the judicial process and the best known is adjudicative supervision mobilized by the procuracy and others. However, what is less known is the fact that the supervision of external bodies is very ineffective. There is a cooperative ethos running through the Criminal Procedure Law (CPL) and the guiding principle in the criminal justice process is mutual cooperation first and mutual supervision second. Indeed, the criminal process is designed to deter any post-conviction supervision by the procuracy. When criminal courts are interested in developing a new institutional identity and a degree of autonomy, supervision through existing mechanism is of little use.

Under Chinese law, defence 'appeals' against a court decision and prosecution 'protests' (*kangsu*) against a trial decision. A second-instance court decision is final and becomes legally effective. However, the CPL empowers the President of the second-instance court, the superior courts, the procuracy and the defendant concerned to initiate an adjudicative review to challenge the second-instance court's decision.[7] The procuracy has a dual role in the criminal process: prosecution and adjudicative supervision. Adjudicative review initiated by the procuracy is also referred to as 'protest'.[8] Chart 2.8 maps the development of trial, appeal/protest and adjudicative review for the past five decades.

Adjudicative review, which is a process external to a criminal proceeding, is therefore a crucial means to control the courts' autonomy in adjudication: the higher the number of adjudicative review cases, the stronger the external control, and hence the lower the autonomy enjoyed by the courts in adjudication.

As shown in Chart 2.9, adjudicative review in both the actual number of cases received by courts and its percentage in the total number of first- and second-instance criminal cases, have been deceasing steadily since the mid-1980s. In 2006, of the 795,471 first- and second-instance criminal cases concluded by the courts, there were only 3,124 adjudicative reviews, accounting for a mere 0.39 per cent of the first- and second-instance criminal cases concluded by the courts in that year.

The procuracy plays a much lesser role in adjudicative review in criminal cases than expected, even though the actual number of adjudicative review initiated by the procuracy may have been on the increase, largely due a conscientious effort of the Supreme People's Procuratorate (Chart 2.10). But generally, procuracy-initiated adjudicative review is small in number and accounts only for a small proportion in the overall number of adjudicative review. Between 1998 and 2006, the number of procuracy-initiated adjudicative review has accounted for less than 14 per cent of the total number of adjudicative reviews received by the courts in the respective years, though the percentage has been increasing throughout those years (Chart 2.11). The low rate of adjudicative review filed by the procuracy during that period was accompanied by an 8–37 per cent rate of withdrawal of the procuracy's adjudicative reviews. Taking year 2006 as an example, of the 415 adjudicative reviews filed by the procuracy, 95 were subsequently withdrawn (Chart 2.12).

In comparison, adjudicative reviews initiated by complainants and presidents of the second-instance courts constituted over 60 per cent of the total number of adjudicative reviews between 2003 and 2007 while adjudicative reviews initiated by the superior courts only accounted for 20–30 per cent throughout those five years (Chart 2.13). Clearly, some of the adjudicative reviews were referred to the courts by the people's congresses, Party organs, members of the Chinese People's Political Consultative Conference and local governments, but the exact percentage remains unknown.

The low level of adjudicative review should be considered in the context that the rate of appeal by procuracy is equally low (Chart 2.14). Indeed, the appeal rate is as low as China's acquittal rate (Chart 2.15).

Another evidence of the increase in autonomy enjoyed by the court is that, over the past decades, the Supreme People's Court (SPC) has become a dominant rule-maker in the area of criminal law.[9] Historically, the SPC worked with the police and the procuracy closely in legal interpretation so that a consensus would be achieved before an interpretation was issued. The judiciary did not dominate in the criminal justice system and a consultative approach could build consensus which gave consistency to legal interpretation and ensured effective enforcement of law across different institutions. This consensus-building process is essential to China given its compartmentalization of law.

Increasingly, the SPC is departing from this traditional approach and becoming more assertive in legal interpretation by interpreting criminal law on its own (Charts 2.16 and 2.17). The SPC has done so notwithstanding disagreement or even open hostility from the police and the procuracy.

Courts are also becoming more assertive in mobilizing existing legal power. They behave more aggressively in dealing with the horizontal relations with the police and procuracy, including selectively expanding its jurisdiction and challenging administrative authorities through accepting administrative litigations.

2.4. Judicial competence

The increase in autonomy allows the courts to expand their power, professional identity and establish new rules of procedures to guide the criminal process. The formal authority of the court has also grown in the criminal process and gradually, China is witnessing a transition from a police-centric criminal justice towards a court-centric criminal justice. Most notably is a new article in the amended CPL. Article 12 of the CPL provides that: 'No person shall be found guilty without being judged as such by a People's Court according to law'. Whether this article implies a presumption of innocence is a debatable issue, but it is beyond doubt that the new article authorizes the court as the final arbitrator of criminal liability, thus highlighting a court-centric criminal process.

As noted in the foregoing section, the SPC has been the primary law-making body for criminal law. Given the lack of cohesiveness, stability and clarity in Chinese criminal law, legal interpretation becomes crucial for the operation of criminal justice. The Chinese legislature historically delegated the power of legal interpretation of criminal law to the police, procuracy and the court. Although now playing a more active role in this area, the legislature is unlikely to play any significant role in guiding judicial practice on the ground and to step in only when there is a significant gap between the law and practice, or when needed to settle a dispute among the criminal justice institutions.

What transpires from the political change is the emergence of an increasingly autonomous judiciary establishing standards for the criminal process. This judiciary-initiated standard-setting ability is creating the momentum for a court-centric criminal justice system.

One excellent example is the self-claimed judicial authority to impose rules of evidence, especially the authority to exclude confessions obtained by investigators through torture and other unlawful means. The exclusionary rules have been on the statutory book of the SPC for more than ten years. The SPC is now formulating evidence rules which are expected to address three major problems that have been undermining the fairness of trial, i.e. failure of witnesses to testify in court; exclusion of illegally obtained evidence; and the lack of pre-trial disclosure of evidence. The new rules, if successfully implemented, will require police testimony in court; will allow the courts to exclude evidence that are unlawfully obtained, especially confession statements; and will compel the prosecution to disclose all the prosecution evidence to the defence.

Can the court make the rules and have them enforced? A more pointed question is whether the court is capable of finding a defendant not guilty because of the new rules. The Chinese court is perceived to be weak, because it rarely finds a defendant not guilty. In the past 60 years since the establishment of the PRC, the number of acquitted defendants was between 1,713 (in 2006) and 6,617 (in 2000), with an acquittal rate between 0.19 per cent (in 2006) and 3.51 per cent (in 1979) (Chart 2.18).[10]

A not-guilty verdict is an open challenge to the prosecutorial and police authority and has been used with great caution. There are internal procedures to ensure that this is a collective decision and endorsed by the court as an institution: Prosecutorial objection is heard after trial, deliberated and overruled, knowing well that such a decision will adversely affect the interest of the individual police officers and prosecutors involved and their institutions. This is an option, while available in law, that judges are eager to avoid if possible.

Because of a cooperative ethos and a politically weak court, judicial authority is exerted less through open confrontation with other institutions characterized by an open announcement of a not guilty verdict, but more through negotiation, compromise and subtle pressure. Armed with an enhanced legal authority in the criminal process, judges are asserting their authorities through other means, notably informal negotiation in which judges persuade and compel prosecutors to withdraw weak cases from proceeding further. Withdrawal is a procedure of dubious legal nature and is not clearly defined in the criminal procedure law. However, this mechanism is less public and carries much less negative incentives on the part of the prosecutors and police for this matter. Because of its informality, it prevents a showdown in an open court and is not confrontational and, more importantly, it is consensual and achieved with the full consent of the prosecution.

Increasingly, judges whisper to the ears of the prosecutors to persuade them to withdraw prosecution on the ground of insufficient evidence to support a guilty verdict. Informal withdrawal is a coping strategy of judges facing conflicting imperatives. The rule of law imperatives demand judges to decide a case on the strength of available evidence. Judges are made responsible for their decisions and a reversal by an appellate court has adverse consequence for a trial judge, therefore, judges have to stop prosecution where the prosecution evidence is insufficient. The imperative of inter-institutional comity and the cooperative ethos demands cooperation, not confrontation, between judges and prosecutors.

Reports from Guangzhou, Anhui and elsewhere have pointed to the common usage of this informal practice during trials. A rough estimate is that as high as 5 per cent of the prosecution's cases may have been withdrawn from courts and there are five to ten informal withdrawals of prosecution for every not guilty verdict in China.[11]

2.5. Judicial fairness

Penalties imposed by Chinese courts are perceived to be harsh. This is so largely because of the wide use of the death penalty. The number of capital offences in China has been on the increase over the past 30 years. There were 28 capital offences among the 115 offences in the criminal code in 1979, accounting for less than 25 per cent. From 1981 to 1993, the legislature promulgated a total of 15 pieces of special legislation, creating more than 40 capital offences, with the average of three new capital offences every year. There are 68 capital offences in the current criminal code. The large number of executions is definitely aggravated by the lack of a minimum degree of procedural protection – over decades China was not following its own criminal procedure in reviewing capital cases, and even the formality of procedural safeguards were not honoured.

The death penalty is of course harsh and China's execution rate remains the highest in the world by a wide margin, although the margin may be narrow if the rate is considered in a per capita term. When the death penalty is treated as the defining characteristic of the Chinese criminal justice system, the system can hardly be anything except harsh and brutal, notwithstanding the current reform to make the trial procedure of the death penalty cases more transparent and tightening the relevant appeal and review procedures.[12]

The picture of harshness and brutality is misleading when legal theory is accepted at its face value and when capital punishment is examined in isolation. Notwithstanding the harsh rhetoric of criminal law, court-imposed punishment is lenient in both absolute and relative terms. Increasingly, punishment imposed by the court is becoming more lenient and the pattern is stabilizing.

As can be seen in Charts 2.19 and 2.20, there are two significant changes in criminal punishment in China in the past three decades. The first change took place between 1978 and 1983 when punishment gained a degree of stability and order, reflecting a rare political stability in the short history of the PRC. Moreover, the second change took place between 1997 and 1998 when the application of punishment of custodial sentence, death penalty and suspended death penalty took a decisive downward trend and the number of non-custodial sentence increased correspondingly. The fall in the former was particularly sharp with respect to the punishment of over five years' imprisonment. The dual change is principally caused by the amendment to the Criminal Law in 1997 which lightened criminal punishment for all criminal offences by restricting the use of death penalty, shortening the term of imprisonment and allowing non-custodial sentencing for a larger number of offences.[13] The change also coincides precisely with the appointment of Mr Xiao Yang as the President of the SPC (Chief Justice), a strong believer of leniency and rehabilitation in the criminal process, reflecting clearly the personal influence of the Chief Justice on punishment.

The SPC initiated this downward trend on its own and without the clear support of other institutions. The court clearly has the power to change sentencing structure. The SPC was better positioned in the criminal justice system after the 1996 amendment to the CPL. The amendment was widely regarded as shifting the focus of the criminal process towards the creation of a court-centric system in which judges weigh the evidence as produced and, on the basis of the evidence, make final decisions.

The lenient penalty movement takes place within the legal framework as provided by the criminal code. Criminal punishment is often broadly framed and there are wide-ranging mitigating factors which allow leniency, including the use of non-custodial sentence. As long as a lenient treatment is justifiable in law and falls within the permissible scope of sentencing guidelines, the prosecution has little legal leverage in challenging a court decision.

While the prosecution is developing a keen interest in protesting against non-custodial sentence (in corruption cases in particular), the current criminal procedure is designed to deter and to frustrate prosecution protest, thus limiting the supervisory function of prosecutors.

2.6. Conclusion

This aforementioned newly found autonomy provides a foundation for courts and their judges to further develop their institutional identity, strengthen their competence and enhance their professional standard. As a consequence, China's criminal courts have developed more space for their own institutional growth and professional development. Courts have become more aware of their institutional interest and are willing to protect, and more capable of protecting, this interest in dealing with other stakeholders in the criminal process. As a result, there is the potential for courts to become an independent actor in the criminal process, playing a more active role in challenging the case of the police and prosecution and in offering better protection for the defendants.

Criminal justice reform lagged far behind legal reform in the social and economic spheres in China and is defective even when benchmarked against constitutional and legal requirements. This chapter does not dispute this claim but merely points out a modest achievement of the court in building an infrastructure that is able to develop a routine, normalized and predictable criminal trial which has brought a degree of order into chaos. Critics of China's criminal process should note the nuance and dynamics of the reform process in which a particular reform measure is initiated, frustrated, negotiated and achieved in a subtle way.

Appendices

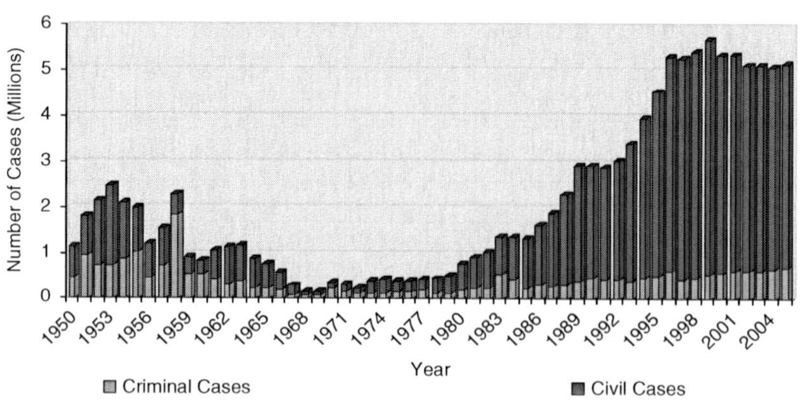

Chart 2.1 Numbers of criminal and civil cases received by courts in China (1950–2005).[14]

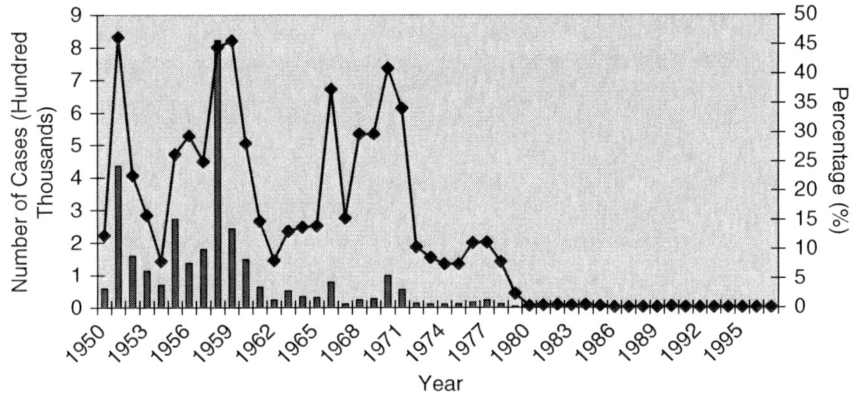

Chart 2.2 Number of first-instance counter-revolutionary cases received by the courts in China (1950–1997).[15]

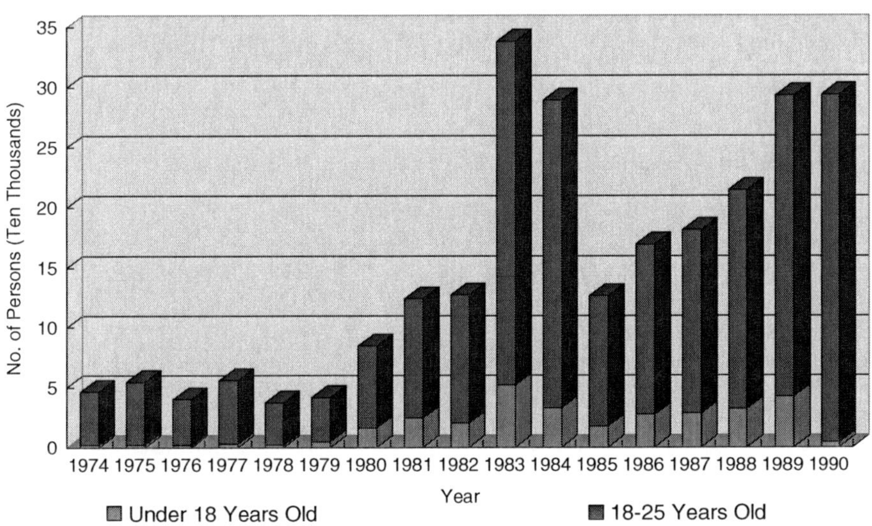

Chart 2.3 Number of convicted persons who were under the age of 25 (1974–1990).[16]

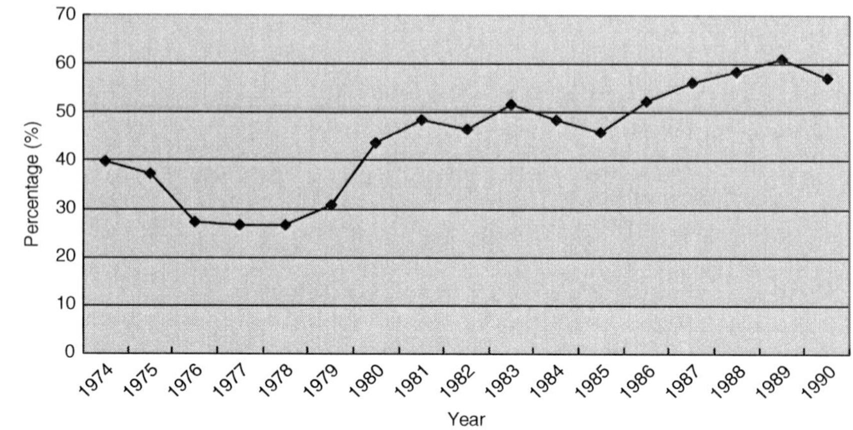

Chart 2.4 Percentage of convicted persons who were under the age of 25 of the total number of convicted persons (1974–1990).[17]

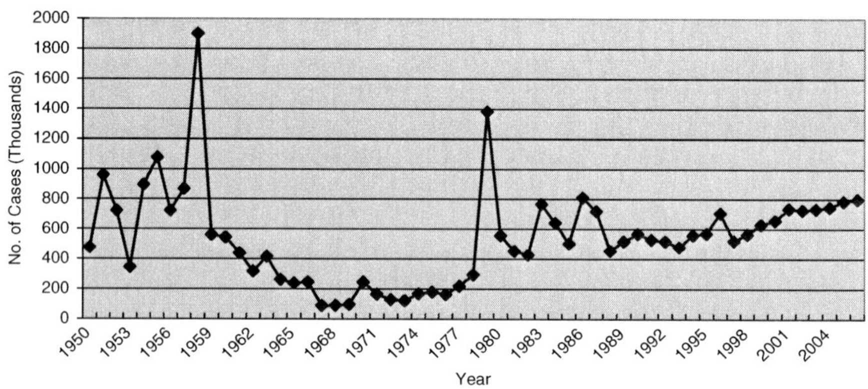

Chart 2.5 Total number of criminal cases received by the courts (1950–2006).[18]

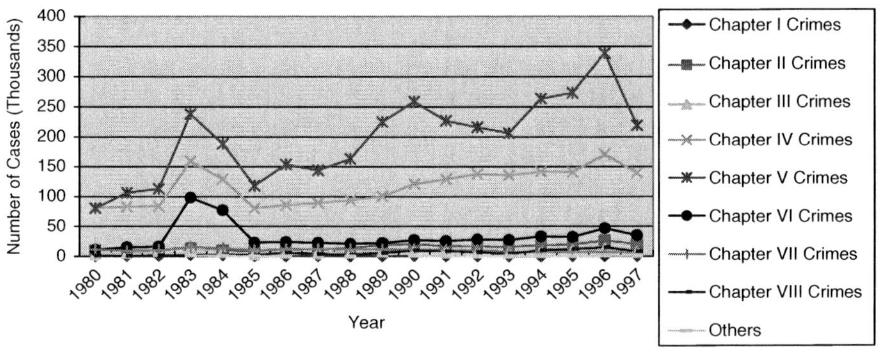

Chart 2.6 Breakdown of first-instance criminal cases received by the courts by category of crimes (1980–1997).[19]

Notes: 'Chapter I Crimes' refers to crimes of counter-revolution; 'Chapter II Crimes' refers to crimes of endangering public security; 'Chapter III Crimes' refers to crimes of undermining the socialist economic order; 'Chapter IV Crimes' refers to crimes of infringing upon the rights of the person and the democratic rights of citizens; 'Chapter V Crimes' refers to crimes of property violation; 'Chapter VI Crimes' refers to crimes of obstructing the administration of public order; 'Chapter VII Crimes' refers to crimes of disrupting marriage and the family; 'Chapter VIII Crimes' refers to crimes of dereliction of duty; and 'Others' includes teaching methods to commit crimes.

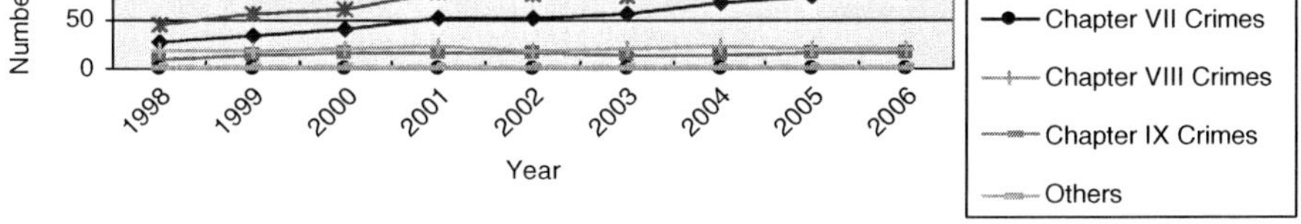

Chart 2.7 Breakdown of first-instance criminal cases received by the courts by category of crimes (1998–2006).[20]

Notes: 'Chapter II Crimes' refers to crime of endangering public security; 'Chapter III Crimes' refers to crimes of disrupting the order of socialist market economy; 'Chapter IV Crimes' refers to crimes of infringing upon citizens' rights of person and democratic rights; 'Chapter V Crimes' refers to crimes of property violation; 'Chapter VI Crimes' refers to crimes of obstructing the administration of public order; 'Chapter VII Crimes' refers to crimes of impairing the interests of national defence; 'Chapter VIII Crimes' refers to crimes of embezzlement and bribery; 'Chapter IX Crimes' refers to crimes of dereliction of duty; and 'Others' include crimes of endangering national security and crimes of servicemen's transgression of duties.

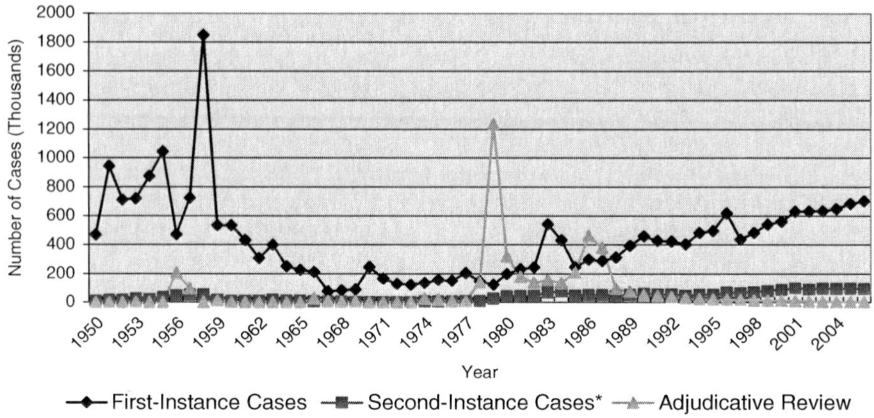

Chart 2.8 Criminal cases received by the courts (1950–2006).[21]

* 'Second-Instance Cases' here include appeals by the defendants and prosecution protests.

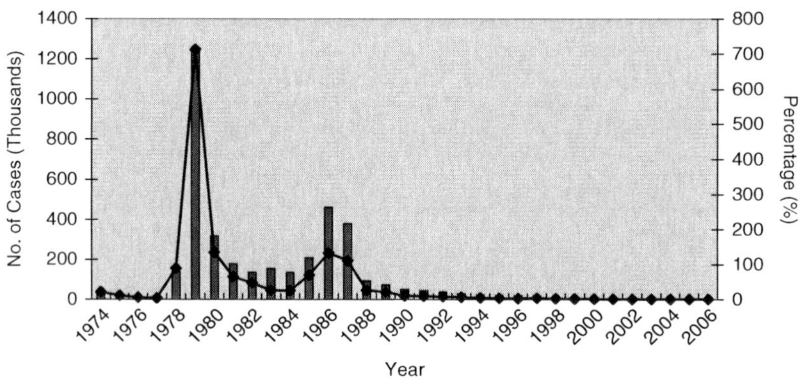

Chart 2.9 Percentage of criminal adjudicative review received by the court in first- and second-instances criminal cases concluded by the court (1998–2006).[22]

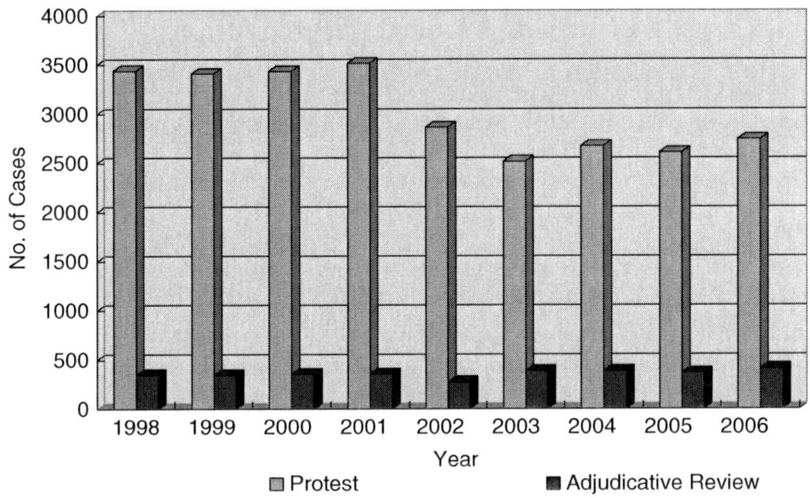

Chart 2.10 Protest in the forms of appeal and adjudicative review by procuratorates (1998–2006).[23]

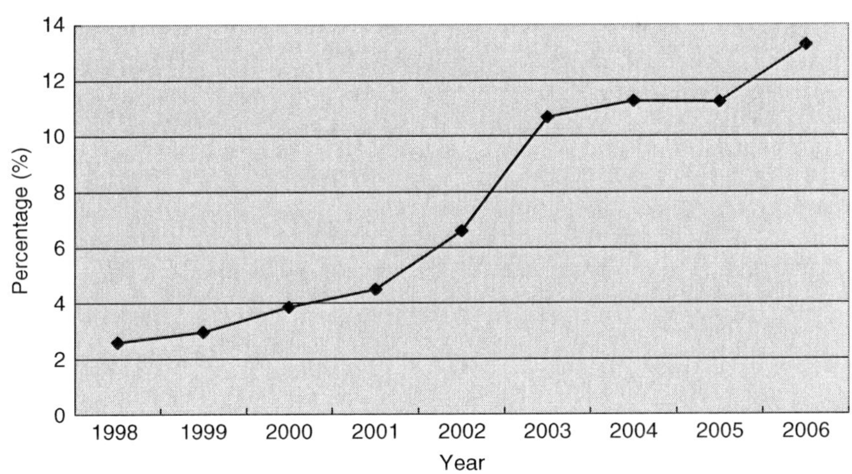

Chart 2.11 Percentage of adjudicative review initiated by the procuracy in the total number of adjudicative reviews received by the courts (1998–2006).[24]

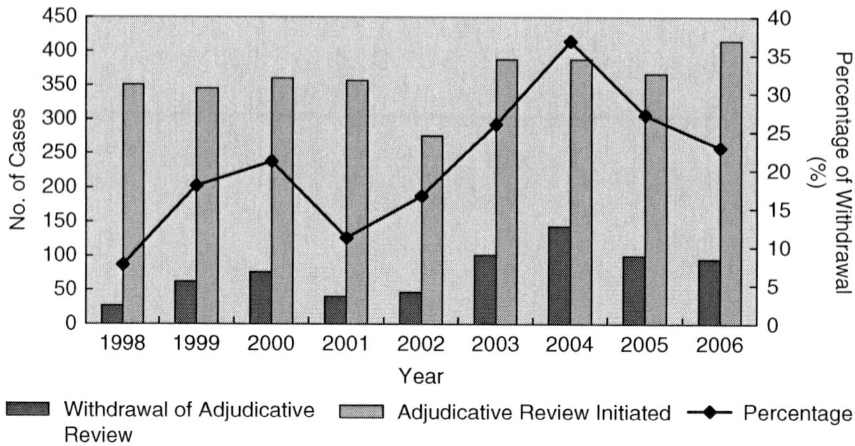

Chart 2.12 Withdrawal of protest (1998–2006).[25]

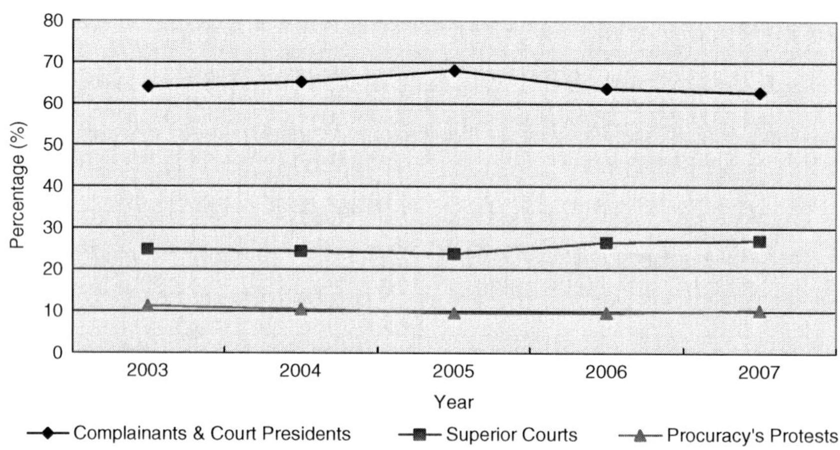

Chart 2.13 Breakdown of adjudicative reviews by sources of cases (2003–2007).[26]

Notes:– 'Complainants & Court Presidents': complaints lodged by the complainants and cases where the president of the court referred to the judicial committee for a decision to retry the case after having discovered that there were mistakes in the judgment.

– 'Superior Courts': cases where the superior courts discovered mistakes in the judgments of the lower courts and therefore decided to retry the cases by themselves and directed the lower courts concerned to retry the cases.

– 'Procuracy's Protests': adjudicative reviews initiated by the procuratorates.

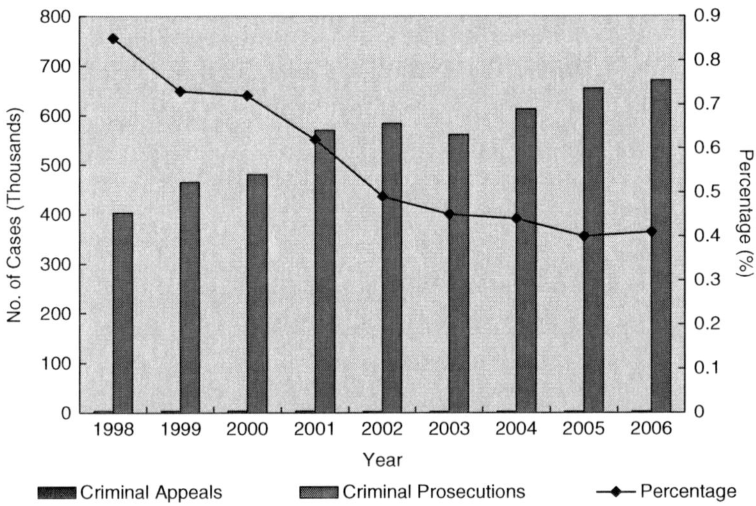

Chart 2.14 Criminal appeals by the procuracy in the total number of criminal prosecutions initiated by the procuracy (1998–2006).[27]

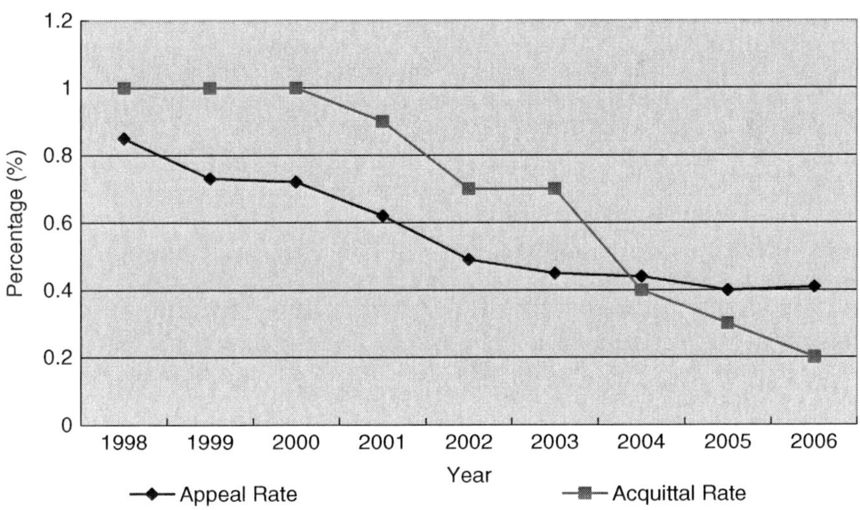

Chart 2.15 Prosecution's appeal rate and acquittal rate (1998–2006).[28]

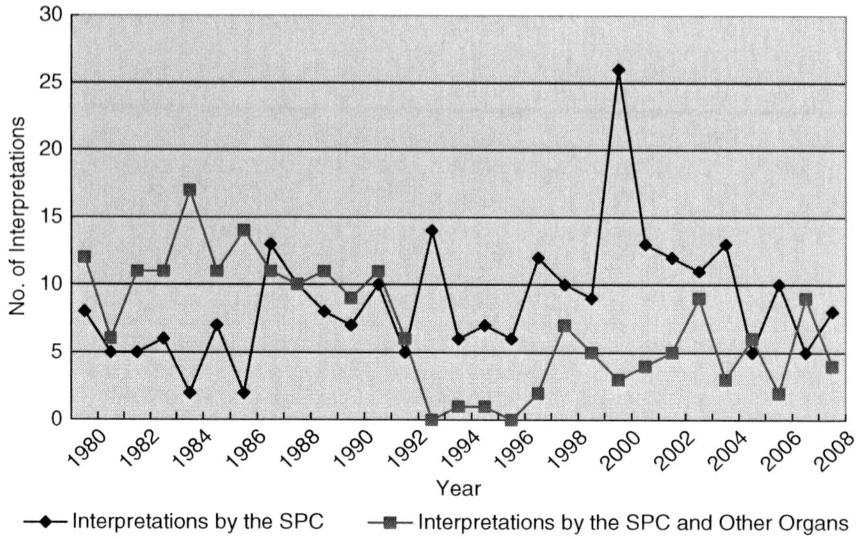

Chart 2.16 Judicial interpretations on criminal law (1980–2008).[29]

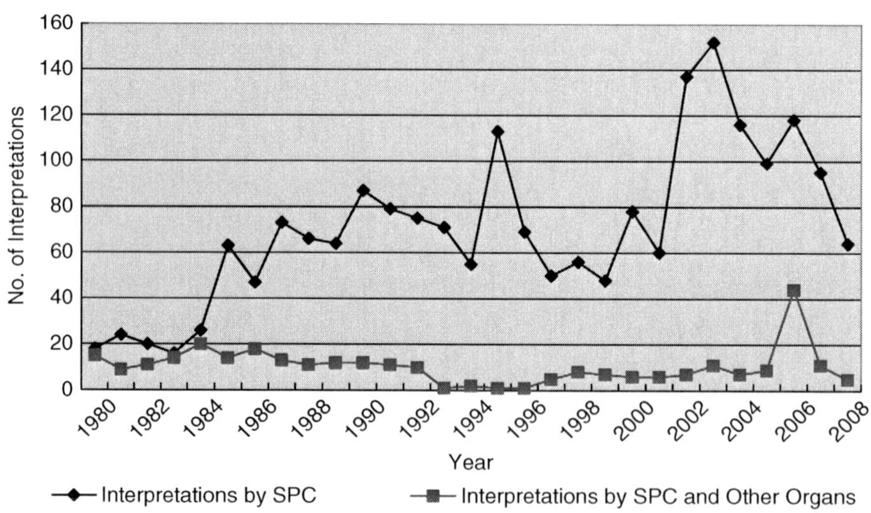

Chart 2.17 Total number of judicial interpretations (1980–2008).[30]

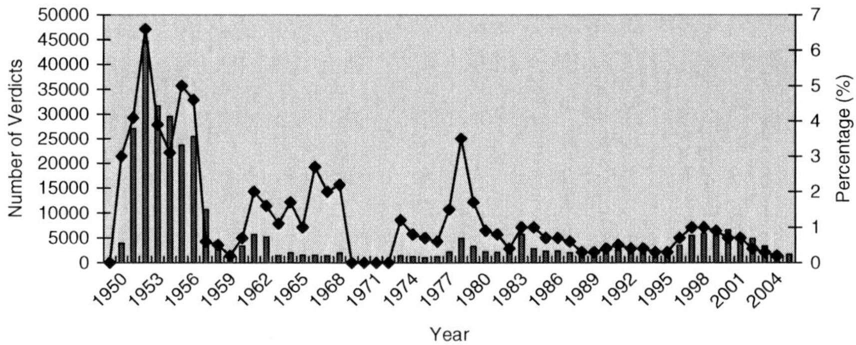

Chart 2.18 Number of not guilty verdicts in the total number of sentences imposed by the courts (1950–2006).[31]

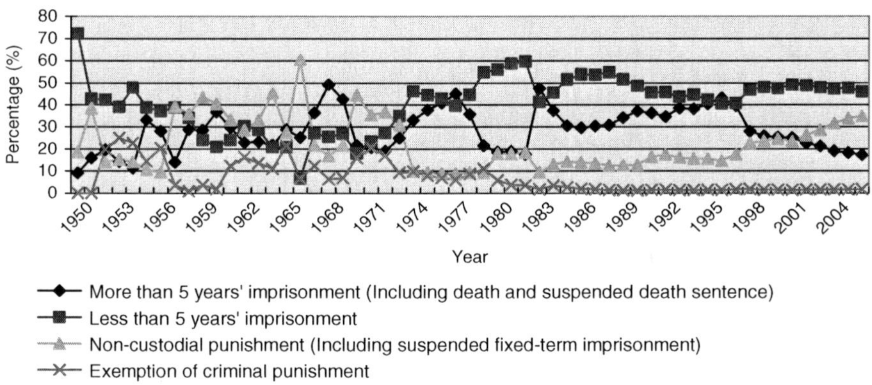

Chart 2.19 Breakdown of the sentences imposed by the courts (1950–2006).[32]

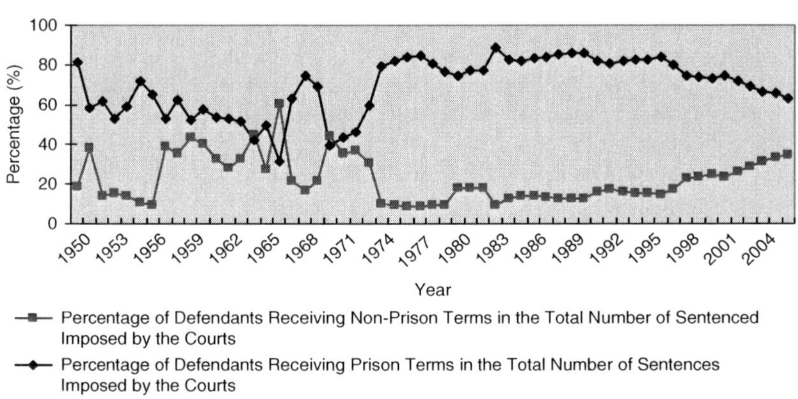

Chart 2.20 Percentages of prison and non-prison sentences in the total number of sentences imposed by the courts (1950–2006).[33]

Notes

1 Preamble to the Constitution of the People's Republic of China 1975.
2 Richard Abel (ed.), *The Politics of Informal Justice*, New York: Academic Press, 1982.
3 Zheng Hanzhou, 'Report on the 2nd National Conference on Civil Trials (22 December 1978)', *Renmin Sifa* [People's Judicature] 1, 1979: 2. Zheng was the Vice President of the Supreme People's Court (SPC).
4 Chen Si, 'Seventy percent of the criminal court judges have above undergraduate academic qualification', *Zhongguo Fayuan Wang* [www.chinacourt.org], 9 November 2006, *<http://www.chinacourt.org/html/article/200611/08/222951.shtml>* (accessed 13 February 2009). In another report, it stated that as of 2006, there were over 18,000 adjudicators in criminal courts in China, and together with the number of persons sitting on the adjudicative committee, there were over 20,000 persons handling criminal adjudication in China. 'China "life and death adjudicators" take turn to receive training in Beijing, Xiao Yang made an important speech', *Zhongguo Renda Xinwen* [News of China's National People's Congress], 16 November 2006, *<http://npc.people.com.cn/GB/15177/53060/5047737.html>* (accessed 13 February 2009) [hereafter '*NPC News*'].
5 Shen Deyong, 'The work of criminal adjudication during the 30 year's reform and opening up', *Fazhi Zixun* (Legal Information) 12, 2008: 5; Wang Shengjun, 'Report of the Supreme People's Court on the Situation of Strengthening the Work of Criminal Adjudication and Safeguarding Judicial Fairness', available at *chinalawinfo.com*, *<http://law.chinalawinfo.com/newlaw2002/slc/slc.asp?db=chl&gid=112997>* (accessed 4 March 2009).
6 *Ibid.*
7 CPL, Articles 203–207.
8 One has to be cautious in viewing 'protest' in Chinese statistics, because, as mentioned earlier, the same term can also be used to describe the prosecution's appeal against a trial court's decision, and very often the two kinds of protests are not clearly distinguished in the statistics.
9 For the past 30 years, the SPC issued, by itself or jointly with other organs, over 440 judicial interpretations regarding criminal matters: 254 were issued by itself or jointly with the SPP between 1978 and 1997; over 190 have been issued since 1997. Shen, *supra note* 5.
10 It is important to note that the not guilty verdict is calculated in a unique way because of the lack of a plea mechanism that is commonly used in common law jurisdictions. Where no plea is taken at the beginning of a judicial process, every defendant must go through a full trial and there must be judicial finding of facts. Nearly every defendant would be found guilty by the court. Where the institution of plea bargaining does not exist, conviction rate has to be high.
11 In Beijing, there were 23 (defendants) acquittals and 137 (cases) withdrawals in the courts between 2003 and 2004. In Guangzhou, there were 24 acquittals and 302 withdrawals between 2000 and November 2002. In Anhui, a city court approved the procuratorate's withdrawal of prosecution in 35 cases in 2002, which was 5.3 times the number of persons acquitted during the same period. 'Not guilty when there is doubt', *Renmin Gongan* [People's Police] 11, 2004: 60; Research Group of the People's Procuratorate of Guangzhou City, 'A survey report of the cases of withdrawal of prosecution and not guilty verdict', *Zhongguo Xingshifa*

Zazhi [China Criminal Law Magazine] 5, 2003: 107; Liu Jiguo, 'Studies on issues regarding withdrawal of public prosecution in criminal litigation', *Renmin Jiancha* [People's Procuratorate] 1, 2004: 37.

12 Since 2006, all death penalty cases are required to be tried in open court; and since 1 January 2007, all death penalty cases have to be approved by the SPC. Since the implementation of these reforms, the death penalty rate has been reduced substantially: according to the then President of the SPC, the decision of imposition of the death penalty in 15 per cent of the death penalty cases submitted to the SPC for approval in 2007 were disapproved. The reduction of death sentence is possibly because of the rigorous effort by the Xiao Yang court. To accommodate the change in approval procedure in death penalty cases, the number of criminal chambers in the SPC was increased from two to five and more than 100 adjudicators were also appointed to take up the job of reviewing the death penalty cases. These new members of the SPC were said to be high-quality judges transferred from the provincial/municipal courts. Similarly, the requirement of opening a court session to adjudicate, as opposed to paper trial, all appeals against death sentence by the higher courts is also responded by increasing the number of criminal court judges in higher courts. Zhang Jun, 'Grand judge's review of criminal adjudication for the past 30 years' reform and opening', *Dongfang Fayan* [www.dffy.com], 14 October 2008, <*http://www.dffy.com/faxuejieti/zh/200810/20081014072632.htm*> (accessed 20 February 2009); 'Announcement of the reports of the Supreme People's Court and Supreme People's Procuratorate', *Wen Wei Po*, 11 March 2008, A10; 'One hundred Supreme People's Court judges will take up their positions to review death penalty cases', *Renmin Wang* [The Website of People's Daily], 2 November 2006, <*http://legal.people.com.cn/BIG5/43027/43034/43049/4987273.html*> (accessed 18 March 2009); *NPC News*, *supra note* 4.

13 Huang Bao, 'Reflections on penal leniency and China's penal reform', *Yunnan Jingxue* (Yunnan Police Studies) 3, 1997: 63–65.

14 'Civil Cases' include civil cases (1950–1998), economic cases (1983–1998) and administrative cases (1987–1998). For the figures for the years 1950–1998, *see* Research Office of the Supreme People's Court, *Quanguo Renmin Fayuan Sifa Tongji Lishi Ziliao Huibian 1949–1998 (Xingshi Bufen)* [Collection of Historical Judicial Statistical Information of the People's Courts in China 1949–1998 (Criminal Section)], Beijing: People's Court Press, 2000 [hereafter '*Criminal Statistics*']; and Research Office of the Supreme People's Court, *Quanguo Renmin Fayuan Sifa Tongji Lishi Ziliao Huibian 1949–1998 (Minshi Bufen)* [Collection of Historical Judicial Statistical Information of the People's Courts in China 1949–1998 (Civil Section)], Beijing: People's Court Press, 2000. For the figures for the years 1999–2005, *see Zhongguo Falü Nianjian* [China Law Yearbook], Beijing: Press of China Law Yearbook [hereafter '*China Law Yearbook*'], vol. 2000–2006.

15 The Amended Criminal Law 1997 abolished the counter-revolutionary offences, so there is no 'counter-revolutionary offence' since 1997. *Criminal Statistics* ibid.

16 For the figures for years 1974 and 1975, they included convicted persons who were between 26 and 28. *Criminal Statistics*, *supra note* 14.

17 *Ibid.*

18 The total number of criminal cases includes the total numbers of first-instance criminal cases, second-instance criminal cases and adjudicative review of criminal cases in China. For the figures for the years 1950–1998, *see Criminal Statistics*,

supra note 14; for the figures for the years 1999–2006, *see China Law Yearbook, supra note* 14, vol. 2000–2007.

19 *Criminal Statistics, supra note* 14; *Zhongguo Falü Nianjian (1987–1997)* [China Law Yearbook (1987–1997)], Beijing: Press of China Law Yearbook, 1998.

20 *China Law Yearbook, supra note* 14, vol. 1999–2007.

21 For the figures for the years 1950–1998, *see Criminal Statistics, supra note* 14; for the figures for the years 1999–2006, *see China Law Yearbook, supra note* 14, vol. 2000–2007.

22 *Ibid.*

23 *China Law Yearbook, supra note* 14, vol. 1999–2007.

24 *Ibid.*

25 *Ibid.*

26 Hu Yunteng and Zhou Haiyang, 'Statistical analysis of criminal cases of second instance, adjudicative review and complaint', *Fazhi Zixun* [Legal Information] 4, 2008: 22.

27 *China Law Yearbook, supra note* 14, vol. 1999–2007.

28 *Ibid.*

29 Data from 1980 to 2001 are extracted from Research Office of the Supreme People's Court, *Zhonghua Renmin Gongheguo Zuigao Renmin Fayuan Sifa Jieshi Quanji* [Collections of Judicial Interpretations of the Supreme People's Court of the People's Republic of China], Beijing: People's Court Press, 2002, vol. I, II and III. Data from 2002 onward are gathered from *Beida Falu Xinxi Wang* [chinalawinfo], <http://www.chinalawinfo.com>.

30 *Ibid.*

31 For the figures for the years 1950–1992, *see Criminal Statistics, supra note* 14; for the figures for the years 1993–2006, *see China Law Yearbook, supra note* 14, vol. 1994–2007.

32 For the figures for the years 1950–1992, *see Criminal Statistics, supra note* 14; for the figures for the years 1993–2006, *see China Law Yearbook, supra note* 14, vol. 1994–2007. This chart does not show the percentages of not guilty verdict.

33 *Ibid.*

Part II

Civil law

3 Public regulation of private relations

Changing conditions of property regulation in China

Pitman B. Potter

Efforts to build a property rights regime in the People's Republic of China (PRC) have been characterized by tensions between acceptance of liberal legal models and retention of socialist principles associated with other areas of China's socio-economic and legal development policy. The globalized international discourse of private property ideals associated with liberal capitalism serves as context for understanding legal reform efforts in China.[1] In the international liberal discourse of property rights, ideals of efficiency and individual liberty privilege private property discourses of economism and republicanism, and result in the entrenchment of private property into law and popular culture.[2] The expansion of these regimes through the process of globalization promotes local acceptance of liberal standards of property law by developing economies even as the expansion invites conflict over assimilation of underlying norms and values. The development of China's legal regime for protecting property rights reveals dynamics and outcomes of ongoing normative tensions between globalized liberal ideology and local legal and political culture. Challenges also arise around the organizational structures and processes for implementing property rights in China.

3.1. Emerging regimes for property rights in China[3]

Under the rubric of internationalization of property rights, Chinese jurists have called for greater reference to be made to foreign law from Japan, Europe and the Anglo-North American tradition as precedents for property rights reforms in China.[4] Chinese civil law notions of property behaviour (*wuquan xingwei*) have been influenced in particular by German law (either directly or through the forms adopted from Japan and Taiwan).[5] Taiwan law scholars such as Wang Zejian have been particularly influential in the transmission of German civil law concepts to China.[6] The recently enacted Property Rights Law of the PRC is particularly influenced by liberal ideals of private property rights, albeit qualified by imperatives of socialist regulation.

3.1.1. *Transitions towards ideals of private property*

While the economic reform policies enacted beginning in 1978 granted enterprises greater autonomy in decision-making and permitted increased diversity of economic actors and transactions,[7] doctrinal norms continued to emphasize the importance of state interests in the enforcement of private law relations. The 1982 Constitution extended protection to property, but only to the extent that it would constitute 'lawful property', the definition of which remained the exclusive province of the state.[8] Constitutional requirements that the exercise of citizens' rights, including the right to own property, not conflict with the state or social interest[9] effectively granted the state a monopoly to interpret those interests and thus to determine the extent to which private property rights would be recognized and enforced. During the period of accelerated reform following Deng Xiaoping's 1992 'Southern Tour' (*nanxun*), property policy and legislation emerged as important agenda items for both academics and government officials. While conventional norms of public ownership and protection of public interest remained well represented,[10] increased attention was also paid to reforming the system of state ownership. Existing discourses on management rights were expanded to address not only issues of managerial autonomy but also managerial responsibility to conserve state property.[11] Problems of corruption and mismanagement of state property (particularly in state-owned enterprises) gave rise to calls for tighter regulation.[12] However, policy changes supporting the transition to a market economy meant that state ownership rights must also evolve and in some instances give way to diverse alternatives.[13]

The PRC Constitution was amended in 1993, to affirm the socialist market economy as the foundation for economic policy.[14] The transition from the socialist commodity economy meant that increased market autonomy for economic actors (including individuals as well as enterprises) could extend beyond the realm of transactions in goods. This invited changes to the existing property rights regime to extend protection not only to immovable personal property such as land and to movables but also to include intangibles such as intellectual property.[15] In 1995, a semi-official proposal on property legislation was published, which suggested that conventional boundaries for property rights as set forth in the General Principles of Civil Law should be re-examined.[16] Jiang Zemin's speech to the Communist Party of China (CPC) 15th National Congress in October 1997 supported the development of property rights in corporations – an essential precursor to expanded private property regimes generally.[17]

Efforts to draft a code of property law in 1998 under the aegis of a Civil Code drafting team revealed ongoing disagreements over the proper scope of private property rights. On one hand, by clarifying property as a civil law relationship, the drafters emphasized the importance of limiting state intrusion. Thus, the draft property law contained a principle that property rights could not be interfered with by third parties (including government organs).[18]

On the other hand, the draft retained the basic principles of protecting 'lawful' rights and interests and safeguarding social and economic order and socialist modernization, as well as a prohibition against property rights harming the public interest.[19] Explanations of this section make specific reference to the constitutional provisions on the market economy – and by extension the limits on full marketization imposed by the Party's policy imperatives on socio-economic order.[20] Thus, even as renewed efforts were made to enshrine property rights into legal codes, the rights that resulted unavoidably remained subject to the general tenor of constitutional provisions favouring socialist public ownership over private property rights.

Confronting those who argued for more expansive private property rights protections in the Constitution, opponents of expanded constitutional protection suggested that this would contribute to problems of corruption and misuse of state property.[21] This reflected the extent to which norms of public ownership remained deeply ingrained in the normative and institutional framework for China's property law regime.[22] Indeed, the importance of conforming to China's particular conditions (*tedian*) remains a powerful orthodoxy governing the scope and terms of property rights reform.[23] Doctrinal norms continued to emphasize the importance of state interests in the enforcement of private law relations.[24] The centrality of public ownership was part of this orthodoxy, and inhibited the recognition of private property rights.[25]

The 1999 revisions to the Constitution did not ultimately include a provision on the sanctity of private property rights (*siying caichan shensheng*) – instead, the language provided that the self-employed, private and other non-public sectors constituted an important component of the socialist market economy, whose lawful rights and interests would be protected by the state.[26] The constitutional amendment originated nominally with the CPC Central Committee,[27] although the CPC Politburo Standing Committee and its politics and law system (*zhengfa xitong*) remain the key arbiters on issues attend to the Constitution and other key enactments. The 1999 amendment confirmed that while the socialist market economy would permit individual enterprises and private firms to play an important role, ultimately property rights would remain subject to the policy priorities of the Party-state, and would not receive unlimited constitutional protection. While this was touted as a major step forward in China's reform process,[28] the reference to state protection of lawful rights and interests signalled that the private sector would remain subject to significant state control. Parallel provisions were to be found in the newly enacted Contract Law of the PRC (1999), which confined contracts to notions of 'lawful rights and interests of the parties', and subject to the imperative to protect 'state and social interests'.[29]

The limits of the 1999 constitutional revision reflected a continuing policy position that privileged socialist public property. While China's socialist system might tolerate or even encourage private property, this would still depend on the policy direction and dispensation of the Party-state.[30] Indeed complaints about the phenomenon of 'unit crimes' (*danwei zui*) such as bribery and tax evasion committed by enterprises suggested further limits to official tolerance of private businesses.[31]

The Constitution was amended yet again in 2004 to provide in Article 13 that lawful private property shall not be violated (*bu shou qinfan*). The language of protection for private property contrasts with the provisions in Article 12 that 'socialist public property is sacrosanct and inviolable (*shensheng bu qinfan*), underscoring to continued privileging of public property.[32] The proposed application of the term sacrosanct (*shensheng*) to private property was rejected yet again, although the constitutional affirmation of an expansive role for private property rights signalled an important change in official orthodoxy on relations between public and private ownership. These constitutional developments in turn paved the way for completion of a draft property law, work on which had begun in the early 1990s.

3.1.2. Property relations in land

Property rights in land are a key feature of China's property rights regime. The post-Mao reforms associated with Deng Xiaoping saw far-reaching changes in PRC land policy. While the Constitution and the General Principles of Civil Law continued to provide that ownership of land remained the exclusive province of the state and the collective, land use rights were increasingly granted to private farming and business operations in rural and urban areas.

The Land Administration Law enacted in 1986 reiterated constitutional principles of public ownership of land, and clarified the jurisdictional arrangements for land administration.[33] Revisions in 1988 to the Constitution and the Land Administration Law of the PRC permitted broader land use rights to be conveyed to private entities. In 1990, China enacted regulations permitting businesses to take long-term interests in land for the purpose of subdivision and development.[34] Local governments began enacting implementing regulations for their own real property markets,[35] giving rise to concerns over jurisdictional conflicts and administrative problems in the system of land administration.[36] The Law of the PRC on Urban Real Estate was enacted in 1994, in an effort both to expand the possibilities of private acquisition and management of land use rights, and to tighten state control over perceived abuses.[37] Land registration rules were enacted shortly thereafter.[38]

As a result, investment in real property for residential and industrial purposes soared, speculation and 'flipping' of property leases was common.[39] Judicial decisions in disputes before the People's Courts reflected confusion over a range of issues, such as the rights of lessor and lessee regarding leased property;[40] real estate valuation;[41] unauthorized sales and leasing of real estate;[42] disregard for licensing requirements;[43] and disputes over building quality.[44] Rights to inherit real estate also arose,[45] as did questions concerning cooperation between agencies and compatibility across regulatory regimes on such issues as resolving real estate issues for firms in bankruptcy.[46] Since real estate transactions involve transfers of two kinds of property interests – ownership of buildings and fixtures, and use rights to the underlying land – the regulatory system struggled to deal effectively with each of these transfers and the rights that underlie them.[47] The focus of law and regulation was increasingly moving beyond the traditional focus of clarifying the respective scope of state and collective ownership, to manage transfers and registration of land use rights.[48] While obligatory recitations of principles of socialist public ownership were unavoidable, increased attention was being paid to the problem of legal protection for land use rights as a property right.[49] With land use rights recognized as enforceable and transferable, mortgages and other ancillary relationships could begin to proceed more easily.[50]

Policy recommendations for resource use, transportation and pollution in urban areas reflected changing approaches to sustainable land use.[51] Recent decisions to rationalize and diversify land use, relocate industrial sites outside the cities and legalize the status of migrant workers suggest a growing appreciation of sustainability issues in some coastal cities.[52] However, interior cities, provincial and prefecture capitals often lag behind. Sophisticated models already exist for achieving sustainability goals through balancing of social and economic needs in land use policy,[53] but systemic implementation remains elusive. Conflicting land use claims – particularly the conflict between preserving agricultural land and the conversion to industrial and residential uses – remains a major point of conflict in rural and peri-urban areas.

In the rural areas, land use policies often conflicted initially with local collectivist sentiments, leading to violence in some cases.[54] The acceleration of agricultural reform, based in part on the appearance of private family farming, did not diminish the importance of collective ideals about land use, leading one prominent observer to describe the result as 'redistributive corporatism'.[55] Reflecting the policies of the CPC Politburo committee from which it emerged, the revised Land Administration Law (1999) reiterated the importance of safeguarding socialist public ownership of arable land.[56] This had particular implications for mining enterprises and other activities where ownership rights affect the value of land and operations licenses.[57]

Land use issues have come particularly to the fore as development and urbanization efforts intrude on local agricultural communities.[58] The resiliency of rural poverty in the midst of China's urban economic boom remains a major concern.[59] Displacement of agricultural communities in peri-urban areas to accommodate suburban economic development zones continues, with attendant problems of land use conflicts and social dislocation.[60] Possible outcomes for China's rural communities depend on resolution of local problems of land use, industrialization, social cohesion (particularly the issue of migrant workers) through planning processes that are informed and responsible to local needs.[61] The Rural Land Contracting Law (2002) permitted limited transfers of land use rights under household responsibility (*chengbao*) contracts with approval of the local authorities.[62] In October 2008, the 17th CPC National Congress approved a rural reform package that removed the government approval requirements for certain land use rights transfers.[63]

Although the increased flexibility of land use rights and the more recent discussions of the possibility of establishing an actual land ownership system suggest a transition towards a more private-oriented property rights regime, the state continues to play a critical role. Registration agencies permit state intrusion in the transfer of property interests in land.[64] The state's Land Administration Bureau (*tudi guanli ju*) remains firmly in control of the approval of land use and the creation and assignment of leases in land. As well, ancillary administrative organs have direct interests in land management. The Environmental Protection Bureau, for example, oversees environmental management on all urban and rural land. The Ministry of Civil Affairs oversees the relocation of families and individuals resulting from changes in land use. Moreover, the residual ownership rights held by the state and the collective mean in effect that rights to land remain subject to the discretion and consent of the state. Rather than beginning with a presumption of individual rights to private ownership of property in land, the Chinese system proceeds from the assumption that the state holds the basic rights of ownership, and that all subsequent uses, transfers, etc., depend on state approval. Thus, individualized notions of liberty and economic utility continue to yield to the Chinese state's conception of public responsibility and collective interest.

3.1.3. The property rights law

The 2007 Property Rights Law of the PRC attempts to formalize and expand legal protection for private property interests by imposing regulatory procedures on the requisition and transfer of property rights in land.[65] Enabled in part by the 2004 revisions to the PRC Constitution that enshrined a right to own private property, preparation of the law accelerated with a public release of a draft statute in July 2005. A 'fifth reading' draft was considered in August 2006. While intended originally to provide greater protection for private property and to lend greater certainty to financing arrangements, the draft law was subject to late-coming criticism from traditionalist intellectuals such as Gong Xiantian of Peking University that it contravened socialist principles and would empower and legitimate land requisitions by local officials for private gain.[66] Other opponents expressed concern that the draft would contravene constitutional provisions distinguishing between public and private property.[67] Proponents of the draft's principles of 'equal protection' for private and public property claimed that while the Constitution affirmed the distinction between public and private property, it nonetheless granted equal legal protection for both forms.[68] The draft was withdrawn in mid-2006 and underwent significant revisions that entrenched the importance of protecting public and state property and protecting rural land use rights by restraining the authority of officials to engage in or approve property transfers (including land acquisition and reallocation). The draft was reconsidered by the NPC Standing Committee throughout late 2006 and submitted to the full NPC for approval in early 2007, after lengthy debate and delay.[69] The Property Rights Law of the PRC came in force from 1 October 2007.

Described as a 'basic civil law', the Property Rights Law acknowledges the increased autonomy of property relations between private social and economic actors, while also underscoring the state's continuing role to regulate these relations.[70] The Property Rights Law aims to 'uphold the basic socialist economic system' and to 'regulate the order of the socialist market economy',[71] by regulating more effectively rights that are already entrenched or implied in China's existing property regimes. Nonetheless, through its emphasis on providing 'equal protection to the property of the state, the collective and the individual', the law clearly signalled further support for property rights in the private economy.[72] The Property Law clarifies the rights and obligations attendant to a wide range of property relationships involving real property, movable property and intangibles. While the statute does not purport to create new property rights, it does clarify the powers of rights holders in matters such as usufruct and condominium relationships. Property security is dealt with at some length, such that mortgages, liens and charges are now more likely to be clearer and more enforceable, and hence more acceptable to lenders.

Of particular importance are the new law's provisions limiting the authority of local officials to expropriate land without lawful process and requiring compensation of villages for land converted from agricultural uses. Such provisions are intended to protect local community interests in cultivated land. The Property Rights Law affirms state interests in natural resources such as water and imposes penalties on local officials for unlawful transfer of state assets, while also providing for procedural limits on transfer of collective property, which includes rural land. Parties with property interests in land will be required to attend more fully to issues of due diligence on property ownership and on the question of a party's authority to transfer property rights in land.

As a result of its procedural requirements for official review and approval of registrations and transfers of property interests in land,[73] the law brings into play the Administrative Litigation Law's provisions on judicial review of specific administrative actions.[74] This may work to impede the patterns of arbitrary and often corrupt abuses of regulatory authority to facilitate conversion of agricultural land to private residential investment. However, the increased emphasis on private interests may also work to insulate private property relations from state intrusion to the extent that registrations and approvals become ritualized practices devoid of serious regulatory scrutiny. Hence, integrity in implementation will be key to achieving the policy goals underlying the new legislation.

By affirming public ownership of land while also allowing for expanded recognition of private interests in land use, the Property Rights Law will undoubtedly raise a host of issues over the boundaries of public and private property relationships. The debate that characterized the last year prior to enactment is certainly not over, as those who seek more public scrutiny over property relations continue to pressure for limits on private autonomy. Implementing regulations and Supreme Court interpretations will be key indicators of the policy direction of private property rights in China under the new regulatory regime. In both process and substance, the Property Law attempts to balance goals of efficiency and fairness in China's attempts to expand property rights in the course of its tumultuous economic growth process. The Property Rights Law represents a major new development in China's property rights regimes, although it remains to be seen whether it can achieve the policy goals for which it was enacted. As former Zhao Ziyang advisor Bao Tong seems to suggest, we cannot yet know whether this latest effort will auger well for a sustained prospect of limiting the intrusion of the state into the social economy of China.[75]

3.2. Understanding property regime performance: norms and structures

The application of globalized liberal models on property law and regulation to China's circumstances is affected by local contexts, particularly socio-cultural norms along with political and administrative structures. The performance of such arrangements may be anticipated through use of the paradigms of 'Selective Adaptation' and 'Institutional Capacity', which allow better understanding of the normative and organizational dimensions of regime performance.[76]

3.2.1. Normative interchange and the role of selective adaptation in China's property rights regime(s)

The reception in China of transplanted legal models entails an interaction between their underlying norms and local values. In contrast to expectations about convergence that suggest development towards a globally unified system of institutional practices and values,[77] Selective Adaptation explains variations in local reception of non-local standards by reference to the extent of normative consensus.[78] Selective Adaptation suggests that local implementation of non-local standards depends on the extent to which their underlying norms are received by local interpretive communities.[79] Interpretive communities are comprised of government officials, socio-economic and professional elites and other privileged groups. These communities exercise authority of political and/or professional position, specialized knowledge and/or socio-economic status to interpret non-local standards for application locally.[80] In the course of this process, interpretive communities interpret non-local legal standards in light of their own normative outlooks. Such interpretation is not necessarily a conscious process of matching foreign models to local interests, but also involves subliminal dynamics of perception, complementarity and legitimacy.

Perception of the content and operation of international law standards determines the ways that interpretive communities will interpret and apply them.[81] China's reception of international legal standards on trade and human rights, for example, depends significantly on perceptions by local interpretative communities of academic and policy specialists about issues of legal development generally,[82] historical contexts for China's participation in international regimes[83] and challenges of globalization.[84] *Complementarity* between international and local practices and values informs the dynamics of local accommodation and resistance to international standards.[85] Factors of complementarity are evident in local analyses of China's participation in the international system which tend to emphasize the need for compatibility with China's systemic and substantive requirements.[86] *Legitimacy* concerns the extent to which both interpretive communities and their local audiences accept the purposes and consequences of transplanted legal forms.[87] Dynamics of legitimacy are evident in China's academic and policy discourses explaining China's increased participation in the international legal system.[88] Working together, these elements inform the process of Selective Adaptation that characterizes the interplay between acceptance of non-local rule regimes and assimilation of underlying norms.

China's property rights regime reflects the influences of Selective Adaptation. The process for enactment of China's Property Rights Law involved a conscious process of borrowing from international sources.[89] In the course of the process, interpretive communities of specialists reviewed international property law models and considered how they might apply in part or in full to China. Such adaptation, however, involves not only conscious efforts at review and comparison of globalized legal standards on property, but also less conscious engagement with underlying norms. This in turn involves dynamics of perception, complementarity and legitimacy.

3.2.1.1. *Perception*

Perceptions about the utility of globalized liberal doctrines on private property rights for economic development is evident in the writings of law specialists on the foundations of property law in China.[90] Lockean themes depicting property as an appropriate mechanism for establishing production and labour incentives and promoting economic accumulation[91] are evident in the attention paid to notions of economic utility in the early drafting efforts on the Property Rights Law.[92] The final version of the Property Rights Law was explained in part by reference to economic and social utility:

> In order to meet the requirements of materializing in an all-round way the scientific concept of development and building of a socialist harmonious society, it is necessary to enact a property law ... to stipulate the questions of a general character in the property system and questions in real life calling for urgent regulation, thus further defining the attribution of

> things to avoid disputes, bring into full play the usefulness of things, protect the property of obligees and improve the Chinese-style socialist property system. ... As the reform and opening-up and the economy develop, people's living standards have improved in general, and they urgently require effective protection of their own lawful property accumulated through hard work, of the right to land contractual management they enjoy in accordance with law and of their other lawful rights and interests. Enactment of the property law will serve to define and protect private ownership, condominium right, right to land contractual management and house-site-use right, for the propose of protecting the immediate interests of the people, stimulating their vigor to create wealth and promoting social harmony.[93]

However, perceptions about liberal concepts of property seldom extend to the entire reach of liberal discourses on property relations. In contrast to liberal principles derived from Roman law supporting private land tenancy and the natural law foundations for private property realms independent of the state,[94] prominent specialists in China emphasize the priority of state policies and interests in public property.[95] Limited perceptions about international liberal discourses of property law are evident in efforts to condition expanded property rights protections under the Property Rights Law to the needs of socialist development.[96] Hegel's call for attention to the material realities of social and economic life as a basis for restraining the unfettered application of abstract concepts of absolute rights to private property[97] is evident in the application of Hegel's philosophy of law to legal reform in China more broadly.[98] In contrast to liberal discourses extolling the political utility of private property rights for protection of individual liberty,[99] authoritative commentary from China emphasizes the role of collective property in strengthening 'democratic management'.[100] Thus, the perception of property specialists concerning international liberal discourses on property remains somewhat partial and selective, drawing upon notions of economic utility but also avoiding embrace of the political implications for individual and private rights.

3.2.1.2. Complementarity

The factor of complementarity is evident in the relationship between the regulatory norms of the international property system and regulatory norms in China. Liberal notions of law as a restraint on state power and social ideals of individualism which have informed many of the legal forms derived from Europe and North America are not endemic to China. The liberal regulatory ethos[101] may be conceived in terms of *Responsible Agency*, a typology by which regulators and their political superiors are accountable to the subjects of regulation, and as a result are expected to exercise regulatory authority broadly in accordance with norms of transparency and the rule of law. By contrast, local norms informing China's official regulatory culture[102] may be described in terms of *Patrimonial Sovereignty*. Drawing on traditional norms of Confucianism combined with ideals of revolutionary transformation drawn from Marxism–Leninism and Maoism, regulatory culture in China tends to emphasize governance by a political authority that remains largely immune to challenge. To the extent that China's property rights regime entails use of legal forms drawn from abroad, their normative foundations of Responsible Agency are often in conflict with local norms of Patrimonial Sovereignty. Issues of complementarity are also evident in tensions about the locus of rights. The orientation of liberal property rights regimes towards individual rights invites conflict with local norms of collectivism, while private rights discourses of liberalism conflict with the public law norms of Chinese tradition and PRC policy.[103]

Yet, the development of property rights in the PRC has long been a process of building complementarity between normative regimes governing private and public interests.[104] Recognizing the centrality of public ownership orthodoxy, proponents of expanded private property rights focused on changing the terms governing standards of public ownership, by distinguishing public ownership of natural resources from collective ownership of land by private economic entities.[105] The market economy is seen by some commentators as requiring diversity in the means of distributing wealth and thus might permit expanded private property rights.[106] Thus, broader civil law autonomy for individuals need not displace the collective imperative of state-centric economic law.[107] The debate of relations of public and private rights continued in the context of the Property Rights Law, as critics and supporters debated the constitutionality of provisions on equal protection of public and private property rights.[108] By bringing this debate within the discourse of constitutional rights and purposes, the interpretive community of legal specialists commenting on the Property Rights Law seem to suggest that, rather than operating in conflict, the two paradigms private and public rights could become mutually sustaining thus supporting complementarity in the selective adaptation of international property rights standards. Thus, the extent of complementarity between globalized norms of private property rights and local norms of socialist public ownership appears limited, as acceptance of globalized legal standards on property is not accompanied by assimilation of underlying norms.

3.2.1.3. Legitimacy

Legitimacy dimensions of Selective Adaptation may be appreciated in light of tensions around property rights and the right to development. As a signatory of and advocate for the 1993 Bangkok Declaration on Human Rights,[109] China places strong emphasis on the right to development over requirements of civil and political rights. In its 1991 Human Rights White Paper, the PRC explicitly adopted a position supporting the primacy of economic growth by stressing the right to subsistence as the primary right from which all other rights derive.[110] In explaining the 1991 White Paper, the Director of the State Council

Information Office stressed the primacy of the state's management of economic conditions as the basis for development:

> '[W]e enable our people to have the economic foundation upon which they can enjoy political rights'.[111] The 1995 and 1997 Human Rights White Papers underscored the regime's commitment to the primacy of the right to development.[112] Achievements in satisfying human rights to subsistence and development were given prominence yet again in the 2000 Human Rights White Paper, subordinating civil and political rights.[113] The 2004 Human Rights White Paper formally integrated themes of subsistence and development, drawing on the international discourse of the right to development to complement China's ongoing emphasis on the right to subsistence.[114] These perspectives are reiterated in the 2008 White Paper on the rule of law that affirms the centrality of Party leadership and asserts China's 'basic stand' on human rights as 'placing top priority on people's rights to subsistence and development'.[115]

The continued emphasis on the people's right to development has contributed to growing popular rights consciousness, particularly in areas of property rights. Public demonstrations over a range of concerns have continued to expand in recent years, such that more than 90,000 disturbances were reported for each of the past three years (2007–2009).[116] The Public Security Bureau reported 87,000 public order disturbances in 2005, up from 74,000 in 2004 and 58,000 in 2003.[117] Many of these concern disputes of rural land use policies.[118] As well, urban and rural residents alike have gradually begun to use legal mechanisms to achieve redress. By the early 2000s, expanded public participation in the legal process is widely evident.[119] Villagers seeking compensation for expropriation of their land in favour of public and private development and neighbourhood residents in urban areas seeking redress for allegedly unlawful relocation and expropriation of housing and other areas suggests the growing awareness of property rights among the populace.[120]

The growing trend of public citizens using the law to enforce their rights against government abuse and against abuse by privileged citizens suggests a new and dramatic phase in China's legal development. This poses a significant dilemma for the governing regime which has, to a large extent, based its legitimacy on a commitment to the rule of law. If the legitimacy of the regime comes to be compromised to the extent that it fails to deliver on commitments regarding the rule of law,[121] an entirely new calculus of political authority may emerge. Although the Party staffing and discipline systems are powerful mechanisms for ensuring compliance by judges and lawyers, the regime's ability to control outcomes is weakened to the extent that the law becomes part of the public domain. The newly enacted revisions to the Lawyer's Law reveal the extent of concern by the government – as new and more stringent requirements are imposed on lawyers upholding the interests of the state in the face of popular rights claims.[122]

To the extent that the state is implicated in denying people access to redress for infringements of property rights that the state has publicly affirmed, legitimacy for the property rights regime is diminished. The Chinese government's support for the right to development invites popular criticism when the benefits of such rights are not delivered. To the extent that both property rights and the socio-economic benefits attached to them are not forthcoming to wide segments of the populace, the resulting legitimacy deficit affects not only government's authority to rule but also the capacity of the property rights regime to modify property relations behaviour effectively is undermined. The challenge of legitimacy, combined with the challenges of perception and complementarity already discussed raise important questions about the sustainability and effectiveness of China's emerging property rights regimes.

3.2.2. *Organizational performance and institutional capacity in China's property regime(s)*

Distinct from but not unrelated to normative interchange, Institutional Capacity is an important factor in legal regime performance.[123] The operation of the Chinese legal regime depends on the Party-state's instrumentalist use of law to pursue policy goals and to maintain political dominance. Law is not intended as a limit on state power, but rather is a mechanism by which state power is exercised. As a result, the capacity of institutions to implement legal rules is critical. Institutional Capacity describes the ability of institutions to perform assigned tasks in the context of local political and socio-economic conditions.[124]

Elements of institutional purpose, location, orientation and cohesion are particularly important indicators of Institutional Capacity. *Institutional Purpose* concerns the goals of institutional behaviour, and the way these reflect consensus and conflict among communities in which institutions operate. Thus, the capacity of local governance institutions to implement new standards on property relations depends on the degree of clarity and consensus regarding policy objectives. Institutional capacity also depends on issues of *Institutional Location*, particularly the question of balancing central authority with local power.[125] In China, practical divisions of power and authority between local and central government departments permit a degree of policy interplay between the central and sub-national governments that reveal marked differences of perspective and practice and affect institutional capacity.[126] Institutional capacity also depends on *Institutional Orientation*, namely the priorities and habitual practices of institutions. Tensions between formal and informal approaches to recognition and enforcement of property rights standards are important examples of institutional orientation.[127] Finally, institutional capacity depends on issues of *Institutional Cohesion*, involving the willingness of individuals within institutions to comply with edicts from leaders and to enforce institutional goals. In the context of implementing newly enacted property rights standards at the local level, institutional cohesion often reflects issues of human resource management and administrative discipline. Thus, the structural features of Institutional Capacity provide an organizational counterpoint to the normative features of Selective Adaptation.

3.2.2.1. *Institutional purpose*

As with virtually all PRC legislation, implementation of the Property Rights Law will continue to depend on policy imperatives of the Party-state. Yet, these are often far from clear or unified. While the Property Rights Law can hardly be said to create new private rights in property where none had existed previously, the statute's provisions clarifying transactional procedures and limiting the authority of officials to intervene echo policy priorities favouring greater autonomy in property relations. Yet, the extent of consensus on these issues remains obscure. Challenges against the constitutionality of the law are not simply the abstract discourses of isolated academics, but rather reflect deep-seated disagreements over the purposes and practices of property law and the implications for Chinese socialism and socialist development.[128] The depth of disagreement is evident as well in Wang Zhaoguo's introductory speech on the law, whose effort to balance economic utility goals with priorities on socialism and fairness was mandated by the extent of political controversy around the basic policies and purposes of the Property Rights Law.[129]

The struggle for consensus has been heightened by disagreement over rural development policies. The CPC's Document No. 1 for 2008 affirmed the importance of rural reform,[130] but policy debates continue as to how this should proceed. The effort by no less than Hu Jintao to press forward at the 3rd Plenum of the 17th CPC Central Committee with a major rural reform initiative granting peasants broader powers to transfer land use rights was partially stymied by conservative opponents.[131] While rural reforms were passed at the Plenum after some 41 revisions,[132] the intended scope of land use rights transfers appeared to be limited to 'non-agricultural development land' (*feinong jianshe yongdi*).[133] While, this small step challenges the monopoly held by government departments on transfers of land use rights, clearly a consensus has not yet emerged in support of unfettered powers of alienation of property rights for rural land users. For the Property Rights Law to fulfil its intended goals of supporting expanded autonomy in the ownership and use of property while still entrenching the supervisory role of the Party-state, a sustainable consensus will need to emerge in favour of expanding the rights of land use holders to register, protect and transfer their rights. At present, this prospect seems remote.

3.2.2.2. *Institutional location*

Debates over the Party's decision on rural development reflect contending perspectives on local conditions. Opponents of expanding land use transfer rights have pointed to the iconic role of land as a foundation for social insurance, questioning whether the purported economic efficiencies to be gained from expanded transfer rights will still protect social needs in rural areas.[134] The reforms are expected to increase migration of surplus agricultural labour to the cities (potentially reaching 700 million by 2020), raising concerns of urbanites over local capacity and social conditions.[135] Still other opponents have expressed doubts that a liberalized land use transfer system will benefit peasants in areas where land quality is poor and access to markets and transportation is limited.[136] Proponents of expanding land use transfer rights have tended to adhere to conventional economic theories extolling the virtues of capital liquidity and mobilization.[137] While such an approach resonates with the experience and training of development and planning officials in Beijing and various provincial capitals, it remains uncertain as to whether it suits the realities of local conditions. Indeed, critiques of the proposal have urged greater attention be paid to local conditions.[138] Demographics also appear to play a role, as older villagers apparently tend to prize landholdings as social security, while younger people seem more eager to leave the land to move to the cities.[139]

Coordination with local conditions is an essential component of institutional capacity. While some attention is paid to the need to facilitate economic growth for the decentralized communities of rural areas, development goals of private property rights are often constructed in terms that conflict with local social arrangements. Basic policy goals underlying rural land reform seem to privilege perspectives on economic organization and behaviour more reminiscent of urban rather than rural realities. Indeed the current world food crisis suggests that conventional economic perspectives on efficiency and comparative advantage may lead to market distortions and unsustainable burdens for rural residents.[140] Resulting dislocation and migration of the peasantry to urban areas may well be a 'natural' consequence of economic imperatives about efficiency, but may also contribute to breakdown of social relations in both the countryside and the cities. Neo-liberal economic approaches centred on accumulation, institutionalization and urbanization, with little attention to preserving local cultures and traditions pose challenges for implementation of the new Property Rights Law, and in the long term challenge traditional patterns of rural life.

3.2.2.3. Institutional orientation

The government's continued reliance on formal systems of regulation at the central and local levels is evident in the new Property Rights Law, with its processes for registration and administration of property rights. State policy decisions and responses to issues of property relations remain subject to the limitations of formal institutionalism, which reflect the influences of liberal property models as well as the state's imperative to ensure (or appear to ensure) regulatory control. Yet, the predominance of informal relations in local socio-economic and political life is well known.[141] The formal regulatory ethos that pervades the Property Rights Law poses significant challenges for inhabitants of rural society, whose reality of socio-economic and political relations is often far removed from the practices of legal formalism.

This tension has the potential not only to impede the effectiveness of the Property Rights Law in controlling unauthorized creation and transfer of private property rights in land, but also puts institutional pressure on traditional social relations in rural areas. To the extent that enjoying the benefits of property rights protection requires compliance with formal regulatory models, this privileges people already adept at communicating and acting in the formal regulatory world, while excludes and marginalizes those who are no so adept. In the short term, this has the potential to aggravate rather than relieve socio-economic tensions, while in the longer term may undermine traditional patterns of socio-economic and political relations. The orientation of China's Property Rights Law remains focused on formal processes of project approvals, licenses, formalized regulation and the 'legalization' of economic relations. In China's rural societies, however, much economic activity is conducted through informal family networks and market networks. Local merchants often consider formal requirements of licensing to be mechanisms for state control, as indeed they are. The new law reveals dynamics of regulatory formalism by the way it confers on local officials authority to approve registration and transfer of property rights in land. Yet, more often than not basic decisions on property-related issues of allocation, development or land use are made informally at the family or community level with little attention to regulatory formalities.[142]

3.2.2.4. *Institutional cohesion*

The Property Rights Law and its extension to land use relations in rural China will depend heavily on implementation by local officials who put the policy purposes of the law ahead of their own parochial interests.[143] Enforcement of property transfer requirements by disinterested officials, the availability of impartial judicial review of administrative action in respect of land use rights; and the effective implementation of remedies (particularly compensation) for unlawful expropriation of land all will depend on a cohort of local officials committed to achieving the policy goals underlying the new regime. A key element of this involves the experience and training of local officials to support relative autonomy in property relations. However, as indicated by the broader lack of consensus on policy goals, the tradition of Party rule is one that has repeatedly denigrated the role of private property.[144] Training materials and seminars at the Central Party School and regional Party training facilities (even in the cosmopolitan centre of Shanghai) often extol the importance of the public ownership system's socialist ideals.[145] At the local level, officials will require comprehensive retraining in order to shed predispositions against private property relations and it remains uncertain as to whether there is the political will or the capacity to bring this about.[146]

Effective constraints on administrative action by local officials either restraining legitimate autonomy in land use transfers or engaging in arbitrary expropriation of land will require more effective judicial review under the Administrative Litigation Law. While courts in the urban areas are well disposed to grapple with the intricacies of property rights relationships, rural courts remain understaffed and often incapable of exercising effective supervision over local Party officials. Surveys of local courts reveal their embeddedness in local communitarian society and their dependency on local political authorities.[147] Acting more like magistrates or justices of the peace, local judges often have neither the training nor the experience – let alone the political protection – to effectively confront administrative abuses by local officials. This further undermines the capacity for institutional cohesion in local property regime institutions.

In addition, corruption is a well-known feature of regulatory life in China, particularly at the local level, with significant costs for economic growth and social well-being.[148] As China's property regime purports to empower government departments to oversee property relations, China's property system also privileges local business interests. For local Party cadres are often invested either personally or for policy reasons with large business interests who are seen as a major component of China's economic growth miracle and are also viewed as essential to maintaining satisfactory levels of employment. Assessments of local cadre performance in rural development are heavily influenced by the imperative to maintain levels of economic growth and employment. As a result, local officials have little incentive to respond to issues of preservation of social relations in land or popular calls for sustainable land use, instead often opting to maintain economic growth at all costs and to protect enterprise autonomy from intrusive regulation.[149] The symbiotic relationship between local officials and large business interests invites problems of corruption and particularly the tendency to place the parochial interests of officials ahead of the policy goals of the new Property Rights Law and associated regulatory regimes. Thus, issues of institutional cohesion, combined with those of institutional purpose, location and orientation, suggest that implementation of the Property Rights Law faces ongoing organizational challenges that augment the normative dynamics of Selective Adaptation.

3.3. Summary

In contrast to the models of Western liberalism, where the norms of individual liberty and economic efficiency constrain the state to limit its regulation of private property, in China the state continues to occupy a central role in mediating property relations. The contours and consequences of debates over inclusion of a private property protection clause in the 1999 constitutional amendments suggest the extent of opposition to liberal private property rights regimes. The 2004 amendment to the Chinese Constitution and the 2007 Property Rights Law reveal that while liberal notions of expanded private property rights are taking hold among certain legal and policy elites, norms about protecting state and social interests remain strong. Selective Adaptation analysis suggests that assimilation of globalized liberal norms of property remain partial, while Institutional Capacity analysis reveals that operational obstacles continue to confront policy initiatives on property rights reform. The outcomes from these processes will determine the ability of the Party-state to manage increasingly private property relations effectively so as to prevent economic development from undermining the security, health and well-being of society.

Notes

1 He Qinghua, 'Fa de yizhi yu fa de bentuhua', (Legal transplanting and localization of law), *Zhongguo faxue* (Chinese legal studies), 3, 2002: 3–15.

2 *See* generally, H. Gibbons, 'Justifying Law: An Explanation of the Deep Structure of American Law', *Law and Philosophy*, 3, 1984: 165–279. For discussion of the dilemmas attendant to challenging liberal private law regimes, *see* e.g. A. Brudner, 'Hegel and the Crisis of Private Law', K. Casebeer, 'The Crisis of Private Law is Not An Ideal Situation' and C. Yablon, 'Arguing From Necessity: A Comment on 'Hegel and the Crisis of Private Law', *Cardozo Law Review*, 10, (1989): 949–1000, 1001–1018 and 1019–1030, respectively.

3 This section updates the author's 'Globalization and Local Legal Culture: Dilemmas of China's Use of Liberal Ideas of Private Property Rights', *Asian Law*, 2, 2000.

4 *See* e.g. Qian Mingxing, 'Lun woguo wuquanfa de jiben yuance' (On the basic principles of our civil law), *Beijing daxue xuebao*, (Peking University Journal), 1, 1998: 29–38; Zheng Chengsi, 'Minfadian zhong de jige gainian xianyi' (Various basic ideas in the civil code), People's University Social Sciences Information Centre, *Minshang faxue* (Civil and commercial legal studies), 7, 1998: 14–15; Yu Nengwu and Wang Shenyi, 'Lun wuquan fa de xiandaihua fazhan qushi' (The development of modernization of property law), *Zhongguo faxue* (Chinese legal studies), 1, 1998: 72–80; Zheng Ruikun, 'Lun woguo de wuquan lifa' (Legislation of our country's property rights), *Faxue* (Legal studies), 3, 1998: 18–19, p. 16; Guo Mingrui, 'Guanyu woguo wuquan lifa de san dian sikao' (Three perspectives on our country's property legislation), *Zhongguo faxue* (Chinese legal studies), 2, 1998: 21–26; Liu Jingwei, 'Cong woguo tudi zhidu zhi biange kan wuquanfa zhi feixing' (Viewing the abandonment of property rights from the transformation of the land system), *Zhengzhi yu falu* (Politics and law), 3, 1996: 47–48.

5 *See* e.g. Liang Huixing, *Zhongguo wuquanfa caoan jianyi gao* (Outline of opinion on a draft Chinese property law), Beijing: Social Science Manuscripts Press, 2000; Sun Xianzhi, 'Wuquan xingwei lilun tan yuan yiqi yiyi' (Exploring the origins and significance of theories of property behaviour), *Faxue yanjiu* (Research in law), 3, 1996: 80–92; Wang Liming, 'Wuquan xingwei ruogan wenti tantao' (Inquiry on several issues of property rights behaviour), *Zhongguo faxue* (Chinese legal studies), 1, 1997: 58–70. Also *see* E. J. Epstein, 'The Theoretical System of Property Rights in China's *General Principles of Civil Law*: Theoretical Controversy in the Drafting Process and Beyond', *Law and Contemporary Problems*, 52, 1989: 179–216.

6 *See* e.g. Qian Mingxing, *Wuquan fa yuan li* (Principles of Property Law), Beijing: Peking University Press, 1994; Ji Yibao, 'Lun wuquan gongshi de xingzhi he zhidu jiazhi' (On the character and systemic value of property public notice), *Zhong wai faxue* (Chinese and foreign legal studies), 3, 1997: 47–51. Also *see* Wang Liming, 'Wuquan xingwei ruogan wenti tantao' (Inquiry on several issues of property rights behaviour), *Zhongguo faxue* (Chinese legal studies), 1, 1997: 58–70.

7 *See* generally, He Guanghui, 'Continue to Deepen Reform by Centering on Economic Improvement and Rectification', *Zhongguo jingji tizhi gaige* (Reform of the Chinese Economic Structure), 2, 1990, translated in *FBIS Daily Report – China*, 23 March 1990, p. 21.

8 *See* Constitution of the PRC (1982), Article 13.

9 *See* Constitution of the PRC (1982), Article 51.

10 *See* e.g. Li Yunhe, 'Dui gongyouzhi we zhuti de yi dian kanfa' (A view on the centrality of public ownership), *Zhongguo faxue* (Chinese legal studies), 5, 1993: 37–38; Wang Shenyi, 'Lun wuquan de shehuihua' (On the socialization of property rights), *Faxue pinglun* (Legal studies commentary), 1, 1999: 56–61.

11 *See* e.g. Xie Zichang and Wang Xiujing, 'Guanyu chanquan de ruogan lilun wenti' (Several theoretical questions about property rights), *Faxue yanjiu* (Research in legal studies), 1, 1994: 42–47.

12 *See* e.g. forum comments in 'Jiaqiang guoyou zichan guanli duse guoyou zichan liushi luodong' (Strengthen management of state property and block the runoff and leakage of state property), *Zhengzhi yu falu*, 1, 1996: 22–25, 45; Wang Jueyu, 'Ezhi guoyou zichan liushi de falu duixiang', (Legal objectives of halting the losses of state-owned property), *Faxue* (Legal studies), 6, 1995: 35–37.

13 *See* e.g. Zou Xi and Shu Sheng, 'Shichang jingji shehui zhong de guojia caichan suoyouquan' (State property ownership rights in the market economy society), *Zhongguo faxue* (Chinese legal studies), 4, 1996: 56–62.

14 *See* 'Draft Amendments to Constitution Discussed' Beijing *Xinhua* English Service, 22 March 1993 in *FBIS Daily Report – China* (FBIS-CHI-93-054) 23 March 1993, pp. 13–14.

15 *See* Gong Xiangrui and Jiang Mingan, 'Zai lun gongmin caichanquan de xianfa baohu' (Again, on constitutional protection for citizens' property rights), *Zhongguo faxue* (Chinese legal studies), 2, 1992: 70–73; Hu Jingguang, 'Shichang jingji huhuan due gongmin caichanquan de xianfa baozhang' (The market economy calls for Constitutional protections for citizens' property rights), *Zhongguo jingji ribao* (China economy daily), 18 June 1998, p. 4.

16 *See* Property Law Research Program of CASS Law Institute, 'Zhiding Zhongguo wuquanfa de jiben sikao' (Basic perspectives on enacting Chinese property law), *Faxue yanjiu* (Research in legal studies), 3, 1995: 3–10.

17 Hu Xiaobo, 'Informal Property Rights and Their Formalization in 1997: A Political Economy Analysis', *China Review 1988*, Hong Kong: Chinese University of Hong Kong Press, 1998: 314–338.

18 *See* 'Zhongguo wuquan fa (caoan)' (Chinese property law [draft]), Article 2, in Liang Huixing, *Zhongguo wuquanfa caoan jianyi gao* (Outline of opinion on a draft Chinese property law), Beijing: Social Science Manuscripts Press, 2000, p. 5.

19 *See* 'Zhongguo wuquan fa (caoan)' (Chinese property law [draft]), Articles 1, 5 in Liang Huixing, *Zhongguo wuquanfa caoan jianyi gao* (Outline of opinion on a draft Chinese property law), Beijing: Social Science Manuscripts Press, 2000, p. 5.

20 *See* Liang Huixing, *Zhongguo wuquanfa caoan jianyi gao* (Outline of opinion on a draft Chinese property law), Beijing: Social Science Manuscripts Press, 2000, pp. 95–97.

21 *See* Huang Rutong, 'Shi fou yiding yao ba "Siying caichan shensheng bu ke qinfan" xiejin woguo xianfa' (Do we really want to write 'the sanctity of private property is inviolable' into our constitution), *Dangdai faxue* (Modern legal studies), 4, 1998: 5–7.

22 *See* Qian Mingxing, 'Woguo wuquanfa de tiaozheng fanwei, neirong tedian ji wuquan tixi' (The scope of adjustment, special contents and property system in our property law), *Zhong wai faxue* (Chinese and foreign legal studies), 2, 1997: 88–90.

23 *See* Guo Mingrui, 'Guanyu woguo wuquan lifa de san dian sikao' (Three perspectives on our country's property legislation), *Zhongguo faxue* (Chinese legal studies), 2, 1998: 21–26.

24 *See* e.g. Yu Nengwu and Wang Shenyi, 'Lun wuquan fa de xiandaihua fazhan qushi' (The development of modernization of property law), *Zhongguo faxue* (Chinese legal studies), 1, 1998: 72–80.

25 *See* generally, Wen Zhiyang, 'Zhanlun Zhongguo minfa wuquan tixi' (Sketching China's civil law property system), *Faxue* (Legal studies), 6, 1997: 37–40. For a poignant example of a reformist scholar responding to orthodox perspectives in times of conservatism, *see* Wang Liming, 'Lun guojia suoyouquan zhuti de quanminxing wenti' (On the issue of the mass character of the bulk of state ownership rights), *Zhongnan zhengfa xueyuan xuebao* (Journal of the Central South Political Legal Institute), 4, 1990: 17–24.

26 *See* 'Text of PRC Constitutional Amendment', Beijing *Xinhua* Domestic Service, 16 March 1999, in *FBIS Daily Report – China* (FBIS-CHI-1999-0316); 'Tian Jiyun on Constitutional Amendments', Beijing *Xinhua* Domestic Service, 13 March 1999 in *FBIS Daily Report – China* (FBIS-CHI-1999-0316), 13 March 1999; 'Li Peng Presides Over Closing of 9th NPC', Beijing *Xinhua* Domestic Service, 15 March 1999 in *FBIS Daily Report – China* (FBIS-CHI-1999-0326), 15 March 1999.

27 *See* 'More on NPC Third Plenary Meeting' Beijing *Xinhua* English Service, 9 March 1999 in *FBIS Daily Report – China* (FBIS-CHI-1999-0308), 9 March 1999.

28 *See* 'Constitution Amendment Gives Solid Legal Support to Private Business', in *China Economic News: Special Supplement for the Second Plenary Session of the Ninth National People's Congres*, 19 April 1999: 2–3; 'Constitutional Amendments Propel China's Reform and Opening-up', Beijing *Xinhua* English Service, 15 March 1999, *FBIS Daily Report – China* (FBIS-CHI-1999-0315), 17 March 1999.

29 *See* PRC Contract Law of the PRC (1999), Articles 1 and 52.

30 *See* Zhang Guangbo, 'Lun caichan de shensheng bu ke qinfan' (On the sanctity of property is inviolable), *Faxue zazhi* (Legal studies magazine), 4, 1999: 10–11.

31 *See* e.g. Dai Jiabing, 'For Public Interest: Breaking the Law and Not Being Punished', *Beijing Fazhi Ribao* (Beijing legal system daily), 23 February 1998, p. 7 in *FBIS Daily Report – China* (FBIS-CHI-98-114), 24 April 1998.

32 *See* generally, Zhang Qianfan, *Xianfa xue daolun* (Guiding theory on constitutional law), Beijing: Law Press China, 2008: 501–502.

33 *See* 'Land Administration Law of the PRC' (1986, rev. 1988). Also *see* 'Nongmuyu bu fubuzhang Xiang Zhongyang xiang quanguo renda changweihui zuo guanyu

tudi fa caoan de shuoming' (Vice Minister of Agriculture, Livestock and Fisheries Xiang Zhongyang delivers an explanation of the draft land law to the NPC Standing Committee), *Zhongguo fazhi bao* (China legal system gazette), 19 March 1986, p. 2.

34 P. B. Potter, 'China's New Land Development Regulations', *China Business Review* March–April 1991: 12–14.

35 *See* e.g. 'Shanghai Municipality, PRC Land Administration Law Implementing Measures', *China Law & Practice*, 15 December 1994: 32–49.

36 *See* Cao Fengying, 'Fangdichan lifa ruogan wenti sikao' (Perspectives on several questions of real estate legislation), *Zhengzhi yu falu* (Law and politics), 3, 1994: 50–52.

37 *See* 'People's Republic of China, Administration of Urban Real Property Law', *China Law & Practice*, 3 October 1994: 23–38. For a review of regulatory conditions leading up the enactment, *see* W. D. Soileau, 'Past Is Present: Urban Real Property Rights and Housing Reform in the People's Republic of China', *Pacific Rim Law & Policy Journal*, 3, 1995: 299–387.

38 *See* D. C. Clarke and N. C. Howson, 'Developing P.R.C. Property and Real Estate Law: Revised Land Registration Rules', *East Asian Executive Reports*, 15 April 1996: 9–17. Also *see* Supreme People's Court Administrative Tribunal, (ed.), *Xingzheng susong yu tudi guanlifa: Xin jie* (Administrative litigation of land administration law: New interpretations), Beijing: Current Events Press, 1999.

39 *See* generally, A. Walker, *Land Property and Construction in the People's Republic of China*, Hong Kong: Hong Kong University Press, 1991.

40 *See* Cases discussed in Wang Liming, (ed.), *Zhongguo minfa anli yu xueli yanjiu – Wuquan bian* (Studies in Chinese civil law cases and theory – chapter on property), Beijing: Law Publishers, 1998; An Conghua *et al.*, (eds), *Renmin fayuan yinan panli pingxi: Minshi zhuan* (Evaluation of difficult cases of the People's Courts: Civil Volume), Changchun: Jilin Chubanshe, 1999: 201, 205, 211, 217, 226.

41 *See* e.g. Case no. 15, in Li Changdao, (ed.), *Shanghai fayuan anli jingxuan – 1997* (Carefully selected cases from the Shanghai Courts – 1997), Shanghai: Shanghai People's Press, 1997: 50.

42 *See* e.g. Case no. 17, in Qiao Xianzhi, (ed.), *Shanghai fayuan anli jingxuan – 1999* (Carefully selected cases from the Shanghai Courts – 1999), Shanghai: Shanghai People's Press, 2000, p. 81.

43 *See* e.g. Case no. 6, in Li Changdao, (ed.), *Shanghai fayuan anli jingxuan – 1996* (Carefully selected cases from the Shanghai Courts – 1996), Shanghai: Shanghai People's Press, 1997: 16.

44 *See* e.g. Case no. 9, in Qiao Xianzhi, (ed.), *Shanghai fayuan anli jingxuan – 1999* (Carefully selected cases from the Shanghai Courts – 1999), Shanghai: Shanghai People's Press, 2000: 44.

45 *See* e.g. Case no. 6, in Li Changdao, (ed.), *Shanghai fayuan anli jingxuan – 1997* (Carefully selected cases from the Shanghai Courts – 1997), Shanghai: Shanghai People's Press, 1997: 43.

46 *See* e.g. Qian Weiqing and Guo Yuyuan, 'Pochan qiye fangdichan chuli yi ji youguan wenti de tantao' (Inquiry on resolution of real estate of bankrupt enterprises and related questions), *Zhengzhi yu falu* (Politics and law), 1, 1995: 51–53.

47 *See* generally, Qian Mingxing, 'Woguo wuquanfa de tiaozheng fanwei, neirong tedian ji wuquan tixi' (The scope of adjustment, special contents and property

system in our property law), *Zhong wai faxue* (Chinese and foreign legal studies), 2, 1997: 88–90. Also *see* Wang Yongxia, 'Lun budongchan wuquan biandong zhong zhaiquan he wuquan de baohu' (Safeguarding creditor and property rights in the transfer of immovable property rights), *Faxue pinglun* (Legal studies commentary), 2, 1998: 121–125.

48 *See* Chen Jian, *Zhongguo tudi shiyongquan zhidu* (China's system of land use rights), Beijing: Machinery Industry Press, 2003; Zhang Shuanggen and Zhang Xuezhe, 'Lun woguo tudi wuquan zhidu' (On our land property rights system), *Zhongguo tudi kexue* (China land science), 3,1997: 7–10.

49 *See* Wang Lanping, 'Lun woguo tudi shiyongquan yu yongyi wuquan' (On rights of use and property rights in usage of land in China), *Shandong shida xuebao* (Journal of Shandong Normal University), 2,1997: 28–30.

50 *See* e.g. Zhang Shaopeng, 'Guanyu fangdichan diya falu zhidu ruogan wenti de yanjiu' (Research on various questions in the legal system for real estate mortgages), *Zhongguo faxue* (Chinese legal studies), 2, 1997: 71–78; Shi Diao, Wang Jin and Du Xueyi, 'Wanshan woguo diya zhidu de ji dian lifa sikao' (Considerations on perfecting various items of legislation in our mortgage system), *Zhongguo faxue* (Chinese jurisprudence), 4, 1997: 45–49.

51 J. Whitelegg, J. Barrett, Dabo Guan and K. Hubacek, 'Resource Consumption in China, Beijing and Shanghai', (CCICED 2005).

52 'Shanghai to test land use measures', *China Daily*, 4 December 2006 (http://www.china.org.cn/english/government/191109.htm); *Shanghai shi tudi liyong zongti guihua 1997–2010* (Comprehensive plan for land use in Shanghai municipality 1997–2010), Shanghai: Shanghai Municipal Government, 1999.

53 Tian Shi and R. Gill, 'Developing effective policies for sustainable development of ecological agriculture in China: the case study of Jinshan County with a systems dynamics model', *Ecological Economics*, 53, 2005: 223–246.

54 Ching-Ching Ni, 'Wave of Social Unrest Continues Across China', *Los Angeles Times*, 10 August 2006; R. McGregor, 'Data show social unrest on the rise in China', *Financial Times*, 29 January 2006.

55 *See* J. C. Oi, 'The Fate of the Collective After the Commune', in D. Davis and E. F. Vogel, (eds), *Chinese Society on the Eve of Tiananmen: The Impact of Reform*, Cambridge MA: Harvard University Press, 1990: 15–36.

56 *See* 'The Law of Land Administration of the People's Republic of China', Articles 1, 2 and 8, *China Economic News*, 26 October 1998: 8–12, and 2 November 1998: 8–11. Also *see* Supreme People's Court Administrative Tribunal, (ed.), *Xingzheng susong yu tudi guanlifa: Xin jie* (Administrative litigation of land administration law: New interpretations), Beijing: Current Events Press, 1999: 108–109.

57 *See* Cui Jianyuan, 'Tudi shang de quanliqun lungang' (Theoretic outline of the cluster of rights in land), *Zhongguo faxue* (Chinese legal studies), 2, 1998: 14–20. Also *see* Wen Zhiyang, 'Zhanlun Zhongguo minfa wuquan tixi' (Sketching China's civil law property system), *Faxue* (Legal studies), 6, 1997: 37–40.

58 E. Cody, 'In the Face of Rural Unrest, China Rolls Out Reforms', *Washington Post* 28 January 2006.

59 Shaohua Chen and M. Ravallion, 'China is Poorer Than We Thought, but No Less Successful in the Fight against Poverty', Policy Research Working Paper no. 4621 (World Bank Development Research Group), May 2008; C. G. Turney and Rong Kong, 'Vulnerability, Trust, and Microcredit: The Case of China's Rural Poor', United Nations University Research Paper No. 2008/52, May 2008.

60 Wong Siu-wai and Bo-sin Tang, 'Challenges to the sustainability of "development zones": A case study of Guangzhou Development District, China', *Cities* vol. 22 no. 4 (2005): 303–316.

61 K. Hallding, A. Huber-Lee, E. Kemp-Benedict, Guoyi Han, S. Kartha, Ke Chen and Ying Li, 'Policy Option Scenarios for Sustainable Urbanization in China', (CCICED 2005).

62 'Law on the PRC on Land Contract in Rural Areas' (Order of the President No. 73) (8 Octobert 2005) http://www.gov.cn/english/2005-10/09/content_179389.htm.

63 'Tudi zhidu gaige bianchu guanjian yibu' (Land system reform takes a key step), Caijing (Finance), 20 October 2008.

64 *See* Ji Yibao, 'Lun wuquan gongshi de xingzhi he zhidu jiazhi' (On the character and systemic value of property public notice), *Zhong wai faxue* (Chinese and foreign legal studies), 3, 1997: 47–51; Sun Xianzhi, 'Lun budongchan quan dengji' (On the registration of rights to immovable property), *Zhongguo faxue* (Chinese legal studies), 5, 1996: 51–62.

65 'Zhonghua renmin gongheguo caiquanfa' (Property Rights Law of the PRC) (16 March 2007), *China Economic News* Supp. No. 9–10, 2007 (hereafter, 'Property Rights Law').

66 Gong Xiantian, 'A Property Law (Draft) that violates the constitution and basic principles of socialism', (12 August 2005) (Eva Cheng tr.), *Links* no 29; G. Powell, 'Not everyone supports law on privatization', *China Economic Review*, 25 February 2007 (http://www.chinaeconomicreview.com/property/2007/02/25/not-everyone-supports-law-on-privatization/html); M. Dickie, 'China delays property law amidst rights dispute', *Financial Times*, 9 March 2006; T. Quek, 'China delays passage of property rights law', *Straits Times*, 10 March 2006. For subsequent indication of Professor Gong's views, *see* Gong Xiantian, 'Guanyu di liu ci shenyi hou de <<Wuquanfa (caoan)>> reng zai wuge zhongda yuanze wenti shang weifan xianfa bixu renzhi xiugai de yijian' (Opinion concerning five important questions of principal in the Draft Property Law following the sixth debate, which violate the constitution and must be conscientiously revised) (9 December 2006).

67 Hao Tiechuan, '<<Wuquan fa (caoan)>> weixian wenti zhi wojian' (My perspectives on the issue of the <<Property Rights Law (draft)>> contravening the constitution), *Faxue* (Legal studies), 8, 2006: 41–42 (10 August 2006); Zhou Gangzhi, 'Gongwu gainian ji qi zai woguo de shiyong' (The concept of public property and its application in our country), *Xiandai faxue* (Modern legal studies), 28, 2006: 62–67 (July 2006).

68 *See* e.g. Gao Fei, 'Ye tan wuquan fa pingdeng baohu caichanquan de xianfa yiju' (Speaking again about the constitutional foundation for equal protection of property rights under the property rights law), *Faxue* (Legal studies), 10, 2006: 128–38 (10 October 2006); Liu Zhigang, 'Lixian zhuyi yujing xia xianfa yu minfa guanxi' (The relationship between constitution and civil law in the context of constitutionalism), *Faxue pinglun* (Legal studies review), 2, 2007: 20–31 (13 March 2007).

69 Wang Zhaoguo, 'Explanation on Draft Property Law' (Delivered at the fifth Session of the Tenth National People's Congress, 8 March 2007) (http://English.people.com.cn/200703/08/print20070308_355491.html).

70 Wang Zhaoguo, 'Explanation on Draft Property Law' (Delivered at the fifth Session of the Tenth National People's Congress, 8 March 2007) (http://English.people.com.cn/200703/08/print20070308_355491.html).

71 *Ibid.*
72 *Ibid.*
73 *See* e.g. Property Rights Law, Chapter 2.1 (on registration of real property transactions); Articles 42 and 44 (on expropriation); Chapter 11 (contracted use of agricultural land); Chapter 12 (contracted use of construction land).
74 'Zhonghua renmin gongheguo xingzheng susong fa' (Administrative Litigation Law of the PRC) (1989), *Chinese Law and Practice*, 3, 1989: 37 (5 June 1989).
75 Bao Tong, 'Of Kings and Bandits', 31 March 2007 (http://rfaunplugged.wordpress.com/2007/03/31/bao-tong-of-kings-and-bandits/html); Bao Tong, 'China Has Come Full Circle', 16 March 2007 (http://rfaunpkugged.wordpress.com/2007/03/17/china-has-come-full-circle-baio-tong-on-the-enlightment-ushered-in-by-chinas-new-property-law/html).
76 P. B. Potter, 'Legal Reform in China – Institutions, Culture, and Selective Adaptation', *Law & Social Inquiry*, 2, 2004: 465–495 (Spring 2004).
77 U. Mattei, *Comparative Law and Economics*, Ann Arbor: University of Michigan Press, 1997; D. Trubek, *et al.*, 'Global Restructuring and the Law: The Internationalization of Legal Fields and the Creation of Transnational Arenas', *Case Western Reserve Law Review*, 44, 1994: 407–498.
78 For discussion of the intersection of norms with identity and community, *see* R. Unger, *Knowledge and Politics*, New York: Free Press, 1975. Also *see* A. Etzioni, 'Social Norms: Internalization, Persuasion, and History', *Law & Society Review*, 34, 2000: 157–178.
79 For discussion of interpretive communities, *see* S. Fish, *Is There a Text in This Class: The Authority of Interpretive Communities*, Cambridge MA: Harvard University Press 1980.
80 For discussion of formation of political groups based on organizational experience, *see* J. Domes, 'Intra-Elite Group Formation and Conflict in the PRC', in D. S. G. Goodman, (ed.), *Groups and Politics in the People's Republic of China*, Cardiff, England: University College Cardiff Press, 1984: 26–39. For discussion recognizing that organizational priorities influence political decision making, *see* K. Lieberthal and M. Oksenberg, *Policy Making in China*, Princeton: Princeton University Press, 1988, pp. 404ff, and sources cited, and S. L. Shirk, 'The Politics of Industrial Reform', in E. J. Perry and Christine Wong, *The Political Economy of Reform in Post-Mao China*, Cambridge: Harvard University Press, 1985: 195. For a contrary view, *see* L. Pye, *The Dynamics of Chinese Politics*, Cambridge: Oelgeschlager, Gunn & Hain, 1981. In the China context, *see* H. Lyman Miller and Liu Xiaohong, 'The Foreign Policy Outlook of China's "Third Generation" Elite' and J. Fewsmith and S. Rosen, 'The Domestic Context of Chinese Foreign Policy: Does 'Public Opinion' Matter?', both in D. M. Lampton, (ed.), *The Making of Chinese Foreign and Security Policy*, Stanford: Stanford University Press, 2001:123–150 and 151–187.
81 *See* e.g. D. Kennedy, 'Receiving the International', *Connecticut Journal of International Law*, 10, 1994: 1.
82 *See* e.g. Zeng Lingliang, '21 shijie falu fuwu maoyi de fazhan qushi yu Zhongguo faxue rencai peiyang de yong you gaige' (Development trends in 21 century trade in legal services and needed reforms in training of China's legal talents), *Faxue pinglun* (Legal studies review), 1, 2001: 3–8; Xiao Yongping, 'Falu de jiao yu xue zhi geming' (Revolution in teaching and studying law), *Faxue pinglun* (Legal studies review), 3, 2003: 153–160.

83 *See* e.g. Li Baojun, *Dangdai Zhongguo waijiao gailun* (Treatise on contemporary Chinese foreign policy), Beijing: People's University Press, 1999; Wang Yinzhou, *Quanqiu zhengzhi he Zhongguo waijiao* (Global politics and China's foreign policy), Beijing: World Knowledge Press, 2003.

84 Rao Geping and Huang Yao, 'Lun quanqiuhua jincheng yu guoji zuzhi de hudong guanxi' (On mutual impacts of globalization processes and international organizations), *Faxue pinglun* (Legal studies review), 2, 2002: 3–13; Liu Shuguang, *Quanqiuhua yu fan quanqiuhua* (Globalization and anti-globalization), Changsha, Hunan People's Press, 2003, esp. pp. 103–166. For response to such resistance, *see* He Qinghua, 'Fa de yizhi yu fa de bentuhua', (Legal transplanting and localization of law), *Zhongguo faxue* (Chinese legal studies), 3, 2002: pp. 3–15.

85 O. Seliktar, 'Identifying a Society's Belief System', in M. Herman, (ed.), *Political Psychology*, San Francisco: Jossey-Bass, 1986.

86 *See* e.g. Li Dexi, Qian Zhen and Lin Zhe, *Quanqiu beijing xia de Zhongguo minzhu jianshe* (Development of democracy in China under the global background), Chongqing: Chongqing Press, 2005, based on a policy conference at the authoritative Central Party School. Also *see* Gao Gangjun, 'Zhongguo de heping fazhan yu guoji fa de jiazhi tixi' (China's peaceful development and the value system of international law), *Faxue pinglun* (Law Review), 3, 2006: 104–110; Zhang Shaodong, 'Ye lun guoji tiaoyue zai woguo de shiyong', (Again examining the application of international treaties in China), *Faxue pinglun* (Law Review), 6, 2001: 73–79.

87 Max Weber, *Economy and Society* (Roth and Wittich, eds), Berkeley and Los Angeles: University of California Press, 1978; F. Scharpf, 'Interdependence and Democratic Legitimation', in S. J. Pharr and R. D. Putnam, (eds), *Disaffected Democracies: What's Troubling the Trilateral Countries*, Princeton: Princeton University Press, 2000; S. P. Turner and R. A. Factor, *Max Weber: The Lawyer as Social Thinker*, London and New York: Routledge, 1994.

88 *See* e.g. Jiang Xiyuan, 'An Analysis on Changing International System and Its Acceptance of China', *International Review*, 39, Summer 2005: 19–36.

89 *See* e.g. Jiang Ping and Li Guoguang, (eds), *Wuquanfa yinan wenti jingda* (Explanation and responses to difficult questions on the Property Rights Law), Beijing: People's Court Press, 1997.

90 *See* e.g. Zhu Guanxin, 'Lun wuquan huntong guize ji qi zai woguo wuquan fa caoan zhong de yingyong diwei' (On provisions for commingled property and the proper place in our property law draft), *Faxue* (Legal studies), 7, 2006: 49–55; Wang Liming, *Wuquan fa lun* (Property rights theory), Beijing: China University of Politics and Law Press, 1998; Guo Mingrui, 'Guanyu woguo wuquan lifa de san dian sikao' (Three points for consideration in China's property rights legislation), *Zhongguo faxue* (Chinese legal studies), 2, 1998: 21–26 (9 April 1998); Zheng Ruikun, 'Lun woguo de wuquan lifa' (On China's property legislation), *Zhongguo faxue* (Chinese legal studies), 3, 1998: 18–19 (15 May 1998); Yu Nengwu and Wang Shenyi, 'Lun wuquan fa de xiandaihua fazhan queshi' (On the phenomenon of modernization development in China's property law), *Zhongguo faxue* (Chinese legal studies), 1, 1998: 72–80.

91 *See* C. Rose, 'Property as a Keystone Right?' supra; S. Coval, J.C. Smith and S. Coval, 'The Foundations of Property and Property Law', *Cambridge Law Journal*, 35, 1986: 457–475.

92 *See* generally, Liang Huixing, *Zhongguo wuquanfa caoan jianyi gao* (Opinion draft of China's property law), Beijing: Social Science Abstracts Press, 2000.

93 Wang Zhaoguo, 'Explanation on Draft Property Law' (Delivered at the fifth Session of the Tenth National People's Congress, 8 March 2007) (http://English.people.com.cn/200703/08/print20070308_355491.html).

94 *See* B. Bouckaert, 'What is Property?' *Harvard Journal of Law & Public Policy*, 13, 1990: 775–816, pp. 785ff.

95 Li Kaoguo, 'Lun woguo chengshi jianshe yongdi de xianzheng houyong yuanze' (On the principle of expropriation first, use second in China's urban development land use), *Xiandai faxue* (Modern legal studies), 29, July 2007: 37–43; Ji jianye, 'Nongmin quanli baozhang yu xin nongcun jianshe' (Safeguarding peasants' rights and the construction of the new countryside), *Faxuejia* (Jurists), 1, 2007: 11–14 (February 2007); Zhou Gangzhi, 'Gongwu gainian yi qi zai wuguo de shiyong' (The concept of public property and its application in our country), *Xiandai faxue* (Modern legal studies), 28, July 2006: 62–67.

96 *See Zhonghua renmin gongheguo wuquanfa shiyi* (Interpretation of the Property Rights Law of the PRC), Beijing: China Economy Publishing House, 2007; Han Dayuan, 'You <<Wuquanfa (caoan)>> de zhenglun xiangdao de ruogan xianfa wenti' (Considering various constitutional issues in light of the debates over the <<Property Rights Law (Draft)>>), *Faxue* (Legal Studies), 3, 2006: 24–32 (10 March 2006).

97 *See* P. G. Stillman, 'Hegel's Analysis of Property in the Philosophy of Right', *Cardozo Law Review*, 10, 1989: 1031–1072.

98 Cf. Lin Zhe, *Hei-ge-er de faquan zhexue* (Hegel's philosophy of legal rights), Shanghai: Fudan University Press, 1999.

99 *See* J. E. Krier, 'The (Unlikely) Death of Property', *Harvard Journal of Law & Public Policy*, 13, 1990: 75–83.

100 Meng Qinguo, 'Wuquanfa ruhe baohu jiti caichan' (How does the property law protect collective property), *Faxue* (Legal studies), 1, 2006: 72–77 (10 January 2006).

101 *See* e.g. *Will Kymlicka, Liberalism, Community and Culture*, Oxford: Clarendon Press, 1991.

102 *See* generally, S. Lubman, *Bird in a Cage: Legal Reform in China After Mao*, Stanford: Stanford University Press, 1999; P. B. Potter, *The Chinese Legal System: Globalization and Local Legal Culture*, Routledge, 2001; R. Peerenboom, *China's Long March, Toward Rule of Law*, Cambridge, Cambridge University Press, 2002.

103 Yin Tian, 'Wuquan zhuti lungang' (Treatise on the locus of property rights), *Xiandai faxue* (Modern legal studies), 28, March 2006: 3–11.

104 *See* e.g. Qian Mingxing, 'Woguo minshi fazhi sishi nian de bianqian' (Changes in forty years of our civil law system), *Zhongwai faxue* (Zhinese and foreign law), 5, 1989: 1–8; Wang Jianrui, 'Wanshen siyou caichan baohu zhidu de falu sizao' (Legal perspectives on perfecting the system of protecting private property), *Faxue zazhi* (Legal studies magazine), 2, 1999: 25–26 and 'Law on Private Economy Called For', *China Economic News*, 23 August 1999: 1–2. Also *see* Hu Jingguang, 'Shichang jingji huhuan dui gongmin caichan de xianfa baohu' (The market economy cries out for constitutional protection for citizens' property rights), *Zhongguo jingji ribao* (China economic news), 18 June 1998, p. 4.

105 *See* Guo Mingrui, 'Guanyu wo guo wuquan lifa de san dian sikao', (Three perspectives on Chinese property legislation), *Zhongguo faxue* (Chinese legal studies), 2, 1998: 21–26.

106 *See* e.g. Qu Maohui and Li Qiang, 'Xianfa ying queren duozhong fenpei fangshi' (The constitution should acknowledge many forms of distribution), *Hunan shifan daxue shehui kexue xuebao* (Social science journal of Hunan Normal University), 5, 1998: 22–25.

107 *See* Liu Shuilin, 'Jingji fa yu minfa de shichang jingji guannian jichu yanjiu' (Basic research on concepts of the market economy of economic law and civil law), *Faxue yanjiu* (Research in legal studies), 1, 1997: 34–39.

108 *See* articles by Tong Zhiwei, Han Dayuan, Zhang Qianfa and Jiao Hongchang in 'Xianfa xuezhe ping <<Wuquanfa (caoan)>> de weixian yu hexian zhizheng' (Constitutional scholars assess the debate over the constitutionality of the <<Property Rights Law (Draft)>>), *Faxue* (Legal studies), 3, 2006: 2–41.

109 *See* 'Final Declaration of the regional meeting for Asia of the World Conference on Human Rights' (Bangkok Declaration) (2 April 1993), Art. 8, *Human Rights. Law Journal* 14, 1993: 370.

110 *See* 'Text of Human Rights White Paper', in *FBIS Daily Report – China* (Supplement), 21 November 1991.

111 *See* 'Interview with Zhu Muzhi, Director of the State Council Information Office', *Xinhua*, (2 November 1991), *FBIS Daily Report–China*, 4 November 1991: 15–16.

112 *See* 'The progress of HumanRights in China', Xinhua Domestic Service, 27 December 1995, *FBIS Daily Report – China* (28 December 1996), pp. 8–26; *See* 'Quarterly Chronicle and Documentation' (April–June 1997), *The China Quarterly,* 151, 1997: 698.

113 State Council Information Office, 'White Paper: Fifty Years of Progress in China's Human Rights' (2000). The 2000 White Paper noted that China's conditions require 'putting the rights to subsistence and development in the first place under conditions of reform, development and stability'.

114 State Council Information Office, 'China's Progress in Human Rights in 2004' (April 2005).

115 State Council Information Office, 'China's Efforts and Achievements in Promoting the Rule of Law' (28 February 2008), pp. 11, 31.

116 J. Garnaut, 'China Insider Sees trouble brewing', *Sydney Morning Herald*, 28 February 2010 http://www.smh.com.au/world/china-insider-sees-revolution-brewing-20100226-p92d.html [8 March 2010].

117 Ching-Ching Ni, 'Wave of Social Unrest Continues Across China', *Los Angeles Times*, 10 August 2006; R. McGregor, 'Data show social unrest on the rise in China', *Financial Times*, 29 January 2006.

118 *See* e.g. Esther Pan, 'China's Angry Peasants', *Council on Foreign Relations Backgrounder*, (15 December 2005), http://www.cfr.org/publication/9425/.

119 N. J. Diamant, S. B. Lubman and K. J. O'Brien, *Engaging the Law in China: State, Society, and Possibilities for Justice*, Stanford: Stanford University Press, 2005.

120 J. Pomfret, 'Chinese Fight A New Kind of Land War', *Washington Post*, 13 September 2003 (http://www.washingtonpost.com/ac2/wp-dyn/articles/A6761-2003-Sep13.html).

121 P. B. Potter, 'Riding the Tiger – Legitimacy and Legal Culture in Post-Mao China', *The China Quarterly,* 138, 1994: 325–358.

122 Law of the PRC on Lawyers and Legal Representation, (October 2007), (http://www.chinanews.com.cn/gn/news/2007/10-28/1061502.shtml). Also *see* Human Rights Watch, 'China: Curbs on Lawyers Could Intensify Social Unrest – New Regulations Cast Doubt on Legal Reforms', (12 December 2006); Human Rights Watch, '"Walking on Thin Ice": Control, intimidation, and harassment of lawyers in China' (April 2008).

123 P. B. Potter, 'Selective Adaptation and Institutional Capacity: Perspectives on Human Rights in China', *International Journal*, 61, 2006.

124 P. Healey, 'Building institutional capacity through collaborative approaches to Urban planning' *Environment and Planning*, 30, 1998: 1531–1546; L. L. Martin and B. A. Simmons, 'Theories and Empirical Studies of International Institutions', in *International Organization*, 52, 1998: 729–757; E. F. Betancourt, A New Approach to Developing Institutional Structure, *Studies in Comparative International Development*, 32, 1997: 3–29; J. A. Desveaux, *Designing Bureaucracies: Institutional Capacity and Large-Scale Problem Solving*, Cambridge: Cambridge University Press, 1995.

125 J. S. Wunsch, 'Institutional Analysis and Decentralization: Developing an Analytical Model for Effective Third World Administrative Reform', in Michael D. McGinnis, (ed.), *Polycentric Governance and Development: Readings from the Workshop in Political Theory and Policy Analysis*, Ann Arbor: University of Michigan Press, 1999.

126 S. Dougherty and R. McGuckin, 'Federalism and the Impetus for Reform in China', *China Law and Practice*, 15, no. 4, 2002; M. Dougherty and J. Radzin, 'How Federalism – Not Just Privatization – Is Driving China's Economy', *Zhongguo jingji pinglun*, China economic forum, 1, no. 2, 2002.

127 P. Pitman B. 'China and the International Legal System: Challenges of Participation', *The China Quarterly*, 191, 2007: 669–715.

128 *See* notes 65–67, supra and accompanying text. Also *see* Huang Rutong, 'Shi fou yiding yao ba "Siying caichan shensheng bu ke qinfan" xiejin woguo xianfa' (Do we really want to write 'the sanctity of private property is inviolable' into our constitution), *Dangdai faxue* (Modern legal studies), 4, 1998: 5–7; 'Xianfa xuezhe ping <<Wuquanfa (caoan)>> de weixian yu hexian zhizheng' (Constitutional scholars assess the debate over the constitutionality of the <<Property Rights Law (Draft)>>), *Faxue* (Legal studies), 3, 2006: 2–41.

129 Wang Zhaoguo, 'Explanation on Draft Property Law' (Delivered at the fifth Session of the Tenth National People's Congress, 8 March 2007) (http://English.people.com.cn/200703/08/print20070308_355491.html).

130 'China vows to deepen rural reform in 2008', *Xinhuanet* 31 January 2008 (http://news.xinhuanet.com/english/2008-01/31/content_7532861.htm).

131 *See* generally, J. Fewsmith, 'Tackling the Land Issue – Carefully', *China Leadership Monitor*, No. 27, Winter 2009, pp. 1–8 (http://www.hoover.org/publications/clm/issues/37361849.html); Edward Wong, 'China May Let Peasants Sell Rights to Farmland', *New York Times*, 10 October 2008; Liang Jing, 'Hu Jintao wei he dubo "xin tugai"' (Why Hu Jintao is gambling on new land reform), 10 October 2008; Edward Wong, 'Hints of Discord on Land Reform in China', *New York Times*, 16 October 2008 (www.nytimes.com/2008/10/16/world/asia/16China/html); M. Magnier, 'China land reform disappears from radar', *Los Angeles Times*, 15 October 2008 (http://latimes.com/news/nationworld/world/la-fg-land15-2008Oct15,0,362260.story).

132 *See* 'Zonggong zhongyang guanyu tuijin nongcun fazhan ruogan zhongda wenti de jueding' (Decision on Major Issues Concerning the Advancement of Rural Reform and Development), *Xinhua* (19 October 2008); 'CPC Closes major meeting with decision on rural reform, development', *People's Daily (English)*, 13 October 2008 (http://english.peopledaily.com.cn/90001/90776/90785/6513620.html); 'Chronology of the CPC's decision on rural reform', *People's Daily (English)*, 20 October 2008 (http://english.people.com.cn/90001/90776/90785/6518136.html).

133 'Tudi zhidu gaige bianchu guanjian yibu' (Land system reform takes a key step), *Caijing* (Finance), 20 October 2008.

134 'Jingti tudi liuzhuan zhong de bu liang xianxiang' (Beware of bad trends in lad transfers), *Banyuetan* (China Comment), 28 October 2008 (http://news.xinhuanet.com/legal/2008-10/28/content_10264151.htm).

135 'China extends rural reform and development in new Party document', *People's Daily (English)*, 20 October 2008 (http://english.peopledaily.com.cn/900001/90776/90785/6517482.html).

136 Sim Chi Yin, 'China to double rural income by 2020', *Straits Times*, (13 October 2008).

137 *See* e.g. comments from CASS research fellow Li Chenggui in 'China extends rural reform and development in new Party document', *People's Daily (English)*, (20 October 2008) (http://english.peopledaily.com.cn/90001/90776/90785/6517482.html).

138 'Jingti tudi liuzhuan zhong de bu liang xianxiang' (Beware of bad trends in lad transfers), *Banyuetan* (Bi-monthly comment), 28 October 2008 (http://news.xinhuanet.com/legal/2008-10/28/content_10264151.htm).

139 M. Magnier, 'China land reform disappears from radar', *Los Angeles Times*, 15 October 2008 (http://latimes.com/news/nationworld/world/la-fg-land15-2008Oct15,0,362260.story).

140 *See* e.g. Penelope Simons, 'Binding the Hand that Feeds Them: Sovereignty, the Agreement on Agriculture, Transnational Corporations, and the Right to Adequate Food in Developing Countries' in W. Shan, P. Simons, D. Singh (eds), *Redefining Sovereignty in International Economic Law,* Hart Publishing, Oxford 2008.

141 T. Gold, D. Guthrie and D. Wank, (eds), *Social Connections in China*, Cambridge: Cambridge University Press, 2002.

142 Ni Guoliang, *Zhongguo xibei diqu xiandaihua zhong de jingji yu wenhua guanxi* (Relations between economy and culture in the course of modernization in China's northwest), Lanzhou: Gansu People's Press, 1998.

143 For early examples, *see* J. C. Oi and A. G. Walder, *Property Rights and Economic Reform in China*, Stanford: Stanford University Press, 1999.

144 Bao Tong, 'Of Kings and Bandits', 31 March 2007 (http://rfaunplugged.wordpress.com/2007/03/31/bao-tong-of-kings-and-bandits/html); Bao Tong, 'China Has Come Full Circle', 16 March 2007 (http://rfaunpkugged.wordpress.com/2007/03/17/china-has-come-full-circle-baio-tong-on-the-enlightment-ushered-in-by-chinas-new-property-law/html).

145 *See* e.g. Zang Zhifeng, 'Woguo gongyouzhi yu fei gongyouzhi jingji xiangtongyi de genju' (The foundation for economic integration of our public- and non-public-ownership systems), *Xuexi shibao* (Study times), 26 April 2004, p. 3; Chi Fulin, 'Yi ren wei ben wanshan shehui zhuyi shichang jingji tizhi'

(Humanism: Perfect the socialist market economic system), *Xuexi shibao* (Study times), 22 September 2003, p. 4.

146 *See* e.g. Willy Lam, 'CCP Campaign for a New Generation of "Red and Expert" Officials' *China Brief*, 9, No. 13, (23 June 2009) (http://www.jamestown.org/programs/chinabrief/single/?tx_ttnews[tt_news]=35170&tx_ttnews[backPid]=25&cHash=a0aad095c4).

147 Zhu Suli, *Song fa xia xiang* (Taking law down to the villages), Beijing: Chinese University of Politics and Law Press, 2000.

148 Xie Ping and Lu Lei, *Zhongguo jinrong fubai de jingjixue fenxi* (Economic analysis of financial corruption in China), Beijing: CITIC Publishing House, 2005.

149 B. O'Rourke, 'China: Rural Discontent Spotlights Those Left Behind', RFE 1 February 2006.

4 The Law of Property and the evolving system of property rights in China

*Albert H.Y. Chen**

The enactment of the *Law of Property* (LP) (*wuquan fa*, alternatively translated as *Property Law*) in March 2007 in China – after a long process stretching over 14 years[1] during which some of the most heated debates[2] in contemporary Chinese legislative history took place – has been hailed as a milestone in the development of contemporary Chinese law. The LP is one of the most important core components of the evolving civil law in the People's Republic of China (PRC). This chapter attempts to understand some of the key concepts and provisions in the LP in the context of the evolving Chinese law relating to property rights, the changing economic system as China moves from a socialist planned economy to a socialist market economy or 'socialism with Chinese characteristics', and from the perspective of comparative law. This chapter also seeks to answer the following two questions. To what extent is the LP a product of borrowing from or transplant of foreign legal ideas, and to what extent is it a reflection of indigenous circumstances and needs in China? And, to what extent has China moved away from the orthodox socialist system of public ownership of the means of production towards a regime of private property rights?

Apart from this introduction, this chapter consists of the following parts. Part 1 reviews the historical trajectory of the evolution of the Chinese law relating to property rights that culminated in the enactment of the LP in 2007. Part 2 examines the transplanted and indigenous elements of the LP from the perspective of comparative law. Part 3 considers the extent to which a regime of private property rights has been established by law in the PRC. Finally, Part 4 summarizes and concludes the chapter.

It should be noted at the outset that the property rights which this chapter focuses on are those covered by the LP or the Chinese term *wuquan* (which may be literally translated as 'rights relating to *wu*' or 'rights over *wu*'). *Wu* may be literally translated as 'things'. In the LP, *wu* is defined to mean movable property and immovable property.[3] Both species of property are tangible property. *Wuquan* is thus property (*caichan*) in a narrow sense, as distinguished from property (also *caichan* in Chinese) in a broad sense, which includes 'invisible' forms of property such as rights under shares in companies and negotiable instruments, intellectual property rights or what are known as 'choses in action' in English common law.[4] Indeed, from the perspective of continental European law, rights under a contract or under the law of tort (the law of contract and the law of tort both being components of the law of obligations in the civil law tradition) also fall within the concept of property in the broad sense.[5]

4.1. The historical trajectory

The 60-year history of the PRC (1949–2009) is commonly perceived as consisting of two periods: the first 30 years of Maoist rule, and the last 30 years of 'reform and opening' (*gaige kaifang*) inaugurated by Deng Xiaoping's rise to power and the Third Plenum of the Eleventh Central Committee of the Chinese Communist Party (CCP) in December 1978. As far as legal history is concerned, the existing legal system and laws of the PRC are largely a product of the era of 'reform and opening',[6] although the basic institutions (such as the system of people's congresses and the legislative, administrative, judicial and procuratorial institutions) were established in the 1950s during which China briefly followed the mode of socialist legality as practised in the Union of Soviet Socialist Republics (USSR).

In the era of 'reform and opening', the fundamental legal source of the regime of property and property rights in the PRC lies in the Constitution of the PRC enacted in 1982. This is the fourth Constitution in the history of the PRC (the former ones were enacted in 1954, 1975 and 1978), and was amended in 1988, 1993, 1999 and 2004.[7]

The 1982 Constitution provides for the 'socialist public ownership of the means of production' which takes two forms – ownership by the whole people (also known as State ownership[8]) and collective ownership by the labouring masses (*laodong qunzhong* or working people) (alternatively translated as 'ownership by collectives of labouring masses').[9] As regards land ownership, it provides that all land in the cities is owned by the State[10] (this provision actually had the effect of nationalizing (without compensation) privately owned urban land on which privately owned residential buildings stood[11] – some such land existed at the time of enactment of the 1982 Constitution); land in the rural and suburban areas is collectively owned (*jiti suoyou*).[12] 'The State may, in the public interest, requisition land for its use in accordance with law. No organization or individual may appropriate, buy, sell or lease land or otherwise engage in the transfer of land by unlawful means'.[13] 'Socialist public property is sacred and inviolable'.[14] 'The State protects the right of citizens to own lawfully earned income, savings, houses and other lawful property. The State protects according to law the right of citizens to inherit private property'.[15]

The first major development relating to property law after the making of the 1982 Constitution was the enactment of the *General Principles of Civil Law* (GPCL) in 1986. The GPCL was largely modelled on the corresponding legislation in the USSR and Eastern European Communist States, such as the

Soviet Union's Basic Principles of Civil Legislation (1961).[16] The GPCL was designed to provide some general principles of the civil law and some rudimentary rules governing particular areas of the civil law pending the enactment of a full civil code in the continental European tradition. Chapter 5 of the GPCL is entitled 'rights in civil law' (*minshi quanli*), and it consists of the following four sections: 'Property ownership and property rights related to ownership'; 'rights over obligations' (*zhaiquan*) (such as rights under a contract); 'intellectual property'; and 'rights of the person' (*renshen quan*). In the first of the four sections, there are express provisions on ownership by the State, by collectives of labouring masses and by individual citizens.[17] 'Property rights related to ownership' provided for in the section include *chengbao* operational rights (*chengbao jingying quan*) under *chengbao* contracts relating to farmland, forests, grassland, waste land, etc.; State-owned enterprises' operational right (*jingying quan*) with regard to property which the State has granted to them for the purpose of operational management; and rights arising from 'neighbourhood relationship' (*xianglin guanxi*) between occupiers of neighbouring land.

The *chengbao* or 'contract responsibility' system that has given rise to the *chengbao* contracts mentioned earlier was a major measure of economic reform in China's rural areas that began in the early 1980s.[18] Under this system, the relevant authority in the rural areas enter into contracts with peasant households pursuant to which the households enjoy the right to possess, control, use and derive economic benefits from (collectively owned) land covered by the contract subject to payment of consideration. For example, the *chengbao* contractor may decide what to grow on the land, sell his produce directly in the market and receive the income. The system may be understood as a partial privatization of agricultural production which had been collectivized since the mid-1950s, and contributed significantly to China's rapid economic growth since the 1980s. The *chengbao* system in agriculture, though such an important element of China's economic reform involving re-allocation of property rights, was largely defined by CCP and government policy documents rather than by formal law, until the enactment of the *Law of Rural Land Contracts* in 2002 as mentioned below.

In another section – Section 5.2 of Chapter 5–the GPCL provides for two forms of property-related security for credit, mortgage (*diya*) of property and lien (*liuzhi*).[19] The context in which these provisions appear is that of security for payment of debt, and the section of which they form a part is that on 'rights over obligations' rather than 'property rights'. The concept of *wuquan* is absent from the GPCL.

In the same year of 1986, the *Land Administration Law* (LAL) (alternatively translated as the *Land Management Law*) was also enacted. The LAL sets out the rules of ownership of both urban and rural land (under State ownership and collective ownership, respectively), and the procedural and substantive rules governing the use of land for various purposes. *Chengbao* contracting of land by collectives or individuals for agriculture, forestry, animal husbandry and fishery is authorized by the LAL.[20] The LAL also provides for requisitioning of land – particularly agricultural land under collective ownership – by the State for purposes of construction and development, and the compensation therefor.

The next major development in Chinese property law came in 1988. In April 1988, the National People's Congress (NPC) adopted the first set of amendments to the 1982 Constitution. One amendment recognizes the importance and legitimacy of 'the private sector of the economy' as a 'supplement to the socialist public economy'. The other amendment provides that 'the right to the use of land may be transferred according to law'.[21] The latter amendment is the constitutional foundation for the emergence of a new regime of private property rights in urban land that will be elaborated in the following section.

Following the constitutional amendment, the LAL was amended in December 1988. According to the amendment, the right to use (*shiyong quan*) State-owned or collectively owned land may be transferred (*zhuanrang*) in accordance with law.[22] A system for the use of State-owned land by payment of consideration (*youchang shiyong*) shall be established.[23]

The legal regime for the acquisition of the 'right to use' State-owned land by real estate developers was established by the State Council when it enacted in 1990 the Provisional Regulations on the Grant (*churang*) and Transfer (*zhuanrang*) of the Right to Use State-Owned Land in Cities and Towns (PRCT). The PRCT provides for various aspects of the operation of the system, including the duration and conditions of grant, modes of grant (agreement, tender and auction), assignment (transfer), leasing and mortgage of land use rights, and requisition by the State. The system of land use rights resembles and was probably influenced in its conception by colonial Hong Kong's system of property rights in land, in which almost all land was owned by Crown and the Crown (i.e. the Hong Kong Government) granted (sold) Crown leases of long duration to developers.[24] It should also be noted that the PRCT distinguishes between grant (*churang*) of land use rights which is subject to payment of consideration, and the allotment (*huabo*) of land use rights which does not require payment of consideration.[25] Although some of the provisions in the PRCT overlap with and may be considered superseded by the *Law on the Administration* (alternatively translated as 'Management') *of Urban Real Estate* mentioned in the forthcoming section, some provisions are still relevant and applicable today. For example, the maximum terms of the grant for various purposes are still governed by the PRCT:[26] 70 years for residential land; 50 years for industrial land; 50 years for land for educational, technological, cultural, public health and sporting purposes; 40 years for land for commercial, tourism and entertainment purposes and 50 years for combined or other purposes.

In 1993, the 1982 Constitution was amended for a second time. The most significant amendment was that the PRC would now practise a 'socialist market economy' instead of practising a 'planned economy on the basis of socialist public ownership' as previously provided in the Constitution.[27] The family household *chengbao* contract responsibility system, which had already been practised in the 1980s as mentioned earlier, was also given constitutional recognition in this amendment.[28]

In 1994, the *Law on the Administration of Urban Real Estate* (LAURE) was enacted. The LAURE raises to the level of law[29] (from the level of administrative regulations) and further elaborates the legal regime mentioned before for the grant of land use rights in urban land to developers and the sale of units in buildings erected on such land to ultimate users. It provides not only for the grant and transfer of land use rights in urban land, but also for property transactions regarding apartments in buildings and houses, including assignment (*zhuanrang*), sale of uncompleted flats, mortgage and leasing and for property agents and registration of title.

The year 1995 saw the enactment of the *Guarantee Law* (GL) (*danbao fa*). The GL sets out the rules governing the creation, effect, operation and enforcement of five legal devices that can serve as security for credit: guarantee (*baozheng*); mortgage (*diya*); pledge (*zhiya*); lien (*liuzhi*) and deposit (*dingjin*). Although the concept of *wu* or *wuchan* is not used in the GL, it may be seen that the mortgage, pledge and lien provided for in it may be used as security over movable and immovable property. It may also be noted that whereas the concept of mortgage (*diya*) as used in the GPCL does not distinguish between mortgage and pledge, these two security devices are now separately provided for in the GL. The pledge is further divided into pledge of movables (*dongchan zhiya*) and pledge of rights (*quanli zhiya*). As explained in Part 2 in the following section, this division is derived from German law.

In 1998, the LAL was amended extensively for better regulation of rural land use. New chapters on the protection of arable land and on arrangements for supervision and inspection were added to the LAL. Some provisions in the amendment relate to the *chengbao* system. It is provided that the term of a *chengbao* contract is 30 years.[30] Adjustments of *chengbao* arrangements and the grant of *chengbao* contracts to persons outside the village shall be subject to the approval of a two-thirds majority in a villagers' meeting.[31] The amendment also improves the compensation arrangements for the requisition of peasants' land for purposes of development.[32]

In 1999, the third amendment to the Constitution was introduced. For our present purposes, the following aspects of the amendment are noteworthy. First, the original provision that 'the basis of the socialist economic system of the PRC is socialist public ownership of the means of production' is amended by adding that China is in 'the preliminary stage of socialism' and its economic system shall be one in which 'public ownership is the main body and the economic activities of multiple forms of ownership shall develop together'.[33] Second, it is provided that the individual and private sectors of the economy (*geti jingji* and *siying jingji*) constitute 'important components' of the socialist market economy.[34] Third, the provision on the *chengbao* system in the rural areas is further refined.[35]

Codification of the legal rules governing the *chengbao* system came in 2002 with the enactment of the *Law of Rural Land Contracts* (LRLC). The declared objective of the LRLC is to ensure that peasants under the *chengbao* system can enjoy secure and long-term rights to the use of *chengbao* land.[36] The terms of the *chengbao* contracts in different contexts are provided for: 30 years for farmland; 30–50 years for grassland; 30–70 years for forest land.[37] Different types of *chengbao* arrangements are provided for, including family *chengbao* (under which every peasant household in a village has a right to be granted a *chengbao* contract),[38] and *chengbao* of wasteland by means of tender, auction or open discussion (*gongkai xieshang*).[39] The LRLC provides in detail for the rights of the *chengbao* contracting party, and for the extent to which rights under a *chengbao* contract may be subcontracted, leased, exchanged, assigned, used as capital contribution to a business, mortgaged or inherited. These provisions suggest that the rights under a *chengbao* contract is in the nature of *wuquan* or property right,[40] but the term *wuquan* does not appear in the LRLC itself.

In 2004, the fourth amendment to the 1982 Constitution was introduced. This amendment contains provisions that are directly relevant to the recognition and protection of private property rights. The most important amendment for this purpose concerns article 13, the original text of which has been quoted earlier. The article is now replaced by the following provision:

> The lawful private property (*siyou caichan*) of citizens shall be inviolable. The State shall protect in accordance with law citizens' private property rights (*siyou caichanquan*) and inheritance rights. The State may, as necessitated by public interest, expropriate (*zhengshou*) or requisition (*zhengyong*) citizens' private property and pay compensation therefor.

Another provision introduced by the constitutional amendment requires the payment of compensation for expropriation or requisition of land by the State in the public interest (in circumstances not limited to those in which private property is affected).[41]

Following this constitutional amendment, the LAL was slightly amended in the same year of 2004 to bring it in line with the language of the constitutional amendment. The existing version of the LAL provided for requisition (*zhengyong*) of land by the State. The constitutional amendment introduces the distinction between requisition (*zhengyong*) (where the State assumes control of the property without, however, transferring ownership of the property to itself) and expropriation (*zhengshou*) (where ownership of the property concerned is transferred to the State).[42] The term *zhengyong* as used originally in the LAL covered both situations, and thus the LAL was now amended to refer to and include both requisition and expropriation.

The aforementioned legislative and constitutional developments thus pave the way for the enactment of the *Law of Property* (LP) in 2007. It may be seen from the foregoing survey that there existed prior to 2007 no code of property law that governed movable and immovable property (or *wu* as now defined in the LP) in a comprehensive and systematic manner. The relevant law has developed in a piecemeal fashion. The relationship between different pieces of law is not easy to understand. In the course of the Chinese economic reform, new practices were often introduced by policy documents and administrative directives before relevant laws and regulations were enacted. For example, in the case of the *chengbao* contracting system for rural land, the practices evolved in the 1980s, the system only received constitutional recognition in 1993, and the precise rights of the *chengbao* contracting party were not specified in law until the enactment of the LRLC in 2002. In the case of the urban land reform involving the grant of State-owned land to developers, the system gradually evolved since the constitutional amendment of 1988, and has been regulated by the LAL, PRCT and LAURE. It is noteworthy that the PRCT – a set of 'provisional regulations' enacted by the State Council in 1990 – is still in force despite the enactment of the LAURE and LAL, and has not been updated or made no longer 'provisional'. Similarly, the GPCL has not been updated, even though the GL has superseded the provisions in the GPCL on mortgage and lien, and even though the land use rights in State-owned land granted to developers should certainly fall within the concept of 'property rights related to property ownership' in the GPCL.

Although the relevant law is by no means well-organized, clear and tidy, the trend since the 1980s of giving increasing scope to private (as distinguished from State-controlled) economic activities on land and to the private sector of the economy may be seen from the foregoing review of legislative and constitutional developments. There has also been an increasing degree of reliance on the Constitution and the law for the purpose of legitimizing, specifying and clarifying the private property rights that have been allowed to emerge in the course of economic reform.

4.2. The transplanted and the indigenous

The LP consists of 247 articles divided into 19 chapters (and two supplementary provisions) organized into five parts. The five parts are entitled, respectively, 'general principles', 'ownership' (*suoyou quan*), 'rights of use and enjoyment over things' (*yongyi wuquan*), 'security rights over things' (*danbao wuquan*) and 'possession'. This part of the chapter examines the basic structure and ideas of the LP from a comparative law perspective, and will demonstrate that in designing the basic conceptual framework of the LP, Chinese lawmakers have borrowed much from continental Europe, particularly the German legal tradition, while the provisions on socialist ownership can be traced back to the legal tradition of the former USSR. On the other hand, the substantive content of the LP caters for the indigenous circumstances of China, and there are important innovations in the LP for this purpose.

The concepts of *wuquan* and *wuquan fa* can be traced directly to the German Civil Code (*Bürgerliches Gesetzbuch*, or 'BGB') enacted in 1896 rather than the Roman civil law tradition generally. Although both the BGB and the French

Civil Code enacted in 1804 were shaped by this civil law tradition which distinguished between actions *in rem* (concerning *jura in re* or real rights) and actions *in personam* and which had developed the concept of *jura in re aliena* (rights of a limited nature over property owned by another, or rights *in rem* other than ownership),[43] the French Civil Code does not contain any textual equivalent of *wuquan fa*. The French Civil Code consists of three books, entitled 'of persons', 'of property (*biens*), and the different modifications of property (*propriété*)' and 'of the different modes of acquiring property (*propriété*)', respectively.[44] Property (*propriété*) (alternatively translated as 'ownership') is defined in Book II of the Code as 'the right of enjoying and disposing of things in the most absolute manner, provided they are not used in a way prohibited by the laws or statutes'.[45] Property (*biens*) is divided into movable and immovable property.[46] Apart from ownership, Book II of the Code also provides for usufruct (*usufruit*),[47] right of common (*usage*), right of habitation, and servitudes. Pledge and mortgage of property are provided for in Book III of the Code (on the modes of acquisition of property), which also contains the law of contract. All these species of property rights are embraced by the concept of *droits réels* (real rights or rights *in rem*, as distinguished from *droits de créance* (rights of credit), such as rights under a contract)[48] developed by French jurists, although this term does not appear in the French Civil Code itself.

The BGB, hailed as the most 'scientific' legal code of its kind[49] at the time of its enactment almost one century after the French Civil Code, is divided into five books, entitled 'the general part', 'the law of obligations' (*Recht der Schuldverhältnisse*), 'the law of things' or 'the law of property' (*Sachenrecht*), 'family law' and 'the law of succession', respectively.[50] For our present purposes, Book III (*Sachenrecht*) of the BGB deserves closer examination.

Sachenrecht means the law relating to *Sachen*, which means corporeal things including movable things (*bewegliche Sachen*) and immovable things (*unbewegliche Sachen*), i.e. land (*Grundstücke*).[51] Book III of the BGB starts with the topic of possession, then stipulates general principles relating to rights over land, and then provides for ownership (*Eigentum*) and other kinds of property rights such as hereditary building rights (*Erbbaurecht*), servitudes (*Dienstbarkeit*), usufruct (*Niessbrauch*), mortgage (*Hypothek*), land charge (*Grundschuld*), annuity charge (*Rentenschuld*), right of pledge on movable things (*Pfandrecht an beweglichen Sachen*) and right of pledge on rights (*Pfandrecht an Rechten*), etc. In German jurisprudence, ownership and the various forms of property rights over things owned by another person (*beschränkte dingliche Rechte*) are collectively known as *dingliche Recht* (real rights). The *beschränkte dingliche Rechte* may be further divided into *Nutzungsrechte* (rights of use and enjoyment) and *Verwertungsrechte* or *Sicherungsrechte* (disposal or security rights).[52]

Thus, a comparison of the text and jurisprudence of the *Sachenrecht* and the Chinese *wuquan fa* would suggest that each of the following pairs of German and Chinese legal terms has the same meaning: *Sachen* (*wu*); *Sachenrecht* (*wuquan* or *wuquanfa*); *dingliche Recht* (*wuquan*); *Eigentum* (*suoyou quan*); *Nutzungsrechte* (*yongyi wuquan*); *Sicherungsrechte* (*danbao wuquan*). Article 2 of the LP, which reads as follows, can therefore be easily understood in the light of German jurisprudence:

> This Law governs the civil relationships arising from the assignment of rights over, and the use of, things (*wu*).
>
> The things mentioned in this Law include immovable and movable property. Where the law provides for rights as objects of rights over things (*wuquan*), such law shall be applied.
>
> The *wuquan* mentioned in this Law means the right of the right-holder to control directly specific things to the exclusion of others, and includes ownership (*suoyou quan*), rights of use and enjoyment over things (*yongyi wuquan*) and security rights over things (*danbao wuquan*).

It should be pointed out, however, that although the term and concept of *wuquan* only appeared for the first time in PRC legislation when the LP was enacted, this was by no means the first time when Chinese law-makers borrowed from the German concepts of *Sachen* and *Sachenrecht*. Actually, the draft civil code produced in 1911 just before the fall of the Qing dynasty (when Chinese law-makers borrowed actively from the contemporary Japanese and continental European law in their attempt to modernize the Chinese legal system) already included *wuquan* as one of its five books, which were on general principles, rights over obligations (*zhaiquan*), rights over things (*wuquan*), family law and law of succession, respectively.[53] It is no coincidence that the BGB and the Japanese Civil Code (1896)[54] consist also of five books on exactly the same subjects as the draft civil code of China.[55] The same structure of books and their topics appeared in the Civil Code of the Republic of China (ROC) enacted in 1929–1930 by the Nanking government of the Chinese Nationalist Party (Kuomintang or KMT). This is the civil code which, subject to various amendments, is still in force in Taiwan today.

Book III of the ROC Civil Code as originally enacted in 1929 consists of 210 articles divided into ten chapters:[56] (1) general principles; (2) ownership (*suoyou quan*); (3) superficies (*dishang quan*);[57] (4) emphyteusis (*yongdian quan*); (5) easements (*diyi quan*, alternatively translated as 'servitudes'); (6) mortgage (*diya quan*);[58] (7) pledge (*zhiquan*), including pledge of movable property (*dongchan zhiquan*) and pledge of rights (*quanli zhiquan*); (8) *dianquan*;[59] (9) lien; and (10) possession. Although the terms *yongyi wuquan* and *danbao wuquan* do not appear in the text of the Civil Code itself, they are used by jurists in Taiwan to explain and categorize the various species of *wuquan* in Book III of the Code: superfices, *yongdian quan* and easements are all *yongyi wuquan*, and mortgage, pledge, *dianquan* and lien are all *danbao wuquan*.[60]

If the concepts of *wuquan*, *yongyi wuquan* and *danbao wuquan* have all been part of Chinese jurisprudence since the enactment of the ROC Civil Code in 1929–1930, why did they disappear completely from Chinese law in mainland China and were only resurrected by the enactment of the LP in 2007? The answer lies in the communist revolution, the abolition at the time of the establishment of the PRC of all laws enacted by the KMT government and the transplant to China of the Soviet Union's Marxist system of property law.[61] Indeed, the provisions on ownership in the LP today are only fully explicable in the light of Soviet property law to which we now turn.

Jurists in the former Soviet Union adopted the Marxist view that law is an instrument of the ruling class. In a capitalist society, property law is thus an instrument of the bourgeoisie to maintain their class domination by legal provisions on the private ownership of the means of production. Private property was therefore a principal target of Marxist criticism of the injustice and oppression of a capitalist society. If the communist revolution means anything, it must mean the abolition of the private ownership of the means of production and its substitution by a system of socialist public ownership. Soviet law-makers and jurists thus embarked upon the task of translating the concept of socialist public ownership into legal provisions and institutions.[62]

The basic sources of Soviet property law included the Constitution, the *Basic Principles of Civil Legislation* enacted in 1961 (BPCL) (which as mentioned before influenced the making of the GPCL in the PRC) and the civil codes of the union republics of the USSR such as the *Civil Code of the Russian Socialist Federal Soviet Republic* (RSFSR). In the USSR Constitution of 1936 (the principal model which the PRC drew upon in drafting its first Constitution of 1954), two forms of 'socialist ownership' were provided for: 'State ownership (the wealth of the whole people)' and 'cooperative–collective farm ownership (ownership by individual collective farms and ownership by cooperative associations)'.[63] Land, natural resources, factories, enterprises, etc. were under State ownership.[64] Citizens had the 'right of personal ownership' (*lichnaya sobstvennost*, as distinguished from *chastnaya sobstvennost* [private ownership])[65] of 'their income and savings from work, dwelling house, … articles of domestic and everyday use', etc., and the 'right to inherit the personal property of citizens'.[66] In the BPCL, a third form of socialist ownership was provided for – ownership by public bodies or social organizations such as trade unions.[67]

As regards ownership by collective farms, it should be noted that under Soviet law, a collective farm was 'recognized as a separate juridical entity with the rights of a legal person'[68] and could therefore own property.[69] (This contrasts with the Chinese system of collective ownership by labouring masses, where the 'collective' that owns property was never clearly defined in law until the LP made some progress in this regard.[70]) Three other features of Soviet law are also relevant for the purpose of comparative study of PRC law. First, there was the concept of the 'right of operative management' on the part of State enterprises in respect of property or assets allocated to them by the State.[71] (This concept also appears in the GPCL as mentioned earlier.) Second, houses or buildings may be privately owned, though not the land on which they stood.[72] (This has also been the case in the PRC.[73]) Third, ownership was the only core concept recognized in Soviet property law, which contained no concepts of *Sachenrecht*, *beschränkte dingliche Rechte* or *Nutzungsrechte*.

(Following the Soviet approach, the PRC law also did not recognize these concepts until the enactment of the LP.) Ownership was defined in the Civil Code of the RSFSR as follows: 'The owner has the right to possess, use and dispose of property within the limits established by law'.[74] (A similar provision may be found in the GPCL.[75])

As mentioned in the preceding section, in both the PRC Constitution and in the GPCL, three types of ownership are provided for: State ownership, collective ownership (being the two forms of socialist public ownership) and ownership by individual citizens. In the course of the drafting of the LP, there was some debate regarding whether the LP should codify this threefold classification of property, or whether an alternative approach closer to that adopted by other civil law jurisdictions should be adopted.[76] One view was that the threefold classification was applicable only to systems of ownership (*suoyou zhi*) and need not be provided for in the LP, which should make provisions for ownership of property rather than systems of ownership which concern the 'economic base' of society (according to Marxist theory) and which belong to the province of constitutional law rather than civil law.[77] A related view is that as the GPCL has already provided that the subjects of civil law are natural persons and legal persons, the subjects of ownership that the LP should recognize are the State, natural persons and legal persons.[78] Another view is that the LP should follow the approach in the BGB and the ROC Civil Code of having separate sets of provisions for ownership of movable property and immovable property (land).[79]

Despite these views, the LP has eventually adopted the conservative or orthodox approach of reiterating the threefold classification of State ownership, collective ownership and ownership by individuals. But the provisions of the LP on ownership do go beyond the existing law in (1) defining the nature and mode of operation of collective ownership,[80] (2) substituting the term 'ownership by private persons' (*siren suoyouquan*, alternatively translated as 'private ownership') for 'ownership by individual citizens',[81] (3) declaring equal protection for the *wuquan* of the State, collectives, private persons and other right-holders[82] – hailed as a major breakthrough in Chinese legal and political thinking and a victory of the reformers over the conservatives who had criticized the draft LP as unconstitutional and a departure from socialism[83] and (4) introducing the concept of ownership by owners of apartments in condominium buildings (*jianzhuwu qufen suoyouquan*).[84] Furthermore, although there is no express provision in the LP on ownership by legal persons, there are provisions in the LP on the property rights of enterprise legal persons (*qiye faren*),[85] other legal persons,[86] and social organizations (*shehui tuanti*).[87]

We now turn from ownership (*suoyouquan*) to *yongyi wuquan* (rights of use and enjoyment over things) and *danbao wuquan* (security rights over things). During the process of the drafting of the LP, some PRC scholars actually suggested that the LP might as well use all the terms for various species of *yongyi wuquan* and *danbao wuquan* in the ROC Civil Code, including *dishang quan* (superficies) and *yongdian quan*, which they considered to be sufficiently similar to the land use rights granted to developers and the rights under the *chengbao* contract, respectively.[88] In the end, the LP adopted neither of the two terms. The *yongyi wuquan* (defined to mean the right to possess, use and derive benefits from immovable or movable property owned by another)[89] provided for in the LP include (1) the *chengbao* operational right in land,[90] (2) the right to use construction land,[91] (3) the right to use land for house sites[92] and (4) easements (*diyiquan*).[93] And the *danbao wuquan* provided for in the LP are (1) mortgage,[94] (2) pledge (including pledge of movable property and pledge of rights – following the dual mode of pledge in the BGB)[95] and (3) lien.[96] Following the two parts of the LP on *yongyi wuquan* (Part III) and *danbao wuquan* (Part IV), respectively, there is a final part (Part V) of the LP on the subject of 'possession' – which is also the subject of a separate chapter in both the BGB and the ROC Civil Code.

The provisions regulating the types and content of *yongyi wuquan* in the LP can be considered the most original features of Chinese property law that distinguish it from its counterparts in other jurisdictions. In non-communist civil law jurisdictions where private ownership of property is the dominant form of ownership, property ownership rather than *yongyi wuquan* (*Nutzungsrechte*) is the central concept in the law of property as well as the most important concept in property practice. The peculiarity of 'socialism with Chinese characteristics' or the 'socialist market economy' in China is such that ownership in land cannot be privately held and cannot enter the market, but *yongyi wuquan* can (and the extent to which each species of *yongyi wuquan* may be considered a private property right will be considered in the next section of this chapter). Hence the crucial importance of the conceptual category of *yongyi wuquan* within the Chinese system of property law.

Actually, the four species of *yongyi wuquan* provided for in the LP are not entirely new, and existed in PRC law and practice well before the enactment of the LP.[97] The most significant advance made by the LP in this regard is the recognition of the *chengbao* operational right in rural land as a *yongyi wuquan*. Before the enactment of the LP, the exact legal nature or status of the rights under the *chengbao* contract was not entirely clear.[98] While many scholars believed that they were in the nature of *wuquan* (property right), some pointed out that insofar as they were derived from contract and the law (at least before the enactment of the LRLC in 2002) did not regulate the content of the contract, they properly belonged to the realm of rights in contract (*zhaiquan*) rather than property rights.[99] In the absence of legislation clearly spelling out the nature of the *chengbao* rights, the courts had for a long time treated them as contractual rights rather than property rights.[100] The ultimate recognition of the *chengbao* rights as a species of *wuquan* has the effect of strengthening the degree of protection afforded to the holder of the rights.[101] For example, the mechanisms and remedies for the enforcement of all *wuquan* specified in Chapter 3 (on 'the protection of *wuquan*') of the LP are now available to the *chengbao* rights holder, and the rights can be enforced against third parties.

In terms of rules of substantive law, the provisions on *danbao wuquan* in the LP introduced more changes to the existing law than those on *yongyi wuquan*. As mentioned earlier, the law on security for credit was previously contained in the Guarantee Law (GL) (*danbao fa*) enacted in 1995. The provisions on *danbao wuquan* in the LP changed considerably the existing law and have largely superseded the GL, although the GL has not been formally repealed. The LP expands the scope of property that may be used as security for credit. For example, one provision stipulates that a mortgage may be created in respect of 'all other property which is not prohibited from being mortgaged by law or administrative regulations', in addition to certain specified categories of property.[102] Moreover, a mortgage in the nature of the floating charge in common law is also made possible by the LP.[103] Moreover, the scope of rights that may be the subject matter of a pledge of rights is expanded to include 'accounts receivables'.[104]

To conclude this section of the chapter, it may be pointed out in terms of the basic conceptual framework and textual structure of property law, the LP has borrowed significantly from the continental European, particularly the German, legal tradition. It has also retained certain crucial ideas on socialist ownership which China imported from the Soviet Union after the communist revolution. However, although conceptual categories such as *yongyi wuquan* and *danbao wuquan* have German origins and formed part of the 'old' jurisprudence of republican China (that had developed before the establishment of the PRC), the precise content of the *yongyi wuquan* and *danbao wuquan* provided for in the LP is largely a response to indigenous circumstances and needs. It also testifies to the unique combination of socialist and private property rights that is a product of the era of 'reform and opening' in China that began 30 years ago, and that is the subject of the next section of this chapter.

4.3. A move towards private property rights?

There is a significant body of literature, by lawyers, economists, philosophers and other scholars in the humanities and social sciences, on theories of property rights[105] and the relationship between the delineation, protection and enforcement of property rights and economic development.[106] It is, however, beyond the scope of this chapter to investigate property law and economic development in contemporary China. The objective of this part of the chapter is much more modest, and it is to examine to what extent the less conventional property rights (less conventional in the sense that there are hardly any counterparts in other jurisdictions) provided for in the LP can be considered private property rights or contain elements of private property rights. The species of rights to be explored here include (1) the right to use construction land, (2) the right to use land for house sites, (3) the *chengbao* operational right in land and (4) collective ownership.

Before we proceed to examine each of these rights, the criteria for determining what are private property rights need to be set out. According to

Harold Demsetz, property should be understood as a bundle of rights, including rights of control, income and transfer.[107] Similarly, Lawrence C. Becker points out that 'to have a property right in a thing is to have a bundle of rights that defines a form of ownership'. In his view, the concept of 'full ownership' comprises 13 elements: the right to possess; the right to use; the right to manage (i.e. to decide how and by whom a thing shall be used); the right to the income; the right to consume or destroy; the right to modify; the right to alienate; the right to transmit (i.e. devise or bequeath); the right to security (immunity from expropriation); the absence of term (time limit); the prohibition of harmful use; liability to execution; and residuary rules. According to Becker, any of the first eight rights, when supplemented by some version of the right to security, can be considered legal ownership.[108]

Becker's detailed analysis of various elements of ownership is useful, and it will be taken into account in our discussion that follows. However, what stands at the core of the concept of private property rights should also be borne in mind, and for this purpose the simpler formulation by Steven Cheung is illuminating:

> Any productive resource is a *private* property if, within well-defined limits, its owners has:
>
> (a) The right to exclude others so that he alone may decide on its use;
> (b) The right to extract exclusive income from its use; and
> (c) The right to transfer or sell the property or resource to anyone as he sees fit.
>
> ... An economic system based on private property rights implies that each individual is necessarily an owner of property (of his own labour, if nothing else), and that he is free to contract with others for its use.[109]

4.3.1. *The right to use construction land*

The right to use construction land ('RUCL') is defined by the LP as the right to possess, use and derive benefits from State-owned land, including the right to use the land for the construction of buildings, structures and ancillary facilities.[110] Two species of this right may be distinguished:[111] RUCL obtained by *churang* (grant by government, usually on the basis of tender or auction, upon payment of premium [*churang jin*] by the grantee),[112] and RUCL obtained by *huabo* (allotment by government for use by government organs or the military, or for urban infrastructural development, etc.,[113] where no payment of premium is required).[114] In both cases, the types of permitted land use are specified.[115] The term of the RUCL obtained by grant varies from 40 years to 70 years depending on the type of land use,[116] while the RUCL obtained by allotment is for an indefinite duration.[117] An important legal rule introduced by the LP is that the RUCL in residential land shall be 'automatically renewed' upon expiry of the term of grant.[118] However, the LP has not made such a guarantee for non-residential land.[119]

The LP provides that subject to any contrary provision in other laws, the holder of the RUCL has the right to assign (*zhuanrang*), exchange (*huhuan*), use as capital contribution (*chuzi*), give as a gift or mortgage the RUCL.[120] It may be noted that lease and inheritance are not mentioned in this provision. The PRCT mentioned in the foregoing section provides, inter alia, for leasing of land use rights together with the buildings or structures on the land.[121] The LAURE mentioned earlier also provides for leasing of housing (*fangwu*).[122] The RUCL may also be the subject matter of inheritance.[123]

The LP provides that where RUCL is assigned, exchanged, made a capital contribution or a gift, the buildings, structures or ancillary facilities shall be disposed of together with the RUCL.[124] Conversely, where the buildings, structures or ancillary facilities are disposed of, the RUCL of the underlying land shall be disposed of together with them.[125]

The right to assign, mortgage or otherwise dispose of RUCL obtained by allotment is subject to more restrictions than RUCL obtained by grant. In the latter case, the LAURE provides that the grantee may not assign the real estate (*fangdichan*) until 25 per cent of the total amount of the required investment has been provided (in the case of housing development) or the conditions for forming industrial or other construction land have been fulfilled.[126] In the case of RUCL obtained by allotment (free of payment of premium as mentioned earlier), the allottee may not assign the real estate until government approval has been obtained and the required premium is paid.[127]

Like other property rights provided for in the LP, RUCL and the buildings thereon are subject to the possibility of expropriation or requisition by the State with payment of compensation.[128] In addition, failure to develop the land in accordance with the conditions in the grant may result in the resumption of the land by the State without compensation.[129]

In the light of the foregoing, it may be seen that the RUCL obtained by grant (as distinguished from allotment) is a private property right close to the right of ownership, subject to the term (limited duration) of the grant. Indeed, the RUCL is very similar to the property right acquired by purchasers of government land in Hong Kong who are lessees of the Government (or the Crown in colonial Hong Kong) for the term of the lease. Where a real estate developer is granted RUCL, constructs buildings on the land and sells the apartments in them to end users, the end users also obtain a property right akin to ownership – including the ownership of the apartment of the condominium building and a share of the RUCL in the land on which the building stands, particularly since the LP now provides for the automatic renewal of RUCL in residential land. In this regard, the system for the development and use of urban land in socialist China is very similar to that in capitalist Hong Kong.

4.3.2. The right to use land for house sites

The LP provides briefly for the right to use land for house sites (RUHS) in four articles. RUHS is defined as the right to possess and use collectively owned land, including the right to use the land for the construction of a residence and ancillary facilities.[130] As in the case of buildings on urban land, the residence so constructed may be privately owned.[131] Apart from recognizing RUHS as a *yongyi wuquan*, the LP does not change but preserves the existing law on house sites on rural land. The LP provides that the LAL and other relevant provisions made by the State shall govern the acquisition, exercise and transfer of RUHS. It also expressly provides that RUHS (and other rights of use over collectively owned land) may not be mortgaged save where authorized by law[132] (and the existing law does not authorize such mortgage).

Before its amendment in 1998, the LAL provided that when rural residents constructed their residence, they should use existing house sites (*zhai jidi*) or vacant land within the village with the approval of the township government.[133] Agricultural land may also be used for this purpose subject to consideration of the application by the township government and approval by the county government.[134] It was also provided that 'if one sells or leases his residence and applies again for a house site, such applications shall not be approved'.[135]

The LAL as amended in 1998 largely preserves the existing rules, but requires all applications for house sites on the part of rural residents to be considered by the township (or town) government and approved by the county government.[136] It also introduces the limitation that each household of villagers is entitled to only one house site.[137] The rule prohibiting fresh applications after the sale or leasing of a residence is preserved.[138]

The RUHS is in the nature of a social benefit made available to rural residents largely for their own use rather than for transfer. Only members of a village are entitled to apply for RUHS.[139] Applicants are households rather than individuals.[140] No payment of consideration is needed.[141] The RUHS is not subject to any time limit,[142] survives the death of individual members of the household,[143] and may be inherited by family members.[144] As regards the extent to which the RUHS and the residence built on the land may be leased or sold, the law is not completely clear. The foregoing rule prohibiting fresh applications after the sale or leasing of a residence seems to presuppose that such sale or leasing may occur.[145] However, a State Council notice in 1999 provides that peasants' residences may not be sold to urban residents, and urban residents should not be given approval to build residences on peasants' collectively owned land.[146] A State Council decision in 2004 prohibits urban residents from purchasing house sites in villages.[147]

There was much debate during the process of drafting of the LP regarding whether free transfer of RUHS should be permitted.[148] In the end, it was decided to leave the question open in the LP.[149] Some localities have, however, started to experiment with the practice of permitting transfer of land use rights in collectively owned land for construction purpose.[150] As regards the interpretation of the existing law, there are different scholarly opinions on whether residences built on house sites by holders of RUHS may be assigned (sold), leased (to fellow villagers or to outsiders) or even mortgaged.[151]

From the perspective of economic efficiency, RUHS should be made freely transferable. There is a demand on the part of some urban residents to live in rural areas either after retirement or for other reasons. Holders of RUHS may want to migrate away from the village or to raise money for their own purposes. However, there is fear on the part of the government that a free market in RUHS may result in many peasants losing their residence and rich people or corporations buying large amounts of RUHS. Similar considerations have also led the government to refrain from allowing the free transfer of the *chengbao* rights to be discussed in the next section.

In light of the foregoing, RUHL may be understood as a private property right of a limited nature, the main limit being on the transfer or other similar dispositions of the right. In other respects, it bears resemblance to RUCL, particularly RUCL as applied to owners of residential accommodation in the urban areas.

4.3.3. The chengbao operational right in land

As mentioned in the preceding section, the *chengbao* operational right in land (CORL) dated back to the rural economic reform of the 1980s, and was first systematically codified in the LRLC. The chapter on CORL in the LP begins by reproducing the provisions in the Constitution that rural collective economic organizations shall practise a two-level operational system based on family *chengbao* operation and the combination of centralized and decentralized operations.[152] It goes on to provide that the system of *chengbao* operation of land is applicable to farmland, forest land, grassland and other agricultural land collectively owned by peasants or owned by the State but collectively used by peasants.[153] CORL is defined as the right to possess, use and derive benefits from the land that is subject to the *chengbao* operation, including the right to engage in various agricultural activities.[154] The periods of *chengbao* operation are specified in the LP, and vary from 30 to 70 years depending on whether the land is farmland, grassland or forest land.[155] The LP provides that on the expiry of the relevant period, the *chengbao* operator may continue to *chengbao* in accordance with relevant provisions made by the State.[156] The grantor of the *chengbao* land may not adjust the land during the *chengbao* period,[157] and may not resume the land save where the law otherwise provides.[158] Compensation is payable for expropriation of *chengbao* land.[159]

Chengbao operation of rural land may be classified into two types – family *chengbao*, and *chengbao* of wasteland (*huangdi*, commonly referred to as *sihuang* [four types of wasteland]).[160] All members of the village are entitled to be granted family *chengbao* contracts;[161] the relevant authority is under a legal obligation to grant *chengbao* contracts to members of the village.[162] *Chengbao* rights are allocated to peasant households (*nonghu*)[163] in accordance with the numbers of persons and manpower of peasant households.[164] On the other hand, *chengbao* contracts in respect of wasteland are awarded on the basis of tenders, auctions or open negotiations (*gongkai xieshang*)[165] and upon payment of a premium (*chengbaofei*).[166] 'Outsiders' (persons who are not members of the village) may bid for such contracts, although members of the village are given some priority in the award of such contracts,[167] and the grant of such contracts to 'outsiders' is subject to the consent of a two-thirds majority at a villagers' meeting and the approval of the township or town government.[168] The *chengbao* periods are usually longer in the case of wasteland *chengbao*.[169] However, the aforementioned provision on the continuation of the *chengbao* arrangement after the expiry of the chengbao period is apparently not applicable to wasteland *chengbao*.[170] In the case of family *chengbao*, the land may be resumed by the grantor before the expiry of the *chengbao* contract if the whole family of the *chengbao* operator has migrated to a city and has become a non-agricultural household (*fei nongye hukou*).[171]

The right to transfer or otherwise engage in dealings in the CORL is more extensive in the case of wasteland *chengbao* than family *chengbao*. The LP provides that wasteland *chengbao* operators who are awarded their contracts on the basis of tender, auction or open negotiation may assign, use as capital contribution, mortgage or otherwise transfer their CORL in accordance with the LRLC and other relevant laws and provisions.[172] In the case of family *chengbao*, the LP provides that the *chengbao* operator may subcontract (*zhuanbao*), exchange or assign their CORL in accordance with the LRLC.[173] The LRLC permits assignment of CORL under limited circumstances: the consent of the grantor (the village authority) must be obtained; the assignor must have a stable non-agricultural occupation or stable source of income; the assignee must be a peasant household engaged in agricultural production.[174] In the case of subcontracting, leasing (note that leasing is not mentioned in the LP but is mentioned in the LRLC) and exchange, no consent by the grantor is required, but the matter should be reported to the grantor for the record.[175] However, mortgage of CORL is not permitted by law.[176]

As regards inheritance, the cases of family *chengbao* and wasteland *chengbao* also need to be distinguished. In the former case, as the grant of the *chengbao* contract is made to the peasant household, the death of an individual member of the household will not affect the continuation of the COLR.[177] If all members of the household die, the COLR is extinguished and the land should be returned to the grantor.[178] Special provision is made in the LRLC regarding *chengbao* of forest land (where the *chengbao* period may be as long as 70 years): on the death of the *chengbao* operator, his or her successor (under the law of inheritance) (irrespective of whether the successor is a member of the household or the village) may continue the *chengbao* arrangement for the remainder of the original *chengbao* period.[179] In the case of wasteland *chengbao* on the basis of tender, auction or open negotiation, upon the death of the *chengbao* operator, the successor may also continue the *chengbao* arrangement for the remainder of the original term.[180]

As in the case of house sites in rural areas, the question of whether to allow free transfer of CORL was much debated in the course of the drafting of the PL.[181] Relaxation of the existing restrictions on transfer would improve economic efficiency: peasants who want to migrate to cities may sell their CORL, and persons or companies which have skills, expertise and capital can acquire large amounts of CORL and introduce large-scale agricultural operations.[182] However, there were reservations about the emergence of large numbers of people from the rural areas (originally peasants) being left without any means of livelihood, and the possible depletion of agricultural land. For a long time, the CORL has performed a 'social security' function for peasants in China's rural areas.[183] With the development of the socialist market economy, economic and social inequality in China has risen sharply. There was concern that marketization of rural land would lead to still greater inequality in China. Thus in the end, the LP did not directly address the issue of such marketization but left it open (for resolution by future legislative change).[184]

To conclude, it may be seen that like the RUHS, the CORL (in the case of family *chengbao*) is a private property right which is fairly extensive in terms of the right to use and derive benefits, and in terms of the long duration which in view of the provision on continuation is almost indefinite. The main limitation on this right concerns transfer and mortgage. In the case of wasteland *chengbao*, the CORL is a more extensive property right because of the existence of the right of transfer and mortgage, although the right (as in the case of RUCL obtained by grant) is not one of indefinite duration.

4.3.4. Collective ownership

As mentioned in the foregoing section, collective ownership by the labouring masses is one of the two modes of socialist public ownership in the PRC. Unlike State ownership, the rights of which are ultimately exercised by the State Council and persons or bodies authorized by it, the subject of collective ownership – the 'collective' – has never been clarified in PRC law.[185] As previously mentioned, in the Soviet Union, there were also two forms of socialist ownership – State ownership and cooperative–collective farm ownership – but the collective farms that were subjects of ownership were separate juridical entities and legal persons.[186] In the PRC, however, there is no corresponding concept of collective farms. The question therefore arises of what is meant by saying that a particular piece of land (in the rural areas, as urban land is State-owned) is under collective ownership. This section of the chapter seeks to investigate the nature and operation of collective ownership as applied to land, particularly in the light of relevant provisions in the LP. Collective ownership of enterprises (as in the case of township and village enterprises), though equally important, is outside the scope of this chapter.[187]

Collective ownership, being one of the two forms of socialist public ownership, was intended to be something other than private ownership or ownership by private individuals. As far as rural land is concerned, the origins of collective ownership can be traced back to the 1950s. The communist revolution was accompanied by a massive redistribution of land; land owned by rich landowners was confiscated. Under the *Land Reform Law* of 1950, peasants were allocated land which they could actually own privately.[188] In subsequent years, however, there was a movement towards the socialization or collectivization of all means of production. By 1957, private ownership of rural land had been largely abolished, with peasants being required to transfer their land to peasants' cooperatives.[189] Thus, the system of collective ownership of rural land was established. The system was elaborated by the Regulations on Rural People's Communes in 1962, which introduced the principle of 'three-level ownership with the production team as the basis'.[190] The three levels were the people's communes, the production brigades (*shengchan dadui*, at a level below the communes) and the production teams (*shengchan dui*, at a level below the brigades).[191] After the end of the Cultural Revolution era, the people's communes were abolished, and a new system of rural governance and rural economic organization was introduced. In this new system, the structural equivalents (in terms of the hierarchy of rural organs) of the people's communes, production brigades and production teams are the townships (*xiang*), the villages (or 'administrative villages') and the villagers' groups (*cunmin xiaozu*, or 'natural villages': one 'administrative village', or village for administrative purposes, may comprise more than one natural village or villagers' group),[192] administered, respectively, by the township governments,[193] the villagers' committees[194] and the heads of villagers' groups (*xiaozuzhang*).[195]

At the time of the enactment of the LP, the existing law recognized three modes of collective ownership of rural land,[196] which correspond to the three levels of rural organization as mentioned before. According to the GPCL, collectively owned land is collectively owned by the peasants of the village, and shall be managed by the agricultural production cooperative of the village or the villagers' committee, except where the land is already owned by the collective economic organization of the township or town.[197] Thus, the GPCL recognized two modes of collective ownership of rural land – at the village level and the township level, respectively. A third mode was provided for in the *Land Administration Law* (LAL), which added the rule that where rural land is already collectively owned by peasants of two or more rural collective economic organizations within a village, it shall be managed by the respective collective economic organizations or villagers' groups.[198] In practice, collective ownership at the township level is rare, and the dominant forms of collective ownership are collective ownership by the village[199] and by the villagers' group.[200]

The law regulates the extent to which those in charge of collectively owned land may deal with or dispose of such land, although it has been pointed out that such restrictive rules are often disregarded in practice.[201] For example, agricultural land may not be used for construction without government approval.[202] Even where rural land has been designated as land for construction purpose, the use by rural collective economic organizations of such land for establishing business enterprises is subject to government approval.[203] The law also provides that the right to use collectively owned land may not be transferred or leased for non-agricultural construction.[204] Generally speaking, those in charge of collectively owned land may not sell it for development purposes; the land (i.e. the right to use land) may only be sold for development purposes after it has been expropriated (requisitioned) by the State and converted into State-owned land.[205]

Before the enactment of the LP, there existed two sets of problems, one theoretical and one practical, relating to collective ownership in rural land. These problems have been addressed in the LP to some extent. The first problem was that the nature of collective ownership had not been clarified by law. According to one leading scholar, there existed at least four schools of thought regarding its nature.[206] The second set of problems flowed from the fact that in practice, those in charge of collectively owned land[207] often abused their powers and engaged in illegal dealings in the land to the detriment of fellow members of the village or the collective that in theory owned the land, who may not even have the standing to take the matter to court.[208]

The LP now defines more clearly the nature of collective ownership, and provides more specifically for the rights of the members of the collective body that owns rural land. It is declared that the immovable and movable property that is collectively owned by peasants is 'collectively owned by *the members of* the relevant collective'.[209] This provision is significant in that it makes it clear that the property does not merely belong to the collective as an abstract entity, but that individuals as members of the collective may enjoy property rights of some kind with regard to the collectively owned property.[210] Although the LP does not define the meaning of the 'collective', it recognizes that, as provided by the existing law, the collective may be the township, the village or the villagers' group by providing that the relevant township collective economic organization, villagers' committee or villagers' group may exercise the ownership on behalf of the collective.[211] The LP seeks to protect the rights of members of the collective by providing that certain matters (e.g. *chengbao* plans or the use and distribution of land compensation) must be decided by members of the collective themselves in accordance with legally prescribed procedures,[212] and that where the collective economic organization, villagers' committee or other responsible persons have made a decision infringing upon the lawful rights and interests of members of the collective, aggrieved members may apply to court for the decision to be quashed.[213] The LP also requires information relating to the State of the collectively owned property to be made available to members of the collective.[214]

In practice, apart from the rights of participation in decision-making and of taking court actions that are expressly provided for in the LP, members of the collective also enjoy the right to share in the income or benefits derived from the use (e.g. leasing[215] or *chengbao* operation[216]) of the collectively owned land managed by relevant authorities such as the villagers' committees or collective economic organizations.[217] This right may be the subject of inheritance, but may not be transferred to others.[218]

As may be seen from the aforementioned, collective ownership of rural land in China is a complex phenomenon that is only partially provided for in law, and much depends on practices that are continuously evolving. It is significant that members of the collective may enjoy certain income derived from the use of the collectively owned property. The LP confers further rights on members by stating that the collectively owned property is collectively owned *by the members of the collective* (rather than by the collective as an abstract entity), and by providing for members' rights of participation in decision-making relating to the collectively owned property. It may thus be argued that although collective ownership is in official theory a form of socialist public ownership, there are elements of private property in it insofar as members of the collective as private individuals may enjoy certain private rights (including income) and assert certain private claims relating to the use of the collectively owned property. Indeed, it has been suggested by a leading Chinese scholar that collective ownership may be conceived of as a special form of common ownership;[219] whereas under the ordinary form of common ownership, the owner may exercise the right of severance over the commonly owned property, or exercise certain rights directly over the commonly owned property, or join together with the other co-owners to dispose of the property, this is not so under collective ownership.[220]

4.4. Conclusion

As this chapter has demonstrated, economic reform in China in the past three decades of 'reform and opening' has been accompanied by significant legal developments relating to property rights that culminated in the enactment of the LP in 2007. The LP has not revolutionized the existing law. The LP's main significance and contribution lies in providing a conceptual framework for the purpose of organizing, consolidating and systematizing the existing law relating to property rights in movable and immovable property. As this chapter has shown, this conceptual framework has largely been borrowed from the continental European, particularly the German, legal tradition. The concepts of *wu*, *wuquanfa*, *suoyou quan*, *yongyi wuquan* and *danbao wuquan* all have their counterparts in German jurisprudence.

This chapter has also pointed out that these concepts, though largely new (except *suoyou quan* which is not new) to the text of Chinese legislation, already existed in the twentieth-century Chinese legal tradition that preceded the establishment of the PRC. The LP suggests that this tradition, embodied in the Civil Code of the Republic of China that is still in force in Taiwan today, is being resurrected in the PRC. From this perspective, there is not only a trend of convergence in the domain of property law between contemporary

Chinese law and continental European law, but also one of convergence between the laws on both sides of the Taiwan Straits.

Nevertheless, the similarity in basic concepts and textual structure might belie the big differences between PRC property law and that in Taiwan or Europe, and the many unique features of the LP that respond to the indigenous circumstances of the PRC. For example, the LP still maintains the system of socialist public ownership that was transplanted from the Soviet Union after the Chinese communist revolution. What is most interesting is that the LP has grafted onto it a regime of *yongyi wuquan* that is uniquely Chinese in content. Such combination of socialist ownership with *yongyi wuquan* represents at once a synthesis of Soviet and German legal ideas, and a synthesis of socialist property and private property.

As this chapter has demonstrated, the main three types of *yongyi wuquan* (including their sub-species) provided for in the LP are to varying degrees private property rights, and collective ownership in respect of rural land also contains elements of private property. The species of *yongyi wuquan* that come closest to private property rights are the right to use construction land (RUCL) obtained by grant and the *chengbao* operational right (CORL) relating to wasteland obtained by auction, tender, etc. The right to use house sites (RUHS) and the CORL in the case of family *chengbao* also exhibit important elements of private property rights, and their limitations as property rights relate mainly to restrictions on sale (transfer) and mortgage.

In his seminal paper on 'Will China Go Capitalist?' published in 1982,[221] Professor Steven Cheung argues that China will go capitalist, and that capitalism depends on an effective regime of private property rights. To a large extent, Cheung's forecast has proved to be accurate. Various species of private property rights (including but not limited to those covered by this chapter) have indeed emerged in China, and have probably contributed significantly to the spectacular economic growth in China in the last three decades. However, in terms of the clarity of legal delineation of private property rights and the security of such rights, there is still much to be desired. As this chapter has shown, there is also scope for the further privatization and commodification of property rights in rural land. Whether that will happen soon or eventually will be a crucial policy choice for the Chinese government and the Chinese Communist Party. However, whatever choice they make, it will be reflected and embodied in new legislative action, which, like the enactment of the LP, may become the subject of intense debate. Thus, the story of Chinese law will continue to unfold, together with the story of China's quest for modernization and for the building of a 'wealthy, powerful, democratic and civilized'[222] nation.

Notes

* The author is grateful to Dr Eva Pils of the Faculty of Law, Chinese University of Hong Kong, for referring him to relevant literature in English for the purpose of writing this chapter.

1 For the history of the legislative process, *see*, Zhihui Liu (ed.), *Wuquan fa lifa guannian yu yinan zhidu pingzhu* (The Law of Property: A Commentary on the Legislative Concepts and Problems in the System), Beijing: Jiangsu Renmin Press, 2007: 15–28.

2 A famous debate was initiated in 2005 by Peking University law professor Xiantian Gong, who criticized the draft Law of Property as an unconstitutional departure from the socialist principles enshrined in the Constitution of the PRC. *See*, e.g. Yiqing Liu and Qinde Zhang (eds), *Gong Xiantian xuanfeng shilu* (Records of the Going Xiantian Storm), Beijing: Zhongguo Caizheng Jingji Press, 2007.

3 LP, art. 2. It is also provided that rights may also be the object of *wuquan* where the law so provides.

4 *See*, *generally*, E. L. G. Tyler and N. E. Palmer, *Crossley Vaines' Personal Property*, London: Butterworths, 1973: 11–14.

5 In the civil law tradition, the law of 'things' (*res*) in the broad sense included the law of 'things' in the narrow sense (i.e. tangible assets such as land and goods), the law of 'obligations' (including the functional equivalents of the law of contract and the law of tort in the common law tradition) and the law of inheritance. *See*, *generally*, B. Nicholas, *An Introduction to Roman Law*, Oxford: Clarendon Press, 1962; Albert H. Y. Chen, 'The Developing Chinese Law and the Civil Law Tradition', in M. Brosseau *et al.* (eds), *China Review 1996*, Hong Kong: Chinese University Press, 1996, Ch. 2, 29–59.

6 *See*, *generally*, Albert H. Y. Chen, 'Legal Thought and Legal Development in the People's Republic of China 1949–2008', in J. Gillespie and Albert H. Y. Chen (eds), *Legal Reforms in China and Vietnam*, London: Routledge, forthcoming 2010, Ch. 3.

7 *See*, *generally*, Albert H. Y. Chen, *An Introduction to the Legal System of the People's Republic of China* (3rd edn), Hong Kong: LexisNexis, 2004, Ch. 4.

8 *See*, arts 7, 9, 10.

9 Art. 6.

10 Art. 10(1).

11 *See*, P. A. Randolph and Jianbo Lou, *Chinese Real Estate Law*, The Hague: Kluwer, 2000: 9–11; T. A. Lo, 'Debate Surrounding the New Property Law in China', *Cambridge Student L. Rev.* 4, 2008: 182, 187–188.

12 Art. 10(2). This rule is subject to the exception that some such land is State-owned as provided by law.

13 Art 10(3), (4). The prohibition on 'lease' was deleted by the 1988 constitutional amendment: *infra note* 21.

14 Art. 12.

15 Art. 13.

16 Chen, *supra note* 5, p. 30; Sun, *Zhongguo wuquan fa zonglun* (General Principles of Chinese Property Law) (2nd edn), Beijing: Law Press, 2009: 190–191; E. L. Johnson, *An Introduction to the Soviet Legal System*, London: Methuen, 1969: 106.

17 GPCL, arts. 73–75. Art. 77 provides for the property of 'social organizations' (including 'religious organizations').

18 *See*, e.g. Chen, *supra note* 7, pp. 249–250.

19 Art. 89(2), (4). The term mortgage (*diya*) in the GPCL covers both mortgage (in English law) and pledge, and no distinction has been drawn between these two security devices in the GPCL. *See*, Chen, *supra note* 5, p. 35.

20 Art. 12.
21 At the same time, the prohibition on lease of land in art. 10 of the Constitution was deleted by this constitutional amendment.
22 *See*, art. 2 of the LAL as amended in 1988.
23 *Ibid.*
24 *See*, e.g. Albert H. Y. Chen, 'The Basic Law and the Protection of Property Rights' *Hong Kong Law Journal* 23, 1993: 31, 40–41.
25 Land use rights obtained by such allotment may not be assigned, leased or mortgaged: *see*, art. 44 of the Provisional Regulations on the Grant and Transfer of the Right to Use State-owned Land in Cities and Towns (PRCT) (which is subject to the exception in art. 45). The circumstances in which allotment of land use rights is permissible are now set out in the *Law on the Administration of Urban Real Estate* (art. 23) and the LAL (as amended in 1998), art. 54.
26 Art. 12.
27 *See*, the amendment to art. 15 of the Constitution.
28 *See*, the amendment to art. 8 of the Constitution.
29 Laws are enacted by the NPC or the NPC Standing Committee, while administrative regulations are enacted by the State Council. *See*, the Constitution, arts 58, 89.
30 Art. 14 of the amended law. In 1993, when many *chengbao* contracts were due to expire, the CCP decide that they should all be renewed for 30 years: *see*, the speech of Suinian Liu introducing the bill for the Law of Rural Land Contracts to the NPC Standing Committee on 26 June 2001, reprinted in Chaoying Wang (ed.), *Zhonghua renmin gongheguo nongcun tudi chengbao fa shiyong wenda* (Practical Questions and Answers on the PRC Law of Rural Land Contracts), Beijing: Zhongguo Fazhi Press, 2002: 204.
31 Arts. 14 and 15 of the new law.
32 Arts. 46–49 of the amended law. Dissatisfaction with the compensation arrangements has been a primary source of conflict and popular unrest in China's rural areas as land was taken away from peasants for purposes of development. *See*, *infra note* 205.
33 *See*, the amended art. 6 of the Constitution.
34 *See*, the amended art. 11 of the Constitution.
35 *See*, the amended art. 8 of the Constitution.
36 Art. 1.
37 Art. 20.
38 Arts 5–6 and Chapter 2 of the law.
39 Chapter 3 of the law.
40 *See also*, Suinian Liu's speech, *supra note* 30, pp. 206–207. According to Liu, the intention of the LRLC was that family *chengbao* should be protected as *wuquan*, while other forms of *chengbao* would only enjoy protection as *zhaiquan* (i.e. as a contractual rather than property right).
41 *See*, the amendment to art. 10(3) of the Constitution.
42 *See*, Dingjian Cai, *Xianfa jingjie* (A Commentary on the Constitution) (2nd edn), Beijing: Law Press, 2006: 197.
43 *See*, Nicholas, *supra note* 5, pp. 140–141.
44 *See*, *The Code Napoleon*, London: C. Hunter, 1824, in HeinOnline.
45 Art. 544.
46 Art. 516.

47 Art. 578: 'Usufruct is the right of enjoying things of which the property is in another, in the same manner as the proprietor himself, but on condition of preserving them substantially'. The concept of usufruct can be traced back to ancient Roman law: *see*, Nicholas, *supra note* 5, pp. 144–148.

48 *See, generally*, C. Dadomo and S. Farran, *French Substantive Law*, London: Sweet & Maxwell, 1997: 11–15, 62–69.

49 E. J. Cohn, *Manual of German Law*, Vol. I (2nd rev. edn), London: British Institute of International and Comparative Law, 1968: 57.

50 *See, generally, The German Civil Code*, transl. by Simon L. Goren (rev. edn), Littleton, Colo.: F.B. Rothman, 1994.

51 N. Foster, *German Law and Legal System*, London: Blackstone Press, 1993: 238.

52 *Ibid.*, pp. 239, 251.

53 For the history of the drafting of civil codes in twentieth-century China, *see*, e.g. Sun, *supra note* 16, pp. 188–190; Jianyuan Cui et al, *Wuquan fa* (Property Law), Beijing: Tsinghua University Press, 2008, 10; Honglie Yang, *Zhongguo falü fazhan shi* (History of the Development of Chinese Law), Shanghai: Shanghai Shudian, 1990 (orig. pub. 1930).

54 *See*, H. Oda, *Japanese Law*, London: Butterworths, 1992: 133.

55 While the five books of the draft civil code of the late Qing dynasty followed the same order as the BGB, in the Japanese Civil Code, the order of the second and third books was reversed: book II is on the law of things, and book III the law of obligations.

56 For the Chinese text of this part of the Civil Code, *see*, *Zuixin liufa quanshu* (The New Book of Six Codes), Taipei: Dazhongguo Tushu Gongsi, 1989: 94–101.

57 This is the right to use another's land for the purpose of owning buildings or other works, trees or bamboo on the land: art. 832.

58 This is the perpetual right to cultivate or raise livestock on another's land subject to payment of rent: art. 842.

59 This is the right to possess, use and derive benefits from another's immovable property on payment of consideration: art. 911. (Art. 912 provides that the duration of the *dianquan* shall not exceed 30 years; art. 913 touches upon the issue of redemption.) This is a form of security for credit in the Chinese tradition.

60 Meiling Chen *et al.*, *Minfa rumen* (Introduction to Civil Law), Taipei: Yuedan, 1994, 393.

61 Sun, *supra note* 16, pp. 190–191. For the Soviet influence on PRC law, *see, generally*, Albert H. Y. Chen, 'Socialist Law, Civil Law, Common Law, and the Classification of Contemporary Chinese Law', in J. M. Otto *et al.* (eds), *Law-Making in the People's Republic of China*, The Hague: Kluwer Law International, 2000, Ch. IV, 55–74.

62 *See, generally*, O. S. Ioffe, *Soviet Civil Law*, Dordrecht: Martinus Nijhoff, 1988: 91–111.

63 Art. 5.

64 Art. 6.

65 Johnson, *supra note* 16, p. 108.

66 Art. 10 of the Constitution.

67 Johnson, *supra note* 16, p. 106; Ioffe, *supra note* 62, p. 96.

68 Johnson, *supra note* 16, p. 107.

69 Ioffe, *supra note* 62, pp. 105–106.

70 *See*, the section of this chapter below on collective ownership.

71 Johnson, *supra note* 16, p. 107; Ioffe, *supra note* 62, pp. 93–95, 98–99.

72 Johnson, *supra note* 16, p. 110.
73 *See, generally*, K. Wilhelm, 'Rethinking Property Rights in Urban China', *UCLA Journal of International Law and Foreign Affairs*, 9, 2004: 227.
74 Art. 92. *See*, Ioffe, *supra note* 62, p. 92.
75 Art. 71.
76 *See*, e.g. Baoyu Liu, *Wuquan tixi lun* (The System of Property Rights), Beijing: Renmin Fayuan Press, 2004: 120–125, 136–145.
77 Sun, *supra note* 16, pp. 26, 122–127.
78 *Ibid.*, p. 123; Liu, *supra note* 76, p. 138.
79 This approach was adopted in the draft Law of Property prepared by Professor Huixing Liang of the Chinese Academy of Social Sciences. *See*, Huixing Liang, *Zhongguo wuquanfa cao'an jianyi gao* (A Proposed Draft Bill for the Chinese Law of Property), Beijing: Shehui Kexue Wenxian Press, 2000, esp. 212–213.
80 LP, arts 58–63.
81 LP, arts 64–66. Ownership by 'citizens' rather than 'private persons' was the concept employed by the 1982 Constitution and the GPCL.
82 LP, art. 4.
83 *See*, e.g. Lo, *supra note* 11, pp. 192–194; Mo Zhang, 'From Public to Private: The Newly Enacted Chinese Property Law and the Protection of Property Rights in China', *Berkeley Business Law Journal* 5, 2008: 317, 343–345; Cui, *supra note* 53, p. 123; Sun, *supra note* 16, p. 138; speech at the NPC cited in *infra note* 184.
84 LP, Ch.6 (arts70–83).
85 LP, art. 68(1). On the question of ownership by legal persons, *see*, e.g., Tia Yin, *Wuquanfa lilun pingxi yu sikao* (The Theory of Property Law: Analysis and Reflections) (2nd edn), Beijing: Zhongguo Renmin Daxue, 2008: 95–110.
86 Art. 68(2).
87 Art. 69.
88 *See*, Zhihui Liu, *supra note* 1, pp. 117–124; Baoyu Liu, *supra note* 76, pp. 120–125, 176–182.
89 LP, art. 117.
90 LP, Ch. 11.
91 LP, Ch. 12.
92 LP, Ch. 13.
93 LP, Ch. 14. These are the main types, but not the only types, of *yongyi wuquan* provided for in the LP. *See*, LP, arts. 12–123; Liming Wang, *Wuquanfa lun* (The Law of Property) (2nd rev. edn), Beijing: Zhongguo Zhengfa Daxue Press, 2008, 216, 306; Ping Jiang, (ed.), *Wuquanfa jiaocheng* (Textbook on the Law of Property), Beijing: Zhongguo Zhengfa Daxue Press, 2007, 176; Cui, *supra note* 53, pp. 178–180.
94 LP, Ch. 16.
95 LP, Ch. 17.
96 LP, Ch. 18.
97 As regards easement (*diyiquan*), this did not exist in Chinese law before the enactment of the LP, but the GPCL provided for a related concept of 'neighbourhood relations' (*xianglin guanxi*). *See*, GPCL, art. 83; Liming Wang, *Wuquanfa lun* (The Law of Property) (rev. edn), Beijing: Zhongguo Zhengfa Daxue Press, 2003, Ch. 17.
98 *See*, e.g. Huixing Liang and Huabin Chen, *Wuquanfa* (Law of Property) (3rd edn), Beijing: Law Press, 2005, 9.

99 *See*, Wang, *supra note* 97, pp. 454–455; Jiang, *supra note* 93, pp. 200–201.
100 *See*, the works cited in *supra note* 99.
101 Wang, *supra note* 93, p. 225.
102 Art. 180.
103 Art. 181.
104 Art. 223(6).
105 For a review of some of these theories, *see*, e.g. Chen, *supra note* 24, pp. 31–39.
106 *See*, e.g. D. C. North, *Structure and Change in Economic History*, New York: Norton, 1981; Y. Barzel, *A Theory of the State: Economic Rights, Legal Rights, and the Scope of the State*, New York: Cambridge University Press, 2002; Albert H. Y. Chen, 'Rational Law, Economic Development and the Case of China', *Social and Legal Studies,* 8, 1999: 97.
107 H. Demsetz, 'Toward a Theory of Property Rights', in E. G. Furubotn and S. Pejovich (eds), *The Economics of Property Rights*, Cambridge: Ballinger, 1975, Ch. 3.
108 L. C. Becker, *Property Rights: Philosophical Foundations*, London: Routledge & Kegan Paul, 1977; L. C. Becker, 'The Moral Basis of Property Rights', in J. R. Pennock and J. W. Chapman (eds), *Property: Nomos XXII*, New York: New York University Press, 1980: 187ff.
109 Steven N. S. Cheung, *Will China Go 'Capitalist'?* (2nd edn), London: Institute of Economic Affairs, 1986: 33 (emphasis in original).
110 LP, art. 135.
111 LP, art. 136.
112 LP, arts 138, 141.
113 *See*, art. 54 of the LAL and art. 23 of the LAURE.
114 Jiang, *supra note* 93, p. 197; Cui, *supra note* 53, p. 212.
115 LP, art. 140.
116 PRCT, *supra note* 25, art. 12 (*see*, text accompanying *supra note* 26); Jiang, *supra note* 93, p. 198; Cui, *supra note* 53, p. 222.
117 Jiang, *supra note* 93, p. 198; Cui, *supra note* 53, p. 213.
118 LP, art. 149(1). 'Automatic renewal' means that there is no need for the holder of the RUCL to apply for renewal. However, the LP has made no provision for the terms and conditions of renewal, including the question of whether, and, if so, how much premium is payable for renewal. It seems that the legislative intention was to leave these matters for future determination. *See*, Songyou Wang (ed.), *Zhonghua renmin gongheguo wuquanfa tiaowen lijie yu shiyong* (The PRC Law of Property: Interpretations and Applications), Beijing: Renmin Fayuan Press, 2007: 446–450.
119 *See*, art. 149(2). *See*, however, the LAURE, art. 21 (regarding applications for renewal).
120 LP, art. 143.
121 PRCT, *supra note* 25, arts 28–31.
122 LAURE, arts 52–55. On the contract of lease, *see*, the PRC *Law of Contract*, Ch. 13.
123 Wang, *supra note* 93, p. 244.
124 LP, art. 146.
125 *Ibid.*, art. 147.
126 LAURE, art. 38. For sale of uncompleted flats, *see*, art. 44.
127 *Ibid.*, art. 39.

128 LP, arts 42, 44, 121. LAURE, art. 19 (on resumption in the public interest before expiry of term). The compensation is generally considered inadequate. The practice of *chaiqian* (demolition and relocation) is such that the protection of urban property rights is weak in China. *See*, e.g. Wilhelm, *supra note* 73.

129 LAURE, art. 25; LAL, art. 37.

130 LP, art. 152. In practice the use of the land is not limited to residential use; small-scale family business operations have not been prohibited: Jiang, *supra note* 93, p. 206; Cui, *supra note* 53, p. 233.

131 Cui, *supra note* 53, p. 231.

132 Art. 184(2).

133 Art. 38(1).

134 Art. 38(1).

135 Art. 38(3).

136 Art. 62(3).

137 Art. 62(1).

138 Art. 62(4).

139 Jiang, *supra note* 93, pp. 206, 208; Cui, *supra note* 53, pp. 177, 232; Wang, *supra note* 93, p. 275.

140 Wang, *supra note* 93, p. 275; Cui, *supra note* 53, p. 177.

141 Jiang, *supra note* 93, p. 207; Cui, *supra note* 53, p. 232.

142 Jiang, *supra note* 93, p. 207; Cui, *supra note* 53, pp. 178, 232.

143 Jiang, *supra note* 93, p. 207.

144 Cui, *supra note* 53, p. 232.

145 Liu, *supra note* 1, p. 96.

146 Wang, *supra note* 93, p. 282.

147 Cui, *supra note* 53, p. 235. In practice it has been common for urban residents to purchase houses in rural areas. The doubtful legality of such practice is referred to by the term *xiao chanquan fang* ('house with mini-property right'). *See*, e.g. '*Wuquanfa de maodun yu chongtu*' (The Law of Property: Contradictions and Conflicts) [notes of a symposium] *Hongfan pinglun* (Journal of Legal and Economic Studies), 10, 2008, 1; Sun, *supra note* 16, pp. 139–140.

148 Wang, *supra note* 93, p. 282.

149 Art. 153 of the LP simply provides that the acquisition, exercise and transfer of RUHS shall be subject to relevant laws (such as the LAL) and provisions. It has been pointed that that this leaves open the possibility of future liberalization regarding the transfer or sale of RUHS. *See*, e.g. Wang, *supra note* 93, p. 282.

150 Wang, *supra note* 93, p. 282.

151 *See, generally*, Wang, *supra note* 93, pp. 276–277, 282; Jiang, *supra note* 93, pp. 207–208; Cui, *supra note* 53, pp. 235–236; Liu, *supra note* 1, p. 95. As regards mortgage, it may be noted that art. 184 of the LP expressly prohibits the mortgage of land for house sites unless otherwise provided for by law.

152 LP, art. 124(1); Constitution, art. 8(1).

153 LP, art. 124.

154 Art. 125.

155 Art. 126(1). Previously this was provided for in the LRLC, art. 20.

156 Art. 126(2). This provision provides an important assurance regarding the long-term nature or indefinite duration of the *chengbao* arrangement. Thus CORL may in practice be the functional equivalent of a property right without time limit

(*wuqi wuquan*): Cui, *supra note* 53, p. 195. *See*, however *infra note* 170 and the accompanying text.

157 Art. 130.

158 Art. 131.

159 Art. 132.

160 LRLC, art. 3.

161 LRLC, art. 5; *see also*, the speech of Liu, *supra note* 30, p. 206.

162 Jiang, *supra note* 93, p. 203; Cui, *supra note* 53, p. 198.

163 LRLC, art. 15.

164 Cui, *supra note* 53, p. 195.

165 LRLC, art. 44.

166 LRLC, art. 45.

167 Art. 47.

168 Art. 48.

169 Originally some contracts for wasteland *chengbao* were for periods as long as 100 years. After 1996 the State Council's policy was that the maximum period for wasteland *chengbao* was 50 years. *See*, Cui, *supra note* 53, p. 195.

170 This means that it is not mandatory for the grantor to renew the *chengbao* contract when it expires: Cui, *supra note* 53, p. 208; Jiang, *supra note* 93, p. 205.

171 Art. 26(3).

172 Art. 133.

173 Art. 128. It should also be noted that art. 184(2) of the LP provides that the right to use farmland and other collectively owned land may not be mortgaged unless there is a contrary provision in other laws.

174 LRLC, arts 37, 41. Members of the same village enjoy priority in obtaining the assignment: art. 33(5).

175 LRLC, art. 37. Again, members of the same village enjoy priority in becoming parties to these transactions: art. 33(5).

176 LP, art. 184; Wang, *supra note* 93, pp. 236, 239–240. Unlike the case of wasteland *chengbao*, the law does not permit CORL to be used as capital contribution. However, localities such as Chongqing have experimented with permitting peasants to use their CORL as capital contribution to a business: *see*, Sun, *supra note* 16, p. 137.

177 Wang, *supra note* 30, pp. 78–79. The benefits due to the deceased under the *chengbao* arrangement may be inherited by his or her successors: LRLC, art. 31(1).

178 Wang, *supra note* 30, p. 78. Thus successors under the law of inheritance who are not members of the original household living in the same village are not entitled to continue the original *chengbao* contract.

179 LRCL, art. 31; Wang, *supra note* 30, p. 79.

180 LRLC, art. 50.

181 *See*, e.g. '*Wuquanfa de maodun yu chongtu*' (The Law of Property: Contradictions and Conflicts), *supra note* 147, p. 3; Sun, *supra note* 16, p. 137.

182 Wang, *supra note* 93, p. 236.

183 *Ibid.*, p. 239.

184 *See, generally*, Wang's speech to the NPC on 8 March 2007 on the bill for the LP, *Zhonghuarenmingongheguo quanguorenmindaibiaodahui changwuweiyuanhui gongbao* (Gazette of the National People's Congress Standing Committee), 2007, no. 3, pp. 309–314.

185 Sun, *supra note* 16, pp. 130–131.
186 *See*, the text accompanying *supra note* 68.
187 *See*, e.g. Wang, *supra note* 93, pp. 150–151; J. C. Oi and A. G. Walder (eds), *Property Rights and Economic Reform in China*, Stanford: Stanford University Press, 1999.
188 Wang, *supra note* 97, p. 292; Yifan Yang and Hanfeng Chen (eds), *Zhong huaren mingongheguo fazhishi* (Legal History of the People's Republic of China), Harbin: Heilongjiang Renmin Press, 1997: 221–224.
189 Wang, *supra note* 97, p. 293; Cui, *supra note* 53, pp. 11, 109; Sun, *Lun wuquan fa* (The Law of Property), Beijing: Law Press, 2008: 363.
190 Wang, *supra note* 97, p. 293.
191 Peter Ho, 'Who Owns China's Land? Policies, Property Rights and Deliberate Institutional Ambiguity', *China Quarterly* 166, 2001: 394, 404–405.
192 Cui, *supra note* 53, p. 109; Wang, *supra note* 97, p. 293; Ho, *supra note* 191, pp. 405–406.
193 *See*, the *Organic Law of Local People's Congresses and Local People's Governments.*
194 *See*, the *Organic Law of Villagers' Committees.*
195 *See*, the *Organic Law of Villagers' Committees*, art. 10. According to figures in the early 1990s, there were 55,800 governments of townships and towns in the rural areas, 743,300 villagers' committees and 5 million villagers' groups: *see*, Wang, *supra note* 97, p. 294.
196 Wang, *supra note* 97, p. 290.
197 GPCL, art. 74.
198 LAL, art. 10.
199 Cui, *supra note* 53, p. 109.
200 Wang, *supra note* 97, p. 295.
201 *Ibid.*, pp. 294, 296.
202 LAL, art. 44.
203 LAL, art. 60.
204 LAL, art. 63.
205 Wang, *supra note* 97, p. 296; Wang, *supra note* 93, p. 145; Cui, *supra note* 53, p. 109. The expropriation of peasants' collectively owned land has been a major source of social unrest in contemporary China. *See*, e.g. E. Pils, 'Land Disputes, Rights Assertion, and Social Unrest in China: A Case from Sichuan', *Columbia Journal of Asian Law,* 19, 2005–2006, 235. It may be noted that in recent years, some provinces and localities (e.g. Guangdong) have experimented with the practice of allowing collectively owned land (i.e. the right to use it) to be directly sold in the market: *see*, Wang, *supra note* 93, p. 282; '*Wuquanfa de maodun yu chongtu*' (The Law of Property: Contradictions and Conflicts) *supra note* 147, pp. 5–6.
206 Wang, *supra note* 97, pp. 283–288.
207 In practice, those in charge of townships, villages or villagers' groups which hold collectively owned land have the power to engage in dealings in the land: Liu, *supra note* 1, pp. 123–124.
208 Wang, *supra note* 97, p. 291; Sun, *supra note* 189, p. 120.
209 LP, art. 59 (emphasis supplied). *See*, the discussion in Wang, *supra note* 93, pp. 146–147.
210 For further analysis, *see*, Cui Jianyuan, *Wuquanfa* (Law of Property), Beijing: Zhongguo Renmin Daxue Press, 2009: 185–188.

211 LP, art. 60. *See*, the discussion in Wang, *supra note* 93, pp. 147–148; Cui, *supra note* 53, p. 113.
212 LP, art. 59. *See also*, the *Organic Law of Villagers' Committees,* arts 5, 19; Wang, *supra note* 93, pp. 148–149.
213 LP, art. 63. *See also*, Wang, *supra note* 93, pp. 149–150.
214 LP, art. 62. *See also*, the *Organic Law of Villagers' Committees*, art. 22; Cui, *supra note* 53, p. 114.
215 Wang, *supra note* 97, p. 296.
216 Members may share in the income derived from the *chengbao* operation of wasteland managed by the collective. *See*, Jiang, *supra note* 93, p. 204; LRLC, art. 46.
217 *Ibid.*, pp. 291–292; Cui, *supra note* 53, p. 112.
218 Wang, *supra note* 97, p. 292.
219 Wang, *supra note* 97, p. 288. However, in the 2008 edition of his book, Wang no longer suggests that collective ownership may be understood as a special form of common ownership, *see*, Wang, *supra note* 93, p. 147.
220 Wang, *supra note* 97, p. 288; Cui, *supra note* 53, p. 112.
221 Cheung, *supra note* 109.
222 Quoted from the preamble to the PRC Constitution.

5 The role of mortgages

A case for formal law

Guanghua Yu

5.1. Introduction

Contract law facilitates exchange in the sense that it makes the gain from trade more predictable. Efficient exchange, however, requires the existence of clear property rights. North claims that 'the inability of societies to develop effective, low-cost enforcement of contracts is the most important source of both historical stagnation and contemporary underdevelopment in the Third World'.[1] Some evidence in China and elsewhere is consistent with North's claim.[2] Enforcement of contracts, however, can be carried out by informal or formal means.[3] The economic theory of self-enforcing contracts suggests that a contract is self-enforcing if the expected future gains from adhering to the contract exceed the current gain from a violation of the contract.[4] It is obvious that self-enforcing agreements are not feasible if the sequence of occasions for transactions has a definite known last period.[5] In addition, highly uncertain conditions are not conducive to self-enforcing agreements.[6] In the modern world, however, unexpected things occur very frequently. The Asian financial crisis, the recent US financial crisis and significant change of cost conditions resulting from commodity price fluctuation are some of the unexpected events which are likely to affect the payoff of contractual parties. To support exchanges, contractual parties may take hostage from the other contractual party.[7] If hostage is used, non-performance by a contractual party will result in the loss of or harm to the hostage.

This chapter argues that hostage used in informal contracts normally only deal with two contractual parties. Built upon and enforced by the formal law, the device of mortgages is able to cope with multiparty conflict of interest. Contrary to the prevailing view that formal legal institutions do not play any important role in China's economic development,[8] this chapter makes a case that the formal legal institutions do make a difference in China's economic development. Part 2 of this chapter explains that a formal legal system is essential to deal with problems arising from mortgages. Part 3 uses empirical evidence on the increasing use of mortgages in China to show the role of mortgages in facilitating bank lending. Conclusions follow in Part 4.

5.2. The device of mortgages and formal law

When the present value of the expected future benefits from maintaining an agreement exceeds that of the expected benefits from a violation of the agreement, the agreement becomes 'self-enforcing'. According to Telser, the only recourse of the non-breaching party in a self-enforcing agreement is to terminate the agreement.[9] Williamson shows that 'the use of hostages to support exchange is widespread and economically important'.[10] Using hostages to support bilateral foreign relations in China can be traced back to 720 BC.[11] Viewed from the perspective of using hostage, the expected future stream of benefits from maintaining a self-enforcing agreement can be viewed as hostage. Violation of such an agreement will result in the loss of the hostage. That is the termination of the agreement and the resulting loss of the expected future stream of benefits.[12]

Klein and Leffler deal with the issue of quality guarantee in sales transactions.[13] A major finding of their paper is that 'market prices above the competitive price and the presence of non-salvageable capital are means of enforcing quality promises'.[14] If the seller cheats by lowering the quality standard in a transaction, the spread of complaints of consumers will result in reduced sales or loss of sales. When reduced sales or loss of sales occur, the seller will either lose the market price above the competitive price or suffer loss on the non-salvageable asset investment. Viewed from that perspective, market price of the seller above the competitive price and the loss of benefits from using the non-salvageable asset because of the reallocation of the asset for the next best alternative can be regarded as hostage. Advertising[15] and developing products with brand names[16] normally indicate that a company is investing in non-salvageable assets and the presence of a current and future price premium.

Klein argues that a franchisor acting as a franchisee's landlord can discipline an opportunistic franchisee by imposing a sunk-cost penalty on him. Franchisors can better

> assure quality by requiring franchisee investments in specific ... assets that upon termination imply a capital loss penalty larger than can be obtained by the franchisee if he cheats. For example, the franchisor may require franchisees to rent from them short term (rather than own) the land upon which their outlet is located. This lease arrangement creates a situation where termination can require the franchisee to move and thereby impose a capital loss on him up to the amount of his initial non-salvageable investment. Hence a form of collateral to deter franchisee cheating is created.[17]

In business franchising, the hostage may be the capital cost of the vulnerable sunk investment.[18] Alternatively, the hostage may be the value of future above-normal profit earnings for the franchisee.[19] Termination of the franchising contract will result in both types of loss. Empirical evidence on franchising relations in the United Kingdom, however, does not strongly support the view that termination of the franchising contract will necessarily result in the loss of location-specific investment.[20] Lease termination is subject to very careful private regulation including the inclusion of arbitration clause, renewal or buy back of franchisee's assets.[21] The purpose of lease control by the franchisor is rather due to the high cost in finding a suitable new site.[22]

The term 'mortgage' refers to a transaction whereby a debtor or a third party ('mortgagor') uses certain property ('mortgaged property') as security for an obligation without the transfer of the possession of such property. If the debtor fails to fulfil his or her obligation, the creditor ('mortgagee') has priority over the mortgaged property.[23] Viewed from the perspective of hostage, mortgaged property can be considered as hostage. This is so because the failure of performing the obligation by the debtor will lead to the disposition of the mortgaged property. When the mortgaged property chosen to secure debt consists of assets whose value in the borrower's business exceeds their market value, the harm to a borrower who defaults under a mortgage contract is the loss of the idiosyncratic value. Since the particular mortgaged property may be used to secure several debts, default on any of the debts will result in the loss of the hostage. Put another way, the probability of losing the hostage in mortgage contracts is greater than in other simple bilateral contracts.

The foregoing discussion on the hostage used in self-enforcing contracts and in mortgage contracts raises a very important question on the institutional difference between simple self-enforcing contracts and mortgage contracts. After all, a simple bilateral mortgage contract is also self-enforcing. When a piece of mortgaged property is used to secure separate debts, the mortgagor faces several secured creditors, mortgagees. The device of mortgages can be used to deal with multiple creditors. The rest of this section will explain why the device of mortgages is different from simple bilateral self-enforcing contracts.

Williamson has remarked:

> The study of contract in both law and economics has mainly emphasized legal rules and technicalities. Such an orientation is supported by the implicit assumption that the courts 'work well'. Whether they work well or poorly, however, requires a comparative institutional assessment.[24]

I take Williamson's suggestion to carry out a comparative institutional assessment to examine the mortgage regime.

In Telser's simple bilateral contract model discussed previously, each contractual party calculates whether it is better off continuing or terminating the relation with the other party. The party terminates the contractual relation if and only if the current gain from termination exceeds the present value of the expected gains from continuing. Such a self-enforcing model becomes problematic, however, when it is extended to multilateral agreements. In the context of international trade, Beth Yarbrough and Robert Yarbrough have observed that 'delicate balancing of costs and benefits may be difficult to accomplish with large numbers of participants'.[25] Different rounds of negotiating multilateral trade agreements show how long and difficult it is to reach multilateral trade agreements. In the case of a mortgage contract, a debtor may face numerous creditors. Furthermore, when a mortgage contract is enforced upon default, the relations between the borrower and secured creditors normally come to an end as far as the particular mortgaged property is concerned.

Klein and Leffler's model deals with promises on quality which cannot be verified by a court. If consumers expect the product to be of high quality but the seller offers a low-quality product to the unsuspecting buyers, the seller can reap a short-run profit. 'Cheating will be prevented and high-quality products will be supplied only if firms are earning a continued stream of rental income that will be lost if low-quality output is deceptively produced'.[26] In their model, a single breach on quality can exact a heavy cost through the costless communication of the breach on the market. As discussed, market prices above the competitive price and the presence of non-salvageable capital are means of enforcing quality promises. Their model, however, does not deal with multiple bilateral transactions when one party faces numerous creditors. In the latter case, contractual devices have to deal with not only relations between the debtor and other creditors but also relations between creditors. In some other cases, legal devices also need to regulate the relations between secured creditors and good-faith purchasers for value.

While Klein and Leffler focused on market forces in contract enforcement, Avner Grief's study of the relations between the Maghribi merchants and their overseas agents in the Mediterranean during the late medieval Commercial Revolution shows how a non-market reputation-based institution worked.[27] In his study, information sharing and multilateral punishment enabled credible commitment of agents to merchants ex ante and effective fulfilment of contractual obligations ex post facto.[28] Similar to Klein and Leffler, Grief does not deal with problems arising from multiple bilateral contractual relations.

In the case of mortgage, a mortgagor may use the same collateral to borrow money from different creditors. When the mortgagor defaults and the value of the collateral is unable to satisfy the claims of all the mortgagees, each mortgagee has the incentive to seize the collateral and thus realize the creditor's right ahead of other creditors. This collective action problem faced by secured creditors requires a third-party enforcement regime. To solve the priority issue, most countries have developed a formal regime. The normal rule is that the order of priority of the several mortgagees must be ascertained, and the first in priority paid in full before anything is given to those who rank below in priority.[29] So far, we have not seen an informal regime which is able to solve the priority competition issue between mortgagees efficiently.

The administration of the formal regime of mortgage law requires a functional court system. In addition, a separate registration system must be established so that mortgaged property can be registered. Such a registration system serves an important purpose of recording the sequence of all mortgaged property of a particular mortgagor. With this registration system, potential mortgagees, trade or financial creditors, can easily search whether a particular debtor has used the same asset to secure debts before. Without a registration system, creditors will have great difficulty finding out whether the debtor has used the same asset to secure debts. When creditors face great uncertainty, they will either reduce credit or lend at a higher interest rate. In either case, the cost of capital formation will be higher.

If a country cannot establish a registration system and a formal legal system, the device of secured debt has to be foregone. Economists claim the importance of the device of secured debt. First, secured debt may solve the debt erosion problem. As a secured lender can usually perfect its security interest easily when there is a registration system, it enjoys priority over subsequent lenders. As a result, the debtor cannot issue subsequent debt of equal or higher priority. Therefore, unless the secured creditor is under-secured, the opportunity to redistribute wealth by the debtor through subsequent debt financing is effectively neutralized.[30] In addition, security interests make the substitution of high-risk for low-risk assets after obtaining the loan more difficult.[31] After obtaining the loan, the borrower may have the incentive to substitute projects with more variable cash flow for projects with less variable cash flow. As creditors are not able to share with the debtor the upside benefits from the borrower's asset substitution but must bear the downside risk, asset substitution transfers wealth from creditors to the debtor. If the debt is secured, however, those secured assets cannot be easily disposed of without permission of the secured creditor. Furthermore, secured debt can ameliorate the underinvestment problem.[32] Some profitable projects will not be undertaken by a borrower which can use only equity or unsecured debt to finance them but will be undertaken if they can be financed with secured debt. Besides, secured interests over specific assets impair their marketability. This is so because the transfer of secured assets not made in the ordinary course of the debtor's business passes title to the purchaser subject to the perfected security interest.[33] Therefore, secured debt makes it difficult for the debtor to transfer wealth from secured creditors to itself. As secured debt serves important purposes of alleviating the above-examined moral hazard problems, the inability of establishing a secured debt regime including mortgages results in a dead-weight social loss.

Williamson argues for the importance of using hostages to support exchange in informal contractual settings. He also cites Klein and Leffler's point that requiring franchisees to rent the outlet from the franchisor can reduce opportunistic behaviours on the part of the franchisee.[34] When the franchisee cheats on quality of the goods or price, the franchisor can require the franchisee to move and 'thereby impose a capital loss on him up to the amount of his initial non-salvageable investment on the outlet'.[35] As discussed previously, Dnes's empirical study in the United Kingdom does not support Williamson's view.[36]

Moreover, while hostages can be used to support exchange, they may also be abused. The person possessing the hostage may have the incentive to expropriate the hostage by creating conditions of contractual termination. In addition, the secured creditor may not have the incentive to make reasonable efforts in obtaining the best possible price on the market when disposing of the collateral, causing harm to the mortgagor and other mortgagees. When a formal legal regime is used to enforce law and contracts, using hostages to support exchange becomes unnecessary.

With respect to the potential of expropriating the hostage, both private contracts and formal law regulates such misbehaviour. Contractual parties in the context of franchising in the United Kingdom insert arbitration, renewal and asset-valuation clauses in their contracts to curb the potential abuse of the hostage.[37] Formal law in the United States also deals with such potential abuse of the hostage.[38]

Formal law also carefully regulates the misbehaviour of mortgagees caused by the lack of incentives in disposing of the mortgaged property. In the United Kingdom, a mortgagee is under a duty to take reasonable care to obtain the true market value of the mortgaged property.[39] A building society has a duty 'to take reasonable care to ensure that the price for which the property is sold is the best price that can be reasonably obtained'.[40] Obviously, the law tries to solve the problem that the mortgagee may not have the incentive to sell the mortgaged property at a reasonable price, causing loss to the mortgagor or other mortgagees. In Australia:

> a receiver owes duties to the mortgagor, primarily to exercise powers in good faith not sacrificing the mortgagor's interest recklessly, to act strictly within the conditions of appointment, to account to the mortgagor for surplus after the discharge of securities and, if property is to be sold, a duty to obtain the best possible price.[41]

In China, the Law on Real Property also requires that the sale of mortgaged property must be done with reference to the market price.[42]

This part explains that the device of mortgages requires the support of a formal legal regime. Under a formal legal system, the use of hostages to support exchange becomes unnecessary. In addition, a formal legal system solves the problem of abusing the hostage relatively well. As the device of mortgages can solve many types of moral hazard problems after the debtor obtains the loan and secures well the principal and interest, secured debt of mortgages is widely used in many developed countries. The increasing use of mortgages in China also provides empirical evidence that mortgages facilitate bank lending. The precondition of developing a formal legal regime of mortgages is, however, the improvement in defining and enforcing property rights. The next Part will examine the evolution of property rights in China. That Part will then explain the relation between the increasing use of mortgages and the expansion of bank lending. Other things being equal, the greater the amount of bank lending, the higher the growth rate of the economy. The case of the developing legal regime of mortgages raises doubt on the claim that formal law does not play any meaningful role in China's economic development.

5.3. Mortgages law and bank lending

In the last ten years or so, as economic reform reaches a more mature stage in China, secured lending through mortgages, a more formal form of financial contract has become more widespread. In a recent study, Haselmann and colleagues conducted an empirical study to examine the relationship between reform of bankruptcy law and collateral law and behavioural changes by banks in their lending activities.[43] One of the findings of their study is that 'collateral law designed to protect individual creditors' claims is of greater importance for expanding bank lending than is bankruptcy law, which is aimed at establishing a collective enforcement regime.[44] One implication of this study is that if secured lending contracts are legally enforceable, the adoption of them will increase bank credits as well as the quality of these credits. Before examining the growing use of mortgages in China, I will briefly discuss the developing legal framework on mortgages.

5.3.1. The legal framework

5.3.1.1. The law of mortgages on immovable property

As urban land is closely related to the real estate market and China's high rate of economic growth, tracing the evolution of the ownership and transfer of real property will provide an institutional explanation of the role of property law. Despite the fact that the Constitution of neither 1954 nor 1978 states as clearly as the 1982 Constitution that urban land is owned by the state,[45] land use had been allocated by the government without any fee payment by users from 1954 to 1979.[46] As the scarcity of land was not well reflected by such an administrative allocation system, there was a great deal of waste.[47] The economic reform program initiated in 1978 started to pay attention to the issue of efficient land use. The *Equity Joint Venture Law between Chinese Partners and Foreign Investors* enacted in 1979 makes it possible for the Chinese partner to use land-use right as equity contribution.[48] If land-use right was not treated as equity contribution by the Chinese partner, the equity joint venture should pay fees for obtaining the land-use right to the Chinese government.[49] This was the starting point of changing the free urban land-use system. In 1982, Shenzhen began to charge land-use fees from users.[50] Since then, the practice of charging land-use fees has spread to the whole nation. Except for a few types of institutions, all profit-oriented enterprises have to pay land-use fee.[51] While the initial purpose of charging land-use fee was to solve the shortage of capital for urban development, the greater significance of the adoption of land-use right system is the reshaping of the administrative allocation of land-use system.

The initial success of charging land-use fee prompted more changes related to land-use transfer. Although the land-use fee system was adopted, the 1982 Constitution still prohibited appropriation, buying and selling or leasing of land or the transfer of land by other unlawful means.[52] Article 80(3) of the *General Principle of the Civil Law* (GPCL) stipulates, among other things, that land cannot be purchased and sold, leased or mortgaged.[53] In July 1987, however, the Office of the Special Economic Zones under the State Council proposed to the State Council that Shanghai, Tianjing, Guangzhou and Shenzhen should be used as trial cities to experiment with the land-use right system.[54] Under this system, applicants may acquire the right of using a specific piece of land for up to 50 years through bidding or auction, or by entering into an agreement with the relevant government upon the payment of a fee. Thereafter, the user may transfer the land-use right to another person for the remaining period.[55] In 1988, the 1982 Constitution was formally amended to permit the lawful transfer of land-use right.[56] Thereafter, the *Law on the Administration of Land*[57] was amended in 1988. One of the amendments was to establish the pay for land-use right system and to incorporate the constitutional amendment that land-use right can be lawfully transferred.[58] The State Council promulgated in 1990 the Provisional Regulation Concerning the Assignment and Transfer of Land-use Right of State-owned Land in Urban Areas.[59] Since then the system of pay for using land and the assignment and transfer of land-use right has been well established. The *Law on the Administration of Urban Real Estate*[60] enacted in 1994 and amended in 2007,[61] and the *Law on Real Rights*[62] enacted in 2007 follow that system.

In addition to the establishment of the system of paying for using land and of the assignment and transfer of land-use right, the housing reform policy in urban areas has also contributed to the better definition and enforcement of property rights of urban real estate.

Before 1988, employees in urban areas all lived in houses or apartments allocated by their enterprises or institutions. They did not have ownership of the houses or apartments and only paid a symbolic rent. The success of market-oriented reform in the areas of trade, investment and employment led to the housing reform. The housing reform was initiated in 1988 when the State Council circulated the Notice Concerning the Implementation Plan of Promoting Housing Reform in Urban Areas.[63] While the immediate objective of the housing reform was to raise the rent, the long-term objective was to realize the goal of allocating houses or apartments through the market.[64] In 1994, the State Council issued the Decision on Deepening the Reform of Urban Housing System.[65] The gist of the Decision was to incorporate the housing benefits into the salary of employees so that the high-income families could buy commercial houses (*shangpinfang*) while the middle- and low-income families could purchase subsidized suitable economy houses (*jingji shiyongfang*) or lease low-rent apartments (*lianzufang*).[66] In addition, the Decision also instructed local governments to gradually establish the system of house accumulation fund (*zhufang gongjijin*)[67] to facilitate policy and commercial bank lending, and to regulate the real estate market.[68] The Decision also urged local governments to sell the then existing houses or apartments to employees.[69] Those who purchased the houses at market prices could later sell their houses right away while those who purchased their houses at cost would be able to sell their houses in five years time.[70] This Decision sent out a very clear signal to the urban residents that buying and selling houses on the market was the future direction. In 1998, the State Council issued the Notice Concerning the Further Deepening of Housing Reform and the Acceleration of Housing Construction in Urban Areas.[71] This Notice urged local governments to terminate the internal allocation of housing property to employees.[72] To address the problem that the least advantaged people in urban areas cannot afford to buy either commercial houses or subsidized suitable economy houses, the Notice required local governments or enterprises to provide low-rent houses to this group of residents.[73] Among other things, the Notice also instructed commercial banks to expand the scope of home-purchasing loans and the local governments to improve the system of registration of mortgage loans.

The housing reform has also led to the development of the real estate registration system. The early registration of land-use right and houses or apartments occurred at the local level. The Administrative Provisions on Commodity Housing in the Shenzhen Special Economic Zone was the earliest local law on the registration of housing ownership.[74] This local law contains detailed provisions regarding the registration of the ownership of houses, transfer of title and mortgage of housing property.[75] The Regulation on the Administration of Land in the Shenzhen Special Economic Zone dealt with the registration of land-use right and mortgages of land-use right.[76] Shanghai, Guangzhou and Beijing had similar local laws in the 1980s.[77] In 1994, the *Law on the Administration of Urban Real Estate* was enacted at the national level.[78] This Law requires the holders of land-use right or owners of housing property to register their property rights.[79] The assignment of land-use right, housing property and the mortgage of these property rights shall also be registered with the relevant authorities.[80] Currently, the registration offices in big cities provide relatively good access for the public to search the title of land-use rights, the title of housing property and the mortgage of land-use rights and housing properties.[81] It goes without saying that the real estate registration system has significantly improved the definition of property rights. Furthermore, the registration system of real estate has also facilitated the provision of mortgage loans.

5.3.1.2. *The law of mortgages on movable property*

An important aspect of the financial reform in China is the reformation of the banking sector. In 1978, there were only two banks in China:[82] the People's

Bank of China, engaged in domestic banking, and the Bank of China, which dealt with foreign currency business.[83] Beginning in 1979, China reconstructed the previously dissolved Agricultural Bank of China and the Peoples' Construction Bank of China.[84] On 1 January 1980, the Industrial and Commercial Bank of China was established.[85] In 1983, the State Council decided to have the People's Bank of China solely exercise the functions of a central bank.[86] In 1984, the Industrial and Commercial Bank of China took over the commercial business from the People's Bank of China. Since then, the People's Bank of China has gradually become the central bank of China.[87] As a result of the banking reform, four specialized banks have emerged: the Agricultural Bank of China, the Bank of China, the Industrial and Commercial Bank of China and the People's Construction Bank of China. Since the enactment of the Law on Commercial Banks in 1995, these specialized banks have become commercial banks.

By the end of 1993, these banks accounted for 80 per cent of the total assets of the banking sector in China.[88] Encouraged to act more like commercial enterprises, these banks are, at least in theory, responsible for raising their own funds and paying interest to depositors.[89] Enterprises are no longer given an automatic right to credit and banks are to allocate funds on the basis of enterprise profitability.[90] To make loans more efficient, banks have started to adopt security devices including mortgages.[91] Before turning to the statistics on the use of mortgage of movables in the next part, I will briefly examine the law of mortgages on movables.

The GPCL[92] contains only one provision on mortgages. This article only provides the definition of mortgages and declares that people may adopt the device of mortgage to secure obligations. As it was difficult to apply this provision to resolve disputes on mortgages, the Supreme People's Court added five provisions when it issued the Opinion Concerning Several Issues related to the Implementation of the General Principles of the Civil Law (GPCL Opinion).[93] Article 115(1) of the GPCL Opinion provides that transfer of mortgaged property without the consent of the mortgagee is invalid. Article 115(2) specifies that priority competition among mortgagees is based on the sequence of the creation of mortgages. The GPCL Opinion, however, does not require the registration of mortgages. Obviously, such a system makes it hard for creditors to decide on whether to take mortgages, as they are not able to search the registration from a third party about the borrower's past record of providing collateral to other creditors.

When the utilization of mortgages increased and when participants and law-makers gained experience, improvement of the law took place. In 1995, the *Security Law* was enacted.[94] Compared with the earlier law, this *Security Law* is far more detailed. In accordance with this law, borrowers can use machinery, means of transportation and other property to secure obligations.[95] For the first time, this *Security Law* dictates that the mortgage of means of transportation, machinery and other movable property of enterprises shall be registered.[96] Also according to this law, the mortgaged contract becomes effective upon registration. In 2000, the Supreme People's Court issued the Interpretation on Several Issues Concerning the Application of the Security Law[97] to clarify some unclear matters in the *Security Law*.

When the use of mortgages further increased and more disputes were dealt with by the courts, the *Law on Real Rights*[98] passed in 2007 further improved the law of mortgages. Pursuant to the *Law on Real Rights*, the mortgage of real property requires registration.[99] The rights and duties between the mortgagor and mortgagee with respect to the mortgage of real property are effective only upon registration.[100] With respect to movables, registration is optional. Non-registration of mortgage of movables, however, will not allow the mortgagee to defeat an innocent third party.[101] The *Law on Real Rights* also adopted the floating mortgage concept whereby the present and future machinery, raw materials, semi-finished products or products of sole-proprietor, enterprises or agricultural production operators can be mortgaged.[102] It goes without saying that the *Law on Real Rights* has considerably enlarged the scope of mortgage of movable property.

The rule on priority competition is relatively clear and easy to administer in practice. In accordance with the *Law on Real Rights*, if the mortgage rights have been registered, the priority among mortgagees is determined by the sequence of registration.[103] If registration of several mortgages occurs on the same date, the claims of mortgagees shall be realized proportionally.[104] Between registered mortgagees and non-registered mortgagees, registered mortgagees prevail over non-registered mortgagees.[105] For non-registered mortgagees, the inadequate assets or proceeds of the debtor will be shared proportionally.[106]

The foregoing short description of the law of mortgage of movable property shows that the Chinese law of mortgage of movables adapted to changing circumstances. It evolved from a very vague provision to a relatively functional regime of mortgage law. The Chinese experience provides a good lesson that it may not be appropriate for developing countries to transplant very sophisticated Western law at the beginning of economic development or economic transition from a planned economy to a market-oriented economy. What is important is for law-makers, participants and enforcement agencies to adapt and solve problems during the development process. When the value of asset increases, people tend to devote more resources to defining and enforcing property rights in mortgages. The next section on statistical evidence will shed further light on this issue.

5.3.2. The evidence and explanations

5.3.2.1. Evidence on mortgage of immovable property

Table 5.1 shows a relatively close correlation between the GDP growth rate and the growth rate of fixed asset investment. Higher growth rate of fixed asset investment are more likely to result in higher growth rate of GDP in the

Table 5.1 GDP, fixed asset investment and investment in urban houses (unit: 100 million yuan)

Year	*Gross domestic product (GDP)*	*GDP growth rate % (calculated at constant prices)*	*Total investment in fixed assets*	*Growth rate of total investment in fixed assets %*	*Investment in urban housing*	*Investment in urban housing in total fixed asset investment %*
1986	10,275.2	8.8	3,120.6	22.7	219	7.0
1987	12,058.6	11.6	3,791.7	21.5	240	6.3
1988	15,04 2.8	11.3	4,735.8	25.4	–	–
1989	16,992.3	4.1	4,410.4	-7.2	359	8.1
1990	18,667.8	3.8	4,517.0	2.4	321	7.1
1991	21,781.5	9.2	5,594.5	23.9	406	7.25
1992	26,923.5	14.2	8,080.1	44.4	411	5.1
1993	35,333.9	14	13,072.3	61.8	637	4.9
1994	48,197.9	13.1	17,042.1	30.4	1,446	8.5
1995	60,793.7	10.9	20,019.3	17.5	1,303	6.5
1996	71,176.6	10	22,974.0	14.8	1,407	6.1
1997	78,973.0	9.3	24,941.1	8.8	3,509	14.1
1998	84,402.3	7.8	28,406.2	13.9	3,799	13.4
1999	89,677.1	7.6	29,854.7	5.1	3,718	12.5
2000	99,214.6	8.4	32,917.7	10.3	3,608	11.0
2001	109,655.2	8.3	37,213.5	13.0	5,616	15
2002	120,332.7	9.1	43,499.9	16.9	5,319	12.2
2003	135,822.8	10	55,566.6	27.7	5,078	9.1
2004	159,878.3	10.1	70,477.4	26.6	8,919	12.6
2005	183,084.8	10.2	88,773.6	26.0	10,727	12.1

Sources: Except for the last two columns, the data in this table has been taken from the *China Urban Construction Statistical Yearbook*, China Architecture & Building Press, 2005, p. 171. The data on investment in urban housing property come from various years in the *China City Statistical Yearbook*, Beijing: China Statistical Press.

same year. This is true for all years except 1998. On the other hand, lower growth rate of fixed asset investment are more likely to result in lower growth rate of GDP in the same year. The best examples are 1989, 1990 and 1999.

This table has also confirmed the importance of investment in urban housing property in China's economic development. When fixed asset investment plays a very important role in China's economic development, the increasing proportion of investment in urban housing property in total fixed asset investment explains the growing importance of investment in urban housing property. The last column of Table 5.1 reveals that the proportion of investment in urban housing property in total fixed asset investment has been doubled since 1997 compared with that in the period from 1986 to 1996. Viewed from the property rights perspective, it is more difficult to have such a considerably increasing amount of investment in urban housing property without clear definition and enforcement of property rights in the property law system. The easy search of titles of land-use rights and housing property and of the burden of mortgage in such real property in large cities in China has significantly facilitated transactions in real estate assets.

The move towards market orientation in allocating land-use rights on the primary market provides good evidence of the improving definition and transfer of land-use rights. While administrative allocation of free land use remains, that proportion has been decreasing. The allocation of land-use rights with fee payment has become more and more relied upon. There are three main methods of allocating land-use rights in the latter case.[107] They include agreement between the relevant governmental authority and the land user, auction whereby the governmental authority publicly sells the land-use rights to the person who is willing to pay the highest price, and bidding where the government authority invites potential users to submit bids and the person who is willing to pay the highest price is normally chosen. In 1993, 152,676 hectares of land were allocated nationwide.[108] Among this allotment, around 89,750 hectares were allocated by administrative methods for free use (*huabo*), accounting for 58.78 per cent[109] while around 62,926 hectares were allocated through auction, bidding or agreement, occupying the remaining 41.22 per cent (*churang*). In 2001, allocation of land through auction, bidding or agreement accounted for 55.5 per cent of the total allocation of 164,000 hectares.[110] Since then, allocation of land-use rights through *churang* has taken a dominant position.[111]

Among the three methods of allocating land with pay, the method of agreement (*xieyi churang*) is becoming less significant. In 1987–1988, allocation of land with pay through agreement accounted for 96.7 per cent of the total area.[112] The percentage of the total land allocation in terms of size through agreement in 1992 remained very high, at 81.2 per cent.[113] Since 2002, allocation of land-use rights through auctions and/or biddings began to increase. The percentage of land allocation through auctions and/or biddings was 15 per cent in 2002, 33 per cent in 2003 and 50.9 per cent in 2007.[114] Higher prices in obtaining land-use rights for urban development reveal that users including developers have confidence in the security of their investment in real estate. Clear definition and transferability of property rights in real estate are the precondition for investment.

Cross-country comparison provides further empirical evidence that formal law on property right is critical to economic development. Writing in the context of Peru, de Soto has the view that the inability to produce capital is a stumbling block to economic development. The source of the problem lies in the legal system. He specifically provides:[115]

> It is the law that detaches and fixes the economic potential of assets as a value separate from the material assets themselves and allows humans to discover and realize that potential. It is law that connects assets into financial and investment circuits. And it is the representation of assets fixed in legal property documents that gives them the power to create surplus value.

While informal systems of contractual arrangements may partly substitute or complement formal contract law,[116] the cost of relying on an informal system of property rights to acquire and enforce land rights can be enormous. De Soto summarized the cost in the following:[117]

> The range of choices open to informals when they decide to acquire land informally is limited. It also involves a tremendous waste of resources because of the high costs of invasion or informal land sales and the uncertainties inherent in illegality. The property rights acquired are diminished by a kind of legal apartheid. And the system is unstable because it does not protect the informals when others try to invade their land. The absence of a legal system of efficient property rights is detrimental to all.

The contrast between China and Peru related to the definition and transfer of property rights in land and houses provides good lessons for other developing countries.

Formal property law not only affects the security of investment in real estate but also influences the way people finance their investment in real property. Palomar observed that 'when land titles and land tenure are secure, landholders may utilize their property rights as collateral for loans'.[118] As the Chinese economy possesses strong characteristics of a dual economy in the sense that urban cities are relatively highly developed while rural areas are underdeveloped, a brief comparison between the outcomes resulting from the formal property law on land use is helpful.

Whereas the definition, transfer and registration of property rights of land and housing property in urban areas are relatively certain as discussed in the previous Part, circumstances are different in rural areas. There were restrictions on the conversion of rural land to land for non-agricultural use from

1987 to 2006. The purpose behind the restrictions is the dominant concern over the quick depletion of arable land in a country with a huge population. Restrictions began to increase when the economy started to grow at a fast rate in the middle of 1980s. The 1986 Law on the Administration of Land still provided three methods of converting rural land to land for non-agricultural use.[119] First, when state-owned enterprises and collectively owned enterprises in urban areas establish joint enterprises (*lianying qiye*) with collectively owned enterprises in rural areas and need to use collectively owned land in rural areas, these joint enterprises may convert the rural land to state-owned land after giving compensation to farmers or the collectively owned enterprises in the rural area may use the land use rights as equity contribution after obtaining governmental approval.[120] Second, housing construction in rural areas, construction related to the establishment of village (township) enterprises, construction of village (township) public infrastructure or construction of village (township) public utilities or welfare projects can be carried out after obtaining governmental approval.[121] Third, when non-rural residents in urban areas have to use collectively owned land in rural areas for the purpose of housing construction, they may use land in rural areas after obtaining governmental approval.[122] A Circular of the State Council in 2006 prohibited the conversion of land for agricultural use to land for non-agricultural use by means of leasing instead of expropriation which has been subject to stricter control.[123]

In the 1998 *Law on the Administration of Land*, the third method for converting rural land provided under the 1986 *Law on the Administration of Land* is no longer possible.[124] Related to the abolishment of this method of converting land from agricultural use to non-agricultural use in this law, using rural land for residential purposes both for farmers and urban residents is very restrictive. The 1986 *Law on the Administration of Land* provides that those farmer applicants who have sold or let their houses shall not be eligible for additional land for building houses.[125] The 1998 *Law on the Administration of Land* further adds a provision that each household shall only have one piece of household land (*Zhaijidi*).[126] Various governmental regulations or rules have also prohibited the purchase of rural houses by urban residents.[127]

The very restrictive approach to the conversion of land from agricultural purpose to non-agricultural purposes and to the purchase of rural houses by urban residents turned many transactions into illegal or informal transactions. Despite some exceptions created by some local governments, using rural land as mortgage asset to finance various projects becomes very difficult.[128]

The situation is very different in urban areas where land title and land tenure are relatively secure. The registration and search of land-use rights or housing title and mortgages of such assets are relatively easy. The statistical data of mortgages related to land use rights and housing property in urban China provide some empirical evidence on the positive correlation between the formal law of property rights and China's economic development. Table 5.2 shows the mortgage of land use rights in urban areas.[129]

Table 5.2 Mortgage of land-use rights in urban China

Year	*Total land turnover on the secondary market (hectares)*	*Mortgage of land-use rights (hectares)*	*Transfer of land-use rights (hectares)*	*Leasing of land-use rights (hectares)*	*Percentage of mortgaged land in total land turnover*
2001	2,290,000	2,140,435	139,304	10,261	93.7%
2002	372,672	288,821	66,757	17,272	77.5%
2003	1,185,168	1,102,207	69,633	9,055	93%
2004	3,565,376	3,422,761	66,842	79,876	96%

Table 5.2 indicates that the mortgage of land-use rights plays a significant role in financing investment in the real estate sector in urban China. There is a positive correlation between the growth of real estate loans and the growth of real estate investment as reflected in Table 5.3.[130] It goes without saying that without the mortgages, the amount of loans from banks would have been considerably smaller.

In addition to the evidence on the mortgage of land-use rights in urban areas, the increasing use of home mortgage for financing the purchase of housing property through bank loans has also contributed to economic growth. From 1999 to 2004, the average annual property development and home mortgage loans grew by 49 per cent.[131] By the end of 2004, the outstanding residential mortgage loans reached 1.6 trillion yuan, 83 times the amount in 1997.[132] In 2005, the outstanding mortgage loans amounted to 1.84 trillion yuan, accounting for 10 per cent of the GDP in that year.[133]

With the high rate of economic development in China, the value of land-use rights and/or housing property has also increased rapidly. The increasing value of such real estate in turn induces people to devote more resources to define or enforce their property rights. Table 5.4 on the increasing number of legal disputes dealt with by courts in China from 1987 to 2001 provides strong empirical evidence.[134] The trend is particularly obvious from 1991.

The discussion in this section shows the close correlation between policy and legal changes related to land-use rights and housing in urban areas and China's high rate of economic development. As urban residents in the past did not have ownership rights in their housing property which used to be small and crowded, reform in this area tend to be less difficult compared with reform

Table 5.3 Correlation between real estate loans and real estate investment

	1999	*2000*	*2001*	*2002*	*2003*	*2004*
Growth of real estate loans	39%	117%	35%	42%	37%	23%
Growth of real estate investment	14%	19%	27%	24%	30%	28%

Table 5.4 Real property disputes dealt with by Chinese courts

Year	*Numbers*
1987	71,110
1988	68,664
1989	68,229
1990	55,704
1991	53,938
1992	58,782
1993	67,736
1994	82,341
1995	94,234
1996	109,822
1997	120,732
1998	140,993
1999	155,782
2000	165,799
2001	172,750

of large, state-owned enterprises, education reform or health care reform. The reform of the real estate market has obviously made most urban residents better off. The adoption of pay for using land has considerably increased the revenue of local governments. This in turn has provided great incentives for local governments to attract investment to their local areas. The relative easy transfer of land-use rights in land and housing has also facilitated investment on the part of enterprises or individuals. The developing legal regime of China's urban real estate market provides some support for Anderson and Hill's theory.[135] The dynamic ways of legal and property market development in China also indicate that the participants on China's real estate market are very adaptive. Decentralized experimentation in finding new ways of solving problems and making most parties in urban areas better off[136] in the reform process shows that adaptive efficiency[137] is vitally important in economic development and transition.

5.3.2.3. *Evidence on mortgage of movable property*

Table 5.5 provides some statistical evidence concerning the use of mortgage of movable property by enterprises in China from 1997 to 2005.

Table 5.5 also shows the increasing use of movable property as collateral for the purpose of securing loans. Although the number of contracts has declined since 1999, the value of contracts for the mortgage of movable property has been increasing except for the minor decrease in the year 2000. It is likely that the newly adopted floating mortgage device will further promote the use of movable property in bank lending.

Table 5.5 Mortgage of movables

Year	*Mortgage of movable property (contract numbers)*	*Mortgage of movable property (contract amount) (unit: 10,000 yuan)*
1997	92,817	36,685,713
1998	114,609	40,903,577
1999	117,459	48,210,788
2000	98,762	44,129,477
2001	91,239	46,672,150
2002	86,161	49,811,313
2003	86,119	58,757,389
2004	73,997	69,958,379
2005	69,580	94,098,771

Source: Various years from the *Administration Yearbook of China Administration for Industry and Commerce*, Beijing: Press of the Industry and Commerce, 2000–2006.

5.3.3. Questionnaire survey

One bank at the national level and seven bank branches or regional banks in Xian responded to my questionnaire survey.[138] When they were asked to explain the proportion of lending requiring security, seven responded that 75–100 per cent of the loans were secured; only one response suggested that 50–75 per cent of the loans were secured. When they were requested to explain whether the use of security will affect the provision of credit by banks, six responded that the use of security will very significantly increase the probability of lending; two replied that the use of security will significantly affect their lending decision. The questionnaire survey provides collaborative evidence that formal contractual arrangements of mortgage have been widely used in business transactions in China. Without the device of secured debts, many bank loans probably would not have occurred. This is especially true during China's high rate of economic growth when firms have to supply goods to new trading partners. With respect to new trading partners, it is far more uncertain whether the suppliers will enter into contracts with these new trading partners in the future. It is equally true in cases where loans are used for infrastructure projects as it is not certain that borrowers will repeatedly undertake similar projects in the future and repeat transactions are likely.

The results of the questionnaire survey suggest the finding that secured lending is already an important part of overall lending by banks today. This is not surprising given the current economic development in China regarding economic actors. It is difficult for banks to establish the appropriate credit rating for borrowers and borrowing firms. Financial reporting procedures are not well established by firms. Most firms are brand new or relatively new. There is insufficient formal information about prospects of proposed investment projects. To protect themselves, banks demand collateral, without which there would be no lending or much reduced lending. However, the collaterals are of no value if the contracts governing them cannot be enforced. Thus, the increased use of secured lending, a more formal financial contract, is to meet the demand for credit from borrowers without putting lenders at an unacceptable risk. The development of secured lending in the last 20 years in China appears to be consistent with North's notion of adaptive efficiency.[139]

5.4. Conclusion

This chapter has examined the increasing definition and enforcement of property rights in China. When the economy develops, people tend to devote more resources to clarifying the property rights of immovable property and movable property. The evidence is relatively clear that there is a positive correlation between the development of the formal legal regime and the expansion of bank lending. In this process, the developing legal regime on property rights has made an important contribution to China's economic development. Without the development of the regime of formal contract and property law, it is much more difficult that China would have had such a high rate of economic growth during the last 30 years. In this sense, this chapter differs from the view that the formal laws related to contract and property rights do not contribute to China's economic development. The evidence from China has implications for other developing or transitional economies that economic development requires a developing legal regime on contracts[140] and property rights. The development of formal law on property rights in China also shows the importance of adaptive efficiency of law making and enforcement. Shaped by the political goal of economic development, formal law on property rights began to change in China. Changes, however, normally occur in a piecemeal way by adapting to changing circumstances and learning from the past experience and lessons. The Chinese experience provides a good lesson that it may not be appropriate for developing countries to transplant very sophisticated Western law at the beginning of economic development or economic transition from planned economy to a market-oriented economy. What is important is for law makers, participants on the market and enforcement agencies to adapt and solve bottleneck problems during the development process. While Milhaupt and Pistor disagree with the static model that good law and enforcement necessarily mean good economic outcome, they do hold the view that the 'relationship between law and markets' is a 'highly iterative process of action and strategic reaction'.[141] Their dynamic approach to the relationship between law and markets from a comparative corporate governance perspective is very similar to my approach of explaining adaptive efficiency in law making and enforcement in China related to the development of the urban real estate market in this chapter and contract law development elsewhere.[142] Another implication from the Chinese experience for relatively large countries like Russia, India and Brazil is that changes on the national level usually follow successful decentralized experiments at local levels.

Notes

1 D. North, *Institutions, Institutional Change and Economic Performance*, New York: Cambridge University Press, 1990: 54.
2 Guanghua Yu and Hao Zhang, 'Adaptive Efficiency and Financial Development in China: The Role of Contracts and Contractual Enforcement', *Journal of International Economic Law* 11, 2008: 459; L. Bernstein, 'Opting Out of the Legal System: Extralegal Contractual Relations in the Diamond Industry', *Journal of Legal Studies* 21, 1992: 115 (The change of resorting to formal dispute resolution in the diamond industry supports the hypothesis that in the presence of a credible formal legal regime, when the need arises to go beyond the ethically derived, extra-legal norms that govern the transactions, it seems likely that the formal law will be more frequently used.); S. Johnson, *et al.*, 'Courts and Relational Contracts', *Journal of Law, Economics and Organization* 18, 2002: 221 (finding that effective courts foster the establishment of new relations and court enforcement is more important when the supplier involves specialized inputs).
3 For a review of the role of informal and formal contracts in economic development, *see*, M. Trebilcock and Jing Leng, 'The Role of Formal Contract Law and Enforcement in Economic Development', *Virginia Law Review* 92, 2006: 1517.
4 L. Telser, 'A Theory of Self-enforcing Agreement', *Journal of Business* 53, 1980: 24, 42.
5 *Ibid.*, p. 44.
6 *Ibid.*
7 O. Williamson, 'Credible Commitments: Using Hostage to Support Exchange', *American Economic Review* 73, 1983: 519.
8 D. Clarke, P. Murrell and S. Whiting, 'The Role of Law in China's Economic Development', in L. Brandt and T. Rawski (eds), *China's Great Economic Transformation*, Cambridge, New York: Cambridge University Press, 2008: 375–428 (observing that it is impossible to make the case that formal legal institutions have contributed in an important way to China's remarkable economic success); G. Mayeda, 'The Role of Different Domestic Norms in Law and Development Reform: Lessons from China and Japan', *McGill Law Journal*, 51, 2006: 547, 582–583 (pointing out by citing others that the Chinese legal system offers little protection to private property rights); T. Ginsburg, 'Does Law Matter For Economic Development? Evidence from East Asia', *Law & Society Review* 34, 2000: 829, 830 (observing that law has not played a major role in Asian economic growth although he raised the possibility that existing evidence is not sufficient and that a more detailed study of Asian legal institutions would elucidate their central importance in Asian growth); for a recent introduction to the Chinese legal system, *see*, Bin Liang, *The Changing Chinese Legal System, 1978–Present: Cenralization of Power and Rationalization of the Legal System*, London: Routledge, 2008.
9 Telser, *supra note* 4, p. 27.
10 Williamson, *supra note* 7, p. 537.
11 Lien-sheng Yang, 'Hostages in Chinese History', *Harvard Journal of Asiatic Studies* 15, 1952: 507.
12 For a similar view in the context of international trade relations, *see*, Beth V. Yarbrough and Robert Yarbrough, 'Reciprocity, Bilateralism, and Economic "Hostage": Self-Enforcing Agreements in International Trade', *International Studies Quarterly* 30, 1986: 7, 11.

13 B. Klein and K. B. Leffler, 'The Role of Market Forces in Assuring Contractual Performance', *The Journal of Political Economy* 89, 1981: 615.
14 *Ibid.*, p. 618.
15 *Ibid.*, p. 630.
16 *Ibid.*, p. 632.
17 B. Klein, 'Transaction Cost Determinants of "Unfair" Contractual Arrangements', *American Economic Review Proceedings* 70, 1980: 356, 359.
18 *Ibid.*
19 *See*, B. Klein, R. Crawford and A. Alchian, 'Vertical Integration, Appropriable Rents and the Competitive Contracting Process', *Journal of Law and Economics* 21, 1978: 297.
20 A. W. Dnes, 'A Case-Study Analysis of Franchise Contracts', *The Journal of Legal Studies* 22, 1993: 367.
21 *Ibid.*, p. 372.
22 *Ibid.*, p. 376.
23 For a discussion of the roles of secured debt in alleviating adverse selection problems and moral hazard problems, *see* G. G. Triantis, 'Secured Debt Under Conditions of Imperfect Information', *Journal of Legal Studies* 21, 1992: 225.
24 Williamson, *supra note* 7, p. 537.
25 Yarbrough and Yarbrough, *supra note* 12, p. 20.
26 Klein and Leffler, *supra note* 13, p. 617.
27 A. Grief, 'Contract Enforceability and Economic Institutions in Early Trade: The Maghribi Trader's Coalition', *American Economic Review* 83, 1993: 525.
28 *Ibid.*
29 P. B. Fairest, *Mortgages* (2nd edn), London: Sweet & Maxwell, 1980: 103, 130; Art. 199 of the *Law on Real Property* in China, available at http://www.chinalaw info.com (accessed 15 October 2009); W. D. Duncan and L. Willmott, *Mortgages Law in Australia* (2nd edn), Sydney: The Federation Press, 1996: 142–146.
30 A. Schwartz, 'Security Interests and Bankruptcy Priorities: A Review of Current Theories', *Journal of Legal Studies* 10, 1981: 1, 31–33.
31 C. W. Smith and J. B. Warner, 'Bankruptcy, Secured Debt, and Optimal Capital Structure: Comment', *Journal of Finance* 34, 1979: 247, 250.
32 R. M. Stulz and H. Johnson, 'An Analysis of Secured Debt', *Journal of Financial Economics* 14, 1985: 501, 515–518.
33 Triantis, *supra note* 23, p. 247.
34 Williamson, *supra note* 7, p. 529.
35 *Ibid.*
36 Dnes, *supra note* 20.
37 *Ibid.*, p. 380.
38 For examples, *see*, *West's Arkansas Code Annotated*, A. C. A. § 4-72-310; *West's Ann. Cal. Bus. & Prof. Code* §20020.
39 *Cuckmere Brick Co. Ltd. v. Mutual Finance Ltd.* [1979] Ch. 948.
40 Fairest, *supra note* 29, p. 98.
41 Duncan and Willmott, *supra note* 29, p. 94.
42 *Law on Real Property*, *supra note* 29, Art. 195(3).
43 R. Haselmann, *et al.*, 'How Law Affects Lending', 1 (Columbia Law and Economics Working Paper No. 285, 2006), available at http://ssrn.com/abstract=846665 (accessed 15 October 2009).
44 *Ibid.*, p. 2.

45 Art. 10 of the 1982 Constitution. Both the Chinese version and an English translation can be found at http://www.chinalwinfo.com (accessed 15 October 2009).

46 Zuotang Wang and Wenzhen Wang, 'On the Reform of Land-Use Right in Chinese Cities', *Beijing University Journal* 3, 1990: 16.

47 *Ibid.*

48 This Law is reprinted in the *Collection of the Laws of the PRC*, Jinlin: Jilin People's Press, 1949–1989: 1239.

49 Art. 5 of the Law, *Ibid.*

50 Youhai Sun, 'A Study of the Land Transfer System', Doctoral Thesis (Nanjing: Nanjing Agricultural University, 2006: 29.

51 *Ibid.*

52 Art. 10 of the 1982 Constitution, *supra note* 45.

53 The GPCL was enacted in 1986. The Chinese version appears in the *Collection of the Laws of the PRC*, Jilin: Jilin People's Press, 1989: 315. An English translation can be found at http://www.chinalawinfo.com (accessed 15 October 2009).

54 Sun, *supra note* 50, pp. 28–29.

55 Regulation Concerning the Administration of Land in the Shenzhen Special Economic Zones, promulgated by the Standing Committee of Guangdong People's Congress on 29 December 1987, available at http://www.law-lib.com/lawhtm/1988/49032.htm (accessed 15 October 2009).

56 Art. 10 of the Constitution, *supra note* 45.

57 This Law was initially enacted in 1986, reprinted in the *Collection of the Laws of the PRC*, Jilin: Jilin People's Press, 1949–1989: 1872.

58 Art. 1 of the Decision Concerning the Amendment of the Law on the Administration of Land; this Decision was approved by the Standing Committee of the National People's Congress on 29 December 1988, reprinted in the *Collection of the Law of the PRC*, Jilin: Jilin People's Press, 1949–1989: 1978.

59 An English translation can be found at http://www.chinalawinfo.com.

60 An English translation can be found at http://www.chinalawinfo.com.

61 An English translation can be found at http://www.chinalawinfo.com.

62 *Supra note* 29. For an evolution of private property and an ideological debate on the protection of private property during the enactment of the *Law on Real Rights*, *see*, Mo Zhang, 'From Public to Private: The Newly Enacted Chinese Property Law and the Protection of Property Rights in China', *Berkeley Business Law Journal* 5, 2008: p. 317; for a legislative history and the content of the *Law on Real Rights*, *see*, G. M. Rehm and H. Julius, 'The New Chinese Property Rights Law: An Evaluation from a Continental Perspective', *Columbia Journal of Asian Law* 22, 2009: 179.

63 Available at http://www.law110.com/law/guowuyuan/2083.htm (accessed 15 October 2009).

64 *Ibid.*

65 Available at http:// www.tsinghua.edu.cn/docsn/fcc/fgzcjzzgl (accessed 15 October 2009).

66 *Ibid.*

67 The house accumulation fund is contributed by employers and employees with no tax levy and can be used by employees to purchase houses and borrow lower interest loans. *See*, Jia Kang and Junmin Liu, 'A Study on the Issue of Housing Reform and Housing Security in China', *Finance and Politics Research* 7, 2007: 8, 17.

68 Decision, *supra note* 65.
69 *Ibid.*
70 *Ibid.*
71 Available at http://www.law110.com/law/guowuyuan/2025.htm (accessed 15 October 2009).
72 *Ibid.*
73 *Ibid.*
74 The Provisions are reprinted in Bingzhi Yang (ed.), *Guidelines on Real Estate Law*, Beijing: Law Press, 1993: 1322.
75 *Ibid.*, Arts 6, 14, 18–19, 39–40.
76 *Ibid.*, Arts 22, 27, 29.
77 *Ibid.*
78 *Supra note* 60.
79 Art. 60.
80 The most recent administrative rule at the national level on land registration is the Land Registration Measures promulgated by the Ministry of Land and Resources on 30 December 2007. The Chinese version and an English translation of the Measures are available at *China Law and Practice*, May 2008, Hong Kong, Asia Law and Practice, 2008: 47. The most recent administrative rule on housing title registration at the national level is the Measures for Building Registration. This Rule was promulgated by the Ministry of Construction on 22 January 2008 and became effective on 1 July 2008. It has replaced the Measures on the Administration of the Registration of Urban Housing Title promulgated by the Ministry of Construction on 27 October 1997 and amended on 15 August 2001. The Current Rule is available at http://www.chinalawinfo.com (accessed 15 October 2009).
81 For an assessment and criticisms of and suggested changes to the land law in China, *see*, J. Palomar, 'Land Tenure Security as a Market Stimulator in China Contents', *Duke Journal of Comparative and International Law* 12, 2002: 7.
82 Jingling Wu, 'China's Economic and Financial Reform', in O. K. Tam (ed.), *Financial Reform in China*, London: Routledge, 1995: 85.
83 Xiaoling Wu, 'China's Financial Institutions', in Tom (ed.), *Ibid*, p. 113.
84 The People's Construction Bank of China, originally established in 1954, was absorbed by the Ministry of Finance in 1958. Established in 1955, the Agricultural Bank of China was dissolved in 1957 and its business was taken over by the People's Bank of China. These two banks re-emerged in the 1960s and continued only for a very short period. *See*, Gong Sun Zhi Yuan (ed.) *Handbook of Financial Law Practice in China*, Beijing: China Economic Press, 1994: 26–27.
85 *Ibid.*, p. 25.
86 These Decisions were issued on 27 September 1983. Decision of the State Council Concerning the Exercise of the Functions of the Central Bank by the People's Bank of China, reprinted in the *Collection of the Laws of the People's Republic of China*, Jilin: Jilin People's Press, 1989: 1353.
87 *Ibid.*
88 Zhengqing Zhou, Explanations Concerning the Commercial Banking Law of the People's Republic of China, Address at the Thirteenth Session of the Eighth Standing Committee of the National People's Congress, (24 August 1994).
89 *See*, D. Eu, Comment, Financial Reforms and Corporate Governance in China, *Columbia Journal of Transactional Law* 34, 1996: 449, 489.

90 *Ibid.*
91 Bank of China, Lending Measures for Foreign Invested Enterprises, issued by the Bank of China on 24 April 1987, available at http://www.infobank.cn (accessed 15 October 2009), legal database; Agricultural Bank of China, Provisional Measures on Lending with Mortgage or Guarantee, available at http://www.infobank.cn (accessed 15 October 2009), legal database.
92 GPCL, *supra note* 53.
93 The Opinion was adopted by the Adjudicative Committee of the Supreme Peoples' Court on 26 January 1988. Both the Chinese version and an English translation can be found at http://www.chinalawinfo.com (accessed 15 October 2009).
94 Both the Chinese version and an English translation of the law are available at http://www.chinalawinfo.com (accessed 15 October 2009).
95 *Ibid.*, Art. 34.
96 *Ibid.*, Arts 41, 42.
97 The Chinese version and an English translation can be found at *China Law and Practice* 2, 2001, p. 24.
98 *Supra note* 29.
99 *Ibid.*, Arts 180, 187.
100 *Ibid.*, Art. 187.
101 *Ibid.*, Art. 188.
102 *Ibid.*, Art. 181.
103 *Ibid.*, Art. 199(1).
104 *Ibid.*
105 *Ibid.*, Art. 199(2).
106 *Ibid.*, Art. 199(3).
107 Provisional Regulation on the Allocation and Transfer of State-Owned Land-Use Rights in Urban Areas, issued by the State Council on 19 May 1990. This Regulation is reprinted in the *Collection of the Laws of the PRC*, Jilin: Jilin People's Press, 1990–1992, p. 1764. Later laws and regulations have followed these three methods of allocating land use rights with fee payment and to some extent have restricted the allocation of free land use.
108 Shouying Liu, 'Property Rights in Land and Real Estate Market Development in China', a lecture delivered at the School of Law of Renmin University, available at http://www.civillaw.com.cn/article/default.asp?id=41228 (accessed 14 November 2009).
109 *Ibid.*
110 *Ibid.*
111 *Ibid.* In 2003, allocation of land-use rights through *churang* accounted for 74.79 per cent of the total 258,860 hectares allocated to users. In 2006, allocation of land use rights through *churang* amounted to 71.5 per cent of the total allocated land of 204,277 hectares.
112 *Ibid.*
113 *Ibid.*
114 *Ibid.*
115 H. De Soto, *The Mystery of Capital*, New York: Basic Books, 2000: 157.
116 For a detailed literature review, *see* Trebilcock and Leng, *supra note* 3.
117 H. De Soto, *The Other Path*, New York: Harper & Row, 1990: 56.
118 Palomar, *supra note* 81, pp. 10–11.

119 *Supra note* 57.
120 *Ibid.*, Art. 36.
121 *Ibid.*, Art. 37.
122 *Ibid.*, Art. 41.
123 Circular of the State Council on Strengthening the Control of Land, available at http://www.gov.cn/ztzl/jqtdtk/content_379776.htm (accessed 14 November 2009).
124 The 1998 *Law on the Administration of Land* is reprinted in the *Collection of the Laws of the PRC*, Jilin: Jilin People's Press, 1998: 2051.
125 1986 *Law on the Administration of Land*, *supra note* 57, Art. 38.
126 *Supra note* 124, Art. 62.
127 Circular of the General Office of the State Council on Strengthening the Administration of Land Transfer and the Prohibition of Speculation and/or Sale of Land, issued in 1999 and available at http://www.bjtd.com/article_view.asp?article_ID=330 (accessed 14 November 2009); Decision of the State Council on the Deepening of Reform and Strict Administration of Land, issued in 2004 and available at http://www.people.com.cn/GB/shizheng/1026/3078631.html (accessed 14 November 2009); Songyou Huang, 'People's Court Shall not Support the Purchase of Rural Houses by Urban Residents' a speech delivered at the Civil Adjudicative Work Conference held on 9 April 2007, available at http://big5.xinhuanet.com/gate/big5/news.xinhuanet.com/legal/2007-04/10/content_5955994.htm (accessed 14 November 2009).
128 Liu, *supra note* 108.
129 *Ibid.*
130 Jiansheng Cheng, 'Reviews on Housing Finance in China', available at http://www.adb.org/PRCM/speech-pres/pboc-jiansheng.pdf (accessed 15 November 2009).
131 Limin Liu, 'Housing Market in Urban China, Master Thesis (University of Nevada, Reno, 2007), 61.
132 Cheng, *supra note* 130.
133 Liu, *supra note* 131.
134 The numbers in this table are compiled by the author based on the *China Legal Yearbook* from 1988 to 2002, Beijing: Law Press.
135 T. L. Anderson and P. J. Hill, 'The Evolution of Property Rights: A Study of the American West', *Journal of Law and Economics* 18, 1979: 163, 176 (arguing that a comparison of the benefits and costs of defining and enforcing property rights explains and predicts the evolution of property institutions).
136 China is currently trying to solve the problem that local governments expropriate land from farmers at prices much lower than market prices and then sell the land-use rights of the expropriated land to investors at higher market prices.
137 North, *supra note* 1, pp. 80–81.
138 The author conducted a questionnaire survey in 2008.
139 North, *supra note* 1, pp. 80–81.
140 For a discussion on the role of contract law in China's economic development, *see*, Yu and Zhang, *supra note* 2.
141 C. J. Milhaupt and K. Pistor, *Law and Capitalism: What Corporate Crises Reveal about Legal Systems and Economic Development around the World*, Chicago: The University of Chicago Press, 2008: 5–6.
142 Yu and Zhang, *supra note* 2.

6 Transplantation and transformation

30-year development of China's IP system

Yahong Li

6.1. Introduction

The year of 2009 marks the 30th anniversary of China's legal reform, paralleling with the State's policy of reform and opening launched in 1978. The intellectual property (IP) law system under the Chinese Communist regime also started around that period. In a nutshell, the *Trademark Law* was passed in 1982 based on several years of preparation and drafting; two years later, in 1984, the *Patent Law* was enacted, and finally, the *Copyright Law* was born in 1990 after many years of drafting. These laws were accompanied by their respective implementing rules and were followed by other IP legislations such as Integrated Circuit Layout Designs Regulations (2001), Software Regulations (2002), Plant Varieties Regulation (1997), Well-Known Marks Regulations (2003) and Internet Transmission Rights Regulations (2006), among others. The three major IP laws have also been amended several times in the past three decades. For example, the *Trademark Law* was amended in 1993 and 2001; the *Patent Law* was amended in 1992, 2000 and 2008; and the *Copyright Law* was amended in 2001. Following the amendments of the laws, the respective implementing rules were also amended.

Enacted and developed during the period in which China was transforming itself from a socialist central-planned economy to a market economy, almost all of the Chinese pieces of IP legislation have a strong imprint of Western IP law. This is particularly true when one takes the following factors into consideration: first, when the Communist Party took power from the Nationalist government, the Communists abolished all laws of its predecessor and thereby completely cut off the Chinese legal tradition in a formalistic way; second, even if the legal tradition was not cut off, China did not have its own IP system developed under the imperial and the Nationalist governments; and third, most of the IP events that happened in China, whether the enactment of laws or the amendment of laws, were prompted by the pressure from the West in the form of trade agreements, the threat of trade sanctions or the mandate from international IP treaties, with only one exception being the 2008 Patent Law amendment. Indeed, all of the Chinese IP laws were more or less modelled after Western IP laws in form and in substance. It is therefore not an overstatement to say that the current Chinese IP system is a transplant from the West.

However, one should also keep in mind that the Chinese IP system is not a total replication of the Western IP system either. For better or for worse, the Western IP law system has been transformed in China into a hybrid system that embraces both Chinese and Western elements and characteristics. In addition to the fact that China's political system and ideologies are completely different from the West, which often gives Chinese IP law a strong 'socialist' flavour, the influence of Chinese culture and tradition on IP law has also been strong and consistent, although Chinese law-makers have not attempted to learn and borrow any provisions from the IP laws of the late Qing Dynasty or the Nationalist (Kuomintang) regime. It may be appropriate to describe the Chinese IP system as a hybrid that consists of Western legal style and substance, old socialist ideologies and Chinese culture and tradition, particularly in the context of enforcement.

This chapter reviews the development of China's IP system since 1978 when China started its open and reform policy. This chapter will identify important IP events such as the enactment and amendment of various IP laws and China's participation in international IP organizations and treaties. From these events, the chapter will critically analyze how China has been transplanting the Western-style IP system to the Chinese society and what difficulties and confrontations China has experienced during this transplantation process, and consequently, how China has transformed the Western-style IP system into a hybrid system that fit both a modern market economy and the unique Chinese political, ideological and cultural circumstances. Based on this analysis, the chapter intends to demonstrate the possibility of a successful transplantation and transformation of one legal system to another legal system with a very distinctive legal tradition and culture.

6.2. The process of transplantation

The transplantation of legal systems from the West to China had already started to take place in the late Qing Dynasty. The process of transplantation during that period bore many resemblances with the transplantation in the early 1980s. Therefore, a sketch of the history may be helpful in better understanding how IP law was transplanted to China and what difficulties had been confronted during this process.

6.2.1. *The first attempt by the late Qing and Nationalist governments*

There are several similarities between the transplantations in the late Qing Dynasty and in the 1980s. The first similarity is that the enactment of IP laws was preceded by the signing of trade agreements with Western powers such as the United States and Great Britain. The second similarity is that trademark law was the first IP law drafted and enacted, probably because trademarks are usually the first targets of infringement when foreign brands expand into the Chinese market. Thus, our following discussion will start from trademark law.

Prior to 1903, there had been no imperial legal regulation of trademarks in China, although guild regulations and clan rules played some role in regulating brand names and symbols. Due to rampant abuses of foreign brands that entered into China in the beginning of the twentieth century[1] and the consequent pressure from Britain, the United States and Japan, the Qing government-signed trade treaties in 1903 with these countries to give their citizens full trademark protection.[2] Subsequently, several drafts of a formal trademark law were produced, which aimed at protecting foreign trademarks regardless of whether the trademarks were registered. These drafts nonetheless failed to be promulgated because of the deadlock between the Chinese government, which insisted in having a centralized Chinese court system to handle all trademark disputes on the one hand, and the foreign governments on the other, which doubted the quality of the Chinese legal system. To be noted is that the drafting of trademark law was closely monitored by the treaty powers, which formed a committee to advise the Chinese in the drafting process.[3] Only about 20 years later in 1923 was a formal trademark law enacted.

The transplantation of copyright law also did not fare as well. Copyright was a novel notion in imperial China and there was no formal copyright law until 1910, although China was the first country to invent printing technology;[4] the imperial governments of several dynasties used penal codes to penalize unauthorized reproduction in order to maintain the state's authority.[5] Similar to trademark law, the concept of protecting copyright was introduced to China only because the Qing government had to fulfil its obligations under the 1903 trade treaty.[6] The Qing government subsequently promulgated laws on printing and newspapers in 1906, 1907 and 1908, which aimed at controlling printers, but the enactment of a formal copyright law[7] was delayed until 1910 due to the resistance from the Qing government.[8]

Patent law was also a product of trade treaties. Under the 1903 US and China treaty, for example, China had to provide a limited term of patent protection 'to citizens of the United States on all their patents issued by the United States, in respect of articles the sale of which is lawful in China, which do not infringe on previous inventions of Chinese subjects, in the same manner as patents are to be issued to subjects of China'.[9] However, such protections were only made available beginning in 1912, which yielded only less than 700 patents in the subsequent 30 years.[10]

From the foregoing discussion, we can see that, in the late Qing Dynasty, the enactment process of IP laws was prolonged; the laws were largely not up to the standards stipulated in various trade treaties[11] and the enforcement of IP laws was even less satisfactory.[12] The attempt of foreign powers to implant a 'modern' IP system in China was a total failure.

The Nationalist government had a vision to modernize China's IP system after taking power in 1928, but it too failed entirely. The government enacted a trademark law in 1930, a copyright law in 1928 and a patent law in 1949.[13] Nevertheless, these laws were not seriously implemented due to the eight-year anti-Japanese war and a series of civil wars.[14]

Alford accurately summarized the reason why the transplantation of IP law during the Kuomintang era failed:

> Yet, more fundamentally, these laws failed to achieve their stated objectives because they presumed a legal structure, and indeed, a legal consciousness, that did not then exist in China and, most likely, could not have flourished there at that time.[15]

6.2.2. The transplantation in the era of opening and reform

After the Communist Party took power in 1949, it abolished all IP laws enacted by the Kuomintang but did not establish its own IP system until the 1980s. During this gap of 30 years, regulations and measures dealing with IP rights–related matters such as trademark registration, author's remuneration, patent rights, etc., did exist, but they were not formal IP laws by any standards. The end of the Cultural Revolution and the beginning of the open and reform policy gave a fresh start for China's intellectual property system. While the reconstruction of the IP system was not completely outside China's internal need for modernization, the matter was mainly forced by foreign powers who wanted China to adopt a Western-style IP system. Through signing trade agreements with China and requiring China to meet certain standards to gain entry to international organizations such as the World Trade Organization (WTO), the Western powers gradually transplanted their IP systems to China.

6.2.2.1 The enactment of IP laws under trade agreements

The first IP area that was subject to transplantation was trademark law. Prior to 1982, only a few regulations existed to deal with trademark registration.[16] These regulations were no more than the government's means to supervise and control the production of goods. Even when the 1950 provisional regulation provided trademark holders with 'exclusive rights', people dared not assert such rights for fear of political consequences. Very few registrations were recorded, unauthorized copying was a massive problem and consumer confusion was rampant.[17] During this period, copyright-related matters were regulated by few administrative regulations. These regulations were issued to deal with some isolated copyright issues such as the payment of '*gaofei*', a very modest remuneration based on number of words, and to prevent unauthorized alteration of authors' works.[18] Similarly, for patent, a regulation was issued in 1950[19] that adopted the Soviet's two-track system, under which either the state owned the patent while inventors received modest rewards, or inventors owned the patents for a short period, from 5 to 15 years. In 1963, the Chinese government changed this system to a one-track system under which only the state enjoyed exclusive patent ownership.[20] Unsurprisingly, both systems attracted very few patent applications during that period.

In summary, in the first 30 years of the PRC, every trace of Western elements in China's IP system was eliminated. The regulations were no more than policy tools of the government to control and regulate very basic IP-related matters and were not aimed at protecting intellectual property right (IPR) holders' rights. This is understandable given that the ideologies and the economic system during that period were totally against the very objectives of the Western IP system. Writers, inventors and entrepreneurs were state workers; enterprises also belonged to the state. There were simply no private property rights to protect.

The situation changed only after 1978 when China started its open and reform policy. In 1979, China signed a trade agreement with the United States (1979 Trade Agreement), under which each side indicated that it 'recognized the importance of effective protection of patents, trademarks and copyrights'.[21] Following this agreement, a trademark law was enacted in 1982, a patent law in 1984, a set of trial copyright regulations in 1984 and finally a copyright law in 1990. China was also mindful of its international obligations and joined the Paris Convention for Protection of Industrial Property in 1985 and the Madrid Agreement Concerning the International Registration of Trademarks in 1989.[22] In a matter of a decade, PRC completed the reconstruction of its IP system, and this time, the West was fairly successful in transplanting its IP system into China.

First, the passage of laws was seen as a necessity for China's socialist modernization and not something forced upon China by foreign powers. For example, patent law's advantages, such as creating incentives for innovations and stimulating earlier dissemination of technologies, were fully recognized.[23] 'Trademark was looked to, at least by some in China's leadership, as providing an interim device for bringing order to a fledgling market'.[24] The recognition of the importance of IP laws to China's modernization is evidenced in Article 1 of the three laws. Second, all three laws were drafted and enacted based on extensive studies of Western IP laws, and the selection of legal principles and rules were based on China's own political, social and economic circumstances at the time rather than blindly borrowing from the West. For example, the following aspects in the 1984 Patent Law were seen as appropriate for China's development then but were criticized by the West as non-conforming to international standards: a ten-year patent-protection term; the lack of protection to chemical and pharmaceuticals; the lack of protection for process patent and state-designated patent agents handling all patent applications, etc. Likewise, the 1982 Trademark Law denied protection to service marks, collective marks, certification marks, defensive marks and denied applications on a multiclass basis.

6.2.2.2. *Amending IP laws under the Sino–US MOU*

Another high point of China's IP law transplantation came ten years later in the early 1990s. The major IP laws enacted during the 1980s were soon deemed to be below international standards, unsatisfactory and ineffective in curbing widespread piracy and IPR infringements. Therefore, in 1992, a 'Memorandum of Understanding on the Protection of Intellectual Property' ('MOU') was signed by the United States and China requiring the latter to raise its IP protection standards.

Following this MOU, China amended its *Patent Law* in 1992 to: (1) expand protection to include pharmaceutical products, food and beverages, flavourings and substances obtained via a chemical process; (2) extend the protection term for inventions from 15 to 20 years, for utility models and designs from 5 to 10 years; (3) narrow the grounds under which a compulsory license may be granted and (4) specify the burden of proof in litigation relating to method patents and adding a provision for domestic priority. A year later in 1993, China amended its *Trademark Law* to extend protection to include service marks, excluded geographical names from protection, allowed one application for several classes, added licensing requirements and expanded criminal liability.

Copyright law was not affected by the MOU, partly because the law was enacted much later than the other two laws and very close to the time the MOU was signed. Prior to its enactment, the Chinese government already issued a Copyright Trial Regulations (CTR) in 1984 that provided many theoretical and practical experiences.[25] The 1990 *Copyright Law* had largely done away with the 'socialist' and 'planned-economy' elements which existed in the CTR[26] and therefore was seen as largely complementary to the spirit of the MOU.

6.2.2.3. *Amending IP laws for the entry of WTO*

The most recent wave of amendments to China's IP laws occurred in the beginning of the twenty-first century, mainly due to the need to join the WTO. To join the WTO, a country must comply with some legal obligations, including the minimum standards required by the Agreement on Trade-Related Aspects of Intellectual Property Rights (TRIPS), which includes 20 years of patent protection term and some subject matters that must be protected (such as computer programs and pharmaceutical products, among others). Although the TRIPS agreement had incorporated most of the provisions of the Berne Convention and the Paris Convention, to which both China had already acceded, Chinese IP laws were not fully in compliance with these Conventions at that time. Joining the WTO required much stricter scrutiny on whether China's IP protection standards are up to the standards of the TRIPS. To gain entry into the WTO, China started amending its three IP laws extensively. Shortly before China joined the

WTO on 11 December 2001, China amended its *Patent Law* on 25 August 2000 and both *Trademark Law* and *Copyright Law* on 27 October 2001.

Specifically, China's *Copyright Law* was amended to add or modify some subject matters of copyright protection such as oral works, *quyi* and acrobatic works, architectural works, cinematographic works, drawings of engineering designs and product designs, etc.[27] The amended *Copyright Law* also lists and defines copyright owners' economic rights more extensively and clearly,[28] adds rental right and the right of communication over Internet, defines the right of public performance and the right to compilation works. These changes made the law more in line with the TRIPS,[29] and narrows down the scope of fair uses in various situations. Lastly, the *Copyright Law* was amended to comply with the requirements under the TRIPS to enable judicial authority to have the authority to order prompt and effective provisional measures to prevent the infringement of IPRs from occurring[30] and to order the alleged infringer to bear the onus of proof.[31]

Major changes made to the *Patent Law* in accordance with the TRIPS include: ownership of 'service invention' can be decided by agreement;[32] the 'offer for sale' of a pirated product can be deemed as acts of infringement for inventions and utility models;[33] judicial review of decisions in re-examination and invalidation processes is allowed;[34] preliminary injunctions and property preservation are permitted;[35] more conditions are imposed on using compulsory licensing[36] and damages can be calculated by multiplying the royalties of licenses.[37]

China's *Trademark Law* also underwent major changes to meet TRIPS standards. For example, protectable trademark is defined as 'any visually perceptible sign capable of distinguishing the goods of one natural person or other entity from those of others'[38] rather than 'a word, device or a combination of words or devices' under the 1993 *Trademark Law*. Registrable marks are extended to certification marks and collective marks;[39] geographic indications are protected,[40] as well as unregistered well-known marks.[41] Judicial review of decisions made by trademark administrative authorities is allowed.[42] Preliminary injunctions along with evidence and property preservation are available.[43] Finally, statutory damages are increased to a maximum of RMB500,000 yuan.[44]

6.3. The evidence of transformation

During the transplantation process, China's IP laws were also gradually transformed from Western laws to a hybrid law system, which consists of both Western and Chinese style and substance. The transformation is a two-way process, from socialist law to Western laws and vice versa, as evidenced by the legal debates during the process of law amendments and the amended provisions in the IP laws.

6.3.1. Transforming a socialist IP law system to a Western-style IP law system

When describing socialist law, Patrick Glenn says

> It is formal law with a difference, however, since its application is entirely in the hands of the guardian of socialist legality, the communist party, which exercises its influence through an entire network of organizations, shadowing those of the state and the courts. Judicial decisions, of allegedly independent judges, are subject to party control and revision.[45]

However, this paragraph does not mention the legislative aspect. In fact, socialist law can also be easily identified from legislation, because they often contain provisions pronouncing socialist oriented legislative objectives and stress the importance of protecting state interests. When Western IP law was transplanted to Chinese socialist soil, the transformation process normally started with legislation. Gradually, the emphasis in legislative objective was switched from protecting socialist states and public interests to private property rights of the individual. One such example is the 1984 Copyright Trial Regulations (CTR).[46] This set of 'Regulations' was classified information, 'not to be published, nor disclosed to foreigners'.[47] It contained many 'socialist elements' of the time. For example, the CTR protects literary and artistic works of literature, art and science created by Chinese citizens and published by state publishing units (emphasis added);[48] authors have the right to retrieve published works due to the author's changed view or a just cause;[49] and the Ministry of Culture, as required by state interests, may purchase the copyright of certain works and lengthen the period of protection for these works by subsuming them under state copyrights.[50] These provisions disappeared altogether in the 1990 Copyright Law. Moreover, although under both the CTR and the 1990 Copyright Law, the purpose of copyright law is to 'encourage the creation and dissemination of works which would contribute to the socialist spiritual and material civilization',[51] the 1990 Copyright Law added a new purpose, that is, to 'protect the copyright of authors in their literary, artistic and scientific works and the copyright-related rights and interests'.[52] Thus, 'copyright grew into a private personal and property right'.[53]

Patent law underwent a similar path towards Westernization. As mentioned in Section 6.2.2.1 of this chapter, in 1950, China adopted a two-track system and then in 1963, virtually eliminated the patent system, because only the state could obtain patents. When the 1984 *Patent Law* was enacted, China started to accept the Western notion of a patent system, which is to protect the rights in 'invention-creations' and to encourage 'invention-creations', even though meeting the need of socialist modernization is still one of the objectives enshrined in Article 1 of the *Patent Law*. However, due to the unclear division of the state, collective and individual ownership at the time, private patent rights were still circumscribed. For example, Article 6 of the *Patent Law* provided that only entities could apply for patents in 'service invention-creations'. Given that almost everything one used or possessed at that time belonged to the state, hardly any inventions could be qualified as non-service invention. Moreover, under Article 14, the State Council and provincial governments had authority to order state entities to license patents they held according to state plan ('state plan licenses') and to order collectives or individuals to license their patents of 'great significance to the interests of the state or to the public interest'. The 1992 revision of the *Patent Law* did not change anything in this respect, but the 2000 revision changed 'state enterprises' to 'state-owned enterprises'. Only state-owned enterprises' *invention* patents, not utility and design patents, can be compelled to be licensed; their invention patents can only be subject to this kind of compulsory license if the 'invention-creations' have great significance to the interest of state or public and not merely according to the state plan.[54] The 2008 revision further abolished the compulsory licensing for the patents held by collectives and individuals for state and public interests. Although the right to apply for patent for 'service invention' still belongs to entities, the economic system has largely changed so that 'inventions' now have more chances to be deemed as 'non-service inventions', because inventors have more channels to get equipments or capital outside of their entities to carry out their inventions. Prior to the 2008 amendment, there was a debate on whether China should adopt the US Bayh-Dole system to allow researchers or research institute undertaking state-funded project to own patents. The final amendment, nevertheless, did not adopt this system. Instead, a version of this amendment was adopted in the *Science and Technology Law*, revised one year earlier in 2007.[55] This left a lingering issue: which law should the court apply when deciding disputes over patent ownership for state-funded inventions?

6.3.2. *Transforming Western law to 'socialist legality with Chinese characteristics'*

6.3.2.1. *In general*

China is an Asian country with a long socialist history and strong influence. Asia's socialist law, as Glenn pointed out, differing from the former Soviet socialist law, is 'a kinder, gentler form of communism, though of course equally savage when necessary'. This is because Asian countries are also influenced by Confucianism. He believes that Confucianism was revived in China since the late 1970s to generate loyalty and preserve structure.[56] With the 'kinder, gentler' socialism and Confucianism coexisting in China, Western influences on China's legal system had its limit. Although 'the socialist legislation looks in many instances just like Western legislation',[57] Chinese laws have not and will not be entirely Westernized. On the contrary, 'just as communism had to bend to deep-rooted Asian thought, however, so too is Western-style law clearly the object of confucianization, as filtered through communist authority'.[58] Many modern Western laws have been gradually confucianized in China. For example, in legal practice, mediation is often preferred over litigation; judges are subject to the 'telephone law of the party'; lawyers' status is still relatively inferior compared with judges and procuratorates and case reporting are often short and general, etc.

More importantly, the concept of rights 'is not found either in indigenous Asian thought or in Asian concepts of communism, and ... it became known only on its arrival from the West in the nineteenth century'.[59] The situation has now changed significantly, but private right in today's China is still not very clear and not well protected. A private right can be compromised or circumscribed when facing state interest, party authority or powerful *guanxi*. This is particularly true in the area of intellectual property protection.

6.3.2.2. Specifically as to IP law

Compared with IP laws of other countries, China is the only country that includes terms of identifying the country's political ideology and system in its IP laws. For example, Article 1 of the *Copyright Law* provides that

> This Law is enacted, in accordance with the Constitution, for the purpose of protecting the copyright of authors in their literary, artistic and scientific works and the copyright-related rights and interests, of encouraging the creation and dissemination of works which would contribute to the construction of socialist spiritual and material civilization, and of promoting the development and prosperity of socialist culture and science.

Trademark Law Article 1 adds the term 'socialist' to 'market economy', and the 2000 *Patent Law* adds the term 'socialist' to 'modernization'. However, interestingly, when the *Patent Law* was amended in 2008, the word 'socialist' was nowhere to be found. Article 1 simply states that

> the enactment of the Law is to protect legitimate rights of patent owners, to encourage invention–creations, to promote the utility of invention–creations, to enhance innovative capacity and to promote the advancement of science and technology and the social and economic development.

Is this a sign of the beginning of 'depolitization' of law in China? It is hard to say unless the word 'socialist' disappear from both *Trademark Law* and *Copyright Law* when they are amended in the future.

The second example that China has modified Western IP law to suit a 'socialist country with Chinese characteristics' is that it used 'public interests' to justify the state intervention or appropriation of private IPRs. For example, *Copyright Law* Article 4 provides that works banned from publication or dissemination in accordance with the law are not protected by the *Copyright Law*, and the use of copyright shall not violate the Constitution and laws or contravene public interest. This provision was entered based on a consensus of the Chinese officials that copyright law should 'take account of ideological considerations and ban items inconsistent with the Four Cardinal Principles, as well as those that split the unity of minority nationalities, advocates theft, pornography, violence and arson, or other criminal activities, and ... are against the Constitution'.[60] In 2007, this provision was challenged by the United States for violation of TRIPS Articles 3, 9.1, 14 and 41, and the allegation was confirmed by the WTO dispute settlement body (DSB) in 2009. Although content review has been a long-standing practice in China, this provision contravenes a basic concept of copyright that copyright automatically protects the form of expression, not the content, of a literary or artistic creation as soon as it is created without any formality. Currently, the Chinese government is preparing to amend this provision to implement the WTO DSB's decision.

Another example of transforming the Western-style IP law into one with Chinese characteristic is the robust administrative protection of IPR in China. Unlike any other countries, China's administrative organs have been extensively involved in enforcing IPRs, in addition to courts. For example, *Copyright Law* Article 47 provides that anyone who commits an infringement act 'may be subject by a copyright administration department to such administrative penalties as ceasing the infringing act, confiscating unlawful income from the act, confiscating and destroying infringing reproductions and imposing a fine; where the circumstances are serious, the copyright administration department may also confiscate the materials, tools and equipment mainly used for making the infringing reproductions'. The Implementing Rules of Copyright Administrative Penalty was issued by the National Copyright Administration in 1997 and was amended in 2003 to provide more detailed administrative penalties.[61] Similarly, patent law also provides administrative measures to deal with patents infringements.[62] The newly amended *Patent Law* not only retains administrative penalties such as an order to stop infringement and confiscation of illegal earning but also further strengthens such penalties by adding the penalty of a fine up to four times that of the illegal gains, or a fine up to RMB200,000 yuan (approximately US$29,250) if there is no illegal gain. The law also grants the patent administrative authority broad power to (1) interrogate relevant parties and investigate suspicious illegal acts; (2) check and duplicate any documents such as contracts, receipts and accounting books; (3) inspect infringing premises and infringing products and (4) seal, seize and detain the product or equipment that infringes on the patents of others.[63] Administrative measures are even more extensive under the *Trademark Law*. One chapter contains seven articles devoted to the administration of the use of trademarks, with three other articles dealing with administrative penalties for trademark infringement.[64] Prior to the entry to the WTO, administrative power was largely unchecked in China. There was no judicial review of administrative decisions on IP-related disputes. The situation changed due to the entry to the WTO. To meet the WTO obligation of providing judicial review for any administrative decisions, all three IP laws were amended to meet this requirement.[65]

In addition to the foregoing examples, a number of other traits in China's IP laws also have strong 'Chinese' and 'socialist' flavour. First, mediation, a favourite method of resolving disputes in China, is preferred when dealing with IP disputes. For example, Article 53 of the *Trademark Law* clearly requires that, where there is an infringement dispute, 'the interested parties shall resolve the dispute through consultation'. Only when the consultation fails may the interested parties bring a suit in court or ask the administrative authority to take action. Similar requirements appear in the *Patent Law* Article 60 and the *Copyright Law* Article 54. Second, compared with IP laws of other jurisdictions, all IP laws of PRC are fairly short and provisions are written in general terms without specific definitions and illustrations as to certain terms and concepts. For instance, the *Copyright Law* only contains 60 articles, the *Trademark Law* 64 articles and the *Patent Law* 76 articles.[66] Although 'oral work' is very controversial because it is not protected under copyright law in most countries, Chinese copyright law lists 'oral work' as a copyrightable work but does not define whether it refers to oral works not fixed in a tangible medium, or to oral works fixed in a tangible medium. As a result, this vagueness causes great difficulties in deciding cases involving copyright disputes between a narrator and a 'ghost writer' of a memoir. As many narrators of memoir are high-level revolutionary veterans, the courts' decisions are normally in their favour over the 'ghost writers'.[67] This is one example among many that China's IP laws lack definitions and illustrations.

6.4. Evaluations

China's intellectual property system is not a homegrown system; instead, it is a Western-bred, imported and transplanted system. As a transplant, it needs conditions and an environment that are suitable for its planting and growth or else it will simply die. This author agrees with Professor Alford that the indigenous IP system was not developed in imperial China because of the character of Chinese political culture and that the first attempt in the late Qing Dynasty to transplant the Western IP system failed, because IP was not relevant to China.[68] The strong tendency to preserve the past and the state's focus on political order and stability rather than on private rights and ownership makes copying possible and even plausible in imperial China.[69] The transplantation of the IP system in the late Qing Dynasty failed not only because of the 'inability of the Chinese to understand such law', but also because of the failure of the Chinese officials to address the implications for China of intellectual property law and to indicate how such a law was to be successfully absorbed; because of the scepticism about the law reform among the higher levels of the Chinese state and their genuine interest in controlling ideas and preserving political stability rather than protecting private rights; and lastly, because of the failure of the treaty powers to show the benefits of IP to China and to educate the Chinese people as to its rationale.[70] In essence, IP law was forced upon China by self-serving foreign powers when China was not ready and without the necessary preconditions to accept the system. As a consequence, introducing the IP system in China was no more than a bargain for the late Qing government to get rid of the extraterritoriality, and later as 'a tool in the struggle to ward off the foreign powers'.[71]

Compared with the first attempt, the transplantation of the IP system from the West to China in the past three decades starting from the 1980s has been fairly successful. It is not an overstatement to say the Western IP system for the first time found its root in Chinese soil, and this root is growing deeper and stronger as the whole system continues to adopt and adjust. The following figures also attest to this success: by March 2009, the total patent applications filed in China had reached five million,[72] and a Chinese company, Huawei, ranked first in the world in filing international patent applications through the Patent Cooperation Treaty (PCT) system, surpassing US and Japanese companies. China's trademark registrations ranked first consecutively from 2001 to 2007, with 600,000 in 2004 alone.[73] In 2007, courts in Beijing handled almost 3,000 IP cases.[74] Almost all intermediate courts have established IP chambers, and the Supreme People's Court is considering establishing a national unified specialist IP court. Since 1980, China has joined 18 international IP treaties or conventions and has become very active in the international IP arena.

There are several reasons why China is relatively successful in its second attempt of transplanting the Western IP system: first, compared with the first transplantation, this transplantation occurred in a much better international environment as Western countries' main purpose of coming to China in the late 1970s was to profit from the Chinese market rather than extraterritorial privileges; therefore, the Chinese did not have to learn the law 'at gunpoint' as their ancestors in the late Qing Dynasty did.[75] It is true that trade agreements, demanding that IP protection be afforded in China, were signed in both the Qing period and the late 1970s, but the status and attitude of the treaty parties in the two different times differed significantly. While economically weak, China was already a political superpower in the late 1970s. Concession to the obligations of the trade agreements was largely out of the Chinese government's own will rather than being forced at gunpoint or as a bargain to get rid of extraterritoriality.

Second, unlike the Qing government, consensus among the highest level of the PRC government on open and reform policy was very strong. Having suffered in the 'lawless' or 'rule of man' period themselves, some high-level government officials actively promoted 'socialist legality' and the idea of 'rule by law'. They also learned quickly to be able to realize that 'market economy' is an 'economy ruled by law'. The introduction of IP laws to China in the late 1970s and early 1980s did not meet much resistance from the top officials. In fact, without the support of senior officials, it would have been impossible to have the three major IP laws and their implementing rules enacted in a matter of eight years because in an authoritarian country like China, legislations are mandated by the government.

Third, the Chinese government's insistence on building a 'socialist legality with Chinese characteristics' may have played a more positive than negative role in the process of transplanting Western IP law to China. When IP laws were first introduced in China in the late 1970s, the Cultural Revolution just came to an end and China remained a socialist centrally planned economy. As shown in previous sections, the ownership system of the IP system had to be modified to suit the property ownership system in China at that time; that is, state ownership was predominant among five other kinds of ownerships. Thus, state interest was given a higher priority and private IPRs were largely circumscribed under the first copyright law, patent law and trademark law. For example, 'state plan license' was provided and patent right to 'service invention' belonged to the state; only copyright works published by state publishing units were protected and only works that passed state content review could have copyright protection; natural persons could not be trademark holder like entities; and foreigners had to register their marks through state designated agencies, etc. These transitional measures helped Western IP law plant its root in China's political, social and economic environment, which differs drastically from where it came. Without these transitional measures, the first batch of IP laws might not have survived to this day, because the Chinese government would not allow a purely unmodified Western-style IP law system to broadly protect IPRs of private individuals or entities when almost everything was still owned by the state.

Fourth, as the reform and opening continued, Chinese IP laws were gradually amended to meet both international standards and domestic needs. The amending process is essential for the success of the transplantation. As shown before, copyright law was amended once, trademark law twice and patent law three times, and each amendment elevated Chinese IP laws to another level. The process of amending is also a process of learning. The first major amendment to trademark law and patent law in 1992 raised the protection level to the standards expected in the Sino–US MOU; for example, patent term was lengthened from 15 to 20 years and patent protection was given to chemical substances and pharmaceuticals. The second wave of amendment in 2000 and 2001 to the three major IP laws forced Chinese law-makers to seriously study and analyze relevant international IP laws such as TRIPS and make extensive revisions to Chinese IP laws according to the standards in these international IP laws. For example, protectable subject matters were further expanded; some legal concepts such as public performance were better defined; more rights such as rental rights and right of communication over Internet were provided; and preliminary injunction, judicial review of administrative decisions and higher statutory damages were introduced.

The process of amendment is also a process of transformation. Through amending the laws, Western concepts of private rights were gradually introduced into the Chinese IP system, which either replaced old Chinese traditional and socialist ideologies or coexisted with them. In the meantime, the amendment process provided Chinese policy and law-makers the opportunity not only to learn the rules set by the West or international communities but also to play with the rules. Specifically, for example, the 2008 patent law amendment requires the disclosure of origins of biological resource used in an invention when filing a patent application. This requirement exceeds the standard in the TRIPS as it is not found in the TRIPS, but it does not violate the TRIPS as the latter only set the minimum standard without any upper limitation.

On the other hand, one should be reminded that, although fairly successful, the transplantation and transformation of the IP system still face tremendous challenges in China. One such challenge is the ideological and cultural differences between the West and China as the latter builds a 'socialist legality with Chinese characteristics'. After several amendments, the 'socialist' ideology in China's IP laws has been reduced; for example, 'state plan license' was abolished, but it is still a guiding ideology in the system. State interest is given a higher priority over the interest of private entities and individuals. Protection of private IP Rights may be undermined when 'state interest' is at stake. This 'socialist legality' coupled with 'Chinese characteristics' may render IP enforcement more difficult. The hierarchical relationship within the society, the importance of '*guanxi*', the heavy reliance on administrative measures and people's general lack of appreciation of private rights are the main obstacles to an effective IPR enforcement. Although cases are increasing rapidly, which shows that more people are resorting to legal actions when their IPRs are infringed, the majority of Chinese are still IPR illiterates and prefer to use '*guanxi*' or administrative channels to solve IPR disputes. In addition, China is still a world 'piracy haven'. There are yet two other most-cited difficulties: the lack of judicial independence and judicial corruption. Without true judicial independence, IPRs provided on paper will be compromised in reality.

6.5. Conclusion

The 30 years of development of the Chinese IP law system witnessed a process of transplantation and transformation of the Western IP system in China. Compared with the Qing and *Kuomintang* governments, the PRC government is fairly successful in this process due to various reasons. With internal demand and external pressure, and through several rounds of amendment, the Western IP law system has been transplanted to China and has transformed into a hybrid system embracing both Western and Chinese elements. The transplantation and transformation process still continues and is destined to face more challenges ahead.

Notes

1 W. P. Alford, *To Steal a Book Is an Elegant Offence: Intellectual Property Law in Chinese Civilization*, Stanford: Stanford University Press, 1995: 34–35, describing how foreign trademarks were being abused.

2 For example, the treaty with the British mentioned that it was to 'afford protection to British trademarks against infringement, imitation or colourable imitation by Chinese subjects'. The Mackay Treaty, art. 7, reprinted in N. F. Allman, *Protection of Trademarks, Patents, Copyrights and Trade-names in China*, Shanghai: Kelly & Walsh, 1924.

3 Alford, *supra note* 1, p. 40.

4 There has been a disagreement among scholars as to whether copyright emerged with the invention of printing. *See*, *Ibid.*, p. 9.

5 For a thorough and enlightening discussion on the history of how Chinese imperial governments exercised their control over publication by using a formal prepublication review system and how this system differs from the earlier IP law system developed in the West, *see*, *Ibid.*, pp. 12–18.

6 For example, under the Shanghai Treaty signed between imperial China and the United States in return for the United States to grant Chinese subjects the benefits of its copyright laws, the Chinese government would 'give full protection, in the same way and manner and subject to the same conditions upon which it agrees to protect trademarks, to all citizens of the United States' with respect to materials 'especially prepared for the use and education of the Chinese people'. The 1903 treaty between the United States and China, Art. II, reprinted in J. V. A. MacMurray (ed.), *Treaties and Agreements*, New York: Oxford University Press, 1921.

7 The Author's Right Law of the Great Qing Empire 1910 and its invocation was suspended after the Revolution of 1911.

8 The Qing government argued that since the 1903 treaties specified that copyright protection was to be provided in the 'same way and manner and subject to the same conditions' as trademark protection, therefore, copyright protection should only be available until the trademark law 'goes into force and proves acceptable and effective'. *See*, Allman, *supra note* 2, pp. 178–179.

9 The 1903 treaty between the United States and China, Art. 10, reprinted in MacMurray, *supra note* 6.

10 Alford, *supra note* 1, p. 42, note 79, some estimated 360 while others put the figure at 692.

11 For example, the *Copyright Law* protected Chinese authors only. Allman, *supra note* 2, p. 107.

12 For a detail account of how foreign IPR holders had to seek other ways of protecting their rights and how IPRs were infringed during that period, *see*, *supra note* 1, pp. 42–45.

13 Prior to 1949, a provisional patent measure, 'Measures to Encourage Industrial Arts', was issued in 1932.

14 David Kaser remarked that 'protection of any kind of literary property was so seldom recognized as deserving of attention in China that very, very few cases of alleged violation went to litigation; precedents, although not unknown, were rare'. D. Kaser, *Book Pirating in Taiwan*, Philadelphia: University of Pennsylvania Press, 1969: 19.

15 For example, only 10 per cent of 2,000 counties had courts with judges and lawyers of limited training, which rendered the enforcement of IPRs through courts impossible. Alford, *supra note* 1, p. 53.

16 For example, the Procedures for Dealing with Trademarks registered at the Trademark Office of the former Kuomintang Government (1950) which invalidated all registrations by the Nationalist government; the Provisional Regulations on Trademark Registration (1950) which provided a new registration-based trademark system; and the Regulations Governing the Control of Trademark (1963) which emphasized quality control of goods rather than protecting trademark holders' rights.

17 Alford, *supra note* 1, pp. 63–64.

18 For example, in September 1950, the National Conference of Publishers issued the Resolution for Improving and Developing Publication Work. In 1953, the General Administration of Publication issued the Rules for Rectifying the Wanton Reproduction of Books. In July 1985, the Ministry of Culture issued the Interim Regulations Concering the Remuneration for Works of Literature and Social Science.

19 Provisional Regulations on the Protection of the Invention Right and the Patent Right.

20 Under the Regulations to Encourage Inventions and the Regulations to Encourage Improvements in Technology.

21 Art. VI of the US–PRC Trade Agreement of 1979.

22 The agreement permits owners of 'international registrations' to obtain trademark and service mark registrations in all other Madrid Union countries upon payment of a fee.

23 D. Kay, 'The Patent Law of the People's Republic of China in Perspective', *UCLA Law Review* 33, 1985: 331–367.

24 Alford, *supra note* 1, p. 75.

25 The Trial Regulations on Copyright Protection for Books and Periodicals, issued by the Ministry of Culture on 15 June 1984 and effective from 1 January 1985.

26 For details, *see* Section 6.3 of this chapter.

27 Art. 2 (6) and (7) list 'drawings of engineering designs and product designs, illustrations, maps and the like graphic works and models'. This is the modified version based on the *Copyright Law* 1990, which listed 'maps, sketches and other graphic works' under art. 3.

28 A total of 12 rights are listed in art. 10 of the *Copyright Law* (2001).

29 Under *Copyright Law* art. 10 (9), the right of public performance not only includes the right of live performance, but also the right to communicate by any means to the public of the performance of a work. For compilation works, art. 14 of the *Copyright Law* provides that 'a work created by compilation of several works, parts of works, data that do not constitute a work or other materials and having originality in the selection or arrangement of its contents is a work of compilation. The copyright in a work of compilation shall be enjoyed by the compiler, provided that the exercise of such copyright shall not prejudice the copyright in the pre-existing works'.

30 Such as preventing the entry of goods into the channels of commerce in their jurisdiction and preserving evidence in regard to the alleged infringement,

see TRIPS art. 50. Arts 49 and 50 of the PRC *Copyright Law* deal with this requirement.

31 *See*, TRIPS art. 43 and PRC *Copyright Law*, art. 52.

32 2000 *Patent Law*, art. 6 (3).

33 *Ibid.*, art. 11.

34 *Ibid.*, arts 41, 57.

35 *Ibid.*, art. 61 (1).

36 *Ibid.*, arts 48–55. The conditions are refusal for dealing, national emergency or urgency and dependent patent. In addition, the Implementing Rules of the *Patent Law* 2001, art. 72 requires that compulsory licensing is limited for domestic market; and in case of semiconductor technology, the exploitation has to be for public non-commercial use or to remedy a practice determined by courts or administrative authority to be anti-competitive.

37 2000 *Patent Law*, art. 60.

38 2001 *Trademark Law*, art 8.

39 *Ibid.*, art. 3 (1), (3).

40 *Ibid.*, art. 16.

41 *Ibid.*, art. 13.

42 *Ibid.*, art. 32.

43 *Ibid.*, arts 57, 58.

44 *Ibid.*, art. 56 (2).

45 H. P. Glenn, *Legal Traditions of the World: Sustainable Diversity in Law* (3rd ed.), New York: Oxford University Press, 2007: 332.

46 The Trial Regulations on Copyright Protection for Books and Periodicals, issued by the Ministry of Culture and on 15 June 1984, and effective from 1 January 1985.

47 Peter Feng, *Intellectual Property in China*, Hong Kong: Sweet & Maxwell, 1997: 50.

48 CTR, art. 2.

49 CTR, art. 5.

50 CTR, art. 14. *See also*, Feng, *supra note* 47, pp. 50–51.

51 CTR, art. 1 and 1990 *Copyright Law*, art. 1.

52 1990 Copyright Law, art. 1.

53 Feng, *supra note* 47, p. 5.

54 Art. 14 of 2000 *Patent Law*.

55 Art. 20 of the revised *Science and Technology Law* clearly allows scientists or their institutions to own patents on inventions, copyrights on computer software, layout design of integrated circuits and rights on new varieties of plants developed from publicly funded research projects.

56 Glenn, *supra note* 45, p. 333.

57 *Ibid.*, p. 334.

58 *Ibid.*

59 H. von Senger, *Chinese Culture and Human Rights*, Munich: C.H. Beck, 1994: 303.

60 Alford, *supra note* 1, p. 79.

61 The 2003 amendment provides that administrative action can be taken only if the case involves 'public interest'; that local copyright authorities have jurisdiction to take administrative actions; that officials can exercise initiative in taking administrative measures even if the case is not emergent; that the suspected

infringers bear the burden of proof; that copyright authorities have no power to decide on damage awards; and the amendment also provides benchmarks for deciding what are 'serious cases'.

62 For example, art. 60 of the *Patent Law* provides that 'In the event that a dispute arises out of any exploitation of a patent without permission of the patentee, that is, the infringement upon a patent right, the parties shall settle the dispute through negotiations. If they are not willing to negotiate or fail to reach an agreement through negotiations, the patentee or any interested party may either bring a lawsuit with the people's court, or request the patent administrative department, for settlement. If the patent administrative department ascertains at the time of settlement that infringement exists, it may order the infringer to immediately stop the infringement act'.

63 Art. 64, PRC *Patent Law* (amended in 2008).

64 Chapter VI and arts 44–50, and 53–55.

65 For example, art. 55 of the *Copyright Law* provides that 'any party who is not satisfied with an administrative penalty may institute proceedings in the People's Court within three months from the date of receipt of the written decision on the penalty. If a party neither institutes legal proceedings nor implements the decision within the time limit, the copyright administration department concerned may apply to the People's Court for enforcement'. Similar provisions are provided in *Trademark Law* art. 50 (with 15 days to institute judicial review) and *Patent Law* art. 60 (also with 15 days to institute judicial review).

66 Compared with 286 articles in the Hong Kong *Copyright Ordinance*, 99 articles in the Hong Kong *Trademarks Ordinance*, and 163 articles in the Hong Kong *Patent Ordinance*.

67 Feng, *supra note* 47, pp. 60–61.

68 Alford, *supra note* 1, p. 2.

69 *Ibid.*, pp. 19–29.

70 *Ibid.*, pp. 45–49.

71 *Ibid.*, p. 49.

72 State Intellectual Property Office (SIPO) Management and Development Bureau, 'Patent applications reached five million', *Patent Statistics*, 23 March 2009, No. 7, accessed www.sipo.gov.cn/sipo2008/ghfzs/zltjjb/200903/P020090330379382318864.pdf (accessed 30 March 2009)

73 Liu Ren, 'China's trademark registration ranked No. 1 for 6 consecutive years'. http://www.sipo.gov.cn/sipo2008/ztzl/zxhd/ggkf/bdpl/hg/200812/t20081218_430597.html (accessed 15 December 2009)

74 Liu San, 'Perfecting IP adjudication through trials', http://www.sipo.gov.cn/sipo2008/ztzl/zxhd/ggkf/bdpl/hg/200812/t20081218_430595.html (accessed 20 April 2009)

75 Alford, *supra note* 1, p. 30.

Part III

Corporate law

7 Who writes corporate law rules?

The making of the 'piercing the corporate veil rule' as a case study

*Chao Xi**

7.1. Introduction

An intriguing, albeit less studied, issue in Chinese law is: What forces have shaped the evolution of legal rules in China? Traditionally, the Chinese law-making process has been seen as a top-down one dominated by the political elite, the Party and government institutions, with minimal input from non-state actors.[1] Enactment and enforcement of laws and regulations have largely been shaped by ideological pursuits and national policies[2] and by the political bargaining and compromise between powerful central-level state actors[3] and between the central and the local governments.[4]

This traditional wisdom has been challenged, however, by many recent studies. Economic reforms, it is argued, have redefined the social structure and are changing the distribution of power between the state and society.[5] Society has exhibited an ability to influence the Chinese state, and there are some encouraging signs a civil society, however fledging, is emerging.[6] It has been suggested that both the process and substance of law- and policy-making have also undergone a fundamental transformation. Although the central government agencies remain powerful policy-makers, they have lost a great deal of control over their policy agency.[7] Therefore, China's national economic laws and policies can no longer be viewed as uninformed intention of a strong state or merely the product of bargaining between government agencies. The process is now far more open, consultative, reactive and adaptive than it was in early post-Mao years.[8]

This chapter represents an attempt to further our understanding of the intriguing issue of who writes legal rules in China by focusing on the corporate law-making in China.[9] The sweeping company law reform in 2005 presents a rare glimpse into the dynamics of corporate law-making in China. Drawing upon first-hand legislative materials, an earlier study argues that the trajectory of board governance reforms in China has been shaped not only by the official ideology and the policy agendas of the China Securities Regulatory Commission and other central government agencies, but also by interest groups politics.[10] Board governance issues, which affect all listed companies, have become ones on which relevant interest groups within the listed companies – the majority shareholders, the minority shareholders, the incumbent managers, the supervisors and the employees – compete to exert their influence. The dynamics of interest group politics explains, in part, the unique pattern of change in formal board governance rules.[11]

Yet, it remains largely unclear as to whether the involvement of interest group politics in the making of corporate board governance rules is an exception or represents an emerging trend. Other rules, in addition to the board governance rules, that were the subject of intense public debate occurring in the 2005 company law reform are in particular useful in our examination of the making of corporate legal rules in China. This chapter looks into the enactment of one of these rules, i.e., 'piercing the corporate veil rule', in the 2005 company law reform.

China embraced the doctrine of piercing the corporate veil in 2005 when it revamped its company law regime. The doctrine is primarily enshrined in the newly added Art 20(3), which reads

> Where any of the shareholders of a company evades the payment of its debts by abusing the independent status of corporate legal person and the shareholders' limited liability, and thus seriously damages the interests of any creditors, it shall bear joint liability for the debts of the company.

This abstract statutory provision has been the subject of criticism. Commentators have noted that the provision gives little guidance to how veil-piercing cases are decided, and fails to indicate whether or not this provision applies to non-voluntary creditors.[12] Numerous proposals have been put forward to substantiate the vague statutory formulation with more clear-cut standards.[13]

This chapter asks a different question: Why did the Chinese law-makers opt to adopt the current version of the veil-piercing doctrine, which is characterized by vagueness and abstraction? There are many possible reasons which have been advanced. The limited capacity and inexperience on the part of the drafters may be a contributing factor;[14] Chinese law-makers might lack knowledge of veil-piercing rules in foreign jurisdictions.[15] Another reason could also be that Art 20(3) has been intentionally drafted in a vague manner that enables the provision to respond to rapid social and economic changes in China.[16]

This chapter argues that the veil-piercing provision in the 2005 *Company Law* is, in part, a product of political compromise. It shows that the Supreme People's Court (SPC) – China's highest-level court – had in effect embraced the doctrine of piercing the corporate veil and developed veil-piercing standards, featured by the test of separateness, prior to the 2005 company law reform. However, opposition from powerful political actors during the legislative process has prevented such standards from being adopted to date.

The chapter proceeds as follows. It first examines the bifurcated veil-piercing regime that the SPC developed before the 2005 company law reform in Parts 2 and 3. Part 4 then looks into the legislative debate leading to the enactment of Art 20(3) of the 2005 *Company Law* – the key veil-piercing provision.

Part 5 introduces the post-2005 development in veil-piercing rules and Part 6 concludes this chapter.

7.2. SPC's 'quasi'-veil-piercing rules: shareholders' personal liability for corporate debts

Prior to the enactment of the 2005 *Company Law*, the SPC developed judicial rules under which the shareholders of a company could be held personally liable for the debts of the company. As we will show in the following section, the shareholder's liability under these rules is, in most cases, not beyond the extent of their stated investments. As such, we call these rules quasi-veil-piercing rules. While these quasi-veil-piercing rules made their first appearance in Chinese law as early as the late 1980s,[17] the focus of our discussion is on three SPC judicial interpretations, which for ease of reference are referred to as 1994 Reply,[18] 2001 Regulations[19] and 2003 Regulations.[20] Under these currently valid SPC normative documents, Chinese courts may hold shareholders liable for the debts of the company under two circumstances: first, where shareholders fail to comply with the registered capital rules and, second, where shareholders are in breach of the capital maintenance rules.

7.2.1. Violation of the registered capital rules

As with many continental European jurisdictions,[21] the 1993 *Company Law* – repealed and replaced by the 2005 *Company Law* – laid down a set of stringent legal capital rules for limited liability companies. Of particular relevance to the present discussion are two rules on registered capital. The first rule is the full payment of registered capital. The 1993 *Company Law* required that shareholders of a company pay in full, either in cash or in kind, the registered capital as a condition precedent of company registration. Partial payment or payment by instalments was not permissible. The second is the minimum capital requirement. The 1993 *Company Law* required that the capital paid in be not lower than the minimum level of capital prescribed by the Law.[22]

A shareholder's non-compliance with the minimum capital requirement constitutes a ground for veil piercing under the 1994 Reply, which governs the determination of the parent company's liabilities for the debts that its subsidiary has incurred, where the subsidiary's is closed down or terminates business. The parent company faces risks of piercing if it has not in fact made any contribution to the subsidiary or the subsidiary paid in capital fails to meet the specific minimum capital thresholds. The court will order that the subsidiary permanently – though not retrospectively[23] – loses its separate legal personality, and its debts and obligations fall on the shoulders of the parent company.[24]

Likewise, the violation of the full payment of registered capital rule on the part of the parent company may also trigger liability for the obligations of the subsidiary. Under the 1994 Reply, the parent will be held liable, if it has met the minimum capital requirement but fails to pay the registered capital in full, for the unsatisfied claims of its subsidiary's creditors. In addition, the parent company's liability is limited to the shortfall between the paid-up capital and the registered capital.[25]

It was unclear, until the 2001 Regulations was issued, as to whether or not the parent's liability for the shortfall is limited or unlimited. This issue arises from the way in which the laws in relation to liquidation of enterprises were administered in China. Under Chinese law, creditors are, like their Western counterparts, required to join in a single liquidation proceeding in which all of the debtor's assets are sold and the proceeds distributed among all the creditors in a prescribed order. For many reasons, the liquidation requirements were not often followed. More often than not, insolvent or otherwise disabled enterprises did not enter into liquidation.[26] This enabled creditors to bring separate lawsuits by virtue of the 1994 Reply to satisfy their individual claims. In some cases, the parent company was held liable to pay each and every creditor the amount of registered but unpaid capital.[27] The 2001 Regulations disapproves of the imposition of, in effect, joint and unlimited liability on the parent company for the subsidiary's debts. For the avoidance of doubt, the 2001 Regulations in its Art 10 makes it explicit that once the parent has been made to pay the shortfall to any one of the debtors, it is deemed to have complied with the requirement for full payment of registered capital and is exempted from the shortfall liability going forward.

7.2.2. *Violation of the capital maintenance rules*

In addition to the registered capital rules, Chinese company law includes some forms of capital maintenance rules. As a general principle, shareholders are prohibited from 'withdrawing' paid-in capital.[28] In other words, paid-in capital may not be returned to shareholders.

The prohibition against asset withdrawal is embodied in a rule in the 2001 Regulations: a gratuitous or unfair value transfer to shareholders will expose the personal assets of the shareholders to the claims of the corporate creditors. As the 2001 Regulations was designed to govern the disputes associated with the enterprises established by public bodies (the Communist Party, government, military organs, legal enforcement departments and judicial institutions),[29] the rule is applicable merely to the determination of the public bodies' liability for the debts incurred by its affiliated enterprises. Moreover, the rule is twofold. First, where the public bodies transferred to themselves, presumably without deceptive intent, funds or property belonging to their affiliated enterprises, they are liable for the enterprises' debts and their liability is limited to the amount that has been transferred.[30] Second, where the public bodies, for the purpose of evading debts, withdrew or transferred funds from, or otherwise concealed assets of, their affiliated enterprises, such funds and assets shall be restituted so as to satisfy the creditors.[31] Apparently, the 2001 Regulations limits the liability of the public bodies for their affiliated enterprises' debts to the amount that they have siphoned out of the affiliates. This is so even if the level of capital of the affiliate falls, as a result of fraudulent transfers, below the statutory capitalization requirements.[32]

By comparison, the rule contained in the 2003 Regulations is far stricter in protecting corporate creditors against opportunistic shareholders. Art 35 of the 2003 Regulations deals with an issue that arises from the so-called enterprise restructuring: the controlling shareholder's liability for the debts incurred by the controlled company where the control is gained by means of acquisition of the controlled company. Art 35 starts with a general provision that the acquisition of the controlled company does not lead to the shift of the controlled company's debts to the controlling shareholder, and the controlled company should be made liable for its own debts. This is in line with a fundamental principle that companies holding shares in other companies enjoy limited liability in respect of their investment.[33] However, the veil of immunity is to be lifted, i.e. the controller will be held personally liable for the debts of the controlled company, if the controller 'withdraws assets from the controlled company in order to evade debts, thereby rendering the controlled company unable to meet its obligations'.[34]

Unlike most other SPC rules examined in this section, the Art 35 rule does not limit the liability of the perpetrating shareholder either to the registered but unpaid capital or to the illegal distribution to the shareholder in violation of the capital maintenance rules. Instead, the liability under Art 35 is joint and unlimited, and it is contingent on the fraudulent behaviour on the part of the controlling shareholder. Some commentators regard it as a useful attempt by the SPC to introduce the veil-piercing doctrine.[35] Important as it is, the Art 35 rule has limited applicability. First, it is restricted to the circumstance where the controlling shareholder is an enterprise. An individual who commits a fraud to the detriment of the corporate creditors by violating the statutory capital maintenance rule could be exempted from Art 35. Second, the Art 35 rule is applicable only to disputes arising from 'enterprise restructuring'.

7.3. Moving towards veil piercing: 2003 SPC draft company law interpretations and practice

While the SPC judicial rules examined in the foregoing section provide corporate creditors with some protection against opportunistic shareholders, the protection tended to be weak. As we have shown earlier, these rules are very narrowly tailored.[36] Only in very limited circumstances can shareholders defrauding the company's creditors be held liable for the company's debts beyond their stated investments in the company, i.e. the registered capital. The SPC began in 2003 to develop a more full-fledged veil-piercing regime, by drafting judicial interpretations of the 1993 *Company Law* and by reporting veil-piercing cases.

7.3.1. 2003 SPC's company law interpretations (consultation draft)

The SPC published in November 2003 a consultation document entitled the Regulations on Several Issues Concerning the Adjudication of Cases Involving Company Disputes (I) (hereinafter, SPC Consultation Draft).[37] The SPC Consultation Draft focuses on four areas of law where 'difficult issues often arose in legal proceedings and much research had been conducted'.[38] Disregarding the corporate entity is one of these areas. Under the heading of 'shareholders' direct liability to the corporate creditors', the SPC Consultation Draft contains six articles (Arts 48–53) setting the parameters of disregarding the corporate entity, to which we now turn.

Art 48 provides that courts strictly adhere to the principles of separate corporate personality and of shareholder limited liability. Only when the case falls into the circumstances prescribed by the SPC Consultation Draft (under Art 51, as we will see immediately below) may courts thrust personal liability upon the controlling shareholder. Art 48 serves two purposes: First, it defines how the veil-piercing doctrine relates to the general principle of limited liability: Limited liability is the general principle and veil piercing exists as an exception to the principle. Second, and more important, this provision constrains the court's discretion to pierce. Art 53 buttresses Art 48 by further providing that a piercing decision has no effect on companies or shareholders who are not involved in the court proceeding.

The SPC's cautious approach to piercing the corporate veil is also embodied in Art 49, which regulates the standing of the plaintiff. Under Art 49, courts are instructed to only accept veil-piercing cases initiated by the corporate creditors who seek to hold the controlling shareholder liable for corporate debts on the ground that the controlling shareholder has abused the privilege of limited liability to the detriment of the company's creditors. Neither the corporation itself nor its shareholders are eligible for petitioning the court to pierce the veil of the corporation.

Having laid down the principles, the SPC Consultation Draft develops a test of separateness in determining whether the privilege of limited liability has been abused. Art 51 provides that the company and its controlling shareholder should be seen to have no separate existence and, consequently, the shareholder should 'bear joint liability' for the corporate debts under three circumstances: First, the corporate income is not separated from the controlling shareholders' own income, thus resulting in the commingling of accounts.[39] The second circumstance is where the company and its controlling shareholder commingle business funds with personal funds, and they continuously use the same accounts.[40] The third circumstance is that there is a constant commingling of corporate business and personal business, and the company's business transactions are under complete control of the controlling shareholder.[41] It is apparent that under Art 51 the separateness between the company and its shareholders is the sole determinative factor as to whether or not the corporate entity has been abused.[42] Unlike the US instrumentality rule, which requires proof of commitment of fraud or wrong on the part of the controlling shareholder,[43] the SPC Consultation Draft has adopted a non-fault standard. The fact that the company has no separate finances and business of its own, standing alone, suffices. Whether the controlling shareholder has used its control to commit a fraud or wrong is not a factor of relevance.

We have seen above that the SPC tried to define with meticulous care the boundaries of the doctrine of piercing the corporate veil. It is worth noting, however, that the SPC Consultation Draft contains two groups of rules that go beyond the standard boundaries. First, regardless of whether or not the shareholders have abused the privilege of limited liability, the SPC Consultation Draft invariably lifts the veil between the de facto one-member company and its shareholders. As one-member companies have been recognized by the 2005 Company Law,[44] this set of rules is not of relevance to our discussion.

The second group of rules is applicable specifically to cases involving parent and subsidiary companies.[45] Art 52 provides that if the controlling company abuses the corporate entity, it should be deprived of the right to set off. In other words, the controlling shareholder would not be allowed to set off the debts due by the subsidiary against this shareholder's own indebtedness to the subsidiary. Should the subsidiary become insolvent, the wrongdoing parent company faces two consequences: First, the parent's claims against the subsidiary ranking in priority to those of the ordinary unsecured creditors are deprived of the priority; and second, the parent's claims, presumably both secured and unsecured, are subordinated to those of other unsecured creditors of the subsidiary. The latter subordination rule is arguably the SPC's first attempt to embrace the doctrine of equitable subordination[46] or the Deep Rock doctrine in the US bankruptcy law.[47]

The Consultation Draft was scheduled to be issued in 2004. The SPC did not, however, finally adopt it for implementation, presumably because of the the NPC's decision in 2004 to put the revision of the 1993 Company Law at top of the legislative agenda.[48] After all, it is unwise to issue interpretations of the soon-to-be-amended law when the new law was in the pipeline. Despite the non-adoption of the SPC Consultation Draft, it is of significant value to the present study for two reasons. First, the SPC Consultation Draft presents a consolidated statement of the SPC's policy, as it was prior to the 2005 company law reform, on, among other things, the veil-piercing doctrine. Second, though the SPC Consultation Draft was not adopted and is consequently not binding on Chinese courts, reported SPC cases seem to have followed the single-factor test of separateness which the Consultation Draft developed.

7.3.2. SPC practice

Since 1985, the SPC has published decided cases in its official Gazette. Though they are not generally regarded as precedents,[49] these Gazette cases are intended to give guidance to Chinese courts on how to apply legal rules and judicial interpretations where there is a legislative lacunae, conflict or ambiguity. For the same purposes, the Second Civil Division of the SPC has published selected cases in its official publication, *Guide on Civil and Commercial Trial*. These reported cases, in particular, the Gazette cases, have played an increasingly significant role in the elaboration and development of legal principles and doctrines in China.[50] Prior to the 2005 company reform, two SPC veil-piercing cases were reported.

In *US Minmetals Inc. v. Xiamen United Development (Group) Co. Ltd*,[51] a Gazette case, the appellant, US Minmetals Inc. (US Minmetals), entered into a series of contracts of sale of goods with Xiamen United Development Import & Export Trading Co. (U&D Trading), a wholly owned subsidiary of the defendant, Xiamen United Development (Group) Co. Ltd (U&D Group). US Minmetals delivered the goods to U&D Trading in accordance with the terms of the contracts, but U&D Trading failed to make full payment for the goods. US Minmetals successfully obtained an arbitration award against U&D Trading, and sought to enforce the award only to find out that U&D Trading had already failed and there were no assets to satisfy its claim. In frustration, US Minmetals brought an action against U&D Group, seeking to hold the latter liable for the amount remaining unpaid, together with interest, under the contracts of sale to which U&D Trading agreed. US Minmetals alleged that U&D Group had violated relevant laws and regulations in establishing U&D Trading, and should thus be made liable for the debts incurred by U&D Trading.

The SPC pointed out that the essence of the plaintiff's allegation is that the corporate entity of U&D Trading should be disregarded. The SPC noted that in China, the privilege of limited liability is granted to all enterprises that are registered with the government agency in charge of industry and commerce administration as 'legal persons'. Promoters or investors of these 'legal person' enterprises are not liable for the obligations of the enterprises beyond their registered investment in the enterprises. The court acknowledged that enterprise registration in China is mostly a legal formality and that no 'substantive and strict examinations' are undertaken to ensure that the enterprises registered as the 'legal persons' have met all the requirements for qualifying as a legal person. As such, the privilege of limited liability may be abused. The court then defined what constitutes the abuse of the privilege of limited liability:

> When a shareholder behind the veil of limited liability abuses corporate personality and harms the interests of the company and its creditors, it means in fact that the shareholder divests assets in order to evade debts and establishes a new company with such assets, or the shareholder withdraws his capital investment in a company after it is established, or the shareholder commingles the assets of the company with those of his own, or the shareholder interferes with the business of the company in such an arbitrary manner that the company has no independent operation of its own.

This definition seems to build on the basis of, first, the separateness test developed by the SPC Consultation Draft and, second, the rationales underlying the SPC normative documents that address the violation of capital maintenance rules, both of which we have examined before.

Applying the definition to the facts of the case, the SPC opined that US Minmetals presented no evidence to prove that U&D Group had diverted assets in order to evade debts or that U&D Group had withdrawn capital invested in U&D Trading. The court also set aside US Minmetals' request to audit the financial accounts of U&D Trading so as to ascertain whether or not the assets or accounts of U&D Trading were commingled with those of U&D Group, ruling that the request was without legal or factual foundation. Taken as a whole, the SPC rejected the allegation made by US Minmetals that U&D Group was to be held liable for the unfulfilled contractual obligations of its subsidiary.

A similar set of criteria was used in another reported SPC case, *China Construction Bank, Chengdu Municipality Jinhe Sub-Branch v. Sichuan Communications Services Co., Sichuan Jinzu Industrial Co. and Sichuan Financial Leasing Joint Stock Co.*[52] to disregard the corporate veil between the parent company and its subsidiaries. Here, Sichuan Communications Services, the parent company, owned 50 per cent of the shares in Sichuan Jinzu Industrial Co., the subsidiary. The subsidiary's chairman and staff were simultaneously employees of the parent. Funds that the subsidiary had secured from banks were used to finance a project of the parent company. The parent was also in possession of various chops belonged to the subsidiary,[53] which, under Chinese law, in effect enabled the parent to enter into transactions that legally bind the subsidiary. The SPC opined that personnel, assets and business operation of the subsidiary were commingled with those of the parent and that the parent company exercised excessive control over the subsidiary by keeping the latter's chops. As such, the court lifted the corporate veil and held the parent company liable for the debts of the subsidiary.

The SPC, in the absence of statutory veil-piercing provisions, was prepared to embrace the doctrine of piercing the corporate veil and it has developed veil-piercing standards, characterized by the test of separateness. Reported SPC cases also show that the SPC had generally adhered to the test of separateness. This leads to an intriguing inquiry: Why has the test of separateness not been adopted alongside the doctrine of piercing the corporate veil? What has happened in the law-making process? It is to this puzzle that we now turn.

7.4. The legislative debate leading to art 20(3) of the 2005 *Company Law*

Law-making in China is a 'multi-stage, multi-arena' process.[54] In order to allow for a more focused discussion, we concentrate on two central stages of law-making: first, the drafting of the amendment bill and, second, the review and passage of the bill as law. Under the 2000 Legislation Law, a wide range of political actors have been formally empowered to put forward a bill for the National People's Congress (NPC) – China's highest legislative organ – or its

Standing Committee to review and enact.[55] In the case of the 2005 company law reform, it was the State Council that sponsored the Amendment Bill of the Company Law. The Amendment Bill, after being approved by the State Council, was then submitted to the NPC Standing Committee for review and passage. In this section, we examine the legislative debate leading to the enactment of Art 20(3) of the 2005 *Company Law*, which took place at the State Council and the NPC Standing Committee, respectively. The debate revolved around two issues: The first and foremost issue was whether or not the doctrine of 'disregarding the corporate entity' should be adopted. Second, if yes, whether or not the law should set bright-line veil-piercing standards?

7.4.1. *Legislative debate at the state council*

The State Council's own ministries, departments and agencies that have authority over the administration of China's corporate regime were naturally key players in the amendment process. This group included the State Administration for Industry and Commerce (SAIC), whose mandates include the registration and supervision of various forms of business organizations, Ministry of Commerce (MOFCOM), a potent regulator of both domestic markets and foreign trade and investment, State-Owned Assets Supervision and Administration Commission (SASAC), the *de facto* owner, manager and regulator of non-financial state-owned assets, especially in state-owned enterprises (SOEs), and China Securities Regulatory Commission (CSRC), the watchdog of China's securities markets. These powerful central government institutions, by virtue of their – sometimes overlapping – mandates and departmental interests, have routinely collaborated and competed in the making of rules affecting Chinese companies. Senior officials from these ministries were key members of the State Council's cross-departmental 'Leadership Group' and 'Working Group' on company law reform.[56]

It would be wrong to assume, however, the concerned State Council ministries and departments had a monopoly on determining how the 1993 *Company Law* was to be reformed. Bargaining, co-optation and consensus building that eventually shaped the Amendment Bill took place not just between State Council institutions. Many other state and non-state actors also played an influential role. Individual NPC delegates (and groups of NPC delegates), members of the National Committee of the Chinese People's Political Consultative Conference (CPPCC), All-China Federation of Trade Unions, localities, industry associations, lawyers' associations, large SOEs, academics and, of course, the SPC all tried to wield some influence over the reform. Moreover, these actors' access to the State Council–sponsored legislative process was through the State Council's Legislative Affairs Office (LAO).

Among its many mandates, LAO's principal task is to resolve legislative disputes – in particular, inter-agency disputes – and help build consensus, so that such disputes would not clog up State Council meetings that consider legislative bills. In order to do so, the LAO frequently organize seminars and colloquiums with, and invite submissions from, parties with vested interests in issues of common concern.[57] Despite their importance, views and concerns received during the drafting process by the LAO are normally not readily accessible to the general public.[58] The drafting process of the Amendment Bill was, however, made much more transparent by the LAO's publication of the three-volume collection of legislative materials.[59] These materials, including LAO's official bulletins on company law amendments, provide a rare glimpse into the dynamics of corporate law-making in China.

As mentioned, the foremost issue facing the Chinese law-makers was whether or not the doctrine of piercing the veil should be incorporated into the amended company law. A consensus on the issue – i.e. the adoption of the doctrine was necessary and compelling – appeared to have been reached among participants in the consultative process resulting in the Consultation Draft of the Amendment Bill.

The consensus began to emerge at the 2004 annual meetings of the NPC and the National Committee of the CPPCC, where 601 NPC delegates and 13 members of the National Committee of the CPPCC submitted proposals and bills urging a revamping of the 1993 *Company Law*.[60] Among them, 36 NPC delegates from Zhejiang Province, 32 delegates from Fujian Province, 31 delegates from Shanghai Municipality and 1 delegate from Beijing proposed that the new company law introduce the veil-piercing doctrine.[61] The fact that the proposal was backed by a large number of NPC delegates representing some wealthy and politically influential provinces presumably gave political momentum to the proposal.

Echoing the NPC delegates' proposal, there was a cross-sector and multi-level support for the establishment in China of 'the institution of disregarding corporate personality' – a term that has been used interchangeably with, but more commonly than, 'veil piercing' in the Chinese literature. SAIC,[62] MOFCOM,[63] large SOEs,[64] local lawyers' associations,[65] local judges,[66] arbitrators,[67] and academics[68] were all vocal advocates of transplanting the common-law doctrine into the new Chinese company law. While the indication of support came mostly in the form of a brief statement that the veil-piercing doctrine should be written into the company statute, the CSRC's amendment proposal contained interesting details, which read

> The connected person [*inter alia*, the controlling shareholder] shall not use his connection with the company to the detriment of the interests of the company; or, he shall compensate the company for the injury suffered, and his claims against the company shall be subordinated to the claims of other creditors. ... Where business and finance of the company commingle with those of its controlling shareholder or its *de facto* controller, the connected person shall be made jointly liable for the debts of the company.[69]

It is worth noting that the CSRC's proposal bore a stunning similarity to the veil-piercing provisions in the SPC Consultation Draft that we have examined earlier: The test of separateness and the equitable subornation rule were both present.

The SPC itself was an equally visible force that pushed for the transplantation of the veil-piercing doctrine. The SPC was commissioned by the LAO, with the aim to assist the drafting of the Amendment Bill,[70] to conduct a study on the issue of disregarding the corporate entity. Two senior judges from the SPC Second Civil Division, with one being a member of the LAO's Export Group on Company Law Amendments, co-authored the report submitted to the LAO.[71] It was commonplace, the report noted, that shareholders in China abused the corporate form and the privilege of limited liability. The report admitted that, based upon a summary and review of the Chinese courts' own experience:

> The existing company law framework in our country has been unable to provide an effective solution to the problem [of rampant abuses of limited liability] … [There was] a sense of helplessness when [the courts] applied the existing laws, regulations and judicial interpretations to relevant [veil-piercing] cases.[72]

As such, the report reiterated, there was a compelling need to adopt the doctrine of lifting the veil which, in the eyes of its authors, has been proven effective in preventing abuses of limited liability in foreign jurisdictions.[73] The report proceeded to make a legislative proposal, drawing upon a comparative survey of veil-piercing rules in the United States, United Kingdom, Germany and Japan.[74] Composed of twenty articles, the proposal was, on the face of it, more sophisticated and comprehensive than, but was in essence not significantly divergent from, the SPC Consultation Draft.

Given the overwhelming support for the codification of the veil-piercing doctrine, it is unsurprising that the Consultation Draft of the Amendment Bill included a new veil-piercing article consisting of two sections:

> The shareholders of a company shall abide by laws, administrative regulations and the company's articles of association, exercise their rights according to law, and shall not abuse limited liability to the detriment of the interests of the company's creditors or the interests of other stakeholders.
>
> [Art 19(1)]
>
> The controlling shareholder of the company shall remain independent from the company in respect of personnel, finance and business. Where personnel, finance and business of the controlling shareholder commingle with those of the company, the controlling shareholder shall be jointly liable for the debts of the company.
>
> [Art 19(2)]

While Art 19(1) represented a general policy statement that shareholders are prohibited from abusing the concept of limited liability, Art 19(2) was undoubtedly a substantive veil-piercing provision. It adopted the separateness test in determining whether or not the veil is to be lifted, and this appears to have been inspired by the SPC and CSRC's earlier endeavours.

When the Consultation Draft of the Amendment Bill was circulated for further comments, Art 19(2) met stiff opposition from a very powerful State Council agency, the SASAC: The SASAC proposed deleting Art 19(2), outright. To many, the opposition came as a surprise: Though the SASAC did not specifically back the adoption of veil-piercing doctrine, Art 19(2) seemed to have entertained the SASAC's initial suggestion that the new company law should seek to regulate the misuse of limited liability by the controlling shareholder.[75] The SASAC provided a justification for its proposal to remove Art 19(2): Art 19(2) originated from the CSRC's requirement that the listed company be kept separate from its controlling shareholder in respect of, *inter alia*, personnel, assets and finance – commonly known as 'three separations'.[76] That requirement was one designed specifically to 'address peculiar corporate governance issues arising from Chinese listed companies at a specific period time'. Hence, it would be inappropriate to extend its application to non-listed companies.[77] That is to say, non-listed companies should not be subject to the CSRC's requirement of 'three separations', since such requirement was no more than a regulatory expedient. It is debatable as to whether the CSRC's requirement of separateness is, as the SASAC alleged, just a regulatory manoeuvre. Even if the requirement was a means to achieving a particular regulatory goal, it does not necessarily follow that it cannot serve other purposes – preventing shareholders in non-listed companies from abusing the corporate entity is one of them.

The real, but unstated, concern of the SASAC in objecting to Art 19(2) may well be that Art 19(2), if adopted, could expose many SOEs to liability to which they had not been subject before. This proposition needs to be understood in light of a key weakness of China's SOE sector: The line between the SOEs and their subsidiaries was, at best, blurred and, in many cases, virtually non-existent. To be fair, the State Council and the Ministry of Finance had issued rules – similar to the CSRC requirement of 'three separations' – requiring the subsidiaries of SOEs to keep accounts, personnel, assets and organization separate from those of the parent SOEs.[78] Unlike Art 19(2), however, none of these pre-existing rules had imposed liability on the non-compliant SOEs for the debts of their subsidiaries. Art 19(2), if passed as law, would immediately make these SOEs vulnerable to claims of the subsidiaries' creditors, consequently, undermine their financial well-being. The perception of PetroChina – a giant SOE – as to the veil-piercing doctrine adds a footnote to our proposition. While PetroChina seemingly supported the adoption of the doctrine, the company's proposal was completely against the genius of the doctrine: In cases of commingling, PetroChina suggested, the shareholder should be held liable for the debts of the company only to the extent of the shareholder's investment.[79]

In what appears to be a response to the SASAC's opposition, Art 19(2) was removed in its entirety from the Amendment Bill submitted for review in

December 2004 by the State Council to the NPC Standing Committee. Art 19(1) remained intact. In the explanatory note accompanying the Amendment Bill, the LAO attempted to provide reasons for not supplementing Art 19(1) with veil-piercing rules.[80] The first reason given was that Chinese courts lacked the actual experience in handling claims to disregard the corporate form, and such experience is prerequisite to the making of the veil-piercing rules. In addition, the LAO noted that courts are the primary law-makers for piercing the veil in many jurisdictions such as United States, Germany, France and Japan.[81] Thus, the LAO suggested that it should be left to the courts to develop the veil-piercing rules in practice.

7.4.2. Legislative debate at the NPC

With the submission of the Amendment Bill, the central arena of company law reform shifted from the State Council to the NPC. The first reading of the State Council's Amendment Bill took place at the NPC Standing Committee in February 2005, after which the Bill was circulated widely for consultation and comments. The SPC was given a second chance to advance its views: The NPC Law Commission and the NPC Standing Committee Legislative Affairs Commission set up a meeting with SPC with a view to seeking advice from selected local courts.[82] In the consultative process, dissenting voices were raised concerning Art 19 of the Amendment Bill. Members of the NPC Standing Committee, NPC delegates, localities, State Council departments and academics all expressed their concern about the prevalent practice of shareholders abusing the corporate entity. More often than not, it was noted, opportunistic shareholders had engaged in unfair value transfers to the detriment of corporate creditors by means of, for example, divesting corporate assets for personal use or commingling corporate assets with personal assets. It was suggested that in such cases the opportunistic shareholders be held jointly liable for corporate debts.[83]

Based upon these and other comments received, a revised version of the Amendment Bill – Amendment Bill (Law Commission Review Draft)[84] – was prepared for the Law Commission's review session on 8–9 August 2005. A veil-piercing provision that differed slightly from what is now Art 20(3) of the 2005 *Company Law* was inserted:

> Where any of the shareholders of a company evades the payment of its debts or breaches statutory duties by abusing the independent status of corporate legal person and the shareholders' limited liability, and thus seriously damages the interests of any creditors or the interests of the general public, it shall bear joint liability for the debts of the company.

In addition, the LAO's suggestion that courts be the maker of veil-piercing standards was translated into a provision in the Law Commission Review Draft: 'The SPC shall determine the specific circumstances under which the shareholders are held jointly liable for the debts of the company'.

The Law Commission examined the two proposed amendments, and opted not to accept the proposed provision that specifically empowered the SPC to make veil-piercing rules. The rejection of the proposed provision does not, however, mean that the Chinese law-makers did not regard it necessary to make bright-line veil-piercing standards or that the law-makers perceived that other institutions are better suited than the SPC to come up with the standards. In fact, the law-makers made a thoughtful observation that any attempt to make an exhaustive list of all factors to be considered by judges when determining whether or not to pierce is set to fail. In the inflexible company law statute, the doctrine of veil piercing is better expressed at a high level of abstraction. The law-makers were also conscious of the risk that in the absence of clear-cut standards, the veil-piercing doctrine could be misapplied by Chinese judges. Nevertheless, they were inclined to believe that the SPC judicial interpretation is the appropriate forum for formulating, and if needed, refining the standards.[85]

The proposed veil-piercing provision was accepted with some minor amendments. The Law Commission felt compelled to adopt the provision in order to 'protect the interests of the creditors and preserve normal economic order'.[86] It also gave credit to the courts, suggesting that the formulation of the provision was based on the Chinese courts' own experience in handling piercing cases, on top of the cases and statutory provisions in foreign jurisdictions.[87] The veil-piercing provision, the Law Commission reiterated, is not to undermine the fundamental principle that the shareholder's liability is limited to its stated contribution to the company. The second and third readings of the Amendment Bill approved of the Law Commission's recommendations, and the provision became what is now Art 20(3) of the 2005 *Company Law*.

7.5. Post-2005 development: *China Cinda Asset Management* case

Since the promulgation of the 2005 *Company Law*, the SPC has issued two sets of judicial interpretations of this law,[88] and two other sets of interpretations are, at the time of writing, under discussion. However, none of the existing and forthcoming interpretations deals with the issue of piercing the corporate veil. Indeed, the SPC has given little formal guidance as to how to approach veil-piercing cases brought before Chinese courts, apart from indicating that Chinese courts may accept claims based upon Art 20(3) of the 2005 *Company Law*.[89] It seems that the SPC has, again, attempted to develop veil-piercing rules by means of publishing decided cases in the SPC Gazette.

It is generally understood that veil piercing under the Art 20(3) is limited to 'vertical piercing', i.e. the corporate veil is lifted in order to reach the assets of shareholders or parent companies. Commentators have proposed that 'horizontal piercing' should be permissible so that creditors could reach the assets of sibling companies under the common control with the pierced company.[90] A recent Gazette case, *China Cinda Asset Management Co., Chengdu Office v. Sichuan*

Tailai Decoration Project Ltd Co., Sichuan Tailai Real Estate Development Ltd Co. and Sichuan Tailai Entertainment Ltd Co.[91] demonstrates the SPC's willingness to allow horizontal piercing. In this case, a Mr Shen controlled, through a holding company, the three defendants, Tailai Decoration, Tailai Development and Tailai Entertainment. The court found that three subsidiaries operated out of the same address, used the same telephone numbers, and – for some time– shared management and financial personnel. In addition, among other things, bank loans extended to Tailai Decoration were used to finance a project of Tailai Entertainment, while the (partial) repayment of the loans was made jointly by the three subsidiaries. Revenue generated from Tailai Entertainment's project was used to pay for house rentals, utility bills and salaries of all three subsidiaries. The issue at question was whether Tailai Entertainment and Tailai Development were to be held liable for the debts, i.e. unpaid bank loans, incurred by Tailai Decoration and, if yes, on what basis.

It is worth noting that the 2005 *Company Law* is inapplicable to this case, since all transactions took place prior to the present law coming into effect.[92] The SPC resorted, again, to the test of separateness. It ruled that, based upon the aforementioned factual findings, there was a 'commingling of corporate personality' between the subsidiaries. That is, because of the way in which the subsidiaries conducted business, they ceased to exist as legal entities independent of and separate from each other. The subsidiaries' misconduct has 'defeated the object of establishing the system of legal person, violated the principles of bona fide, and fairness and harmed the interests of the creditors'.[93] This, the SPC concluded, allowed the courts to pierce the corporate veil between the sibling companies.

7.6. Concluding remarks

This chapter highlights the significant law-making role that the Chinese judiciary – in particular, the SPC – plays, and the political constraints and limits of the role.[94] Prior to the sweeping company law reform in 2005, the SPC attempted to embrace the doctrine of piercing the corporate veil, gradually developing both quasi-veil-piercing rules to hold shareholders personally liable for corporate debts and, more notably, veil-piercing standards characterized by the single-factor test of separateness. In the legislative process, however, the SPC's preference had to be weighed against the discrete, and sometimes, conflicting preferences of other political institutions, including powerful ministries. Outcomes of the process are likely to be the product of compromise. This helps to explain the mixed fate that the doctrine of piercing corporate veil has met: The doctrine, together with the test of separateness, was initially written into the Amendment Bill sponsored by the State Council, but was removed almost altogether amidst the stiff opposition of the SASAC. When the doctrine was eventually reinstated by the NPC Law Commission as Art 20(3) of the 2005 *Company Law*, it lost most of its teeth and is left in a state of vagueness and abstraction. The development of the veil-piercing rules in China does not end here, for certain. The SPC will continue to play a highly significant role in the elaboration, development and, perhaps, even innovation of veil-piercing rules, as evidenced by the recent development, including, the *China Cinda Asset Management* case.

This chapter represents a modest attempt to further our understanding of the nature of China's corporate law-making. The judiciary, interest group dynamics, official ideologies, national policies, powerful government agencies and forces of globalization all seem to have a role to play in corporate law-making. It remains far from clear, however, as to precisely how these forces interact to determine the trajectory of corporate legal rules in China. An inquiry into other corporate legal rules that were the subject of legislative debate in the 2005 company law reform would shed more light on this puzzling issue.

Notes

* The author would like to thank Donald Clarke, Jing Leng, Mike McConville, Randall Peerenboom, Roman Tomasic and Xianchu Zhang for their comments and discussion.

1 *See, generally*, S. Lubman, *Bird in a Cage: Legal Reform in China After Mao*, Stanford, Calif.: Stanford University Press, 1999.

2 *See*, e.g. D. Clarke, 'Corporate Governance in China: An Overview', *China Economic Review* 14, 2003: 494; Chao Xi, "Transforming Chinese Enterprises: Ideology, Efficiency and Instrumentalism in the Process of Reform' in J. Gillespie and P. Nicholson (eds), *Asian Socialism and Law Change: The Dynamics of Vietnamese Renewal and Chinese Reform*, Canberra: Asia Pacific Press, 2005: 91.

3 W. P. Alford and B. L. Liebman, 'Clean Air, Clean Processes? The Struggle over Air Pollution Law in the People's Republic of China', *Hastings Law Journal* 52, 2001: 703.

4 S. Green, *The Development of China's Stock Market, 1984–2002: Equity Politics and Market Institutions*, London: Routledge, 2004; A. C. Mertha, *The Politics of Piracy: Intellectual Property in Contemporary China*, Ithaca: Cornell University Press, 2005.

5 T. Saich, *Governance and Politics of China* (2nd edn), New York: Palgrave Macmillan, 2004.

6 M. Goldman, *From Comrade to Citizen: The Struggle for Political Rights in China*, Cambridge, Mass.: Harvard University Press, 2005.

7 M. S. Tanner, *The Politics of Lawmaking in China: Institutions, Processes, and Democratic Prospects*, Oxford: Clarendon Press, 1999.

8 K. S. Tsai, *Capitalism with Democracy: The Private Sector in Contemporary China*, Ithaca: Cornell University Press, 2007.

9 For excellent recent studies, *see*, e.g. Guanghua Yu, *Comparative Corporate Governance in China: Political Economy and Legal Infrastructure*, London: Routledge, 2007.

10 Chao Xi, 'In Search of an Effective Monitoring Board Model: Board Reforms and the Political Economy of Corporate Law in China', *Connecticut Journal of International Law* 22, 2006: 1.

11 For potential benefits that civil society institutions may bring to Chinese corporate governance, *see*, D. C. Clarke, 'Law Without Order in Chinese Corporate Governance Institutions', *Northwestern Journal of International Law & Business* 30, 2010: 125.

12 *See*, e.g. B. C. Reed, 'Clearing Away the Mist: Suggestions for Developing a Principled Veil Piercing Doctrine in China', *Vanderbilt Journal of Transnational Law* 39, 2006: 1643, 1667–1675; M. Wu, 'Piercing China's Corporate Veil: Open Questions from the New Company Law', *Yale Law Journal* 117, 2007: 328, 332–334.

13 For example, Xiaoming Xi and Jianfeng Jin, *Gongsi Susong de Lilun yu Shiwu Wenti Yanjiu* [Research on the Theory and Practice of the Company Litigation], Beijing: People's Court Press, 2008, Chapter 11; Ciyun Zhu, *Gongsifa Renge Fouren Zhidu Lilun yu Shijian* [Theory and Practice of Disregarding the Corporate Entity in Company Law], Beijing: People's Court Press, 2009.

14 C. Ross and L. Ross, 'Language and Law: Sources of Systemic Vagueness and Ambiguous Authority in Chinese Statutory Language', *University of British Columbia Law Review* 31, 1997: 205, 209.

15 This may not be the case though, as there was an informed debate within China about whether to adopt the veil-piercing doctrine, *see*, D. M. Albert, 'Addressing Abuse of the Corporate Entity in the People's Republic of China: New Thoughts on China's Need for a Defined Veil Piercing Doctrine', *University of Pennsylvania Journal of International Economic Law* 23, 2002: 873, 890–894.

16 P. H. Corne, 'Creation and Application of Law in the PRC', *American Journal of Comparative Law* 50, 2002: 369, 375; R. Peerenboom, *China's Long March Toward Rule of Law*, Cambridge: Cambridge University Press, 2002: 251.

17 For the early development of 'veil-piercing' rules, *see*, Xianchu Zhang, 'Piercing the Company Veil and Regulation of Companies in China' in Guiguo Wang and Zhenyin Wei (eds), *Legal Developments in China: Market Economy and Law*, Hong Kong: Sweet & Maxwell Asia, 1996: 129; Tingmei Fu, 'Legal Person in China: Essence and Limits', *American Journal of Comparative Law* 41, 1993: 261, 291–295.

18 *Guanyu Qiye Kaiban de Qita Qiye bei Chexiao Huozhe Xieye hou Minshi Zeren Chengdan Wenti de Pifu* [Reply on the Assumption of Civil Liability after Enterprises Established by an Enterprise Have Been Closed down or Have Terminated Business Operation], issued by the SPC on 30 March 1994.

19 *Guanyu Shenli Jundui, Wujing, Budui, Zhengfa Jiguan Yijiao, Chexiao he yu Dangzheng Jiguan Tuogou Qiye Xiangguan Jiufen Anjian Ruogan Wenti de Guiding* [Regulations on Several Issues of Adjudicating Disputes Involving the Enterprises Handed over or Closed down by the People's Liberation Army, the Armed Police Force and the Political–Legal Organs and the Enterprises Separated from the Party and Government Organs], promulgated by the SPC on 6 February 2001.

20 *Guanyu Shenli yu Qiye Gaizhi Xiangguan de Minshi Jiufen Anjian Ruogan Wenti de Guiding* [Regulations on Several Issues of Adjudicating Civil Dispute Cases in Relation to Enterprise Restructuring], promulgated by the SPC on 3 January 2003.

21 For discussion of legal capital rules in Europe, *see*, L. Enriques and J. R. Macey, 'Creditors versus Capital Formation: The Case against the European Legal Capital Rules', *Cornell Law Review* 86, 2001: 1165; J. Armour, 'Legal Capital: An Outdated Concept?', *European Business Organization Law Review* 7, 2006: 5; E. Ferran, 'The Place for Creditor Protection on the Agenda for Modernization of Company Law in the European Union', *European Company & Financial Law Review* 3, 2006: 178.

22 The minimum level of capital was commensurate with the nature of business in which the company is engaged. It was RMB500,000 yuan for a company engaged primarily in manufacturing or in wholesale, RMB300,000 yuan for a company engaged primarily in retail and RMB100,000 yuan for a company engaged primarily in R&D, consultancy or service provision. Art 23, 1993 *Company Law*.

23 It was unclear under the 1994 Reply as to whether the subsidiary loses its legal personality *ab initio*. The SPC issued in 1997 another Reply to provide that the contracts that the subsidiary has entered into prior to the revocation of its business licenses are not invalid. *See*, *Guanyu dui Zhuce Zijin Touru wei Dadao Fagui Guiding Zuidi Xian'e de Qiye Faren Qianding de Jingji Hetong Xiaoli Ruhe Queren Wenti de Pifu* [The Reply on the Determination of the Validity of the Contracts Entered into by Enterprise Legal Persons Whose Paid-Up Capital Has Not Reach the Minimum Thresholds Provided by Regulations], issued by the SPC on 25 February 1997. It seems to suggest that the piercing order does not have retrospective effect.

24 Art 1(3), 1994 Reply; Art 3, 2001 Regulations.

25 Art 1(2), 1994 Reply; Arts 2 & 10, 2001 Regulations. It is thus also commonly known as 'short-fall liability'.

26 Xiaoming Song, Yongjian Zhang and Min Liu, 'Zuigao Renmin Fayuan Guanyu Shiyong "Zhonghua Renmin Gongheguo Gongsifa" Ruogan Wenti de Guiding (Er) de Lijie yu Shiyong' [Interpretations and Application of the Regulations on Several Issues Regarding the Application of the PRC Company Law (II)], in Xiaoming Xi (ed.), *Minshangshi Shenpan Zhidao* [Guide on Civil and Commercial Trial], Beijing: China Law Press, 2008, Issue 2, pp. 26, 37.

27 Jianfeng Jin, 'Gongsi Renge Fouren Lilun Jiqi zai Woguo de Shijian' [Disregarding the Corporate Entity: Theories and Practice in Our Country], *Zhongguo Faxue* [China Legal Science] 2, 2005: 117, 123.

28 Art 34, 1993 *Company Law*; Art 36, 2005 *Company Law*.

29 For the rise and fall of the enterprises affiliated to public bodies in China, *see*, Dali L. Yang, *Remaking the Chinese Leviathan: Market Transition and the Politics of Governance in China*, Stanford, Calif.: Stanford University Press, 2004: 125–144.

30 Art 4, 2001 Regulations.

31 Art 5, 2001 Regulations.

32 Xiaoming Song, Yongjian Zhang and Xuemou Zhang, 'Gongsifa Yinan Wenti' [Difficult Issues in Company Law], in Xiaoming Xi (ed.), Minshangshi Shenpan Zhidao [Guide on Civil and Commercial Trial], Beijing: China Law Press, 2006(2): 22, 25. Xiaoming Song and Yongjian Zhang are Chief Judge and Deputy Chief Judge, respectively, of the Second Civil Division of the SPC, the division in charge of the adjudication of, among other things, company law cases.

33 E. Ferran, *Principles of Corporate Finance Law*, Oxford: Oxford University Press, 2008: 33.

34 Art 35, 2003 Regulations.

35 Junhai Liu, 'Xin Gongsifa Zhong Jiekai Gongsi Miansha Zhidu de Jieshi Nandian Tanxi' [Analysis of the Controversial Issues Regarding Piercing Corporate Veil in the Context of New Corporate Law], *Tongji Daxue Xuebao (Shehui Kexue Ban)* [Tongji University Journal (Social Science Section)] 17(6), 2006: 111, 112.

36 Albert, *supra note* 15, p. 883.

37 *Guanyu Shenli Gongsi Jiufen Anjian Ruogan Wenti de Guiding (Yi) (Zhengqiu Yijian Gao)*, promulgated by the SPC at its own official website on 3 November 2003 and at the *People's Court Daily* and the *China Securities News* on 5 November 2003.

38 Dongmin Wang, 'Gongsifa Sifa Jieshi Zhunbei Gongzuo Dashi Ji' [Major Events in the Preparation Work of the Draft Interpretations of the Company Law], available at http://www.zwmscp.com/list.asp?unid=17 (accessed 15 June 2009). Wang is a judge at the SPC Second Civil Division.

39 Art 51(1), SPC Consultation Draft.

40 Art 51(2), SPC Consultation Draft.

41 Art 51(3), SPC Consultation Draft.

42 Piercing based on a single factor is not entirely unfamiliar even to the US courts though. *See*, K. A. Strasser, 'Piercing the Veil in Corporate Groups', *Connecticut Law Review* 37, 2005: 637, 642–644.

43 R. C. Clark, *Corporate Law*, Boston: Little, Brown and Company, 1986: 37.

44 For a comparative study of laws on one-member companies, *see*, Jianlin Chen, 'Clash of Corporate Personality Theories: A Comparative Study of One-member Companies in Singapore and China', *Hong Kong Law Journal* 38, 2008: 425.

45 It appears that the SPC Consultation Draft does not draw a distinction between the liability of a parent company with respect to the debts of its subsidiaries and that of an individual investor with regard to the debts of the company of which he is a member. Art 51 applied indistinguishably to the controlling shareholder of all types, be it a natural person or an incorporated parent company.

46 As early as in 1999 a local court in Guangdong Province proposed to resort to the doctrine of equitable subordination in an insolvency proceeding. The Higher Court of Guangdong Province rejected the proposal, suggesting that there was no statutory basis for subordinating the claims of the controlling shareholder to those of outsider shareholders. *See*, Wenhui Wu, 'Pochan Fa zhong Kongzhi Qiye Congshu Qiuchang Yuanze Chutan' [A Study on the Equity Subordination of the Controlling Shareholder Claims in Insolvency Proceedings], available at http://www.law-lib.com/lw/lw_view.asp?no=700 (accessed 2 April 2009).

47 Comparative studies show that Germany has also developed a highly sophisticated regime of subordination of shareholder claims, and a number of continental European countries, including Austria, Italy and Spain, have followed the German example. For an introduction to and assessment of German law on subordination, *see* P. O. Mülbert, 'A Synthetic View of Different Concepts of Creditor Protection, or: A High-Level Framework for Corporate Creditor Protection', *European Business Organization Law Review* 7, 2006: 357, 394–399. The key difference between the US doctrine of equitable subordination and the German regime of subordination lies in the US requirement of misconduct on the part of the controlling shareholder. *See*, R. I. Pardo, 'Beyond the Limits of Equity Jurisprudence: No-Fault Equitable Subordination', *New York University Law Review* 75, 2000: 1489 (arguing that the 'use of a no-fault standard of equitable subordination by a bankruptcy court exceeds the limits of its equitable powers'.)

48 Ye Lin, *Gongsifa Yanjiu* [Studies on Company Law], Beijing: Renmin University Press, 2008: 112.

49 *Cf.* Nanping Liu, '"Legal Precedents" with Chinese Characteristics: Published Cases in the Gazette of the People's Republic of China', *Journal of Chinese Law* 5, 1991: 107.

50 Chenguang Wang, 'Law-Making Functions of the Chinese Courts: Judicial Activism in a Country of Rapid Social Changes', *Frontiers of Law in China* 4, 2006: 524, 541–542.

51 Judgment No. 4 (2004) of the SPC Fourth Civil Division, published in the SPC Gazette, 2005, Issue 12, 24–28. An English translation is published at *Chinese Journal of International Law* 7, 2008: 257.

52 Judgment No. 111 (2003) of the SPC Second Civil Division, reported in Min Liu, '"Faren Renge Fouren Zhidu" zai Ge'an zhong de Shenzhong Shiyong' [Cautious Use of the 'System of Disregarding Corporate Legal Personality' in Specific Proceedings],

in Xiaoming Xi (ed.), *Minshangshi Shenpan Zhidao* [Guide on Civil and Commercial Trial], Beijing: China Law Press, 1, 2005: 192.

53 For the roles and functions of company chops in China, *see* Pricewaterhouse-Coopers, 'Facing the Company Chops in China', available at http://www.pwccn.com/home/eng/cn_co_chops_may2009.html (accessed 19 May 2009).

54 M. S. Tanner, *The Politics of Lawmaking in China: Institutions, Processes, and Democratic Prospects*, Oxford, Clarendon Press, 1999: 209.

55 These include the State Council, Central Military Commission, SPC, Supreme People's Procuracy and NPC Standing Committee's own Sub-Committees. Art 24, 2000 *Legislation Law*.

56 *Legislative Materials III*, *infra* note 59, 379–380.

57 Tanner, *supra note* 54, p. 220.

58 Wu, *supra note* 12, p. 329 (noting that 'one can only speculate about why Chinese law-makers felt compelled to include veil-piercing provisions in the new Company Law', 'because of the relative lack of public transparency surrounding China's statutory drafting process'.).

59 Qiong Zhong (ed.), *Xin Gongsifa Xiuding Yanjiu Baogao* [Research Reports on the New Amendments to the Company Law], Beijing: China Legal Publishing House, 2005. The three volumes are referred, hereinafter, to as *Legislative Materials I*, *Legislative Materials II* and *Legislative Materials III*, respectively.

60 *Legislative Materials III*, *supra note* 59, 379.

61 *Legislative Materials I*, *supra note* 59, p. 20.

62 *Ibid.*, p. 46.

63 *Ibid.*, p. 75.

64 PetroChina Co. Ltd. *Legislative Materials I*, *supra note* 59, p. 56.

65 Beijing Lawyers' Association. *Legislative Materials I*, *supra note* 59, p. 52.

66 A division chief judge of the Chongqing Higher People's Court. *Legislative Materials I*, *supra note* 59, p. 8.

67 An arbitrator of Chongqing Arbitration Comission. *Legislative Materials I*, *supra note* 59, p. 8.

68 China Commercial Law Society, and a number of leading company law experts. *Legislative Materials I*, *supra note* 59, pp. 39, 84.

69 *Legislative Materials I*, *supra note* 59, p. 73.

70 *Legislative Materials III*, *supra note* 59, p. 380.

71 They are Judge Yongjian Zhang and Judge Jianfeng Jin. Judge Zhang was then the Deputy Chief Judge of the SPC Second Civil Division, and now a Vice President Judge of Heilongjiang Higher People's Court.

72 *Legislative Materials III*, *supra note* 59, p. 18.

73 *Ibid.*

74 *Ibid.*, pp. 3–13.

75 *Legislative Materials I*, *supra note* 59, 71.

76 The requirement of 'three separations' has been expanded to 'five separations' to include separation of organization and separation of assets.

77 *Legislative Materials I*, *supra note* 59, p. 106.

78 For example, Art 5, *Guoyou Qiye Xingban Qiye Ruogan Caiwu Wenti de Zanxing Guiding* [Provisional Regulations on Several Financial Issues Regarding Enterprises Established by SOEs] (issued by the Ministry of Finance on 9 February 1995); Sec 2.4, *Guowuyuan Pichuan Caizhengbu Guanyu Jiaqiang Guoyou Qiye Caiwu Jiandu Yijian de Tongzhi* [Circular of the State Council on Forwarding the Ministry of

Finance's Opinions Regarding Strengthening Financial Supervision of SOEs] (issued by the State Council on 27 February 1997).

79 *Legislative Materials I*, *supra note* 59, p. 56.

80 'Guanyu "Zhonghua Renmin Gongheguo Gongsifa (Xiuding Cao'an) de Shuoming"' [Explanations of the PRC Company Law (Amendment Bill)], in Jian An (ed.), *Zhonghua Renmin Gongheguo Gongsifa Shiyi* [Annotations of the PRC Company Law], Beijing: China Law Press, 2005, pp. 349, 355–356. This book is prepared by the Legislative Affairs Commission of the NPC Standing Committee, and contains authoritative annotations of the 2005 *Company Law*. It is referred to, hereinafter, as *Legislative Annotations*.

81 A survey of pierce-the-corporate-veil rules in various jurisdictions was conducted by the State Council. The conclusion was that, in an overwhelming majority of the jurisdictions surveyed, the doctrine of piercing has been created and developed by the courts and has no explicit statutory basis. *See Legislative Materials II*, *supra note* 59, p. 135.

82 Jian An, 'Gongsifa de Quanmian Xiuding he Xiuding de Zhuyao Neirong' [Wholesale Amendments to the Company Law and the Main Contents of the Amendments], *Legislative Annotations*, *supra note* 80, pp. 1, 4.

83 NPC Law Commission, *Quanguo Renda Falü Weiyuanhui Guanyu Zhonghua Renmin Gongheguo Gongsifa (Xiuding Cao'an) Shenyi Jieguo de Baogao* [The NPC Legal Committee's Report on the Review Outcomes of the PRC Company Law (Amendment Bill)]. *Legislative Annotations*, *supra note* 80, pp. 414, 415–416.

84 On file with the author.

85 *Legislative Annotations*, *supra note* 80, pp. 44–45.

86 *Ibid.*

87 *Ibid. Cf.* the LAO's argument that local judicial experience was inadequate to buttress the codification of veil piercing, text accompanying *supra note* 81.

88 *Zuigao Renmin Fayuan Guanyu Shiyong 'Zhonghua Renmin Gongheguo Gongsifa' Ruogan Wenti de Guiding (Yi)* [Regulations on Several Issues Regarding the Application of the PRC Company Law (I)], issued by the SPC on 28 April 2006 (concerning mainly with the applicability of the 2005 *Company Law*); *Zuigao Renmin Fayuan Guanyu Shiyong 'Zhonghua Renmin Gongheguo Gongsifa' Ruogan Wenti de Guiding (Er)* [Regulations on Several Issues Regarding the Application of the PRC Company Law (II)], issued by the SPC on 12 May 2008 (dealing with issues arising from dissolution and liquidation of companies).

89 *Minshi Anjian Anyou Guiding* [Regulations on the Causes of Civil Cases], issued by the SPC on 4 February 2008, effective on 1 April 2008.

90 Junhai Liu, *supra note* 35, p. 114.

91 Judgment No. 55 (2008) of the SPC Second Civil Division, published in the SPC Gazette, 2008, Issue 10, p. 27.

92 Art 2 of the SPC Regulations on Several Issues Regarding the Application of the PRC Company Law (I), *supra note* 88.

93 *Supra note* 91, p. 37.

94 There is an emerging literature on the Chinese courts' rule-making outside of their routine judicial decision-making. *See*, e.g. Chenguang Wang, 'Law-Making Functions of the Chinese Courts: Judicial Activism in a Country of Rapid Social Changes', *Frontier of Law in China* 1, 2006: 524; R. Peerenboom, 'Courts as Legislators: Supreme People's Court Interpretations and Procedural Reforms' (The Foundation for Law, Justice and Society, 2007); B. L. Liebman and T. Wu,

'China's Network Justice', *Chicago Journal of International Law* 8, 2007: 257; N. C. Howson, 'The Doctrine That Dared Not Speak Its Name: Anglo-American Fiduciary Duties in China's 2005 *Company Law* and Case Law Intimations of Prior Convergence' in H. Kanda, *et al.* (eds), *Transforming Corporate Governance in East Asia*, London: Routledge, 2008: 193.

8 Looking at corporate governance in China's large companies

Is the glass half full or half empty?

Roman Tomasic

8.1. Introduction

Although it has a much longer history, the national and multilateral pursuit of enhanced corporate governance has been strongly articulated in the rhetoric of capitalist markets over the last two decades. Western-inspired corporate governance models have been heavily oriented towards self-regulatory approaches to regulation. This has seen the development of model corporate governance codes; these have often been motivated by the desire to prevent government intervention in markets. Where the state has intervened and passed laws that seek to affect the structure of corporate governance, these are sometimes seen as merely putting in place rules that market actors would have devised themselves had they sought to negotiate appropriate rules. However, in China, the corporate governance project has been a top-down exercise with the State playing a major role in fashioning and implementing this agenda.

After the events of the recent global financial crisis, assumptions about the value of the corporate governance project, as currently conceived, must be called into question. Such questioning was evident when the former Chairman of the US Federal Reserve, Alan Greenspan, expressed his amazement at the failure of financial markets to self-correct because of the selfishness of banks that were not prepared to support other financial institutions that were in crisis. As Greenspan admitted: 'Those of us who have looked to the self-interest of lending institutions to protect shareholders' equity, myself included, are in a state of shocked disbelief'.[1]

The effectiveness of corporate governance often depends upon the readiness of those who control corporations to voluntarily apply widely accepted corporate governance rules. Not surprisingly, corporate law is also often seen as largely self-enforcing.[2] Associated with this has been the idea of light-touch regulation and the reliance upon the self-interest of market actors to ensure that markets are well regulated.[3] However, the recent global financial crisis has shown that over-reliance upon minimal State intervention in markets and the self-regulatory features of markets can be disastrous. This has seen a rebalancing with a greater space being given to regulation and enforcement. This also applies to corporate governance norms. The recent crisis has demonstrated massive failures in the spirit of corporate governance ideas, despite widespread compliance with the letter of corporate governance codes. Not only is there a case for stronger regulatory oversight of markets, but we also now know that corporate governance norms are most effective when they are embedded within the culture and fabric of the corporation.[4] The challenge is to get this balance right.[5]

In recent decades, multilateral bodies such as the World Bank and the Organization for Economic Cooperation and Development (OECD) have played a major role in promoting the dissemination of corporate governance ideas well beyond the countries in which these ideas were first developed. Some have pointed to the pernicious aspects of this process of fostering narrow Anglo-American models of corporate governance in transitional economies.[6] Such outside efforts have usually been promoted within the context of various assumptions regarding the manner in which transition economies should advance. In regard to the dominant State-owned enterprise sector, in transitional economies such as China, Peter Nolan, for example, points out that

> The World Bank ... conceived of only one feasible path for large SOEs in all former command economies: privatization. It was *completely* disinterested in the construction of big businesses as a policy goal. It *totally* failed to distinguish between the privatization of former command-run *plants* as opposed to the building of multi-plant *firms*. It visualized only four possible ways for the performance of large SOEs in former command economies to be improved, each of which put privatization at the forefront: 'sales to outsiders', 'management–employee buyouts', 'equal-access voucher privatization' and 'spontaneous privatization' ... Each of these is now acknowledged, even by the World Bank, to have large problems, which were not anticipated when it confidently gave its advice in the early phase of the 'transition'.[7]

As Nolan points out, China did not adopt any of these models or methods in transforming its SOEs into large businesses and listed companies that the country was positioning to compete internationally in accordance with China's own industry policy. As a result of this kind of local institutional experimentation, it is expected that local corporate governance patterns will also emerge and that externally derived models of appropriate corporate governance structures will be as questionable as the World Bank's efforts to foster privatization in former communist economies.

Nevertheless, multilateral agencies have provided a template of 'good' corporate governance measures, usually leaving it to local legislatures and local interest groups to select from the range of options in response to their particular circumstances. However, and not surprisingly, there is no single picture of what a good or well-developed system of corporate governance will look like; one reason for this is that there are varieties of capitalism and that explanations of market development that may have emerged in Northern

Europe and the United States are often difficult to transplant to other parts of the world.

Notions of efficiency and of the corporation that may be seen as self evident to some Western scholars, such as American economists and corporate law scholars, are not always accepted in other counties as providing a balanced public policy framework. The rise of stakeholder ideas and their institutionalization in some countries, such as the United Kingdom, has for example, been criticized by some American economists as offending against ideas of efficiency.[8] A similarly narrow approach can be seen in the work of other economists, such as La Porta and his colleagues,[9] as well as in the efforts of leading corporate law scholars to distil the essential features of corporate law.[10]

Although many ideas are readily transportable between nations and cultures, there are clearly some limits to this, especially in regard to the movement of corporate law and corporate governance ideas. This is clear to anyone who sees law as being a socially constructed institution. This inevitably leads to some diversity in modes of business activity. Insofar as China is concerned, this conclusion was reached some time ago by S. Gordon Redding in his classic study of 'the spirit of Chinese capitalism'. Although he was largely discussing overseas Chinese businesses operating in Hong Kong, Taiwan, Singapore and Indonesia, Redding noted that Max Weber's characterization of capitalism did not translate well to discussions of Chinese business structures. This insight has subsequently been applied to other Western-derived governance ideas.

The influence of distinctive cultural factors was seen by Redding to play an important role in differentiating Chinese business from business practice in Weber's Europe.[11] As the work of the World Bank and its advisers has also shown, we have often failed to appreciate this reality.[12] A related assumption is that economic development assumes the pre-existence of a well-developed legal system that will protect property rights that are a key element of economic markets,[13] something that has not been the case in China where the development of a nuanced collection of commercial law rights has usually followed, rather than preceded, economic development that has been overseen by the State.

Another reason for the lack of a single measure of 'good' corporate governance is that there may be functional equivalents for particular corporate governance institutions that may work better in some countries than the forms developed elsewhere. As a result, surrogate measures of success are often developed; the most obvious of these are the enactment or adoption of corporate law and corporate governance codes, often based upon Western models; in addition, these may be supplemented by the creation of institutional structures that again resemble Western models, such as Stock Exchanges and corporate regulatory commissions.

But, as we well know, merely having a new law 'in the books' does not mean that it will operate effectively or that it will be used in the same way as it may have been used in the society from which its core ideas were derived. Often, the enactment of new laws, such as the 1994 PRC *Company Law* and the PRC's more recent 2005 *Company Law* and its 2005 *Securities Law* may serve symbolic purposes for the outside world. This is not to say that these laws do not serve particular purposes within their own society and generate some important changes in behaviour.

Nevertheless, the 1993 *Company Law* fell far short of being a broadly based corporate law statute and largely served to facilitate the corporatization of State-owned enterprises without any significant privatization. Nolan suggests that the introduction of joint-stock companies in China was a reflection of a broader industry policy of providing SOEs with managerial independence from government control. He notes that by this means 'the state intends through State holding companies to maintain a controlling share ownership in the 'pillar industries' and 'key enterprises in the basic industries'. As for general enterprises where non-State-owned capital will be absorbed as much as possible, the State will have equity participation, not a controlling interest.[14]

The use of the joint-stock company mechanisms provided a flexible means of transforming property rights whilst maintaining strong State oversight or control in key areas. Newly corporatized entities were seen as a mechanism for the movement to a 'modern enterprise system'. Under this Chinese approach, an array of interests coalesced within each new large corporate entity:

> Behind each of the emerging large joint-stock SOEs lay a multiplicity of institutions, large and small, each of which had an interest in the firm's performance, mainly, but not exclusively, attributable to their share in the firm's ownership ... [such as the local government authority, the relevant central ministry, other domestic institutional shareholders, a foreign joint-venture partner and foreign shareholders] ... This was a potentially powerful network of institutions, each of which had some common interest in promoting the firm's performance, none of which had the interest or capability to run it directly, all of which perceived that their best interest was served by having a strong management team running the firm.[15]

The process of enacting new laws may produce quite confusing outcomes, such as the use of overlapping systems like the German-derived supervisory board structure and the Anglo-American-derived independent director model that is used in China's *Company Law*. The process of law making may also rework some basic ideas which may be drawn from foreign legal systems, such as the concept of the lifting of the corporate veil,[16] and the idea of a shareholder derivative action procedure.[17] However, the implementation of such ideas is often problematic, especially when one is dealing with a large, state-controlled company.

Yet, efforts to introduce other complex corporate governance ideas, such as the fiduciary duties of directors and other officers, which are said to play a crucial role in fostering corporate accountability structures in Western legal systems, have had a mixed success in China. The complexity of these ideas is such that they may be poorly understood by law-makers or awkwardly applied by judges. Significantly, whilst Article 148 of the 2005 PRC *Company Law* has now sought to institutionalize the idea of a 'duty of loyalty and duty of diligence to the Company', this has occurred against a background of resistance based on arguments concerning China's civil law origins and the alien nature of fiduciary ideas in civil law systems. However, the language of Article 148 does not speak of fiduciary duties as such, although foreign commentators have been pleased to describe it in this way. Teubner has pointed to the difficulties of transplanting common-law-derived legal concepts, such as good faith, to civil law systems.[18] The transplantation of the concept of fiduciary duties is even more problematic.

However, taking an optimistic perspective, Howson argues that great progress has been achieved in this area as, even before the enactment of the 2005 *Company Law*, Chinese courts and regulators have informally relied upon what he sees as fiduciary law ideas in dealing with the relationship between Chinese directors and their companies.[19] This may reflect ongoing 'palace wars' amongst Chinese elites,[20] especially judges and regulators, but it is too early to see how well these ideas have actually been implemented in Chinese corporations. Even in UK companies, the implementation of the fiduciary duties of directors leaves much to be desired.[21]

Furthermore, even in seemingly similar systems, such as those of the United States and the United Kingdom, there may be wide gulfs in corporate governance arrangements; for example, US corporations will generally have a powerful chief executive, in contrast to the United Kingdom's preferred position (as stated in the UK Code on Corporate Governance) of a separation between the office of chairman and the CEO in listed companies.

The use of legal mechanisms to structure a market economy may also vary sharply between different Western countries; for example, in the area of corporate rescue, US Chapter 11 reorganization procedures are heavily dominated by lawyers and the courts, whilst in the United Kingdom and Australia corporate rescue often takes place out of the courts and involves insolvency practitioners or turnaround professionals who are usually trained as accountants.[22] This also points to another major difference between developed legal systems, namely the size of their respective legal professions; the United States is unusual for the relative size of its legal profession; however, 'law jobs' may be carried out by non-lawyers in other systems, and the latter work perfectly well using such strategies.

Applying these kinds of concerns to the Chinese case presents an array of issues that are of considerable relevance in regard to any discussion of the progress that has been achieved in the advancement of corporate governance ideas. What is clear, however, is that we need to look beyond the narrow confines of legal institutions or legal rules to the wider economic and social framework within which these institutions and rules are located.

8.2. The gulfs between different corporate governance systems

Comparisons between different capitalist systems are hard enough at the best of times and become fraught with difficulty where there are major variations in cultural contexts, history and political structure.[23] Finding appropriate measures to allow fair comparisons to be made is similarly difficult and is often affected by the observer's own assumptions or experiences; this is perhaps best illustrated by the problems that arise when one seeks to compare many countries and identify key differentiating variables, as La Porta and his colleagues have done when looking broadly at the nature of investor protection as a proxy for corporate governance in countries with different legal origins.[24]

This kind of research has been popular with multilateral funding bodies such as the World Bank, as they look for quantifiable measures to assist them in allocating their limited resources or funds. However, these bodies have been criticized for fostering their preferred political models, such as the so-called Washington Consensus.[25] Perhaps we can also talk of a Paris Consensus when we point to the liberalization efforts forested by the OECD and the IMF.[26] The IMF's efforts during the Asian Financial Crisis clearly imposed these kinds of externally derived preference or models in areas such as bankruptcy reform in Asia.[27] Ohnesorge has observed that the legal origins literature, although deserving of study, can be criticized for adopting overly formalistic variables and excessive reliance upon various political and policy prescriptions; in the end, it fails to offer significant insights in regard to China's legal developments.[28]

One example of the dangers of an overly zealous approach promoted by bodies such as the World Bank has been the fostering of rapid privatization. This is based on an economic developmental model that assumes that privatization is the most effective way forward. Nolan describes this approach as the 'transitional orthodoxy' which has been responsible for developmental failures in former communist countries such as Russia. This orthodoxy assumes that only privatization is capable of solving the industrial problems of countries such as Russia and China.[29] As Nolan has observed: 'China's incrementalist approach to economic reform may have been correct and the attempt in the former USSR to move rapidly towards a market economy may have been a serious mistake. There seems to be a growing consensus that this was indeed the case'.[30]

Nolan adds that the presence of a strong State which is able to give priority to the overall national interest is likely to be a more effective means of making this transition from communism to a market-based society.[31] Contrary to the transition orthodoxy which called for the closure of large, State-owned enterprises and the support for new small- and medium-sized enterprises,[32] China has instead chosen to strengthen its big State-owned enterprises and keep these under State control, whilst getting rid of smaller firms, such as by selling these off to private investors.[33] This has constituted a significant institutional innovation, albeit different from the dominant models fostered by many Western experts. In such a context, we also need to consider the relevance to transitional economies of Anglo-American models of corporate law and corporate governance, especially ones that assume a widely held body of shareholders and a minimal degree of government intervention in economic markets.

Economists tell us that the protection and growth of large-scale firms is essential to economic performance and prosperity in advanced countries;[34] this is how large firms initially arose in many Western countries (such as through the provision of tariff protections and monopolies); it is clear that this pattern is also likely to be evident in transitional economies such as China. Paradoxically, as the credit crisis has shown, the operation of large firms in Anglo-American economies also calls into question the relevance of prevailing corporate law theory which assumes advanced economy models of shareholder capacity to influence the actions of corporations and aims to protect the rights of these shareholders.

Economists La Porta *et al.* have suggested that good corporate governance can be determined by the degree of shareholder legal protection in different countries; these economists tend to argue that such protection is likely to be greater in common-law-derived legal systems than in those systems derived from civil law models;[35] however, this view ignores functionally equivalent protections found in different systems. It also is somewhat naive to assume that investor protection is actually high in Western legal systems; if the UK legal system is any guide, for example, the level of protection available has been quite disappointing.[36] Another useful intervention that has challenged the focus on shareholder legal protections has been made by John Coffee who has hypothesized that

> substantial differences in corporate law may matter far less than differences in enforcement practice. In turn, enforcement may depend more upon the strength of the incentives to assert legal remedies than upon the availability of legal remedies themselves. Even this hypothesis, however, over simplifies, because once one closely examines the differences between various systems of corporate governance, the assumed homogeneity of even common-law legal systems begins to break down. Another possibility is that differences in substantive corporate law are less important than the differences in the level of regulation that different nations impose on their securities markets. Under this latter hypothesis, the focus shifts from the minority shareholder to the investor generally.[37]

Superficially, some key contours of the commercial world, such as the existence of the corporate form and the establishment of stock exchanges, have come to look increasingly alike in many parts of the world. Most commonly, the adoption of similarly named bodies of commercial laws has given the impression that the gaps between systems are rapidly narrowing. However, the institutional and social context of such laws varies greatly and may project vastly different meanings upon those affected by them. Often these new laws have been adopted by developing countries to persuade foreign investors and multilateral bodies that they have a similar business environment; they may also have a variety of objectives, some of which may not be shared by foreign observers, such as the preservation of significant State ownership and party control of major corporations. Of course, this is often little more than a symbolic exercise akin to a letter of comfort. Ultimately, it is a question of the degree to which laws can be readily enforced in any one country.

For this reason, it has been suggested from the study of other transitional economies, such as Russia, that any effort to measure the degree to which 'good' corporate governance has emerged should look at the pathologies or failures that predominate in any one system. As Fox and Heller have suggested, it is necessary to 'link poor corporate governance to real economy effects' or to identify a 'complete set of vulnerabilities to corporate governance'.[38] They also argue that such vulnerabilities 'are far more visible when approached from the transition angle, but they are present in rich economies, just harder to spot'.[39] Just as we learnt a great deal about the effectiveness of corporate governance arrangements in particular companies by studying corporate failures, such as Enron (in the United States), Parmalat (in Europe), HIH (in Australia) and Satyam (in India), so too we can learn from a wider inquiry into common pathologies of corporate governance in transitional economies.

If we adopt a value maximization perspective, these pathologies can be divided into the failure to maximize the availability of the company's residual assets and the failure to distribute assets in an equal fashion. Some of the pathologies of corporate governance identified by Fox and Heller are as follows:

1. An unreformable value-destroying firm failing to close
2. A viable firm failing to use its existing capacity efficiently
3. Where a firm mis-invests internally generated cash flows
4. Where a firm fails to implement positive net present value projects
5. Where a firm fails to identify positive net present value projects
6. Where firms fail to prevent the diversion of claims against it
7. Where firms fail to prevent the diversion of its assets[40]

Of course, these pathologies may be seen as socially desirable where a more stakeholder–oriented view of the corporation is adopted. One of the problems in being able to apply these criteria is that the real financial and legal affairs of companies in transitional economies are often notoriously difficult to penetrate so as to establish the true nature of their corporate governance arrangements. This is also the case in China, despite the existence of increasingly professional annual reports and detailed listed company disclosure regimes. This calls for a much closer engagement with Chinese companies, of the kind pioneered by Redding two decades ago.

A more meaningful evaluation of the quality of corporate governance in Chinese companies will be greatly assisted by resorting to such empirical methods. Such empirical studies are likely to be more illuminating than a review of corporate governance codes and legal rules and other public documents, such as company annual reports and stock exchange filings. This is also likely to be more useful than seeking to measure the performance of Chinese companies on the basis of performance measures that have been developed for economies such as those in the West.

Studies of corporations in crisis or corporate failures are likely to tell us much more about the true state of corporate governance in Chinese companies than we have recognized in the past; this is well illustrated in the recent collection of essays from Milhaupt and Pistor.[41] However, such research can have its dangers as it may trip over State secrets laws,[42] as was originally suggested in regard to China-based employees of Rio Tinto plc who undertook market research in regard to mineral resources trading in China.[43] However, this is an extreme situation that has been coloured by other broader political factors.[44]

Corporate governance scholars, such as Richard Leblanc have long pointed to the importance of researching the actual processes of decision making within corporations.[45] However, as the conduct of this kind of research may present some challenges to legal researchers, we have not seen as much of this kind of research as might have been expected. This is in part due to the larger problem of obtaining access to business and other elites for research purposes.[46] Most of those who undertake fieldwork into socio-legal topics in China tend to be non-lawyers, even though most foreign 'experts' in the field of Chinese legal studies tend to be lawyers working in law schools.[47] Consequently, it is often prudent for foreign researchers to work with local Chinese institutional partners rather than to undertake what Gold has referred to as 'guerrilla interviewing' in China; this was described as 'unchaperoned, spontaneous but structured participant observation and interviews as opportunities present themselves'.[48] This style of research may be contrasted with Potter's Chinese business research survey undertaken with local collaborators.[49]

Not surprisingly, there has been relatively little such empirical research into corporate governance practices within Chinese companies, although some business-school-based researchers have made some progress in this regard.[50] Extended empirical research into particular Chinese companies and sectors, of the kind undertaken by Peter Nolan and his students and collaborators, is also an important means of advancing our understanding of Chinese corporate governance practices.[51] Some empirical work has begun into areas such as the work of Chinese lawyers[52] and law enforcement and the work of courts in China.[53] Some empirical survey work by Chinese economists has begun to look more closely at what actually happens or is said to happen in Chinese companies in regard to corporate governance.[54] Regrettably, we have yet to study in any great depth or intensity corporate governance within Chinese companies; a range of research tools for studying elites may be appropriate to facilitate this. If we are serious about looking more closely at corporate governance in China, this will need to be done.

Empirical research into Chinese corporate governance also often needs to look more broadly at other factors, such as the pivotal role of the Party in structuring relationships at senior levels of the company.[55] It could be argued that the Party's role is somewhat paradoxical; it may be seen as both a pivot of the current system as well as the principal obstacle to change in China's major listed companies. This pattern has not changed much insofar as corporate governance outcomes are concerned; for example, in 1999 Tam's empirical work revealed that: 'corporate governance arrangements in Shanghai's public companies were dominated by managers who often chaired the boards of directors as well as the enterprise Party organization'.[56] However, the dominance of the Party does have some advantages in terms of managing the process of incremental change in China's economy aimed at facilitating the emergence of new economic institutions. As Nolan has observed: '[a] self reforming communist party may be the least bad vehicle available to accomplish this [successful transition away from a communist economy]'.[57]

More recent empirical work in China's listed public company sector has found that the pattern of Party dominance in China's major listed companies is still very evident.[58] Whilst Party control does serve a useful purpose in a transitional economy of linking the old systems of governance in China with the new system by, for example, allowing the positions of Party secretary and the chief executive or chair to be held by the same person, it does concentrate power somewhat dangerously and lead to the dominance of one person or the 'key man' system to which many, including the Shanghai Stock Exchange, have pointed.[59] This concentration of power has meant that cases of corrupt practices in Chinese companies have sometimes been very serious.

The listing of Chinese companies on stock exchanges has not dramatically changed their corporate governance practices. This has been well demonstrated by Alice de Jonge in her case studies of the first nine PRC companies to list on the Hong Kong Stock Exchange in 1993–1994.[60] As de Jonge concludes, despite the time that these nine PRC firms have had to adopt corporate governance ideas associated with outsider systems, '[y]et, even these firms, it seems, remain stubbornly the same in the way they actually operate on a day-to-day basis, despite ostensible compliance with regulatory requirements aimed at promoting shareholder protection and market efficiency in "outsider" systems'.[61]

Whilst much has been written about the evolution of corporate governance in China, there is considerable room for more intensive empirically based research which also connects with research undertaken by other students of the transformation and development of China's State-owned enterprises.

8.3. Progress in China's corporate governance practices?

This chapter started with a hard question; like all such questions, there is no simple answer to it. Yes, there has been significant progress in many areas of China's market economy, whilst in some areas there has been little if any progress and even backsliding. Where progress has been readily achievable, this has often been in regard to things that are relatively superficial or of relatively minor importance in regard to corporate governance. Nevertheless, China's circumstances in this regard are sometimes matched by similar patterns of mixed outcomes in other parts of the world. The achievement of corporate governance goals has been found to be much more complex than it was at first perceived to be, as the global financial crisis has recently demonstrated.

Even in developed countries, there have often been political pressures on corporate regulators to minimize interference with business, such as the use of so called light touch regulation, in an effort to enhance the attractiveness of their respective financial centres to foreign business; this happened with such catastrophic outcomes in the United Kingdom prior to the onset of the global financial crisis in late 2007. In addition, in developed countries, enforcement of commercial laws and norms may not take place through the courts at all, with companies sometimes being shamed or forced to remedy harms that they have caused; this remedial action may arise out of informal pressure from regulators or as a consequence of media campaigns or due to public campaigns and protests. These alternative approaches often depend on the existence of a parallel informal system that draws upon the mechanisms of civil society. Such mechanisms are, however, less effective where the State frowns upon such forms of social ordering or campaigning. Inevitably, the absence of such an alternative system, places an almost impossible burden upon any legal system to provide adequate remedies to its citizens who are adversely affected by corporate misconduct.

Much has been achieved in the development of corporate governance dialogues, soft law Codes and enhanced legal obligations. In 2001, we even had some leading corporate law scholars proclaim the end of history in corporate law development, suggesting that corporate law had reached its highest state of development in countries such as the United States.[62] Whilst the collapses of companies such as Enron, WorldCom, AIG and Lehman Brothers may have left proponents of such views somewhat embarrassed,[63] there remains a persistent view that the main outlines of corporate law have now been settled, at least in key Western countries.[64] End of history rhetoric also arose following the collapse of the Soviet Union with writers such as Fukuyama[65] predicting that the State would become less important in what others, such as Ohmae,[66] have described as a borderless world. Instead, we have seen the persistence and indeed the strengthening of the nation-State in transition economies; this is especially evident in China itself.[67] The recent global financial crisis seems to have seen the re-emergence of the State in many countries with governments becoming owners of large proportions of shares in major banks; this process of State expansion has also been evident in China.[68] This must affect the way we look at corporate governance.

Parallel to this line of thought, others have advanced the somewhat weak argument that there is increasing convergence between different market economies, despite the existence of long-established patterns of legal action in different countries; this convergence has arguably been accentuated by economic globalization[69] which is often seen as being most evident in regard to financial markets and international trade. Nevertheless, there remain powerful forces of localism and resistance to such convergence.[70] For this reason, as Branson has noted, the prospects for global convergence in corporate governance remain very uncertain.[71] Others have argued that whilst formal convergence may not occur, functional convergence may arise through the use of contractual mechanisms.[72]

What we do know is that the proponents of the Anglo-American model are no longer able to comfortably assert that Western systems of law and corporate governance are as robust as had previously been believed.

Of course, another strand of thinking, looking at the varieties of capitalism, has championed the persistence of diversity in market societies.[73] This would cover the approach that is adopted to the closely related topic of corporate governance, as Milhaupt and Pistor have recently illustrated.[74] These authors point out that 'just as there are varieties of capitalism, there are varieties of legal support for capitalism'.[75] In other words, the complexity of a legal system and its social supports will vary from one capitalist system to another. It may also be that functionally equivalent institutions may fill the gap that is taken by law in other countries. Empirical research has highlighted the importance of Government influence as the dominant shareholder in China as well as the influence of the Chinese Communist Party in shaping major corporations.[76]

Companies that are seen by the State as being 'national champions' would also be treated differently from other companies.[77] If anything, since China's entry into the WTO, the country has begun to more aggressively support its national champions and their growth both within China and abroad.[78] The position of the Party in Chinese companies has also been strengthened by the reformulation of the PRC *Company Law* in 2005 by the insertion of Article 19 which is wider than a similar provision in the 1993 PRC *Company Law*.[79] The fact that the 2005 Law applies to a much broader range of companies than the 1993 Law has perhaps signalled a deepening of Party monitoring of all companies. Of course, entrepreneurs were invited to join the Party as long ago as 2001 when President Zhang Zemin announced that they could become Party members.[80]

This development in a way mimicked the old pattern of private enterprises seeking to pass themselves off as 'red hat' enterprises so that they could more easily have access to much needed loans from government-controlled banks.[81] However, it also served as a means of enhancing Party control of Chinese companies. Empirical evidence from corporate governance fieldwork suggests that such control continues to be significant and apparently growing.[82] Nevertheless, many Chinese firms also seek to structure themselves as foreign firms so as to avoid some of the regulation that may otherwise be imposed upon them by government; the weight of this regulation is especially felt by smaller firms.[83] Others have also pointed to the important role that non-legal institutions may perform in regard to Chinese corporate governance.[84] These non-legal institutions have had varying degrees of impact on the nature of Chinese corporate governance and include banks and institutional investors, the State as a large shareholder and gatekeepers such as lawyers, accountants and the financial press.[85]

However, as the recent global financial crisis has demonstrated, there remains much to be done in properly embedding corporate governance ideals within the processes of the modern corporation. This applies as much to China as it does to corporate governance in more 'developed' markets. Indeed, the recent banking and financial crisis has shown that corporate governance practices in 'developed' countries such as the United Kingdom and United States have fallen well short of the rhetoric of the proponents of enhanced corporate governance. In other words, the crisis may have shown that we have failed 'to walk the talk' insofar as corporate governance has been concerned.

The Chinese economy has witnessed a massive transformation over the last thirty years.[86] This transformation has been followed by the development of a legal system that serves as one of the key supports for the market economy. However, legal rules do not exist in isolation and need to be based upon a social and political system if they are to be effective. The record of Chinese economic growth has shown that legal rules have not been a pre-requisite to this growth. As a result, the mere passage of new commercial laws and codes of conduct will not take a country very far unless these rules and norms are supported by society and embedded within society's governmental and business processes.

This means that civil society institutions such as professional associations, industry-based business groups, shareholder activists and the commercial press should be allowed to play more important roles in fostering corporate governance ideas and uncovering corporate failings. This has, however, been a major sticking point in China and if anything we have seen more monitoring and control of civil society activism in recent times.[87] This problem, however, will no doubt be dealt with in a gradual way as has been the pattern with China's opening up experiment.

It is clearly very easy for formal rules and norms to be displaced or downgraded by other more powerful norms and institutions in a society, such as by religion, political authority or the use of force. Informal mechanisms such as corruption and blatant disregard of legal rules can have a similar effect on the status of these rules. In addition, euphoric markets and market bubbles, as well as commitment to economic expansion and development at all costs, may also undermine the effectiveness of legal and ethical values by privileging reckless risk taking. This undermining of the effectiveness of established legal rules and codes of good business practice is well illustrated, for example, by the widespread existence of foreign corrupt practices or the payment of bribes by otherwise well-regarded companies (e.g. BAE Systems in the United Kingdom,[88] Siemens in Germany,[89] Halliburton in the United States[90] and AWB in Australia,[91] to mention but a few recent examples).

The extent of such corrupt practices which serve to undermine the rule of law and the embedding of new cultural values has been well documented by groups such as Transparency International. Although much progress has been made in combating corruption in China, business-related bribery remains extensive in China; this is an important indicator of the true nature of corporate culture in China's leading corporations. In this regard, Transparency International has reported that China was perceived as 72nd out of 180 countries in terms of the level of corruption.[92] At 72 out of 180 countries, China is in the top half of nations, between the best and the worst levels of corrupt practices that are to be found in the world today. Given its world leadership aspirations, it might be expected to do better than this. Corruption is a corrosive problem that undermines the integrity of the rule of law and corporate cultures and needs to be addressed in transitional economies such as China as well as in 'developed' economies such as the United Kingdom.

8.4. Whither corporate governance in China?

The use of the term corporate governance has had a relatively short history in China, probably not going back much earlier than the passage of the first PRC *Company Law* in late 1993, although China has of course had earlier company laws.[93] A common lawyer might have been struck by the odd nature of this law if one did not look at it in terms of the process of seeking to transform and corporatize the old State-owned enterprises.[94] To this extent, it was not until the passage of the 2005 *Company Law* that we saw a law with more traditional corporate governance objectives.[95]

Professor J.V. Feinerman, for example, has recently reviewed this 2005 Law and asked whether it was a sign of 'new hope' for Chinese corporate governance. He suggested that the provisions of the new law 'hold out some promise for improving corporate governance in China'.[96] Feinerman relied upon the OECD Principles of Corporate Governance to provide a benchmark against which to evaluate China's new company and securities laws, even though these principles had their origins in work by US and UK corporate governance advocates, such as Ira Milstein and Sir Adrian Cadbury and international investor groups, such as the International Corporate Governance Network. The law's origins are also to be found in a different kind of corporate entity to China's State-controlled and largely State-owned listed companies. Whilst Feinerman gives 'a generous appraisal' of China's new laws, Tang has correctly observed that many other real-world problems remain to be solved.[97]

There is room for these kinds of legislative overviews as they certainly demonstrate some of the many achievements that have been made in China's legal system. However, such efforts need to be supplemented by deeper forms of analysis if we are to obtain a more embedded perspective. It is easy to be optimistic about Chinese corporate governance if we merely look at law making and institutional structures both within the large Chinese corporation and outside it. However, there is a dark side that remains to be more adequately explored by China corporate governance scholars.

Whilst Chinese reformers seem to have been much impressed by Anglo-American models of corporate governance, these models do not fit very neatly upon the social context and structure of large Chinese listed companies, as On Kit Tam has argued.[98] This is in part because the history of the recent introduction of corporate governance in China has been a top-down or State-driven process. This has of course been characteristic of the whole pattern of developing legislation for China's market economy, as Donald Clarke has shown.[99] Instead of being market-driven, legal reform has been driven from the top-down by the State. This pattern of reform seems destined to continue, given the nature of the current State system in China. Anglo-American-based models have been built upon the existence of widely dispersed corporate shareholdings in listed companies and the operation of a system of 'outsider' control that facilitates a market for corporate control.[100] However, as we know, China's major listed companies generally have major blocks of usually State-owned shares and only a small proportion of their shares are freely traded on stock exchanges.[101]

Chinese stock exchanges fall far short of Western 'outsider'-control models as they allow for only a small proportion of shares to be traded on the exchange. This will remain so as long as the State remains the dominant shareholder in major listed companies in China. Despite recent reforms under China's so-called split share scheme, there is not much reason for optimism that this will change quickly.[102] This probably does not matter in the short term, unless we assume that these exchanges are like Anglo-American stock exchanges. Chinese equity markets are dominated by firms which have a large, State-ownership stake with the number of active individual share traders being much less than is often assumed, with the consequence that they have little influence as minority shareholders. Donald Clarke has explained the implications of this pattern of ownership and stock market activity as follows:

> Understanding who the investors are and how they behave has critical implications for corporate governance. First, it helped us understand whether equity markets can in fact serve a disciplining function. Do they respond to failures of corporate governance? Second, it helps us to assess the necessity and urgency of measures to help the small investor who, in the popular image of the stock market, is getting roughed up by the big boys. If small investors gave up hope and left, would it matter?[103]

Clarke verges towards the view that it does not matter as 'while a great deal of speculation does take place on the market, it is driven by institutional investors and not individuals'.[104] It is clear that minority shareholder interests receive little serious attention from the boards of listed companies, largely because of their relative insignificance in the overall structure of ownership.[105] Transforming the ownership structure of Chinese firms will be essential if corporate governance ideas are to serve a transformative purpose in China.[106]

A key issue underlying any market-based system of corporate governance must be concerned with the overall effectiveness of the system in enhancing firm performance.[107] Because of the mixed goals that have been given to China's national champions, enhanced economic performance is by no means their only or even their primary goal. A complicating factor here is the extent to which leading Chinese companies engage in related Party transactions; something that was seen as normal within a large, State-owned enterprise in a planned economy, but related Party transactions potentially threaten the integrity of listed companies that still have connections with their former SOE. Minority shareholders were most likely to be adversely affected by the existence of such transactions and the system of independent directors is ill suited to controlling these kinds of transactions. On the other hand, it seems natural for the parent company, out of which the listed entity was formed, to seek financial transfers or favourable treatment (such as the provision of guarantees) from the listed company.[108]

Various efforts have been made to chart the history of corporate governance related reform efforts in China.[109] Reference can be made to the early history of Chinese business,[110] but recent history is more relevant for current purposes.[111] Any review of the state of corporate governance in China is therefore necessarily impressionistic, as it must draw upon a variety of studies each with its own perspectives and assumptions; it must also address some of the problems that have been addressed in this chapter.

8.5. Some conclusions

It is not the intention of this chapter to be overly critical of Chinese (or Western) achievements with regard to corporate governance, or to 'throw the baby out with the bathwater', but there is clearly a need for more intensive empirically based legal research into the key drivers and processes of corporate governance in Chinese companies.

We can have unrealistic expectations about corporate governance ideas, such as the value of independence of directors and the need to give minority shareholders more control or influence.

Although much research work has been done in regard to the development of commercial law and legal institutions in China, much remains to be done in regard to the actual practices of corporate governance in leading Chinese companies. This necessitates some caution in seeking to impose foreign-derived governance models in what is clearly a period of considerable institutional innovation.

Just as Western systems of corporate governance can be seriously criticized (as we saw in official responses to the recent banking crisis in the United Kingdom and the United States), it is also possible to raise some serious questions about inadequate Chinese corporate governance practices and their effects as reflected in recent scandals in China. We are still very much in the early stages of such research activity.

Notes

1 *See*, T. Bawden, 'Alan Greenspan admits some mistakes', *Times Online*, (London 23 October 2008), available at: http://business.timesonline.co.uk/tol/business/economics/article5003610.ece?print=ye (accessed 5 April 2010); and E. L. Andrews, 'Greenspan Concedes Error on Regulation', *The New York Times*, (New York 23 October 2008), available at: http://www.nytimes.com/2008/10/24/business/economy/24panel.html?_r=1&hp (accessed 5 April 2010).

2 B. Black and R. Kraakman, 'A Self-Enforcing Model of Corporate Law', *Harvard Law Review*, 109, 1996: 1911–1982.

3 *See, generally,* OECD, 'Corporate Governance Lessons from the Financial Crisis', OECD Steering Group on Corporate Governance, Paris, 2009; International Corporate Governance Network, *Second Statement on the Global Financial Crisis*, 23 March 2009, at para 1.2; available at: http://www.icgn.org/files/icgn_main/pdfs/news/icgn_statement_on_the_financial_crisis_23_march_09.pdf (accessed 5 April 2010); Treasury Committee, House of Commons, The *Run on the Rock – Fifth Report of Session 2007–2008, Volume 1*, HC 56-1, London: The Stationery Office, 2008.

4 *See*, S. M. Jacoby, *The Embedded Corporation – Corporate Governance and Employment Relations in Japan and the United States*, Princeton: Princeton University Press, 2005.

5 *See*, D. McBarnet, A. Voiculescu and T. Campbell (eds), *The New Corporate Accountability – Corporate Social Responsibility and the Law*, Cambridge: Cambridge University Press, 2007.

6 *See*, e.g. S. Soederberg, 'The promotion of "Anglo-American" corporate governance in the South: who benefits from the new international standard?', *Third World Quarterly*, 24, 2003: 7–27.

7 P. Nolan, *Transforming China – Globalization, Transition and Development*, London: Anthem Books, 2004: 174.

8 *See*, e.g. M. C. Jensen, 'Value Maximization, Stakeholder Theory, and the Corporate Objective Function', in D. H. Chew and S. L. Gillan (eds), *U.S. Corporate Governance*, New York: Columbia Business School Press, 2009: 3–25. Jensen takes the view (at p. 4) without the 'clarity of mission provided by a single valued objective' (i.e. the value maximization perspective) it is likely that 'companies embracing stakeholder theory will experience managerial confusion, conflict, inefficiency, and perhaps even competitive failure'.

9 *See*, e.g. R. La Porta, *et al.*, 'Law and Finance', *Journal of Political Economy*, 106, 1998: 1113–1155; A. Shleifer and R. Vishny, 'A survey of corporate governance', *Journal of Finance* 52, 1997: 737–778.

10 R. Kraakman, *et al.*, The *Anatomy of Corporate Law – A Comparative and Functional Approach* (2nd edn), Oxford: Oxford University Press, 2009.

11 S. G. Redding, *The Spirit of Chinese Capitalism*, Berlin: Walter de Gruyter, 1993: 8–16.

12 *See, generally*, J.Stiglitz, *The Roaring Nineteies – Seeds of Destruction*, London: Allen Lane, 2003.

13 *See*, C. J. Milhaupt and K. Pistor, *Law and Capitalism – What Corporate Crises Reveal about Legal Systems and Economic Development Around the World*, Chicago: Chicago University Press, 2008: 17–25.

14 Nolan, *supra note* 7, p. 164.

15 *Ibid.*, p. 165.

16 Art 20 imposes a liability upon shareholders who abuse the independent status of the company as a legal person. This is only a partial treatment of lifting of the veil issues. However, this does not deal effectively with situations where the company form is used as a sham or a front, or as an instrument for fraud. Perhaps this is a matter that will be clarified by the Supreme People's Court when it lays down criteria to be used by judges applying this provision.

17 Article 152 of the 2005 *Company Law* provides shareholders with a right to bring an action against a director or senior manager who has caused loss to the company (making this individual liable under Article 150 to pay compensation); the shareholder will be entitled to bring a legal action in their own name, but 'in the

interests of the company' after first making a written request to the company to take such legal action and this request has not been acted upon within 30 days. This is a curious provision as it requires the shareholders to bring the action in their own names and not in the name of the company. However, under China's *Civil Procedure Law*, only the company's legal representative can bring an action in the name of the company. Shareholders are also empowered by Article 153 to bring legal proceedings directly against a director or senior manager who has violated the law or a provision of the company's articles with the effect of damaging the interests of shareholders. *See*, J. Fu and J. Yuan, *PRC Company and Securities Laws – A Practical Guide*, Singapore: CCH Asia Pte Limited, 2006: 96–98.

18 G. Teubner, 'Legal Irritants: Good Faith in British Law or How Unifying Law Ends Up in New Differences', *Modern Law Review*, 61, 1998: 11–32.

19 N. C. Howson, 'The Doctrine That Dared Not Speak Its Name: Anglo-American Duties in China's Company Law and Case Law Intimations of Prior Convergence', in H. Kanda, *et al.* (eds), *Transforming Corporate Governance in East Asia*, London: Routledge, 2008: 193–254.

20 *See, generally,* Y. Dezalay and B. G. Garth, *The Internationalization of Palace Wars – Lawyers, Economists, and the Contest to Transform Latin American States*, Chicago: University of Chicago Press, 2002.

21 R. Tomasic, 'Raising Corporate Governance Standards in Response to Corporate Rescue and Insolvency', *Corporate Rescue and Insolvency*, 2, 2009: 5–9.

22 *See, generally,* V. Finch, *Corporate Insolvency Law – Perspectives and Principles* (2nd edn), Cambridge: Cambridge University Press, 2009: 178 ff.

23 In regard to comparing company law, *see, generally,* K. J. Hopt, 'Comparative Company Law', in M. Reimann and R. Zimmerman (eds) *The Oxford Handbook of Comparative Law*, Oxford: Oxford University Press, 2006: 1161–1191. Alas, even the company law harmonization program in Europe has been slow to develop: *see* further, P. De Cruz, *Comparative Law in a Changing World* 3rd edn, London: Routledge, 2007: 395.

24 La Porta, *et al.*, *supra note* 9; A. Shleifer and R. Vishny, 'A Survey of Corporate Governance', *Journal of Finance* 52, 1997: 737–783.

25 *See*, R. Peerenboom, *China Modernizes*, Oxford: Oxford University Press, 2007.

26 *See, generally,* R. Abdelal, *Capital Rules – The Construction of Global Finance*, Cambridge: Harvard University Press, 2007.

27 *See, generally,* T. C. Halliday and B. G. Carruthers, *Bankrupt: Law's Global Markets: How International Organizations Shaped Bankruptcy Law After the Asian Financial Crisis,* Stanford: Stanford University Press, 2009.

28 J. K. M. Ohnesorge, 'China's Economic Transition and the New Legal Origins Literature', *China Economic Review* 14, 2003: 485.

29 Nolan, *supra note* 7, p. 132. Nolan refers to World Bank publications which have taken this approach, such as *Bureaucrats in Business*, New York: Oxford University Press, 1996; and *From Plan to Market*, Washington DC: Oxford University Press, 1996.

30 *supra note Ibid.*, p. 126.

31 *Ibid.*, p. 127.

32 *Ibid.*, pp. 136 and 150–151.

33 This is sometimes referred to as the policy of 'Grasp the Large, Let Go of the Small' or *zhua da, fang xiao*. *See*, Nolan, *supra note* 7, p. 156.

34 *Ibid.*, p. 151.

35 This also ignores the different patterns in some common-law-derived legal systems, such as in India. *See*, J. Armour and P. Lele, 'Law, Finance, and Politics: The Case of India', *Law and Society Review* 43, 2009: 491–526.

36 *See*, R. Tomasic, 'Shareholder Litigation and the Financial Crisis: The Northern Rock Shareholder Appeal Considered', *Company Law Newsletter*, 262, 2009: 1–5. *See, generally,* A. Reisberg, 'Derivative Claims under the Companies Act 2006: Much Ado About Nothing?', in *Rationality in Company Law – Essays in Honour of DD Prentice*, Oxford: Hart Publishing, 2009: 17–55.

37 J. C. Coffee, 'Privatization and Corporate Governance: The Lessons from Securities Market Failure', in M. B. Fox and M. A. Heller (eds), *Corporate Governance Lessons from Transition Economy Reforms*, Princeton: Princeton University Press, 2006: 265–314.

38 M. B. Fox and M. A. Heller, 'What Is Good Corporate Governance?', pp. 3–31 in Fox and Heller, *supra note* 37, p. 4.

39 *Ibid.*, p. 3.

40 *Ibid.*, p. 5.

41 Milhaupt and Pistor, *supra note* 13.

42 Article 8 of China's 1988 *Law of the People's Republic of China on Guarding State Secrets* provides a broad definition of the category of 'State secrets', including: '(1) secrets concerning major policy decisions on state affairs … (4) secrets in national economic and social development … and (7) other matters that are classified as state secrets by the state secret-guarding department'. In 2001, the Supreme People's Court issued an Interpretation of the Law on Guarding State Secrets: Supreme People's Court, *Interpretation of Certain Issues Regarding the Specific Application of the Law When Trying Cases of Stealing, Gathering, Procuring or Illegally Providing State Secrets or Intelligence Outside of the Country;* Document No: Legal Interpretation No. 4 (2001); Promulgated on 17 January 2001 and Effective from 22 January 2001. Implementing Measures have also been promulgated to enforce this Law: National Administration for the Protection of State Secrets, '(Document No. 1) Measures for Implementing the Law on the Protection of State Secrets of the People's Republic of China'; Promulgated 25 May 1990; Effective from 25 May 1990. Section 111 of the 1997 *Criminal Law of the PRC* is also relevant here, but discussion of these is beyond the scope of this chapter.

43 *See*, J. Garnaut, 'Undiplomatic Relations: Stern Hu's Trial Has Not Only Put China in the Spotlight but also Sino–Australian Relations', *The Age*, 27 March 2010, Insight, p. 1.

44 *See*, T. Macalister, 'Rio Tinto Rights Issue Imminent after Controversial Chinalco deal Collapses', *The Guardian*, 5 June 2009: 28.

45 R. Leblanc and J. Gillies, *Inside the Boardroom – How Boards Really Work and the Coming Revolution in Corporate Governance*, Mississauga: John Wiley & Sons Canada Ltd, 2005. For other types of empirical research into corporate governance issues, *see*, J. W. Lorsch, *Pawns or Potentates – The Reality of Amercia's Corporate Boards*, Boston: Harvard Business School Press, 1989; M. Huyse, *Boards, Governance and Value Creation*, Cambridge: Cambridge University Press, 2007; A. Kakabadse and N. Kakabadse, *Leading the Board – The Six Disciplines of World-Class Chairmen*, Houndmills: Palgrave, 2008; R. Tomasic and S. Bottomley, *Directing the Top 500 – Corporate Governance and Accountability in Australian Companies*, Sydney: Allen & Unwin, 1993; and the broad ranging empirical study by R. M. Kanter, *Super*

Corp – How Vanguard Companies Create Innovation, Profits, Growth, and Social Good, New York: Crown Business, 2009.

46 Some of the difficulties of empirical research within companies are discussed in: R. J. Thomas, 'Interviewing Important People in Companies', in R. Hertz and J. Imber (eds), *Studying Elites Using Qualitative Methods*, London: Sage, 1995: 3–17.

47 N. J. Diamant, S. B. Lubman and K. J O'Brien, 'Law and Society in the People's Republic of China' in N. J. Diamant, S. B. Lubman and K. J. O'Brien, *Engaging the Law in China,* Stanford: Stanford University Press, 2005: 3–27. *See, generally,* E. G. Jensen and T. C. Heller (eds), *Beyond Common Knowledge – Empirical Approaches to the Rule of Law*, Stanford: Stanford University Press, 2003.

48 Quoted by M. Heimer and S. Thogersen (eds), 'Introduction' to *Doing Fieldwork in China*, p. 11. *See*, T. B. Gold, 'Guerilla Interviewing among the Getihu' in P. Link, *et al.* (eds), *Unofficial China – Popular Culture and Thought in the People's Republic*, Boulder: Westview Press, 175–192.

49 P. B. Potter, 'Socialist Legality and Legal Culture in Shanghai: A Survey of Getihu', *Canadian Journal of Law and Society* 9, 1994: 41–72.

50 *See, generally,* O. K. Tam, *The Development of Corporate Governance in China*, Cheltenham: Edward Elgar, 1999; D. N. Sull and Y Wang, *Made in China – What Western Managers Can Learn from Trailblazing Chinese Entrepreneurs*, Boston: Harvard Business School Press, 2005. Similar research methods have been used in other studies of China's corporate leaders; *see*, e.g. D. Guthrie, *Dragon in a Three-Piece Suit – The Emergence of Capitalism in China*, Princeton: Princeton University Press, 1999: 219–242; and Pearson's study of Chinese managers in foreign business firms in China: M. M. Pearson, *China's New Business Elite – The Political Consequences of Economic Reform*, Berkeley: University of California Press, 1997: 169–174. *See also*, X. Jia and R. Tomasic, *Corporate Governance and Resource Security in China*, New York: Routledge, 2010.

51 *See*, e.g. P. Nolan, *China and the Global Business Revolution*, Houndmills: Palgrave, 2001.

52 *See, generally,* K. C. Wong, 'Studying Policing in China: Some Personal Reflections', *International Journal of the Sociology of Law* 35, 2007: 111–126; M. Dutton, *Policing and Punishment in China*, Cambridge: Cambridge University Press, 1992; D. C. Clarke, 'Power and Politics in the Chinese Court System: The Enforcement of Civil Judgments', *Columbia Journal of Asian Law* 10, 1992: 1–92. Also in regard to studies of Chinese lawyers, *see*, E. Michelson, 'The Practice of Law as an Obstacle to Justice: Chinese Lawyers at Work', Law and Society Review 40, 2006: 1–38; and S. Liu, 'Client Influence and the Contingency of Professionalism: The Work of Elite Corporate Lawyers in China', *Law & Society Review* 40, 2006: 751–781.

53 *See, generally*, Dutton, *supra note* 52.

54 *See*, e.g. Wei-An Li, *Corporate Governance in China: Research and Evaluation*, Singapore: John Wiley & Sons (Asia) Pte Ltd., 2008; L. Tong, *Corporate Governance Assessment Report of Top 100 Chinese Listed Companies*, Beijing: Chinese Academy of Social Sciences, 2005. *See, generally,* R. Garnaut, L. Song, Y. Yao, and X. Wang, *Private Enterprise in China*, Canberra: Asia Pacific Press, 2001; and R. Garnaut, L. Song, S. Tenev and Y. Yao, *China's Ownership Transformation – Process, Outcomes, Prospects, Washington*: International Finance Corporation and the World Bank, 2005.

55 *See*, e.g. C. A. McNally, 'Strange Bedfellows: Communist Party Institutions and New Governance Mechanisms in Chinese State Holding Corporations', *Business*

and Politics, 4, 2002: 91–115. Also see further, R. Mc Gregor, The Party – The Secret World of China's Communist Rulers, London, Allen Lane, 2010: 34–69. This is important if one was to look at some of the obstacles to significant change in Chinese corporate governance practices, such as more extensive privatization of state-owned companies; this may help to explain why it might be argued that the development of Chinese corporate governance is somewhat trapped or at least has not advanced in significant respects. *See*, M. Pei, *Trapped in Transition – The Limits of Developmental Autocracy*, Cambridge: Harvard University Press, 2006. *See, generally,* D. L. Yang, *Remaking the Chinese Leviathan – Market Transition and the Politics of Governance in China*, Stanford: Stanford University Press, 2004.

56 Tam, *supra note* 50, p. 75.

57 Nolan, *supra note* 7, pp. 127–128.

58 *See*, R. Tomasic and J. Fu, 'Legal Regulation and Corporate Governance in China's top 100 listed companies', *The Company Lawye*r 27, 2006: 278–287.

59 Shanghai Stock Exchange, *China Corporate Governance Report 2003*, Shanghai: Fudan University Press, 2004. For further evidence of this phenomenon, *see*, R. Tomasic and N. Andrews, 'Minority Shareholder Protection in China's Top 100 Listed Companies', *Australian Journal of Asian Law* 9, 2007: 88–119.

60 A. de Jonge, *Corporate Governance and China's H-Share Market*, Cheltenham: Edward Elgar, 2008. De Jonge notes (pp. 233–234) that despite the fact that the-Hong Kong stock exchange has operated within a British common law legal tradition and fostered corporate governance ideas, it is far from being an outsider controlled market of the kind that is said to be typical of Anglo-American stock exchanges. Clarke has also shown that China's mainland stock exchanges also do not behave like typical outsider control exchanges, despite the number of shares said to be traded on them. *See*, D. C. Clarke, 'The Role of Non-legal Institutions in Chinese corporate governance', in H. Kanda, *et al.* (eds), *Transforming Corporate Governance in East Asia*, *supra note* 19 (pp. 172–175). Tam has also pointed to the seeming paradox of China's approach to corporate governance systems which pay homage to outsider-control system ideas, whilst in realty remaining an insider control system; Tam, *supra note* 50.

61 De Jonge, *supra note* 60, pp. 234–235.

62 H. Hansmann and R. Kraakman, 'The End of History for Corporate Law', *Georgetown Law Journal*, 2001: 89, 439–471.

63 *See*, R. Gilson and R. Kraakman, 'The Mechanisms of Market Efficiency Twenty Years Later: The Hindsight Bias', in J. Armour and J. McCahery (eds), *After Enron – Improving Corporate Law and Modernising Securities Regulation in Europe and the US*, Oxford: Hart Publishing, 2006: 29–64.

64 *See*, R. Kraakman, *et al.*, *The Anatomy of Corporate Law – A Comparative and Functional Approach* (2nd edn), Oxford: Oxford University Press, 2009.

65 F. Fukuyama, *The End of History and the Last Man*, Harmondsworth: Penguin Books, 1992.

66 K. Ohmae, *The End of the Nation State*, London: Harper Collins, 1996.

67 *See*, Nolan, *supra note* 7, pp. 144–149.

68 *See, generally,* J. Anderline and G. Dyer, 'Beijing Accused of Launching Attack on private enterprise', *The Financial Times*, 26 November 2009: 7.

69 *See, generally,* T. Friedman, *The World is Flat – A Brief History of the Globalized World in the 21st Century,* London: Allen Lane, 2005; J. Frieden, *Global*

Capitalism – Its fall and rise in the twentieth century, New York: WW Norton & Company, 2006.

70 *See, generally,* C. Antons and V. Gessner, *Globalisation and Resistance: Law Reform in Asia Since the Crisis*, Oxford: Hart Publishing, 2007.

71 D. Branson, 'The Very Uncertain Prospects of "Global" Convergence in Corporate Governance', *Cornell International Law Journal* 34, 2001: 321–362. *See also*, L. Bebchuk and M. Roe, 'A Theory of Path Dependency in Corporate Ownership and Governance', *Stanford Law Review* 52, 1999: 127–170.

72 R. Gilson, 'Globalizing Corporate Governance: Convergence of Form or Function', *American Journal of Comparative Law* 49, 2001: 329–357.

73 P. Hall and D. Soskice (eds), *Varieties of Capitalism*, Oxford: Oxford University Press, 2001.

74 Milhaupt and Pistor, *supra note* 13.

75 *Ibid.*, p. 3.

76 *See*, Tomasic and Fu, *supra note* 58; R. Tomasic and N. Andrews, 'Minority Shareholder Protection in China's Top 100 Listed Companies', *Australian Journal of Asian Law*, (2007) 9(1): 88–119; Andrews and Tomasic, *supra note* 59. *See, generally,* Qiu, Jian-Qian, *Ownership Structure, Corporate Governance and Institutional Shareholder – The Case of Chinese Listed Companies*, Beijing: Law Press China, 2005.

77 *See*, P. Nolan, *China and the Global Economy – National Champions, Industrial Policy and the Big Business Revolution*, Houndmills: Palgrave, 2001. *See, generally*, Nolan, *supra note* 7.

78 This is a point that has been made by Zhang, who points to a 2005 report of the Ministry of Commerce which sets out a plan for China to form 30–50 super-sized state-owned enterprises by 2020. X. Zhang, 'Commentary on "Legislating for a Market Economy in China"', in D. Clarke (ed.) *China's Legal System: New Developments, New Challenges*, Cambridge: Cambridge University Press, 2008: 34.

79 Article 18 of the 1993 Act stated that 'The grass-roots organizations of the Communist Party of China in companies shall carry out their activities in accordance with the Constitution of the Communist Party of China'; In contrast, Article 19 of the 2005 Law is similar to this, but adds that 'Companies shall provide the necessary conditions for the Party organizations to carry out their activities'.

80 *See, generally,* G. Wang and Y. Zheng (eds), *Damage Control – The Chinese Communist Party in the Jiang Zemin Era*, Singapore, Eastern Universities Press, 2003.

81 Garnaut, *et al.*, *supra note* 54, p. 59.

82 *See*, e.g., Tomasic and Fu, *supra note* 58, pp. 282–285. *See*, A. Young, G. Li and A. Lau, 'Corporate governance in China: the role of the state and ideology in shaping reforms', *Company Lawyer*, 28, 2007: 204–211.

83 *See, generally,* Y. Huang, *Capitalism with Chinese Characteristics – Entrepreneurship and the State*, Cambridge: Cambridge University Press, 2008: 5.

84 Clarke, *supra note* 60.

85 *Ibid.*

86 *See, generally,* L. Brandt and T. Rawski (eds), *China's Great Economic Transformation*, Cambridge: Cambridge University Press, 2008.

87 The importance of this kind of approach has been noted by D. Clarke, 'The Ecology of Corporate Governance in China', 2008, at ssrn.com/abstract=1245803.

88 In regard to BAE Systems, see, A. Wilson and R. Mason, 'SFO to pursue bribery case against BAE Systems', The Daily Telegraph, 1 October 2009, available at:

http://www.telegraph.co.uk/finance/newsbysector/epic/badot/6249542/BAE-facing-bribery-case-after-SFO-talks-fai.html (accessed 5 April 2010).

89 In regard to Siemens, *see*, 'At Siemens, Bribery Was Just a Line Item', *The New York Times*, 21 December 2008, available at: http://www.nytimes.com/2008/12/21/business/worldbusiness/21siemens.html?_r=3&pagewanted=1&th&emc=th (accessed 5 April 2010).

90 In regard to Halliburton, *see*, 'Editorial: More Annals of Global Greed Inc.', *The New York Times*, 14 February 2009 available at: http://www.nytimes.com/2009/02/15/opinion/15sun3.html (accessed 5 April 2010).

91 In regard to AWB, *see*, L. Wood, 'Review flagged AWB bribes', *The Age*, 22 October 2009, available at: http://www.theage.com.au/business/review-flagged-awb-bribes-20091021-h96f.html (accessed 5 April 2010).

92 Transparency International, *Global Corruption Report 2009: Corruption and the Private Sector*, Cambridge: Cambridge University Press, 2009: 253–261.

93 *See*, W. Kirby, 'China unincorporated: Company law and business enterprise in twentieth-century China', *Journal of Asian Studies* 54, 1995: 43–63.

94 *See*, G. Wang and R. Tomasic, *China's Company Law: An Annotation*, Singapore: Butterworths Asia, 1994.

95 *See*, J. Fu and J. Yuan, *PRC Company & Securities Laws – A Practical Guide*, Singapore: CCH Asia Pte Limited, 2006.

96 J. Feinerman, 'New Hope for Corporate Governance in China ?', in D. Clarke (ed) *China's Legal System: New Developments, New Challenges*, Cambridge: Cambridge University Press, 2008: 36–58.

97 X. Tang, 'Commentary on "New Hope for Corporate Governance in China?"', in Clarke (ed), *supra note* 96, pp. 59–65.

98 Tam, *supra note* 50, p. 39 ff. *See*, O. K. Tam, 'Models of corporate governance for Chinese companies', *Corporate Governance: An International Review* 8, 2000: 52–64.

99 D. Clarke, 'Legislating for a Market Economy in China', in Clarke (ed) *supra note* 96, pp. 13–35.

100 However, as we know, this so-called 'market for corporate control' does not always operate as economic theories would assume. *See, generally,* N. O'Sullivan and P. Wong, 'The Governance Role of Takeovers', in K. Keasey, *et al.* (eds), *Corporate Governance – Accountability, Enterprise and International Comparisons*, Chichester: John Wiley & Sons Ltd, 2005: 155–181.

101 For a discussion of the distinction between insider and outsider systems of ownership and control *see* further: C. Mayer, 'Stock-markets, Financial Institutions, and Corporate Performance', in N. Dimsdale and M. Preverzer (eds), *Capital Markets And Corporate Governance*, Oxford: Oxford University Press, 1994: 179–194 ff.

102 *See*, G.S. Liu and P. Sun, 'Ownership and Control of Chinese Public Corporations: A State-dominated Corporate Governance System', in Keasey, *et al.*, *supra note* 100, pp. 389–414., *See*, S. L. Lee, 'From non-tradeable to tradeable shares: split share structure reform of China's listed companies', *Journal of Corporate Law Studies* 8, 2008: 57–78.

103 Clarke, *supra note* 60, p. 174.

104 *Ibid.*, p. 175.

105 *See, generally,* Tomasic and Andrews, *supra note* 59.

106 *See, generally*, Garnaut *et al.*, *supra note* 54.

107 *See, generally,* G. S. Liu and P. Sun, 'The Class of Shareholdings and Corporate Performance – A Case of State Shareholding Composition in Chinese Publicly Listed Companies', *Corporate Governance – An International Review* 13, 2005: 46–59; D. Qi, W. Wu and H. Zhang, 'Shareholding Structure and Corporate Performance of Partially Privatized Firms: Evidence from Listed Chinese Companies', *Pacific-Basin Finance Journal* 8, 2000: 587–610; Q. Sun, W. H. S. Tong and J. Tong, 'How Does Government Ownership Affect Firm Performance? Evidence from China's Privatization Experience', *Journal of Business Finance and Accounting* 29, 2002: 1–27.

108 *See*, W. G. Zhang, 'Shareholding Structures, Related Party Transactions and Corporate Governance in China', (pp. 27–53) in F. A. Gul and J. S. J. Tsui (eds) *The Governance of East Asian Corporations – Post Asian Financial Crisis*, New York: Palgrave, 2004: 42–44.

109 *See, generally,* Y. Wei, *Comparative Corporate Governance – A Chinese Perspective*, The Hague: Kluwer, 2003.

110 For discussions of some early history, *see*, W. Goetzmann and E. Koll, 'The History of Corporate Ownership in China – State Patronage, Company Legislation, and the Issue of Control', in R. Morck (ed.) *A History of Corporate Governance around the World*, Chicago: University of Chicago Press, 2005: 149–181; W. C. Kirby, 'China unincorporated: Company law and business enterprise in twentieth-century China', *Journal of Asian Studies* 54, 1995: 43–63; W. A. Thomas, *Western capitalism in China: A history of the Shanghai Stock Exchange*, Ashgate, 2001. *See also*, D. Faure, *China and Capitalism – A History of Business Enterprise in Modern China*, Hong Kong: Hong Kong University Press, 2006; and Redding, *supra note* 11

111 *See*, e.g. Z. J. Lin, L. M. Liu and Z. Xu, 'The development of corporate governance in China', *Company Lawyer*, 28, 2007: 195–203; S. Shim, 'Corporate governance reform in China', *Company Lawyer* 26, 2005: 375–378.

Part IV

The regulation of banking and the stock market

9 China's banking reforms at the time of global economic recession

Yuwa Wei

9.1. Introduction

In an era of 'fictitious economy' or 'financial deepening', no economic transformation or reform can be truly realized before a financial reform being effectively completed in the system.[1] It is true to say that finance has become the core section of a modern economic system. China's economic reforms had started by the time the concept of 'finance deepening' had just gained its influence and has progressed through out the period in which the practice of fictitious economy has reached the peak and begun to send warnings of how destructive it can be when the balance between fictitious economy and real economy is broken.

Against such a background, the Chinese have become more conscious than ever before of the importance of China's financial reforms to the ultimate success of the country's economic transition. While the attention of the world was directed to China's enterprise reforms and the reforms undertaken in its agricultural sector, financial reforms have been cautiously, but steadfastly carried out. After the completion of separating commercial banking from the central banking during the 1980s and 1990s, Chinese banks have accelerated the pace of commercialization. Various types of financial products have been introduced, and Chinese banks have been eager to embrace the idea and practice of securitization. In the meantime, a legal framework has been built up to facilitate the structural transformation.

However, the current economic recession in the global scale has posed the question of how far China may go down the path. Studying the Chinese case in the context of global development of fictitious economy, one may notice that while the Chinese endeavour to expand the program of banking privatization, the United States and some European countries have moved to nationalize their banks.[2] It is very interesting to note that these developed nations have been vigorously advocating and selling the idea of financial liberalization and fictitious economy for a few decades. The tide in these countries has turned quietly recently. How does China decipher such initiatives? To what extent should the Chinese connect the current global economic recession with finance deepening? Should China rethink its reform strategies concerning the banking sector reforms and make adjustments accordingly?

This chapter sets out to assess China's efforts in transforming its banking sector in order to facilitate the nation's economic reforms, through investigating the impact of the philosophy of fictitious economy on China's banking reforms, and examining the development of banking law and regulation. In doing so, this chapter deliberates on feasible reform strategies that the Chinese may need to formulate in order to develop an efficient market economy, as well as secure the country's future financial safety. The discussions will be divided into three sections. The second part of this chapter will examine the importance of banking development to economic growth. The third will introduce the banking reforms and regulation in China. The fourth will discuss the character of the current economic crisis sweeping the developed world and analyse the challenges that it poses to China in the process of growing into a mature market economy. The fifth part will seek solutions for China in developing a healthy banking system.

9.2. The importance of the banking sector and banking law to China's economic development

Investigation into the relationship between banking development and economic growth started since the nineteenth century. As early as 1873, Bagehot argued that well-functioning banks promoted economic growth.[3] This view was reiterated and confirmed by other economists, including Joseph Schumpeter and Levine.[4] Recent decades have observed increased attention being paid to the causal relationships between banks and economic development and between law and economy. King and Levine, based on their empirical research, argued that the level of financial development could act as a predictor of long-term economic growth.[5] Levine and Zervos developed a new formula, Bank Credit, to measure banking development. Bank Credit only took into account the loans issued by commercial banks and other loan-taking banks to the private sector. In doing so, it filtered out the credit issued by the central bank or other intermediaries and the credit issued to the government, and thus was able to more accurately indicate how well the banks identify profitable activities, mobilized resources, manage risks and facilitate transactions. Based on research, Levine and Zervos held that banking development positively predict economic growth, capital accumulation and productivity improvements.

At the same time, research on the connection between law and banking development has been progressing. In this field, the studies by LaPorta, Lopez-de-Silanes, Shleifer and Vishny are the most fruitful. Their research outcomes published in 1996 revealed that legal systems providing better protection to creditors and contract parties facilitated better functioning financial markets.[6] The fact that their analyses were based on extensive data collection (Information from 49 countries over fifteen years was collected, examined and analysed) has gained credibility for their conclusions. Levine further developed the research and discovered that legal systems giving a high priority to banks receiving the full present value of their claims against firms had better-developed banks than countries failing to do so.[7] His research also revealed that law enforcement was as important as the legal codes themselves, since the data indicated that countries effectively complying with laws were likely to have better-developed banks than countries with lax enforcement.[8]

On the other hand, arguments opposing the foregoing views claim that the role of the financial system has been over-stressed.[9] Some argue that banks were unlikely to respond actively to economic growth.[10] Some go further to point out that empirical evidence suggests that legal development did not play a crucial role in the rise of some economies, particularly those emerging economies in East Asia.[11]

Despite the opposing arguments, the attention on the financial sector and on law and economic development has gained increasing momentum in recent decades worldwide. This is evidenced by the development of regulatory regimes in both mature markets and emerging markets. Banking regulation in world's leading economies has generally experienced the transition from the domination of self-regulation to the domination of legal regulation. For instance, before 1933, the banking sector in the United States was basically unregulated. Since 1933, US banks have been subject to stringent legal regulation. Although US financial laws have undergone reforms for the purpose of loosening the control over banks since the 1980s,[12] legal regulation over the financial market and the banking sector has remained dominant. Meanwhile, financial laws in emerging economies have also experienced significant development.

In China, with the deepening of the economic reforms, increasing importance has been attached to the banking sector. This is because the financial turmoils which occurred in some emerging and transitional economies from the 1990s onwards have made the Chinese realize that financial crises are more costly to a developing country. In recent years, literature on the financial sector and economy has grown in China. For example, Hongping Song in *Currency Wars* illustrated the essential role of banks and currency control in an economy by reviewing the history of the fights for the power of issuing currencies in the developed world. In *Storms Striking Wall Street*,[13] a group of leading economists of China, including Wuchang Zhang, Jinglian Wu and Xianping Lang, enunciated their views on economic development in contemporary China and discussed the relationship between the financial sector and economy and the destructive effect that financial crises may cause to an economy. Facing the increasingly frequent and devastating economic crises resulting from financial failures in both developed and developing worlds, the Chinese have become more aware than ever of the essential part of banks in the healthy development of the economy.

Many researchers have called for the establishment of a financial safety net in China. Some generally equal a financial safety net with a banking safety net, and regard the financial safety net as a risk control system designed to protect banks and the public using bank services.[14] Some hold that a financial safety net should cover a broader scope of security strategies and institutional network, including a banking safety net.[15] This system comprises an internal safety net and an external safety net, which combines internal governance, external regulation, financial market admission control, performance and products evaluation and a set of remedial measures.[16] It is expected that with the formation of the safety net, the risk of financial crisis will be reduced to minimal and China's economy will eventually benefit from financial stability and sustainability.

It is clear that law will form the foundation of this financial safety net. Economic globalization has posed challenges to banks. First, with the progress of globalization, many countries have abolished or loosened capital control. This allows capital to flow swiftly and easily at a global scale and consequently increases the risk of financial crisis.[17] Second, globalization enables countries to borrow with less restrictions and difficulties. Large amounts of debts can drag a country into debt crises and can drive the banks acting as the intermediaries into insolvency.[18] Finally, due to lax control, exchange rates have become increasingly volatile, and this further exposes banks to greater financial and moral risks.[19] The aforementioned facts indicate that developing a set of practicable and effective laws to regulate financial transactions, control financial risks and monitor the business activities of financial institutions is an indispensable precondition for ensuring a country's economic safety in the context of globalization.

9.3. Banking reforms and regulation in China

Before the economic reforms, China's banking system, under the planned economy, was a mono-banking system, with the People's Bank of China (PBC) conducting the functions of both a central bank and a commercial bank.[20] Chinese banks adopted a unified manner of cooperation, with the PBC and its branches controlling and providing all types of financial services including credit issues, money supply, extension of loans, acceptance of deposits and savings.[21] With the framework of a market economy being established in China, reforms to the nation's banking/financial sector have been undertaken gradually.

Generally speaking, China's financial reforms have typically lagged behind its enterprise reforms. The government was particularly keen to maintain the stability in the banking sector and has been extremely cautious about taking drastic strategies to reform the banking system. Consequentially, the progress of China's banking reforms has been less impressive.[22] This has, however, not been a result of the reformers' negligence or confusion, but their deliberate arrangement. To be precise, this is the price that China needs to pay for achieving the objects of its overall economic reforms. Economic transformation comes with a cost. Any transitional economy has to pay this price in one way or another. Some transitional economies, such as those in Eastern Europe, took a radical reform step by rapidly privatizing their enterprises and financial institutions and thus paid their transitional costs in the form of inflation, massive unemployment, diminution of welfare and social instability. China took a gradualism approach to achieve its reform goals. This has been a top-down process of social and economic changes, in which the Chinese government plays the role of a guide and organizer. In this process, the government has extensively relied on state-owned banks to financially sustain the reforms in the rural and industrial sectors.[23] In other words, the Chinese banks have been paying for China's economic transitional costs. Since 1978, millions of Chinese enterprises have completed institutional transformation through corporatization; and many have been admitted into securities markets. Without the financial backing up of the state banks, this could hardly be achieved. Hence, the fruition of thirty years' economic reforms comes with a price – a banking system heavily burdened by bad loans. This is a price that the Chinese have been willing and believed worthwhile to pay.[24] Today, the enterprise reforms have come into the final stage, and now is the time for China to undertake thorough reforms to its financial sector.

Reviewing the path of China's banking reforms, one can see that important reform tasks were implemented in three phases. The first phase of banking reforms started in the mid-1980s. By then, China's enterprise reform was in its initial period and corporatization has just started. The main object of the reforms during this period was to restructure China's highly centralized and unified banking system into a diversified banking system in order to satisfy the demand of the expanding economic activities.[25] The most significant outcome of the reforms during this phase was the introduction of the two-tier banking system, which has since established the framework of China's banking sector. The two-tier banking system separated the country's central bank from other banks by defining the PBC as the central bank of the nation and other banks as specialized banks.[26] The specialized banks, including the Agricultural Bank of China (ABC), the Bank of China (BOC), the China Construction Bank (CCB) and the Industrial and Commercial Bank of China (ICBC), took over the commercial bank business from the PBC. In the meantime, China extended the enterprise reforms into its banking sector by establishing the first corporatized bank – the Bank of Communications, China (BoCom).[27] During this period, the important regulatory piece was 'The Decision of the State Council on Reforming the Financial System of China' (the Decision), which laid the legal foundation for China's banking system. The decision reaffirmed that the framework of China's banking system was an organizational system comprising an independent central bank to implement monetary policies and macro-control and state-owned commercial banks, coexisting with a variety of other financial institutions.[28]

The reforms in the first phase did not truly bring commercial banks into existence in China. The newly established specialized banks were not commercial banks yet in the strict sense. These institutions were, in fact, still in the transitional process from state-owned enterprises to modern corporations.[29] In this stage, the banks' main objects were to facilitate China's enterprise reforms and advance social welfare, rather than to maximize their profits. They were obliged to continue to provide financial support to state-owned enterprises and would not legally enforce an overdue debt against an enterprise.

The second phase of the banking reforms took place from 1994 to 2003. During this period, state-owned commercial banks emerged. In 1994, three policy banks were established to take over the policy lending business from the specialized banks. In fact, these banks were founded to provide finance for government projects of national priority, in order to ensure that macro-economic policies of the central government would be implemented and the objectives of national economic development would be achieved. The policy banks shouldered the task of financing and supporting the newly corporatized state-owned industrial firms – the products of the enterprise reforms. However, most of these newly corporatized enterprises lacked the initiative and the awareness of improving their management efficiency and credit records; rather, these enterprises continued to rely on the traditional ties between the state banks and themselves for finance.[30] As a result, the policy banks were heavily burdened with bad loans. The bad loans were so extensive that there was the danger that the banks might be dragged into bankruptcy soon. The Chinese government resolved the problem by setting up four state assets management companies. In 1997, four state assets management companies were established to take over and deal with the bad loans of the state commercial banks. By 1999, about ¥1400 billion assets were transferred from state commercial banks to the four state assets management companies, among them ¥980 billion were non-performing loans.[31] In the meantime, the government issued ¥270 billion of treasury bonds and the capital raised was used to improve the capital to debt ratio of the state commercial banks.[32] The banking reforms at this stage aimed to introduce the concept and mechanisms of risk management. This was an important step towards corporatization of state commercial banks.[33]

A legislative framework regulating the banking sector and the financial market began to take shape. Important banking laws enacted during the period included the *Law of the People's Republic of China on the People's Bank of China* (1995), the *Law of the People's Republic of China on Commercial Banks* (1995) and *Negotiable Instruments Law of the People's Republic of China* (1995).

During the second phase of the banking reforms, the Chinese government demonstrated great determination to deal with the bad-loan problem and introduced drastic measures to reduce the amount of non-performing loans accumulated by Chinese banks. The Asian financial crisis at the end of the 1990s served as a lesson to the Chinese and rang an alarm for the policy-makers. The Chinese acutely sensed the importance of financial health to a nation's economic safety.[34] The government speeded up the pace of banking restructuring. Policy banks were introduced for releasing specialized banks from policy lending, and treasury bonds were issued for cashing up these specialized banks. All these efforts were made for catalyzing the birth of real commercial banks in China. However, there was still a long way to go before Chinese banks could fully break away from their past practice and completely turn into profit-making institutions.

The third phase of China's banking reforms has been carried out from 2003 to present. With China's entry into the WTO, reforms to its banking sector have been accelerated. To fulfil its WTO commitments, China has to open its financial market to the world. Foreign banks, financial institutions and investment funds are able to enter into China's financial market. Foreign banks and financial institutions will gradually be allowed to carry on financial business in China. They will be able to compete with Chinese banks on equal terms. This has, in fact, put Chinese banks in a disadvantageous position, since China's banking sector has been in the process of transition from a banking system designed for facilitating the planned economy to a banking system working for the market economy. Compared with commercial banks in some mature markets, Chinese banks were less experienced in handling complex banking business in a market economy. Facing the challenge, the government sped up the banking reforms. The goal was to transform state-owned banks into 'real commercial banks'. An important strategy adopted was to corporatize state-owned banks in order to improve the internal governance of the banks, as well as introduce insolvency mechanisms into these banks.[35] In 2004, the BOC and CCB were the first to be corporatized. After corporatization, the BOC and the CCB have become commercial companies, in which the state controlled the dominant shareholdings. Since 2005, the BOC, the CCB and the BoCom have been admitted into the Hong Kong Stock Exchange and Shanghai Stock Exchange.

Legislation for banking and finance has made remarkable progress. The most significant step forward in law making during this stage was the amendments to the *Law on the People's Bank of China* and the *Law on Commercial Banks*, and the promulgation of a number of new laws and regulations including the *Law of the People's Republic of China on Supervision and Administration of the Banking Sector* (2003); the *Anti-money Laundering Law of the People's Republic of China* (2006); the *Regulations of People's Republic of China on Administration of Foreign Banks* (2006); and the *Methods of Administrating Trust Companies* (2007).

Research suggests that the third phase of banking reforms has begun to generate positive outcomes. For instance, three of the four commercial banks were listed on securities markets, and their reserve capital, competitive capacity and managerial transparence were improved substantially. The share prices of these banks increased steadily and their profitability rose dramatically.[36] All these have paved the way for further profound financial reforms.

Reviewing the historical development of China's banking sector, one can see that China's banking reforms have followed the trend of globalization and the Chinese have closely followed the banking practices in the world leading economies. This is evidenced by the promotion of a series of practices such as the move from fragmented banking to universal banking, the introduction of pilot projects undertaking trials of securitization and the adoption of modern corporate governance arrangements for internal control.

9.4. The difficult road to a market economy

The Chinese government has officially declared that the current banking reforms are necessary and crucial to the final success of China's transition from a planned economy to a market economy.[37] Today, many perceive that the banking reforms have basically achieved the goals of improving the strength and capacity of China's commercial banks to survive and compete in a market economy and an environment of economic globalization.[38]

Generally speaking, the banking reforms in the past twenty years have yielded positive results and visible improvements have been made to China's banking sector. First, the internal governance of Chinese banks has been improved significantly. The commercial banks have adopted the practice of modern corporate governance by setting up the board of directors and the supervisory board and by including foreign strategic investors and appointing financial experts to be independent directors.[39]

Second, economic performance and operational efficiency of the commercial banks have been enhanced. The capital adequacy ratios of the four commercial banks have increased from 2.11 per cent to 12.58 per cent between 2003 and 2008.[40] In the meantime, the non-performing loan ratio of these banks decreased from 16.84 per cent to 2.55 per cent.[41] The average return on assets (ROA) of the banks has exceeded 0.7 per cent, very close to the 1 per cent ROA performance of the top 100 banks in the world.[42]

Third, after the banking reforms Chinese commercial banks' ability to manage and withstand financial risks has been greatly enhanced. Chinese commercial banks have endeavoured to introduce advanced risk management mechanisms including stress test and the risk measure technique of Value at Risk (VAR) in order to accurately identify and forecast financial risks and develop timely strategies for risk control and management.[43]

However, beneath the success, there are worrying facts. First of all, the reforms to China's enterprise system, financial market and banking sector have extensively exposed China's financial market to possible international speculation at an early stage. Without first establishing a working financial safety net, such exposure makes China's banking sector vulnerable to financial crisis. Since the beginning of the new millennium, international hot money has been manipulating China's securities market and property market.[44] By the end of 2007, China has further opened its financial market to the world in fulfilling its WTO commitments. Nowadays, an increasing number of foreign banks and financial institutions have obtained permission to carry on businesses across finance, insurance, investment, securities dealings and banking services sectors. China's fledgling market system and legal regime are experiencing growing difficulties in exercising capital control. Its securities market and property market have faced more frequent and unbridled speculation. Without effective control, the crash of the securities market could happen at anytime, which may trigger financial crises.

Looking back at the financial crisis in Japan in the 1990s, the Chinese may be able to learn some lessons. Right before the financial market crash in the beginning of 1990, some international speculators were aggressively purchasing stock index put options. When the stock index put options accumulated to a sufficient amount, the speculators unleashed their attack on the Japanese capital market. Since January 1990, with the plunge of the stock index put option, the confidence of Japanese investors was eroded. Soon, all stocks dipped to historical lows and the Japanese capital market crashed. The crisis on the capital market quickly spread to Japan's banking sector, insurance business and finally the industrial sector, and Japan eventually sank into decades-long economic recession. Japan's experience tells the Chinese that an economic crisis could become a real threat, when China's capital market and banking sectors are under stress at the same time.[45]

Furthermore, since the financial reforms, China has loosened governmental control over its currency, and its financial market is therefore susceptible to speculation. In this aspect, the Chinese may be able to draw experience from the Asian economic turmoil at the end of the twentieth century. The success of the Asian emerging economies owed much to their policies for sustainable economic development. However, with the promotion of economic globalization, these countries eventually accelerated the pace of liberalizing their financial markets and freed exchange rates since the 1980s. This made these countries' currencies and securities markets extensively exposed to international speculative money.[46] Consequently, the financial markets of these countries crashed, and their economies ran into stress by the end of the 1990s. After ending its isolation, China has seen the opportunity of integrating itself into the global market. It has been gradually but steadfastly opening up its financial market and loosening the Renminbi exchange rate control. However, China, in every respect, is still a Third World developing country. Its securities market is in its infant stage and Chinese investors are immature. If China loosens the control over its currency and exposes its financial market prematurely, the country's financial safety will be in jeopardy.[47]

In addition, with foreign banks surging into China and introducing various new financial products, China's central bank may eventually lose its firm control over China's currency and finance.[48] Once China's central bank and banking sector are unable to function effectively in defending the country's currency, the Renminbi will become unstable and the risks of inflation and deflation will haunt China's economy all the time.[49] The introduction of various financial products and securitization of different types of bank loans in some developed countries have brought huge profits to banks on the one hand and shift financial risks to a wide range of investors on the other. They are also the main factor causing inflation and bubbles in the securities and property markets in these countries. Eventually, the bubbles will burst and millions pay a high price for the consequence of the financial adventures. The aftermath will affect every corner of a country's economy including collapse of industrial firms, inflation and crash of the capital market. In a country of lesser economic power such a crisis may be orchestrated by some mammoth international speculators. This actually happened in some emerging economies not long ago. Hence, it is crucial for China to establish an efficient regulatory and monitoring system over the banking activities in the country in order to limit such financial risks to a minimal degree.

Today's world economy has evolved into something beyond description of all classic economic theories and ordinary people's imagination.[50] Michael Hudson characterizes today's US economy and other leading market economies of the developed world as 'financial capitalism' or 'rentier capitalism'.[51] In such a system, ancient economic wisdoms cease to work, and people are encouraged to believe that earning capital gain in real estate and the stock market should be the main economic object. Hence, economic savings are recycled 'into real estate and the stock market to bid up land and equity prices, not to create new assets'.[52] The problem is that such an economic system will not sustain itself. The real estate bubble and the securities bubbles eventually burst and dragged the United States and the world into an unprecedented economic crisis.

On 2 April 2009, the G20 summit was held in London. The summit aimed mainly to achieve the following goals: (1) to stabilize financial markets; (2) to reform and strengthen the global financial and economic system to restore confidence and trust; and (3) to put the global economy on track for sustainable growth. Combating the current liquidity crisis was the focus of attention.[53] However, there is no sign of any efforts to bring fundamental changes to the current economic model by political powers and economic elites. With no reform to the current financial system being made, the rescue plans so far introduced will not really cure the disease. Hence, the most challenging task that China has to confront in the coming years will be how to achieve the goal of defending its financial and economic safety on the one hand, and continue to develop its economy and improve people's living standard on the other. Right now, colossal amounts of hot money have swarmed at the door of China's real estate market and securities market, and a battle between speculation and resisting speculation may take place at any moment. It was reported that the amount of international capital inflow in the second quarter of 2009 reached US$170 billion, an increase of 23 times of what it was in the first quarter.[54] Currently, the purpose of the capital is somewhat unclear. Some predicted that this hot money would target China's capital market and real estate market. Some warned that the money would target the industrial sector aiming to take over manufacturing enterprises.[55] It is evident that without guidance and supervision the hot money will do more harm than good. First, past experience indicates that hot money makes huge profits by creating chaos in a country's financial and real estate markets. Second, hot money usually takes over industrial firms for realizing profitability by selling the property and assets of the firms, rather than for the long-term prosperity of these firms. At a time of economic slow down, this will raise the unemployment rate and aggravate a country's economic difficulties.

It is interesting to note that while banks in the United States and some other developed countries are plagued by liquidity crisis, Chinese banks have performed reasonably well. The net profits of Chinese banks increased 30.6 per cent in 2008.[56] This growth rate is expected to continue in 2009.

For this reason, the Chinese government has no plan to slow down the bank reform engine. Instead, the banks are encouraged to increase their share capital and continue to expand their businesses. Some have warned that Chinese banks are likely to repeat the path of US banks and thus expose themselves to future financial crises.[57]

Currently, some Chinese people are more interested in the stability of the US dollar, but give less attention to assessing and examining the measures and outcomes of the bank reforms. This is another worrying fact.

9.5. Defending the nation's financial safety in an era of bubble economy and gambling nations

The development of China's economy since the economic reforms has benefited from the government's economic policies. The Chinese government has been very aware of the importance of maintaining capital control and the balance of international payment. The government has introduced mechanisms for controlling capital flows and defining borrowing limits. To ease its foreign capital shortages, China has endeavoured to attract foreign investments. The preference has been given to direct foreign investments. The Chinese government believes that direct foreign investment will not cause the problem of debt service.[58] China has effective control over foreign debts. As a result, it enjoys a comfortable position in foreign borrowing and external debt levers. Foreign loans are under tight governmental control. The Ministry of Commerce (the former Ministry of Foreign Trade and Economic Cooperation) is the only institution that can borrow from foreign governments.[59] In addition, the government has carefully designed the strategy of developing China's securities market investment, and in doing so, has limited the risk of excessive speculation by international hot money by dividing shares of Chinese companies listed on domestic stock exchanges into A shares and B shares.[60]

The aforementioned policies have allowed China to efficiently utilize foreign capital, maintain the stability of the Renminbi and sustain a low interest rate to stimulate domestic consumption and the economy. However, the foregoing mechanisms of capital control are under severe erosion and challenge in recent years. Today, China's financial safety is under the most serious threat. It is not an exaggeration to say that China has never been so vulnerable financially since the economic reforms. The first challenge or erosive element is internal. There exist serious irregularities in capital flows, resulting in evasion of capital control. The perpetrators include Sino–foreign joint ventures, wholly foreign-owned enterprises, transnationals and Chinese enterprises and citizens. The forms of evasion are many. For instance, some foreign enterprises use domestic collateral to borrow Renminbi.[61] It has become more prevalent that foreign investors use Chinese citizens as agents to buy A shares. Transfer of price by transnationals is not a rare incident. Corruption inside Chinese financial institutions and enterprises has further exposed China's financial safety to risks. Many Chinese enterprises invest abroad without authorization. Many of them resolve to forge documents to obtain foreign exchange as advances for non-existing imports.[62] There are also increased reports on cases where individuals falsify certificates or commercial documents to purchase foreign exchange.

It is imperative that China puts in place effective mechanisms of controlling and regulating capital inflow and outflow, in order to encourage long-term investments and direct international capital to flow into the economic sectors in need of foreign capital input. In the meantime, the government needs to tighten the control over the inflow of short-term capital and closely monitor their movements. This requires improvement of the regulation over international balance of payments, and establishment of a financial crisis management system combining the functions of financial risk identification, risk analysis, risk monitoring, risk forewarning and risk control. In the meantime, the government must strictly scrutinize foreign exchange businesses and transactions in state-owned enterprises and state banks and endeavour to crack down on illegal foreign exchange trading, so as to ensure the healthy development of the foreign exchange market.

The second erosive element or challenge that China has encountered comes from the WTO and the United States. China has been cautious in developing financial markets and liberalizing its capital account. The Chinese government has made great efforts to maintain a fixed Renminbi exchange rate and to control its financial market.[63] However, some economic powers and interested groups have put mounting pressure on the Chinese government to free up its exchange rate and increase the Renminbi value against the US dollar. In July 2005, China announced that the exchange rate between the US dollar and the Renminbi would be reduced to 1:8.11.[64] Soon, the value of the Renminbi against the US dollar was pushed up again. Since May 2007, the floating range of the exchange rate of the Renminbi has increased from 0.3 per cent to 0.5 per cent.[65] It means that within a single trading day, the Renminbi value could increase 0.5 per cent against the US dollar. It also means that China's foreign exchange reserves accumulated over the past few decades could shrink dramatically.[66]

In an age of economic globalization and debt capitalism, it is not realistic for China to return to strict Renminbi exchange rate control. In future, it is inevitable that the Renminbi will eventually become a fully convertible currency.[67] Before the Renminbi becoming fully convertible, it is necessary for the government to formulate rational Renminbi exchange rates against the US dollar and other hard currencies and at the same time, speed up the process of making the Renminbi exchange rate more market-oriented. However, it has never been an easy task to determine a rational Renminbi exchange rate against the US dollar or another currency, since the Renminbi exchange rates may have certain political, trading and financial impacts, and may have some effects on the regional or global economy.[68] For the time being, ending the anticipation of the financial market that the Renminbi will continue to appreciate unilaterally against the US dollar should be at the top agenda of the Chinese government. The employment rate in China has been under pressure in recent years. Since the global economy went to recession, many multinational and foreign companies residing in China have been cutting staff. This has further deteriorated the job market. Under such a circumstance, an appreciation of Renminbi will further lead to rise of the unemployment rate, due to the decline of export and increase of import.[69] At the time when social stability has been put on the top agenda, such an outcome will no doubt to be the most desirable to the Chinese. To avoid the risk, it is necessary for the Chinese to send a clear message to international speculators that China is not prepared to further relax its control on Renminbi exchange rate against the US dollar. Only in this way, China may be able to restrain hot money from speculating on the securities market, the real estate market and the Renminbi itself, in order to stabilize Renminbi exchange rates and the financial market.[70]

Another challenge to the Chinese is that China's banking sector is also under pressure to further open up. Like a beginner swimming in the rough sea, Chinese banks are forced to jump into fierce competition before they are ready. It is crucial that China's banking sector survives the competition, since the banking sector is the cornerstone of a country's financial arch.[71]

It is, therefore, extremely important for China to promote constructive financial policies and improve its regulatory framework for the banking sector in order to defend its financial safety and safeguard its economy. First of all, China's banking laws and regulations require further improvement. In this aspect, the most critical actions to be taken include: enhancing regulation over financial fraud and irregularities by introducing criminal liability for financial misconduct; establishing a working system for credit registry; introducing comprehensive laws governing financial institutions and businesses and improving the enterprise insolvency law.[72]

In the meantime, it is essential for China to develop an investigatory and monitory system to supervise the operation of foreign banks and financial institutions in the country. In recent years, with the enhancement of financial investigation, an alarming amount of financial misconduct by foreign financial institutions has been discovered.[73]

Currently, the PBC has the responsibility of making and implementing currency policies, averting financial risks and maintaining financial stability.[74] In fulfilling these duties, the PBC exercises investigative and supervisory rights, including information collection. Detailed strategies and procedures need to be introduced to guarantee the effective implementation of these powers.

Apart from the aforementioned strategies, China also needs to institutionalize its working policies regulating the financial sector through strengthening legal instruments. Due to the banks' essential role in shaping a healthy financial system, special attention should be given to developing sound banking laws. Overall, China's legal framework for the banking sector requires further enhancement. First of all, there is the need to perfect China's banking legislation. Although China has been productive in enacting laws regulating the banking sector in the past two decades, gaps and loopholes still remain in the banking legislation. For example, there are insufficient rules governing bank insolvency. Regulation over foreign banks is not addressed in the law either.

Furthermore, there is a lack of supporting rules in some related legal areas such as accounting, audit and insolvency, etc. An efficient banking sector requires the support of a carefully designed legal system. Hence, improving regulatory mechanisms should be regarded as a matter of urgency.

Second, there is the need to increase the practicability of the current banking law. Some banking rules are too general and lack details for implementation. For instance, the law stipulates that a banking regulatory institution may place a commercial bank under its administration, when a credit crisis is impending or has actually occurred, and depositors' interests are in jeopardy. However, the law fails to define a credit crisis and the situations endangering the interests of depositors.[75] The law has also omitted to provide for the authorities and the obligations of the banking regulatory agency in the course of taking over and administrating a commercial bank under stress. Another example is that the banking law does not clarify whether or not the *Insolvency Law* applies to banks. Moreover, the *Insolvency Law* does not provide specific rules regulating the substantive and procedural matters concerning the insolvency of a financial institution. It is not practicable to apply some general rules in the code to banks and other financial institutions.

Third, there is the need to maximize the co-ordination of various legislative pieces regulating the banking sector. Currently, three pieces of legislation have formed the three pillars of the banking law. They are: the *Law of the People's Republic of China on the People's Bank of China* (1995), the *Law of the People's Republic of China on Commercial Banks* (1995) and the *Law of the People's Republic of China on Supervision and Administration of the Banking Sector* (2003). Apart from these principal banking laws, there exist a number of specific regulations. In addition, more than 500 administrative rules, provisional rules, decrees and announcements have been produced by the State Council of China, the PBC, China Banking Regulatory Commission (CBRC), the CSRC and China Insurance Regulatory Commission (CIRC). There is a lack of co-ordination between these pieces of legislation. Moreover, some contents of these legal documents overlap, and sometimes, even contradict each other.[76] Time is up for Chinese law-makers to update these laws by repealing obsolete provisions and by amending conflicting rules. At the same time, efforts should be made to systematize China's banking legislation. Furthermore, the legislators should formulate legislative plans according to the objects and schedule of the financial reforms. Only through such comprehensive and coordinated efforts can the legislative costs be reduced and the efficiency of law enforcement increased.

9.6. Conclusion

Since China initiated the transition from a planned economy to a market economy, China's highly centralized banking system could no longer meet the needs of commercial activities in the changing economic environment. Reforms to its banking sector have become inevitable. In the past thirty years, reforms to China's banking system have been carried out in a gradual fashion.

Up to today, a banking sector compatible with a market economy has evolved. However, much work ought to be done to improve Chinese banks' economic efficiency and ability to weather financial risks, so as to ensure the final success of the economic reforms.

Since its entry into the WTO, China has extensively deregulated its financial market and opened much of its banking sector to foreign banks and financial institutions. This has urged Chinese banks to accelerate the pace of internationalization on the one hand and exposed these banks to increasing competition and challenges on the other. The Chinese government has taken key steps to assist the banks to survive and develop through out the transitional period. Between 1998 and 2005, the government injected huge amounts of capital into the four big commercial banks. In the meantime, the government relieved its largest banks from billions of US dollars in bad loans. As a result, the banks' capacity to resist financial crisis has improved significantly and are able to develop their businesses steadily, even in the current environment of global economic slowdown. Nevertheless, China still has a long way to go to fully modernize its banking sector. Some serious vulnerabilities remain to be addressed.

It is unclear how far and how fast the reforms will go. Immediately before the global economic slow down in 2008, some of the loudest calls for accelerating China's banking reforms both inside and outside China were made.[77] However, the recent financial crisis has reminded Chinese people to rethink their reform objects and strategies and has also made the people outside China to review their expectations on the progression of China's banking reforms. While debates continue, most Chinese people seem have the common understanding that developing an efficient financial system to support the market oriented economy is the only way out for China.

Notes

1 The concept of 'fictitious economy' or 'finance deepening' was firstly introduced by American economists Ronald McKinnon and Edward Shaw in the beginning of the 1970s. See R. McKinnon, *Money and Capital in Economic Development*, The Brookings Institution, Washington, 1973; and E. Shaw, *Financial Deepening in Economic Development*, Oxford University Press, New York, 1973.

2 *See* W. C. Zhang, J. L. Wu, X. P. Lang *et al.*, *Storms Strike Wall Street*, China Encyclopaedia Press, Beijing, 2009: 74, 150–152.

3 *See* W. Bagehot, *Lombard Street*, Richard D. Irwin, Homewood, 1873.

4 *See* J. A. Schumpeter, *The Theory of Economic Development* (Translated by Redvers Opie) Harvard University Press, Cambridge, MA, 1934; and R. Levine, 'The legal environment, banks, and long-run economic growth', *Journal of Money, Credit and Banking*, 30, 1998: 598–599.

5 *See* R. G. King and L. Ross, 'Finance and growth: Schumpeter might be right', *Quarterly Journal of Economics*, 103, 1993: 717–737.

6 *See* R. Laporta, F. Lopez-de-Silanes, A. Shleifer and R. W. Vishny, 'Law and finance', *National Bureau of Economic Research Working Paper* (No 5661,1996); and

R. Laporta, F. Lopez-de-Silanes, A. Shleifer and R. W. Vishny, 'Legal determinants of external finance', *Journal of Finance*, 52, 1997: 1131–1150.

7 *See* Levine, *supra note* 4, pp. 598–599.

8 *Ibid.*, p. 599.

9 *See* R. E. Lucas, 'On the mechanics of economic development', *Journal of Monetary Economics*, 22, 1988: 3–42.

10 *See* J. Robinson, 'The generalization of the general theory', in J. Robinson (ed.) *The Rate of Interest and Other Essays*, MacMillan, London, 1952: 67–142.

11 *See* T. Ginsburg, 'Does law matter for economic development? Evidence from Asia', *Law and Society Review*, 34, 2000: 829.

12 *See* the Depository Institutions Deregulation and Monetary Control Act of 1980; the Competition Equality Banking Act of 1987; and the US Financial Institutions Reform, Recovery and Enforcement Act of 1989.

13 *See* Yuan Lu (ed.), *Storms Striking Wall Street*, China Encyclopaedia Press, Beijing, 2009.

14 *See* P. Lin, 'The reflection on the theories and policies concerning financial safety nets', *South China Finance*, 11, 1999; and Longguang Yan, 'Designing a safety net for banks', *China Finance*, 2003: 7.

15 *See* X. Q. Zeng and Y. Yang, *A Study of the Legal System of Financial Safety Nets*, China Economic Publishing House, Beijing, 2009: 5.

16 *Ibid.*

17 *Ibid.*, p. 34.

18 *Ibid.*

19 *Ibid.*

20 *See* Kumiko Okazaki, 'Banking system reform in China: the challenges of moving toward a market-oriented economy' (Occasional Paper published by the Rand Corporation: Santa Monica, 2007), p. 6.

21 *Ibid.*

22 *See* J. Wang, *A Study of Strategic Transformation of China's State-Owned Commercial Banks*, Economic Science Press, Beijing, 2009: 125.

23 *See* X. Tang, *China's Financial Reform: Theories, Approaches and Devices*, China Finance Press, Beijing, 2008: 3–4, 14–15.

24 As Xu Tang stated: 'Without RMB 300 billion bad loans born by Chinese banks, there would not be realization of RMB 20,000 billion worth of Chinese listed companies in market value'. *See Ibid*, p. 15.

25 *See* J.C. Yang (2008), 'Reforming big banks: moving forward from a new starting point', pp. 2–3, available at <http://news.stockstar.com/Info/Darticle.aspx?id=JL,20081118,00000281&columnid=1823> [accessed 17 June 2009].

26 *See* Okazaki, 'Banking system reform in China: the challenges of moving toward a market-oriented economy', pp. 7–13.

27 At that time, all banks were wholly state-owned institutions adopting a governance system complimentary to the planned economy, which differed from the practice of corporate governance of a modern corporation, except the Bank of Communications, China.

28 *See* paragraph 1 of the 1993 *Decision of the State Council on Reforming the Financial System of China*.

29 *See* Tang, *supra note* 23, p. 13.

30 *Ibid.*, p. 3.

31 *See* Yang, *supra note* 25, p. 1.

32 *Ibid.*
33 *See* Y. W. Wei, 'The banking reforms in China: a move leading to financial safety or vulnerability?', *International Company and Commercial Law Review*, 9, 2009: 329.
34 *See* Wang, *supra,* note 22, p. 90.
35 *Ibid.*, pp. 91–92.
36 *See* Tang, *supra note* 23, p. 4.
37 *See* the remarks made by Mingkang Liu (the Chairperson of the Banking Regulatory Commission of China) in Mingkang Liu, 'China's banking reforms: the development and historical changes', *Qiu Shi,* 20, 2007: 25–28.
38 *See* Wei, *supra note* 33, p. 330.
39 *See* Yang, *supra note* 25, p. 1.
40 *Ibid.*
41 *Ibid.*
42 *See* M. K. Liu, *supra note* 37, p. 26.
43 *See* Yang, *supra note* 25, p. 3.
44 *See* Z. L. Yin (2005), 'Hot money attacks China', available at <http://news.sina.com.cn/c/2005-12-31/11348743853.shtml> [accessed 17 June 2009].
45 *See* Wei, *supra note* 33, p. 330.
46 *See* Yin, *supra note* 44, pp. 99–104.
47 *See* Wei, *supra note* 33, p. 331.
48 *See* H. B. Song, *Currency Wars*, China Citic Press, Beijing, 2007: 272.
49 *Ibid.*
50 *See* M. Hudson, 'Financial capitalism v. industrial capitalism'. Paper presented at *The Other Canon Conference on Production*, Oslo, 3–4 September 1998: 1.
51 *Ibid.*, p. 8.
52 *Ibid.*, p. 15.
53 *See* London Summit 2009. 'Global plan for recovery and reform' (The official communiqué issued at the close of the G20 London Summit), p. 1, available at <http://www.londonsummit.gov.un/resources/en/news/15766232/communique-020409> [accessed 17 June 2009].
54 *See* P. Xu, 'Hot money's re-entry into China', available at <http://news.xinhuanet.com/fortune/2009-07/31/content_11803789.htm> [accessed 17 June 2009].
55 *See* X. P. Lang, 'Well-engineered economic crisis: Hot money is not here just for speculating the stock market', *Zhongshan Business Daily*, available at <http://finance.sina.com.cn/stock/stocktalk/20090218/15345871445.shtml> [accessed 17 June 2009]. *See also* X. J. Qian, 'The inflow of US$120 billion hot money has created the historical high', *Shanghai Securities Daily*, available at <http://www.china.com.cn/economic/txt/2009-07/23/content_18186053.htm> [accessed 17 June 2009]
56 *See* China Banking Regulatory Commission, 'The report on opening up China's banking sector' (2007), p. 5, available at <http://www.china.com.cn/policy/txt/2007-03/22/conent_9252691.htm> [accessed 17 June 2009].
57 *See* Editor, 'How far China is away from financial crisis?' p. 1, Available at <http://cn.chinareviewnews.com/doc/1007/6/3/8/100763845.html?coluid=7εkindid=0εdocid=100763845> [accessed 17 June 2009].
58 *See* Y. D. Yu, 'China: the case for capital control', in W. Bello, N. Bullard and K. Malhotra (eds), *Global Finance: New Thinking on Regulating Speculative Capital Markets*, Zed Books, London & New York, 2002: 177.
59 *Ibid.*, p. 181.

60 Before 2003, A-shares could only be purchased by Chinese investors in Renminbi, while B-shares were offered to foreign investors to be purchased in foreign currencies. Usually, only about 30 per cent of a company's shares are freely transferable. State shares and legal person shares are not freely tradable on the stock market. This arrangement is called 'the split share structure'. In 2005, the China Securities Regulatory Commission initiated the program aiming at reforming the split share structure. Following certain procedures, companies are able to trade the shares previously classified as non-tradeable shares (i.e. state shares and legal person shares). However, the split share structure reform did not touch the arrangement of dividing company stocks into A and B shares. There are speculations that A and B shares will eventually merge into one category of shares, with the deepening of the share structure reform.

61 *See* L. H. Zhao, 'An analysis of the forms of irregular capital flows in China', *International Economic Review*, 1, 1999: 3–4.

62 *Ibid.*

63 *See* Y. L. Chen, 'National and international regulation of the Renminbi', in Z. P. Wu (ed.), *Jurists in Economic Law*, Beijing University Press, Beijing, 2003: 273.

64 *See* Wei, *supra note* 33, p. 332.

65 *Ibid.*

66 *Ibid.*

67 The increase of the demand on Renminbi and the loosening of Renminbi control all suggest the necessity of allowing Renminbi exchange rates to float according to the market needs. Chong Li made detailed analysis on the advantages and disadvantages of fixed exchange rates and floating exchange rates to an emerging economy. *See* Chong Li, *Financial War: Methods of Plundering Wealth in the Era of Fictitious Economy*, The Publishing House of the Capital City University of Business and Trade, Beijing, 2009: 223–233.

68 *See* C. Xu, 'The challenge of reforming Reminbi exchange rates in the era of globalization', *China Finance* (17 February 2008), available at <http://news.xinhuanet.com/fortune/2008-02/17/content_7616276_1.htm> [accessed 17 June 2009].

69 *See* M. J.Trebilcock and R. House, *The Regulation of International Trade*, Routledge, New York, 2005: 93.

70 *See* Wei, *supra note* 33, p. 332.

71 *Ibid.*

72 *Ibid.*

73 *See* China Banking Regulatory Commission, 'The report on opening up China's banking sector', p. 5.

74 *See* Section 2 of the 2003 *Law on the People's Bank of China*.

75 Section 64 of the *Law of the People's Republic of China on Commercial Banks* states: 'the State Banking Regulatory agencies can take over a bank that is experiencing or has experienced a credit crisis, and thus seriously affects the interests of its depositors'.

76 *See* the Business Unit of Shanghai Lawyers Association, 'The special report on the forum on reviewing and forecasting China's banking legislation, and the most vigorously debated topics concerning the development of the banking sector', available at <http://www.lawyers.org.cn/info/11bc41487936a516179b38187e02a873> [accessed 17 June 2009].

77 *See* L. Zhang, 'An inevitable change: WTO and economic analysis of the development of China's banks', available at <http://www.studa.net/jingjililun/080729/14464269.html> [accessed 17 June 2009].

10 The political logic of securities regulation in China

Jiangyu Wang

10.1. Introduction

The development of the securities market in the People's Republic of China (hereafter China or PRC) is truly a legend. No shareholding company existed in the PRC from the late 1950s to the early 1980s. A national securities market began to emerge only after 1993. In 1991, a year after the Shanghai Stock Exchange and Shenzhen Stock Exchange were established, there were only 14 listed companies in China, with total market capitalization of merely RMB10.9 billion yuan.[1] By the end of 2009, 1718 companies were listed on the two stock exchanges, and the total market capitalization exceeded RMB24,393.9 billion yuan.[2] In addition, 28 companies are listed on the ChiNext, China's NASDAQ-like growth enterprise board (*chuangyeban*) opened on 23 October 2009.[3] Today, the Chinese stock market, excluding Hong Kong, is the second largest in the world.[4] Meantime, starting from scratch in the early 1990s, China has now established a very sophisticated national regulatory framework for governing the securities market.

The orthodox theories of economic regulation, such as the public interest theory and public choice theory, are hardly able to help us understand the logic of securities regulation in China. This is because the relationship between state and business, and the politics therein, are very different in China. Regulation theories were originally developed to explain how regulation arises, develops and declines in Western democracies. From a public interest perspective, it is first of all extremely difficult to identify the interest-orientation of a public policy in China, given the many conflicting objectives and vested interests which have to be included in the decision-making process. The main idea of the public choice theory is understood as

> on the one hand, that citizens and interest groups use their *voting* power to extract from collective decision-making the maximum benefits for themselves, and, on the other hand, that politicians and political parties act as entrepreneurs to provide those benefits in exchange for *voting* them into power.[5]

The economic and political systems of China present a different picture:

> Significant public ownership of industrial assets inevitably leads to conflict of interest for the government in its roles as both owner and regulator. The ambition of the Chinese Communist Party … to retain a monopoly of political power prevents the full emergence of the rule of law. Powerful provincial governments have discretion over a wide range policy and can act autonomously, often undermining the coherence of national policy. Moreover, limited private-sector involvement in the economy and the policy-making process itself, as well as the lack of electoral competition, means that public actors are largely insulated from external pressures when they develop institutions. This is in contrast to Western experience where private-sector interests often lead institutional development.[6]

This chapter adopts a political approach to explain the philosophy and practice of securities regulation in China in the context of the unique developmental path of the country's economic and political systems. It argues that securities regulation in China is part of the Chinese government's political legitimacy management efforts. For this reason, government regulation of securities market in China shall not be understood merely as economic regulation. Seen in a broader picture, securities regulation is a government-controlled process to rebuild and maintain political legitimacy of the Chinese state. This explains, in part, the often-conflicting regulatory objectives and self-contradictory regulatory practices in the Chinese securities market. In this endeavour, the paper also borrows some elements from the public interest and public choice theories which offer some powerful explanatory tools for use in the Chinese case.

10.2. Legitimacy management and government regulation in China

10.2.1. A conceptual framework of legitimacy management

Political legitimacy can be broadly defined to include 'both citizens' trust in public officials and their conviction that government institutions are fair, responsive and valuable'.[7] It deals with a fundamental question about 'who deserves to have authority and why'.[8] As Weber noted, 'So far as it is not derived merely from fear or from motives of expedience, a willingness to submit to an order … always in some sense implies a belief in the legitimate authority of the course imposing it'.[9] Put in a simple way, a legitimate regime, no matter whether it is good, peaceful, democratic, etc. is accepted by the people (or the majority of the people) as a government with political authority.

Broadly, political legitimacy contains two elements, namely the control of power and popular acceptance. Legitimacy, however, cannot be taken for granted by the ruler or ruling party. As Lipset points out, legitimacy also 'involves the capacity of a political system to engender and maintain the belief that existing political institutions are the most appropriate and proper ones for the society'.[10] In other words, legitimacy must be managed in order to remain viable and sustainable. Political legitimacy management involves the tasks of gaining legitimacy, maintaining legitimacy and repairing legitimacy.[11] A political regime, after gaining power, must constantly take measures to win and maintain public acceptance of its authority to rule. Specifically, the regime must fulfil the following tasks, which, as often conflicting with each other, not only need to be deployed concurrently, but also be balanced:

- Concentration and preservation of power
- Promotion and maintenance of the ruling group's ideology
- Coordinating interest groups politics
- Control of bureaucratic politics (departmentalism) and official rent-seeking (corruption)
- Pursuance of good policy to rationalize governance, including institutional building.

10.2.2. Legitimacy management in China

As an authoritarian Party-state, the Chinese government cannot base its legitimacy on democratic elections. This, however, does not mean the regime is one without legitimacy. Guo argues that political legitimacy in the Chinese context can be understood from the perspective of original justification and utilitarian justification. Original justification, tracing the origin of the ruling authority, refers to four Chinese concepts: mandate of Heaven (*tianming*), rule by virtue (*dezhi*), popular consent (*minben*) and legality (*hefa*).[12] Utilitarian justification deals with the capacity of the rulers to meet people's needs, such as material well-being or physical security.[13] Utilitarian justification is directly related to maintaining legitimacy, namely 'how to maintain people's belief that the political system is legitimate'.[14] In the Chinese context, this entails that the government, as a provider of benefits, should implement public policies which are consistent with the concepts of 'benefiting the people' (*limin*) and 'equality of wealth' (*junfu*).[15] In short, the Chinese cognitive pattern of political legitimacy can be stated as follows:

> A ruler, who has the mandate of Heaven, possesses the quality of virtue, shows respect to his subjects, follows the rules of the ancestors, and tries to win the hearts and minds of the people, will be considered a just and legitimate one. A just ruler will strengthen his legitimacy by promoting policies that will benefit the people, not himself, by ensuring relatively equal distribution of these benefits, and by allowing the people to do what they do the best.[16]

In the Reform Era, political legitimacy management has focused on the following agenda, with the ultimate goals of preserving power base of the Chinese Communist Party (CCP), maintaining the dominant status of the CCP's evolving ideology, maintaining social stability, pursuing good policy to build institutions and rationalize governance, balancing the conflicting objectives of interest groups and containing departmentalism and corruption:

(1) *Preserving the CCP's Power Base:* It is no surprise that the primary purpose of the CCP is to maintain its status as the ruling party of the state. For the CCP, staying in power is not achieved through elections. Instead, the CCP must use other means to hold on to power, the most important of which is to deliver sustained improvements in consumption and living standards to the Chinese people through economic growth. Apart from this, the regime also has to ensure that it controls sufficient financial and other resources. This objective determines, to a large extent, the state's policy-orientation to state- and private-owned enterprises.

(2) *Maintaining Official Ideology:* 'Ideological adaptation and innovation are thus seen as *the* prerequisite of relegitimating party rule'.[17] Party scholars in China believe that 'ideology fulfils various functions crucial to political, social and economic life, such as interpreting political order, cementing national security, mobilizing support and reducing economic transaction costs by enhancing social trust'.[18]

   In the 1980s and early 1990s, the battle over Marxism and capitalism in China remained intense. Reflected in economic regulation, reformers at that time face tough questions from conservatives whether a particular public policy would turn China into a capitalist society. Reformers had to convince the conservatives that a public policy or project was not only in line with the official socialist ideology, but would also promote it. For example, Liu Hongru, the first Chairman of the Chinese Securities Regulatory Commission (CSRC), was pressed by conservative legislators at the National People's Congress (NPC) with the allegation that all systems of shareholding and stock markets would lead to privatization (and hence the collapse of socialism), during a committee meeting of the National People's Congress in 1992.[19]

   With the gradual demise of the Marxist ideology, nationalism now 'serves as an integral part and important ingredient of ideological modernization',[20] increasingly employed by the Chinese state to justify its legitimacy. Any major public policy, if characterized as something which may contribute to China's rise to a superpower, to 'national unity' or to 'national self-confidence and pride', will be much easier to gain public support. In this context, the securities market has been promoted as something crucial to China's 'peaceful ascendancy to the status of a great power' by the authorities.[21]

(3) *Maintaining Stability:* Bearing in mind the chaos and turmoil during the Mao Era, the Chinese leadership since Deng Xiaoping has been obsessed

with maintaining social stability.[22] Deng Xiaoping's 1989 phrase, 'stability above everything', has been carried out throughout the Reform Era. All government agencies at the central and local levels are required to vigorously maintain political and social stability. As the major report to the 2002 Sixteenth CPC Congress has required, 'It is essential for the Party to give top priority to development', but 'stability is a prerequisite for reform and development'.[23] The stability orientation has had a significant impact on officials' (including regulators') behaviours. In the case of economic regulation, this may mean that regulators have to intervene in the market activities to maintain stability, even though doing this may undermine market efficiency. As will be discussed in the following section, from time to time, China's securities regulators have tried a variety of means to meddle in the securities market for the political sake of achieving political and social stability.

(4) *Managing Interest Groups:* The absence of democracy does not necessarily mean that China is lacking special interests. As ownership gets increasingly dispersed and the society more diversified, different interest groups have begun to emerge. In the area of economic regulation, the regulatees are having a subtle relationship with the regulators. The 'life-cycle' accounts of the regulatory capture theory suggest that regulatory agencies go through various stages, from vigorous enforcement at the beginning of its establishment to becoming the protectors of the regulated in the end.[24] Regulatory capture in China takes place in a different context: at the beginning, the regulated enterprises were usually the 'children' of the regulators, namely they were initially created or sponsored by the regulators. During the planned economy period, China established a central power structure that divided the administration of all aspects of the national economy among different agencies, with state-run enterprises under most agencies. Premier Zhu Rongji's Government Restructuring Project in 1998 deprived most economic agencies of their direct powers and interests over domestic industries and significantly weakened the ministries-industries complex. But even after this reform, state-owned enterprises (SOEs) found protégés in the remaining government agencies. The agencies, prompted both by ideological traditions and by departmental benefits such as 'soft money income', are willing to be the industries' representatives and fight for their interests in the decision-making process. Over time, a Chinese style of departmentalism (*benwei zhuyi*) has emerged as one of the most salient features in Chinese politics.[25]

(5) *Official Rent-seeking:* The public sector in China has a notorious reputation of being corrupt. As Pei observes, corruption 'undermines the legitimacy of the ruling [CCP], fuel social unrest, contributes directly to the rise in socioeconomic inequality'. Ultimately, 'if the party fails to curb corruption, China will most likely witness the rise of a form authoritarian crony-capitalism that marries unaccountable political power with ill-gotten private wealth'.[26] Corruption tends to concentrate in sectors that involve

extensive state investment or heavy state regulation.[27] As will be discussed in the following section, the securities regulators were also tainted by corruption, with a number of its senior officials convicted in the past years. The Chinese government acknowledges the problem, but whether it is able to wage an effective war against corruption is still an open question. Fighting corruption needs not only the rule of law, but also the commitment of the political elites to relinquish opportunities to use public office to gain private benefits. Many anti-corruption measures have been adopted in China, but their success within the current political framework eventually depends on whether the CCP's good policy pursuance can override the rent-seeking temptations. At least for now, the central leadership has been successful in casting itself as an enemy of corruption.

(6) *Pursuance of Good Policy:* Political approaches based on public choice theory to interpreting economic regulation in China tend to underestimate the Chinese leadership's commitment to pursue good public policy. Leaving aside the controversial debate over Mao Zedong's motives of launching the Cultural Revolution, it is widely recognized that the central leadership after Mao has been consistently seeking the correct course through which China can achieve modernization.[28] For example, in the wake of Mao's death, Deng Xiaoping arguably could have become another dictatorial ruler. Rather, Deng used the chance to put into practice his beliefs that China could become prosperous and strong only after firms and individuals in the country were allowed to pursue their own fortune and to face competition from outside China. Lieberthal identifies the major motives underlying Deng's reform measures, and observes that most of them were good-policy driven.[29] Another example was China's accession to the World Trade Organization (WTO). In fact, domestic opposition was at its strongest point when the Chinese leadership accepted the packages drafted by the United States in 1999. The reason was that Chinese leaders felt the need of using the outside pressure from the WTO to push for bolder and wider domestic economic and regulatory reform.[30] As Lardy remarks, although 'political leaders rarely are willing to impose high short-term economic costs in order to reap benefits in the medium and long run', China appeared to be an exception.[31]

Good policy in the contemporary Chinese political context first means that the ruling party must deliver sustained economic growth, which is one of the primary pillars of the Party-state's legitimacy. Lardy notes that, although Chinese elites have hotly debated many details of the economic reform, 'the view that economic growth is the *sine qua non* for retaining political power seems almost unanimous'.[32] At the operational level, pursuing good policy has led to substantial regulatory reform in China, featuring efforts to improve legalism, transparency, accountability and independence of the regulatory systems.[33]

10.3. Legitimacy management and the establishment of a national securities market and regulatory framework

CSRC notes that the growth of China's securities market has gone through three stages.[34] From 1978 to 1992 was the formative period, during which shareholding enterprises, shares, bonds and securities intermediaries emerged in the form of informal markets in many places across China as a result of Deng Xiaoping's economic reform programme which encouraged a market-oriented approach to resource allocation.[35] The second stage, from 1993 to 1998, witnessed the development of more formal structures, such as stock exchanges, corporate law and regulatory framework. At the third stage (1999–present), more significant additional reforms have been implemented, marked by the 1998 Securities Law which codified the central government's exclusive authority over the securities market, as well as the 2005–2006 Split Shareholding Structure Reform (*guquan fenzhi gaige*) which converted, legally, all non-tradable shares into tradable ones.

In praise of the initially market-oriented approach to developing capital markets, the World Bank Development Report 1996 cited China's experience: 'China is an example of bottom-up regulatory development: the emergence of regional exchanges prompted regional regulators to formulate their own rules first, which were later absorbed into an overarching national regulatory framework'.[36] That is to say, the development of the securities market was initially driven by spontaneous innovation by market participants and local authorities, until the central government intervened in the early 1990s to establish a national, uniform regulatory framework. The legitimacy management model could effectively explain the motives behind this unification movement. In this process, legitimacy related considerations, such as concentration of state power, maintaining the mainstream ideology, political and social stability and establishing and institutionalizing a market-oriented regulatory framework, all played significant roles.

10.3.1. Securities market and SOE reform

In order to overcome the objections and doubts held widely among conservative senior officials and some members of the public, the exponents of securities market initially advanced two arguments: one was that the securities market could bring private capital to finance the ailing SOEs, and the other was that securities market could improve corporate governance of SOEs.[37] Obviously, the first argument is directly related to concentration of state power, and the second is concerned with good public policy.

As Naughton notes, 'Chinese stock markets were given the go-ahead by the top political leadership – and especially [the] premier at that time, Zhu Rongji – because of the role they could play in reforming the state-enterprise sector'.[38] SOEs form the most important part of the state's power base. Li Rongrong, the chief officer supervising China's SOEs, once granted to SOEs a title of the 'eldest son of the [People's] Republic' (*gongheguo zhangzi*), indicating that they had the greatest financial and social responsibility to the state.[39] In fact, at the inception of China's economic reform in 1978, China's industry was largely state owned, with traditional SOEs producing 77 per cent of industrial output and employing 76 per cent of all industrial workers.[40] For most years in the 1980s and 1990s, SOEs were facing serious difficulties, including deteriorating financial performances.[41] The SOEs were initially financed by the state budget and then bank lending as reform of the financial system progressed. In the late 1980s, organized reformers began to persuade the senior leaders that the securities market could provide a more efficient and cheaper channel for industry financing. In the words of a report about the Shanghai stock market, which was submitted in 1991 to the State Council (China's central government) by a joint investigative group comprising representatives from the then State Commission for Restructuring the Economic System, People's Bank of China and State Administration for Foreign Exchange:

> Seen from Shanghai's situation, it is really necessary to implement a shareholding system dominated by public ownership and to modestly develop the securities markets. First, this may raise relatively larger amounts of funds to finance technological restructuring of backward SOEs as well as important infrastructural projects. At this stage, state-run large- and medium-sized enterprises are seriously backward in equipments and technology, and could have sustained development. The major contradiction is that they are short of funds because the state is facing fiscal constraints and difficulties [and hence cannot inject more capital], and the banks lending cannot be so large to meet all the needs. For this reason, raising funds through issuing shares to the public could not only absorb the huge amount of unused money in the civil society, but also could convert consumption money into capital for production and construction …[42]

Similarly statements appeared in a number of other internal reports.[43] In fact, throughout the history of China's securities market, its major patrons have always been SOEs. Today, most of the listed companies are directly or indirectly controlled by the state.[44] By the end of 2007, the stock market as a source of funding supplied about RMB1.92 trillion yuan to Chinese companies in the form of corporate shares and bonds,[45] and most of the funds went directly to SOEs, strengthening significantly the Chinese state's financial capacity.

As for pursuing good policy, the securities market was expected to be a tool to improve SOEs' corporate governance from the very beginning of the economic reform. The aforesaid report to the State Council also stated that '[raising funds from the securities market] could improve the transparency of SOE's management, leading to SOEs' self-constraints, self-development and self-responsibility with respect to profits and losses'.[46] In a national conference on securities market development in October 1991, Liu Honghu, then a vice governor in charge of coordinating capital markets in the People's Bank of China and later the first Chairman of the CSRC, urged the audience to recognize the securities market's ability to improve SOE governance by introducing into the SOE non-state shareholders. Traditionally, attention was mainly paid to the fund-raising function of the securities markets.[47] In the 1990s, the accelerated development of the securities market, together with the adoption of the 1993 PRC *Company Law*, fundamentally changed the landscape of industrial enterprises in China by 'corporatizing' the traditional SOEs – namely converting them into the form of companies with an independent legal personality, which paved the way for their further privatization.

10.3.2. Managing the ideological debate on a securities market: socialism, capitalism and nationalism

After the government's crackdown of the 1989 Tiananmen demonstration, the battle over socialism and capitalism revived. The conservatives were able to press their advantage and lead the economic development towards re-emphasizing state planning and public ownership.[48] Conservatives were mounting attacks on market-oriented reforms, arguing, 'opposing bourgeois – not developing productive forces – was the key to ensuring political stability'.[49] In such a climate, the biggest fear for the reformers was the possibility of political prosecution once they carried out their ideas, although they still hoped to gain support from open-minded leaders.

The most immediate threat was the call by the conservative faction to close the local securities markets, in particular, in Shanghai and Shenzhen. Liu Hongru recalled that, in a 1992 meeting with members of the NPC's Financial and Economic Affairs Committee, tough questions and statements concerning whether the securities market would lead to departure from socialism were raised by Committee members. One member alleged that 'worldwide experience suggests that no shareholding system would not lead to [complete] privatization'.[50] Similar criticisms were already directed to the proponents of securities markets, from both senior officials and ordinary citizens, in those years.[51] Fearing possible political backlash, Liu, in a meeting with President Jiang Zemin, pleaded with the undecided President:

> No matter what, we should continue our stock market experiment – our reform must not go backward. Please trust me, as an old Party member, I would not carelessly push for privatization. But since mistakes are unavoidable, I hope that we don't punish people or affix political labels. If that happens, no one would be willing to take responsibility.[52]

President Jiang eventually decided that the markets in Shanghai and Shenzhen could be kept, however on the condition that they might not be expanded further and that no more new markets would be established until China gained more experience.[53] The real breakthrough could only be made by Deng Xiaoping, China's Paramount Leader. In his famous 'South Tour' in which he declared that China would replace its planned economy with a market economy and encouraged people to boldly conduct experiments in all aspects of the economy irrespective of the socialistic or capitalistic nature of the activities, Deng made the following comment: 'Securities and stock markets, are these things good or bad? ... Are they peculiar to capitalism? Can socialism make use of them? We allow people to reserve their judgment, but we must try these things out'.[54]

These statements, carrying the political authority of Deng, eventually silenced the opponents and ended the debate on the securities market in respect of its ideological nature. However, there is no way for the reformers to claim a full victory, as they had to, as a reconciliatory gesture to the conservatives, promise that 'public ownership should dominate the market' – in particular, state ownership in public companies should generally not be less than 51 per cent, and that the transfer of state shares should obtain special approval from the authorities in charge of state assets.[55] This was the origin of the split shareholding structure in China's securities market. It is however worth mentioning that the split share structure was considered a good policy even by reformers at that time.[56]

Over the years, the securities market has gradually taken root in China, but it still faces challenges as to its relevance to the Chinese economy. In January 2001 Wu Jinglian, one of China's pre-eminent 'mainstream' economists,[57] proclaimed that China's stock market was 'worse than a casino'.[58] Another economist, Xu Xiaonian, allegedly said in public that China's stock market should be knocked down first and then rebuilt from scratch (*tuidao chonglai*). Those statements triggered remarkable reactions, leading to an intensive debate in the following years on the utility of the securities market to the Chinese economy.[59] In response to this, the central government has taken a number of measures to stimulate public confidence in the securities market. In January 2004, the State Council released the Opinions of the State Council on Promoting the Reform, Opening and Steady Growth of Capital Markets.[60] As the State Council's first policy paper on the securities market, the Opinions emphasized the importance of strengthened rule of law enforcement in the market. It, however, also reminds the people that the securities market is of 'strategic importance' to the development of a socialist market economy.

In recent years, nationalism is increasingly deployed as a tool to inspire public support of the securities market. Thus Shang Fulin, the current Chairman of the CSRC, stated that '[t]he competitiveness and viability of the capital markets have become important components of national competitiveness'.[61] In an article titled 'Capital Markets and the Rise of Great Powers', Qi Bin, the Director of CSRC's Research Center, argues that international experiences suggest that the rise of all great powers had all been supported by a strong capital market, such as the role Wall Street played for the US hegemony, and that the battle among today's great powers will be one competing for international capital flow. As such, the resurgence of China as a great power and great civilization cannot be achieved without the driving force generated from a strong securities market.[62]

10.3.3. Establishment of a national regulatory framework: power concentration and institutional building

As noted previously, securities activities, such as share and bond issuance and over-the-counter (OTC) trading, emerged as early as the 1980s, driven mainly by initiatives of market participants and local governments. The central government did not make substantial efforts to regulate the markets until 1992, when the CSRC was established with the aim to implement a very preliminary national regulatory framework. The CSRC acquired the full power to regulate a nationally united market only after 1999, when the national *Securities Law* took effect. Two legitimacy-management-related motives present themselves in this 'national unification' process: the determination to reassert state control over the capital markets by transferring the regulatory power fully to the central level, and the good-policy-based belief that the central government should take the lead in establishing a national market and building regulatory institutions in order to balance the popular demands for shares and curb irregular securities activities.

In the early 1980s, a few small SOEs and collective enterprises experimented with share offerings, initially only to their own employees. After 1986, some large SOEs joined in and issued shares publicly or semi-publicly, in response to the central government's call for expanding the SOE restructuring programme. Investors started to trade the shares and bonds privately in the so-called black markets.[63] In short, the answer to the question 'how did it start', in the words of commentators, is that the experiments arose 'spontaneously all across the country, wherever people needed money … and no longer feared political repercussions'.[64]

Although regulatory authority was lodged with the People's Bank of China (PBC), which is China's central bank, central officials largely stood aside and tended to ratify existing practices during the 1980s and early 1990s. There were no local securities rules until 1984, when Shanghai Municipal Government adopted the nation's first rules on share issues.[65] Since then local governments, in collaboration with the local branches of the PBC, enthusiastically stepped in to regulate the market largely in the spirit of encouraging securities activities.[66] Most significantly, the establishment of both the Shanghai and Shenzhen stock exchanges resulted from local initiatives.[67]

The central government acted in response to the '8.10 riot' in Shenzhen. In the early 1990s, the public's enthusiasm in buying shares had evolved into 'a stock fever' in a market which had only a few issuers.[68] In August 1992, about 1.2 million investors flooded into Shenzhen to participate in an IPO. As most of them were not able to buy the IPO application forms (the owners of which were allowed to subscribe to IPO shares through lottery), they suspected that most of the forms went to corrupted officials and their families and friends through the 'backdoor'. On 10 August, 'this dissatisfaction spilled over into rioting, the most serious social disturbance in China since the 1989 Tiananmen Square protests'.[69] Two days later, Zhu Rongji, the State Council's Vice Premier in charge of economic affairs, announced the central government's intention to establish a national regulator for the securities market. On 12 October 1992, the State Council decided to form the State Council Securities Committee (SCSC) and the CSRC. The SCSC was a ministerial level government agency in charge of macro-management of the securities market, comprising of representatives from a number of ministries. The CSRS was designed to be a non-government organization and an implementing agency for the SCSC.[70]

The establishment of the SCSC/CSRC combination represents the state's reassertion of the regulatory power over the securities market. The reassertion of power ignited a prolonged securities regulatory battle between the central and local governments, which was the main theme of securities politics in the 1990s. The SCSC was mainly a meeting forum; the CSRC was regarded as a securities supervisor which, however, was not granted the supervisory powers to make rules or to punish illegal behaviours. More significantly, the two stock exchanges were still under the control of the local municipal governments.

'Dual supervision' has been used to characterize the period between 1993 and 1997,[71] which featured a political battle between the CSRC with the Shenzhen and Shanghai governments over the power to regulate the exchanges – and the markets. The two local governments offered the exchanges great autonomy to supervise the stock markets, and the exchanges developed innovative regulatory tools, combined with the local governments' industrial, fiscal and bank-lending policy, to expand the listing and trading of shares. Local governments benefited from rapidly increased stamp tax and flood of domestic and foreign investment in their jurisdictions. Risk management was hardly a major consideration.[72] However, as Green observes:

> Local leaders equity developmentalism during 1993–1997 was especially frustrating for the central leadership because of their new ambition to enlist the share market in support of SOE reform on a much larger scale than before. While the secondary market was so volatile, manipulation so extensive, the risks of a market crash so high, the CSRC's regulatory abilities so limited and local administrative influence so far-reaching, their programme could not be effectively rolled out.[73]

The CSRC, on behalf of the central government, gradually seized the regulatory powers from the local governments through a variety of political manoeuvres. In this process, the CSRC has brought a variety of institutional changes to the regulatory framework. In 1996, the SCSC issued the Measures for the Administration of Securities Exchanges which granted

> the CSRC *de jure* authority over the appointment of the exchanges' senior management; the power to request the exchange to punish their members

> and listed companies; to suspend trading; and to sanction the exchanges for failure to enforce any regulation.[74]

The regulation also theoretically excluded the local governments from exerting any jurisdiction over the stock exchanges. Despite the strong resistance from the local leaders, the CSRC sent its staff to take over the key management positions in the two stock exchanges in 1997.[75] These measures were codified in the 1998 national Securities Law. Further measures were adopted to take away the self-regulatory powers of the exchanges, reducing them to the CSRC's *de facto* administrative arms in the disguise of 'self-regulatory organizations'. As a result, the CSRC now controls the exchanges in the following aspects:

> appointment powers; direct supervision of day-to-day exchange activities; full-time CSRC staff based at the exchanges; CSRC control of all aspects of market development (including research on new instruments); CSRC control of all investigations; and CSRC control of the issuance and listing process.[76]

In addition, the share of stamp tax collected by the Shenzhen and Shanghai governments decreased from 50 per cent to 3 per cent, tremendously reducing the financial incentive for the local governments to regulate the markets.[77]

Thus, although the development of China's securities market was initially driven by market forces and local initiatives, it was eventually integrated into China's market socialism through the creation of a centralized legal and institutional framework.[78] For the central government, this institutional capture is a typical legitimacy management process. On the one hand, it caused the stock exchanges to completely lose their autonomy and innovative capacity, as well as their self-regulatory powers. Market forces are now successfully under the control of the government, and would grow within only the cage designed by the central government. On the other hand, from the good-policy perspective, '[c]entral capture has provided more coherence in policy-making and implementation; better quality and more standardized implementation of regulation; and seems to have prevented a repetition of the stock market crisis of the 1990s'.[79]

10.4. Legitimacy management and the battle of regulatory philosophies

The philosophical approach to securities regulation determines the mission or goals of the regulators. The philosophy also indicates the orientation of administrative and judicial policies on the relationships between the regulator and the regulated, as well as the line between legal and illegal behaviours in the market. For example, the mission of the US Securities and Exchange Commission (SEC) is set to 'protect investors, maintain fair, orderly, and efficient markets, and facilitate capital formation'.[80] Put simply, it is the so-called disclosure philosophy. The adoption of the disclosure approach in the United States followed a battle of conflicting regulatory philosophies in the late 1920s and early 1930s.[81] The liberal view preferred a non-interventionist, anti-fraud approach, namely 'stern enforcement of the penal laws without even the power somewhere to enjoin frauds'.[82] 'Any preventive law, even of the purely injunction type, would not work … and would only hinder honest business'.[83] At the other extreme, the merit doctrine based on state blue-sky laws of the 'merit standards' endorsed government revocation of securities issuance upon administrative finding that 'the enterprise or business of the issuer … or the security is not based upon sound principles, and that the revocation is in the interest of the public welfare', or that the issuer 'is in any other way dishonest' or 'in unsound condition or insolvent'.[84] But eventually, the Securities Act of 1933 adopted the disclosure approach based on Louis D. Brandeis' publicity philosophy.[85] As the SEC points out

> The laws and rules that govern the securities industry in the United States derive from a simple and straightforward concept: all investors, whether large institutions or private individuals, should have access to certain basic facts about an investment prior to buying it, and so long as they hold it. To achieve this, the SEC requires public companies to disclose meaningful financial and other information to the public.[86]

China's securities regulation obviously practices 'merit standards' especially with regard to securities issuance. Under the PRC Securities Law and CSRC rules, public offering of securities is subject to an ex-ante review and approval system by the CSRC, otherwise known as the *hezhun* system, under which the CSRC requires potential issuers to fulfil certain substantive conditions, procedural requirements, as well as mandatory disclosure obligations.[87] It is a typical merit-based system, which obligates the issuers to meet the following substantive requirements:

- *Capital adequacy*. The issuer's register capital must have been fully paid up, and there is no major ownership dispute over its main assets.
- *Industrial policy*. The issuer's business operation must comply with the state's industrial policy.
- *Stability*. There is no significant change in the issuer's core business, directors and senior management personnel, as well as in the company's actual controller, during the past three years.
- *Independence*. The issuer should have an integral business operation system. The senior management personnel of the issuer must be independent of its controlling shareholder. The issuer should have an independent financial and accounting system, as well as an independent management structure.
- *Standardized operation*. The issuer must have established a sound corporate governance structure as well as international control system. It must not

have been involved in any illegal activities within the most recent 36 months. In addition, it must have in place a stringent funds management system which is able to prevent misappropriation of corporate funds by the controlling shareholders.

- *Finance and accounting*. The issuer should maintain good financial status, having quality assets, a reasonable assets–liability structure, good profitability and normal cash flow. Specifically, the issuer should have reported profit in each of the past three years, with an aggregate profit exceeding RMB30 million yuan. Its total cash flow generated within the past three years exceeds RMB50 million yuan (or its total business revenue in the past three years exceeds RMB300 million yuan). The total pre-IPO share capital is not less than RMB30 million yuan, and the value of intangible assets must not exceed 20 per cent of the net assets. In addition, there are no unrecovered losses.
- *Use of funds*. The proceeds raised through the public offering must be used for specified purposes, mainly for developing the issuer's core business, rather than purchasing, holding or trading in financial assets (such as securities).[88]

In addition, the CSRC also closely monitors and controls the process of public offerings through regulating the sponsoring, share pricing, information disclosure and listing mechanisms.[89] In short, government control in public offering of securities demonstrates a strong degree of paternalism. Numerous legal and regulatory restrictions are employed to control firms' access to the capital markets. As the present author has noted, 'China's IPO market is dominated by the mentality of a centrally planned economy in which the government directly controls the IPO process as well as any follow-up issuance, determining which enterprise is able to issue shares'.[90]

In stark contrast, the government, including the regulators and the judiciary, has taken quite a relaxed attitude towards the enforcement of securities laws on market manipulation, insider trading and misrepresentation. For a long time, the CSRC was rather reluctant to take serious punitive actions against fraudulent activities. As Tondkar and co-authors observed:

> [the] CSRC tends to take a reactive rather preventive approach to the enforcement of securities laws. It would normally not initiate an enforcement action against a firm unless a complaint was received from the public or a significant disaster or scandal occurred in the market.[91]

Judicial protection of shareholders' rights in disputes concerning securities litigation is also weak. For years, courts in China were unsympathetic to minority shareholders, refusing to adjudicate most of the cases filed. In the wake of a spate of shareholders' lawsuits concerning a listed company's false disclosure in its share offering documents, the Supreme People's Court (SPC) issued, on 21 September 2001, the famous (or infamous) judicial interpretation requiring all lower courts not to accept securities lawsuits concerning insider trading, fraud, market manipulation and the like, based on the 'constraints created by the current legislative and judicial conditions'.[92] Several months later, the SPC released two more judicial interpretations, including significantly the Provisions concerning the Adjudication of Civil Compensation of January 2003, opening the door for private securities litigation in China. However, the new SPC rules confine the lower courts' jurisdiction only to misrepresentation cases, and precondition judicial acceptance of these cases on the prior penalty report of the CSRC establishing facts and evidence.[93]

The conflicting regulatory approaches with respect to public offerings and enforcement against illegal market activities can also be understood from the perspective of legitimacy management. The starting point is that the CSRS is stuck between two conflicting regulatory objectives: one is to facilitate the 'development' (*fazhan*) of the market, and the other one is 'regulating' (*jianguan*) the market in terms of enforcing the anti-fraud rules. It is expected for both to do well.[94] Presumably, both are good policies, albeit they seriously conflict with each other.

The initial decision of the Chinese central government to establish the securities market in the early 1990s was supposed to pursue a good policy towards further liberalization of the economy. The decision had two goals: '1) to mobilize private savings in order to finance SOEs and 2) to improve SOE performance through public listing'.[95] Clearly the securities market has opened the door for corporatization and even privatization of the SOEs – and hence in theory a good public policy. One may, however, argue, as many small investors did, that the mere purpose of this policy was to channel private funds to support the ailing SOEs, thus advancing mainly the interest of the state as a shareholder – the biggest private interest in China. As a result of this policy, the overwhelming majority of the listed companies in China are state owned.[96] The rationale is clear: taxes and dividends collected by the state from the SOEs constitute indeed one of the major pillars supporting the Party-state's legitimacy. As a commentary published on the Web site of the State-owned Assets Supervision and Administration Commission of the State Council nakedly admits:

> state-owned enterprises are not only one of the major characteristics of the modern enterprise system and the modern market economy, they are also an indispensable and important economic foundation for the rule of the Chinese Communist Party, embodying the distinctive advantage of socialism with Chinese characteristics or the 'Chinese model'.[97]

The tight control over public access to the securities market reflects also a broader concern relating to ideology and political stability. The CSRC's first Chairman, Liu Hongru, once sighed that the biggest lesson he had learnt from the development of China's securities market was that the regulatory work in China is always about '*sanfen yewu, qifen zhengzhi*' (30 per cent business,

70 per cent politics).[98] Liu pointed out that, after its establishment, China's securities market has always been faced with some cognitive problems, one of which is how to politically treat the market.[99] He noted that China's top leadership and the regulators always tend to impose limits on the size of the market for political reasons, as the officials were afraid that market risks would lead to political unrests which might shake the ruling status of the communist party.[100] The judiciary's reluctance to permit private securities litigation, especially those based on class actions involving a large number of plaintiffs, reflects also the regime's determination to prevent the emergence of any organized forces outside the political establishment of the Party-state.

In order to 'develop' – or grow, put simply – the market, the regulators have to tolerate some fraudulent activities. As a Wall Street Journal report remarked, 'moves against insider trading are likely to only go so far ... Digging too deep, especially at big state-owned firms, risks undermining broader market confidence and implicating businesspeople with ties to politicians who have the power to overrule regulators'.[101] One example is, in 2001, after Zhou Xiaochuan was appointed as CSRC Chairman, he launched immediately enforcement campaigns against illegal securities activities by enacting and strictly enforcing disclosure and anti-fraud rules. In 2001 alone, the CSRC introduced 51 new regulations and disciplined more than 81 listed companies and 10 intermediaries. The result was obvious: the Chinese securities market entered its longest bear period from 2001 through 2005, and Zhou Xiaochuan's CSRC had since been a subject of constant criticism by both the public investors and senior government officials for causing the market losses.[102] However, despite the criticism, the CSRC under the leadership of Zhou and Shang Fulin, Zhou's successor who is now the incumbent CSRC Chairman, has never completely given up enforcement efforts, although its regulatory philosophy has to switch constantly between 'development' and 'regulation'. The regulatory framework has been substantially strengthened with stricter investor protection rules, disclosure rules and increasingly clearer anti-fraud rules, although the overall regulatory culture remains interventionist and opaque. In short, the tension between 'development' and 'regulation' highlights a fundamental phenomenon in China's emerging market economy, namely the state must create or help create a market and, simultaneously, regulate it.

The Chinese government's legitimacy management efforts have, however, been greatly compromised by CSRC officials' rent-seeking activities. Despite the mounting public appeal for a registration system in which public offerings of securities would not be subject to government approval, the CSRC has been adamant in refusing to make any change. Apart from the political considerations relating to legitimacy management, the CSRC's unwillingness to relinquish control over the power to review and approval securities issuance could also demonstrates its determination to keep the 'private benefits of control' brought by the *hezhun* system to the CSRC and its officials. Put simply, *hezhun* is a convenient rent-seeking machine for CSRC officials. Because of the CSRC's unfettered administrative licensing power, potential issuers will have to spend tremendous financial resources lobbying – or simply buying – the CSRC approval through corrupt CSRC officials. Since its establishment, a number of senior CSRC officials have been sentenced for securities-issuance-related corruption charges. In December 2005, Wang Xiaoshi, an official with the CSRC's securities offering supervision department, was sentenced to 13 years in jail, for leaking the officially secret names of the members of CSRC sharing issuance committee to an issuer. Wang received bribes worth RMB720,000 yuan for selling the names.[103] In June 2008, Wang Yi, a former CSRC vice chairman, was arrested for corruption charges relating to several major securities scandals, including the insider trading by Guangfa Securities as well as the unusual IPO of Pacific Securities. Reportedly, Wang Yi received more than RMB17 million yuan as bribes.[104] For system in which rent-seeking benefits are almost unlimited, the regulatory officials have great personal interest to hold tightly the power of approving securities issuance.

In summary, the apparently conflicting regulatory philosophies in China's securities market could indeed harmoniously coexist in the country's securities regulatory system, if understood from the perspective of legitimacy management. In dealing with the regulation of issuing, listing and trading of securities, as well as the enforcement of laws against securities market frauds, the regulators would have to consider a variety of political-legitimacy-related factors, such as the use of industrial policy to channel the capital flow to benefit SOEs, social and political stability, preventing the loss of state-assets, and of course, developing a healthy securities market in which the investors are duly protected. In addition, the regulators have also strived to create rent-seeking opportunities through regulation.

10.5. Concluding remarks

This chapter explores the political logic of securities regulation in China and argues that political legitimacy management is the rationale behind the often-conflicting regulatory philosophies and practices in the Chinese securities market. In this system, the Party-state's overriding concern is preserving its rule, for which it believes it must solidify its financial base, and maintain political and social stability by preventing the rise of organized challengers. Meanwhile, it must also deliver economic growth to improve the people's living standards, and be ideologically flexible to respond to the changing environment brought about by globalization and economic liberalization. Securities regulation in China, like a bird in cage, must serve this purpose and could only develop within the boundaries that do not undermine this purpose. As this chapter illustrates, the establishment of a centralized securities market and national securities regulatory framework, as well as the regulatory philosophies of the CSRC, embodies perfectly the legitimacy management model.

As China's securities market gets larger, more sophisticated and more market-oriented, managing political legitimacy through securities regulation is becoming increasingly difficult for the political establishment. The problems of the existing legitimacy-management-based regulatory model have already revealed themselves in the past decade.

First, the government often misperceives and misplaces the priorities. The government uses the securities market to take excessive care of the SOEs, while significantly limiting the private sector's access to the capital market. Without vibrant privately owned listed companies, the Chinese securities market could only be an ATM machine for SOEs and will never be a true driving engine to support China's newly acquired status as an economic superpower.

Second, if political legitimacy considerations conflict with regulatory legitimacy considerations, the former will always prevail, resulting in tremendous inefficacy of securities regulation in China. For example, the government, usually oversensitive to public opinions and obsessed with maintaining social and political stability, tend to use administrative actions to control the price movements of the market and is often hesitant to adopt necessary institutional reforms.

Third, the political-legitimacy-management model leaves significant administrative discretion to the regulator, namely the CSRC, without imposing institutional accountability. There has been a lack of checks and balances to the regulatory powers of the CSRC. The opaque work style of the CSRC is not subject to any institutional scrutiny and supervision, and the CSRC always invokes political legitimacy consideration to justify its tight administrative control over public offering, listing and trading of securities. Although it has been obvious that the CSRC's greedy appetite for power is mainly for creating rent-seeking opportunities for itself and its officials, under the current legitimacy-management-based regime very little can be done to hold the CSRC accountable. Ironically, corruption cases involving senior CSRC officials have greatly undermined the political legitimacy of the Party-state, although the initial purpose of granting such huge administrative discretion to officials was supposed to be maintaining and strengthening this legitimacy.

Using the term of Pistor and Xu, the legitimacy management model can be characterized as 'administrative governance'.[105] The two authors argue that, in the substantial development of China's securities market, 'formal law and law enforcement have played at best a marginal role'.[106] Instead, 'during the initial period of stock market development China relied primarily on an administrative governance structure built upon the quota system'.[107] In transition economies where there were only 'undeveloped and/or largely untested legal systems, as well as inexperienced and frequently corrupt enforcement agencies',[108] administrative governance may provide a viable alternative to formal law and could prevent regulatory failures. However, administrative governance always suffers from a major weakness: it is hardly sustainable in the long run.[109] At a certain point of market development, a country should grow out of the administrative governance structure and rely on formal legal mechanisms of governance based on the rule of law. Now may be the right time for China to do so.

Notes

1 Qingquan Ma, *Zhongguo Zhengquan Shi 1978–1998* (*History of Securities in China 1978–1998*), Beijing: Zhongxin Chubanshe (CITIC Publishing House), 2003: 163.
2 Statistics of the China Securities Regulatory Commission (CSRC), December 2009.
3 More information about the ChiNext can be found at its official Web site at www.szse.cn/main/chinext/ (accessed 1 December 2009).
4 'China's Market Value Overtakes Japan as World's No. 2', Bloomberg News, 16 July 2009 (stating, on 16 July 2009, 'the Shanghai Composite Index rose 1.4 per cent yesterday, sending the value of China's domestic stock market to [US]$3.21 trillion, compared with Japan's $3.20 trillion'). It is worth mentioning that the ranking is not static: except the fact that the US stock market has always been the largest in the world, the relative position of other major economies in the ranking constantly changes in response to the economic environment. For instance, this was not the first time that China surpassed Japan in stock market capitalization. The size of the Chinese market temporarily exceeded that of Japan from 4 to 24 January 2008.
5 A. I. Ogus, *Regulation: Legal Form and Economic Theory*, Oxford: Hart Publishing, 2004: 59 (emphasis added).
6 S. Green, *The Development of China's Stock Market, 1984–2002: Equity Politics and Market Institutions*, London and New York: Routledge Curzon, 2004: 7.
7 B. Useem and M. Useem, 'Government Legitimacy and Political Stability', *Social Focus* 57, 1979: 841.
8 Baogang Guo, 'Political Legitimacy and China's Transition', *Journal of Political Science*, 8 (1 and 2), 2003: 2.
9 M. Weber, *The Theory of Social and Economic Organization,* Talcott Parson (ed.), New York: The Free Press, 1964: 132.
10 S. M. Lipset, *Political Man: The Social Bases of Politics* (2nd edn), London: Heinemann, 1983: 64.
11 M. C. Suchman, 'Managing Letigimacy: Strategic and Institutional Approaches', *The Academy of Management Review*, 20, 1995: 586.
12 Guo, *supra note* 8, pp. 3–5.
13 *Ibid.*, p. 3.
14 *Ibid.*, p. 5.
15 *Ibid.*, p. 6.
16 *Ibid.*, p. 7.
17 B. Gilley and H. Holbig, 'The Debate on Party Legitimacy in China: A Mixed Quantitative/Qualitative Analysis', *Journal of Contemporary China* 18:59, 2009: 346.
18 *Ibid.*
19 Hongru Liu, *Tupo – Zhongguo Ziben Shichang Fazhan Zhi Lu* (*Breakthrough – The Pathway of China's Capital Markets*), Vol. 1 and Vol. 2, Beijing: Zhongguo Jinrong Chubanshe, 2008: 19.
20 Gilley and Holbig, *supra note* 17, p. 349.
21 Bin Qi, 'Ziben Shichang yu Daguo Jueqi' ('Capital Markets and the Rise of Great Powers'), available at: http://www.csrc.gov.cn (accessed 1 December 2009).
22 J. Fewsmith, *China Since Tianmanmen,* Cambridge: Cambridge University Press, 2001: 79 (noting 'Chinese policymakers [not just 'hardliners'] and intellectuals ... are keenly aware of the turmoil of twentieth-century politics and worry openly about the costs of political imposition').

23 K. Lieberthal, *Governing China: From Revolution Through Reform*, New York and London: W. W. North & Company, 2004: 317.

24 Ogus, *supra note* 5, p. 57.

25 For example, departmentalism in the legislative process was said to have the four common manifestations: '(1) Using the law to expand a department's rights beyond its own sphere; (2) Using law to push one department's duties onto another department; (3) Using law to force resolution of larger problems a department cannot solve in its daily work; (4) Drafting laws which are either illegal or unconstitutional'. *See*, M. S. Tanner, *The Politics of Lawmaking in China: Institutions, Processes, and Democratic Prospects*, Oxford: Oxford University Press, 1999: 120–121.

26 Minxin Pei, 'Fighting Corruption: A Difficult Challenge for Chinese Leaders', in Cheng Li (ed.), *China's Changing Political Landscape: Prospects for Democracy*, Washington D.C.: Brookings Institution, 2008: 230.

27 *Ibid.*, p. 238.

28 *See*, Lieberthal, *supra note* 23, p. 127 (stating 'Deng [Xiaoping], like most other twentieth-century Chinese leaders, sought to make the country prosperous and strong']. *See also*, S. L. Shirk, *The Political Logic of Economic Reform in China*, Berkley, California: University of California Press, 1993; J. D. Spence, *The Search for Modern China*, New York and London: W. W. Norton & Company, 1999; R. Baum, 'The Road to Tiananman: Chinese Politics in the 1980s', in Roderick MacFarquhar (ed.), *The Politics of China: The Eras of Mao and Deng* (2nd edn), Cambridge: Cambridge University Press, 1997; J. K. Fairbank and M. Goldman, *China: A New History* (2nd edn), Cambridge: The Belknap Press of Harvard University Press, 2006; and D. Shambaugh, *China's Communist Party: Atrophy and Adaptation*, Washington D.C.: Woodrow Wilson Center Press, 2008.

29 Lieberthal, *supra note* 23, pp. 129–130.

30 J. Fewsmith, 'China and the WTO', *NBR Analysis*, 10 (5), 1999.

31 N. R. Lardy, *Integrating China into the Global Economy*, Washington D.C.: Brookings Institution Press, 2002: 10.

32 *Ibid.*, p. 11.

33 Dali L. Yang, *Remaking the Chinese Leviathan: Market Transition and the Politics and Governance in China*, Stanford: Stanford University Press, 2004.

34 CSRC (China Securities Regulatory Commission), *China Capital Markets Development Report,* 2008, 153. *See also*, OECD, *China in the World Economy: The Domestic Policy Challenges*, Paris: OECD, 2002: 499.

35 CSRC, *supra note* 34, pp. 155–160.

36 World Bank, *World Development Report 1996: From Plan to Market*, Oxford: Oxford University Press, 1996: 107.

37 OECD, *supra note* 34, p. 499.

38 B. Naughton, *The Chinese Economy: Transitions and Growth*, Cambridge: MIT Press, 2007: 468–469.

39 'Li Rongrong says SOEs deserve to be called the Republic's eldest son' ('Li Rongrong: Guoqi Wuweiyu Gongheguo Zhangzi Diwei'), China News Services newswire, 5 August 2009.

40 L. Brandt, T. G. Rawski and J. Sutton, 'China's Industrial Development', in L. Brandt and T. G. Rawski (eds), *China's Great Economic Transformation*, Cambridge: Cambridge University Press, 2008: 571.

41 OECD, *Reforming China's Enterprises*, Paris: OECD, 2000.

42 Liu, *supra note* 19, p. 96.
43 Personal interview.
44 Lay-Hong Tan and Jiangyu Wang, 'Modelling an Effective Corporate Governance System for China's Listed State-Owned Enterprises: Issues and Challenges in a Transitional Economy', *Journal of Corporate Law Studies,* 7, 2007: 1–47.
45 CSRC Research Center, *Zhongguo Ziben Shichang Ruogan Wenti Baogao* (*Report on Several Issues Concerning China's Capital Markets*), 2008: 1. *See also*, CSRC, *supra note* 34, 188.
46 Liu, *supra note* 19, p. 96.
47 *Ibid.*, p. 99.
48 *See, generally*, J. Fewsmith, *supra note* 22, Chapters 1 and 2.
49 *Ibid.*, p. 50.
50 Liu, *supra note* 19, p. 150.
51 *Ibid.*, pp. 79–80, 150–151.
52 R. L. Kuhn, *The Man Who Changed China: The Life and Legacy of Jiang Zemin*, New York: Crown Publishers, 2004: 202. *See also*, Liu, *supra note* 19, p. 19.
53 Kuhn, *supra note* 52, p. 202; Liu, *supra note* 19, p. 19.
54 Deng Xiaoping, 'Excepts from Talks Given in Wuchang, Shenzhen, Zhuhai and Shanghai', (18 January and 21 February 1992), in Deng Xiaoping, *Selected Works of Deng Xiaoping, Vol. III*, Beijing: Renmin Chubanshe, 1992. Available at: http://web.peopledaily.com.cn/deng (accessed 1 March 2010).
55 The proposal was first made in a 1990 report of a joint investigation group organized by the State Council to review the development of the Shenzhen stock market. The chairman of the group was Liu, *supra note* 19, p. 68.
56 *Ibid.*, p. 124.
57 In the Chinese context, 'mainstream' economists (*zhuliu jingji xuejia*) refer to the leading economists who are also advisors to the government. The mainstream economists are normally followers of the neo-institutional economics.
58 Jiangyu Wang, 'Dancing with Wolves: Regulation and Deregulation of Foreign Investment in China's Stock Market', *Asian-Pacific Law & Policy Journal*, 5, 2004: 38.
59 'Is it Right to Destroy the Current Stock Market and Set Up a New One?', *Beijing Review*, No. 51, 18 December 2001.
60 State Council, *Guowuyuan Guanyu Tuijin Ziben Shichang Gaige Kaifang he Weiding Fazhan de Ruogan Yijian* [Opinions of the State Council on Promoting the Reform, Opening and Steady Growth of Capital Markets], 31 January 2004.
61 CSRC, *supra note* 34, VI.
62 Qi, *supra note* 2.
63 CSRC, *supra note* 34, 155–157.
64 C. E. Walter and F. T. Howie, *Privatizing China: The Stock Markets and Their Role in Corporate Reform*, Singapore: John Wiley & Sons, 6.
65 *Ibid.*, pp. 23–24.
66 Liu, *supra note* 19, pp. 40–61; Qingshan Tan, 'State, Institution Building, and Emerging Stock Markets in China', *Communist and Post-communist Studies,* 37, 2004: 378–380.
67 Liu, *supra note* 19, pp. 103–124.
68 S. Green, *China's Stock Market: A Guide to Its Progress, Players and Prospects*, London: The Economist, 2003: 12.

69 *Ibid.*, p. 14. *See also*, Liu, *supra note* 19, pp. 96–203.
70 State Council, *Guowuyuan Guanyu Jinyibu Jiaqiang Zhengquan Shichang Hongguan Guanli de Tongzhi* [State Council Circular on Further Strengthening the Macro-management of the Securities Market], 17 December 1992.
71 S. Green, 'Equity Politics and Market Institutions: the Development of Stock Market Policy and Regulation in China, 1984–2003', paper presented at the Association of Asian Studies Conference, San Diego, United States, 4 March 2004 (on file with the author), pp. 11–26.
72 *Ibid.*, pp. 14–18.
73 *Ibid.*, pp. 18–19.
74 *Ibid.*, p. 20.
75 *Ibid.*, p. 21.
76 *Ibid.*, p. 22.
77 *Ibid.*, p. 25.
78 Tan, *supra note* 66, p. 391.
79 Green, *supra note* 71, p. 26.
80 SEC (US Securities and Exchange Commission), 'The Investor's Advocate: How the SEC Protects Investors, Maintains Market Integrity, and Facilitates Capital Formation', Washington D.C.: US Securities and Exchange Commission 2010, available at: www.sec.gov (accessed 1 March 2010).
81 L. Loss and J. Seligman, *Fundamentals of Securities Regulation*, Aspen Law & Business, 1995: 22–33.
82 *Ibid.*, p. 25.
83 *Ibid.*
84 *Ibid.*, p. 25 [quoting the original legislative bills of the 1933 Securities Act, S. 875 and H.R. 4314, 73d Cong., 1st Sess., §§6(c), (e), (f) (1933)].
85 *Ibid.*, p. 25.
86 SEC, *supra note* 80.
87 Jiangyu Wang, 'Regulation of Initial Public Offering of Shares in China', *China Law,* 76, 2009: 56.
88 *Ibid.*, pp. 57–59.
89 *Ibid.*, pp. 58–65.
90 Wang, *supra note* 58, p. 34.
91 R. H. Tondkar, Songlan Peng and C. Hodgdon, 'The Chinese Securities Regulatory Commission and the Regulation of Capital Markets in China', *Advances in International Accounting,* 16, 2003: 153–174.
92 Jiangyu Wang, 'Rule of Law and Rule of Officials: Shareholder Litigation and Anti-dumping Practice in China', Foundation for Law, Justice and Society, *Developments in Dispute Resolution in China* policy brief series, No. 4, Oxford: Foundation for Law, Justice and Society, 2008: 4.
93 Wang, *supra note* 58, p. 44.
94 *Ibid.*, p. 34.
95 OECD, *China in the World Economy: The Domestic Policy Challenges*, p. 497.
96 Wang, *supra note* 58, p. 11 (noting the average government ownership in China's stock market was 45 per cent as of 31 January 2002). *See also*, Shanghai Stock Exchange Research Centre, *China Corporate Governance Report (2006): The Governance of Listed Companies Controlled by the State*, Shanghai: Fudan University Press, 2006, 1 (noting the state is the controlling shareholder in 70 per cent of the companies listed on the Shanghai Stock Exchange).

97 Luo Zhir*ong, 'The Resurgence of State-Owned Enterprises Is an Important Indication of the Advantages of the 'Chinese Model' of Development'*, available at: www.sasac.gov.cn/n1180/n6881559/n6987010/6987066.html (accessed 17 March 2010).

98 Liu, *supra note* 19, p. 289.

99 *Ibid.*, p. 322.

100 *Ibid.*

101 R. Carew, 'The Battle against Insider Trading', *Wall Street Journal (Chinese) Online*, 27 June 2007, available at: http://cn.wsj.com (accessed 4 April 2010).

102 Wang, *supra note* 58, pp. 26–27; K. Wilhelm, 'Casinos by Another Name?' *Far Eastern Economic Review*, 8 March 2001, p. 46. *See also*, Liu Hongru, 'Guanyu Zhongguo Zhengquan Shichang Jige Renshi Wenti' [Several Cognitive Issues on China's Securities Market], speech at the 2002 High Level Forum for China's Securities Market, 21 March 2002 (on file with the author); and Zhou Zhengqing, 'Zai Guifan he Fazhan Zhong Jiejue Gezhong Maodun he Wenti' [Solving All Kinds of Contradictions and Problems of the Securities Market in Its Stable Development], speech at the 2002 High Level Forum for China's Securities Market, 21 March 2002. Available at: www.people.com.cn (accessed 1 March 2010).

103 Xinhua newswire, 12 December 2005.

104 Bihua Liu and Huiwei Tang, 'From Wang Xiaoshi to Wang Yi, Seven CSRC Officials Had Fallen Down and All were in Powerful Departments', *Legal Daily*, 21 May 2009, at www.legaldaily.com.cn (accessed 18 March 2010). *See also*, 'Former Vice President of State Development Bank Wang Yi Has Been Indicted for Receiving 17 Million in Bribes', *Legal Daily,* 2 February 2010, available at: www.legaldaily.com.cn (accessed 4 April 2010).

105 K. Pistor and Chenggang Xu, 'Governing Stock Markets in Transition Economies: Lessons from China', *American Law and Economics Review*, 7, 2005: 207–208.

106 *Ibid.*, p. 185.

107 *Ibid.*

108 *Ibid.*, p. 186.

109 *Ibid.*, p. 185.

Part V

Procedural law

11 Civil justice reform with political agendas

Xianchu Zhang

In 2009, the People's Republic of China (PRC) celebrated its 60th birthday and 30th anniversary of its opening-up and economic reform. As far as civil justice is concerned in this period, the impressive achievements that have been made are well reflected in the White Paper published by the State Council as part of the national endeavour to modernize the legal system in the country's social and economic transition towards a market economy.[1] However, given the size of the country and the complexity of the national conditions, there will always be different sides of stories to tell. The limited space would not allow this chapter to engage in a full-scale deliberation of the debate on the direction and future of the civil justice reform in China.[2] Instead, by reviewing the recent developments, the author argues that in dealing with the social conflicts in the transitional period the judiciary of China has been assigned increasingly and disproportionately more political tasks. As a result, to a large extent, the agenda of the civil justice reform has been changed, at least momentarily, at the cost of judicial efficiency and professionalism.

11.1. An overview of the civil justice reform in the past 30 years

The civil justice development and reform have experienced four stages since the economic reform was implemented in late 1970s. In the first ten years, a legal order and a legislative framework were restored after the ten-year lawlessness during the Cultural Revolution. The promulgation of the Constitution (1982), together with *Organic Law of the People's Court* (1979), *Law of Criminal Procedures* (1979) and *Law of Civil Procedures* (on trial, 1982) in the same period was considered the milestones of the return to the 'socialist legality' model under the 1954 Constitution.[3]

In the second ten years, the *Law of Civil Procedures* was comprehensively amended and formally adopted in the course of the national reorientation to develop a socialist market economy. The new ideology of giving more respect to litigants' autonomy and to judicial efficiency was clearly reflected. As a result, the traditional inquisitional trial system began to give way to the adversarial model with the introduction of the parties' burden of proof, increased parties' autonomy in civil litigations and the reduced judicial responsibility in adjudicating civil cases.[4]

With the new momentum provided by the Constitutional Amendment in 1999 to officially introduce the concept of the rule of law into China,[5] the civil justice reform entered into a new stage with professionalization, independence of collegial panels, judicial efficiency and public supervision as its major themes.[6] For example, as a measure to raise the professional standard of judges, the amendment to the *Law of Judges* in 2001 has transformed the original bar examination to the national judicial qualification examination for all judges, prosecutors and lawyers to be. As a symbol of the normative reform, the judicial gown and gavel were officially introduced into the People's Courts in early 1990s. Moreover, two five-year reform plans were promulgated by the Supreme People's Court in 1999 for 1999–2003 and in 2005 for 2003–2008, respectively.[7]

In addition to the impressive developments on professionalizing the judiciary, the dynamic judicial reform has also aroused the judicial activism. In a speech made in 2002, Jintao Hu, the Secretary General of the Communist Party of China (CPC), called for full-scale implementation of and compliance with the Constitution and promotion of governance under the rule of law for the entire society.[8] Against this background, the Supreme People's Court issued its historical instruction to the lower courts to directly apply the Constitution provisions in civil adjudication, which made the Constitution a live-law in the judicial process for the first time in PRC history. In the Yuling Qi case, the college admission letter of the plaintiff was taken by the defendant and the ruse was not discovered until the defendant had graduated from a business institute and had a job in a local bank. The Supreme People's Court took the opportunity to address the plaintiff's claim for compensation for violation of her education entitlement as a constitutional right and instructed the lower court to recognize the damage claim on the constitutional ground.[9] According to Songyou Huang, then the Vice President of the Supreme People's Court, the opinion was of tremendous and far-reaching importance like *Marbury v. Madison* in the United States[10] in a sense that the decision changed the long practice since the adoption of the first Constitution in 1954 not to use the Constitution as a law alive in adjudicating process. The Supreme People's Court's instruction on the Yulin Qi case virtually declared that even without specifically applicable laws, a citizen's basic constitutional rights should still be protected.[11] As such, the case was hailed as beginning of the new era of constitutional governance.[12]

China's accession to the World Trade Organization (WTO) with the firm commitments to its fundamental legal principles, such as impartial administration of law, transparency, non-discrimination and independent judicial review,[13] has further challenged the existing regime and accelerated the civil justice reform in China. In order to prepare the People's Courts for China's WTO membership, the Supreme People's Court further rationalized the structure of the civil trial divisions of the entire judiciary system, verified and amended a large number of judicial interpretations and circulars, heightened the internal supervision and enhanced judicial training and transparency, particularly on the quality of judgment making. The goals in this course were clearly identified to improve judicial justice, openness, efficiency, authority and professionalism for a new image of the Chinese judiciary in the international society.[14]

Despite the progress of the civil justice reform, the national reform and opening thus far have not changed the fundamental nature of China as a socialist country. As a result, the deepening of the judicial reform will inevitably clash with the totalitarian regime and ideology. In promoting the ambitious reform Mr Yang Xiao, then the Chief Justice and the President of the Supreme People's Court, once stated that the authority of law should give its expression to the authority of the judiciary, and the public and private interests would only be safeguarded through judicial justice and efficiency. As such, the independence of the People's Courts was an indispensable means to realize the rule of law.[15] He further asked the People's Courts to change their passive and weak condition and as a serious political discipline to hold an unequivocal stand with determined and resolute measures against the intensifying administrative interference with the judicial functions.[16] Such a new mindset, together with the brave reform measures, was even considered as 'a quiet revolution' in China.[17] In a sense, this period was the golden years of the reform.

The enthusiasm of civil justice reform apparently was dampened in the amendments to the *Law of Civil Procedures* in 2007. With the reform experience, there was a high hope for overhauling the law to reflect the new social reality and to meet the demands of the rapidly developing market economy.[18] However, the final revision with many reform proposals being shelved by the legislature disappointed many scholars and experts, although there has been wide consensus on the ripeness of the conditions to introduce the new reform measures to enhance the judicial authority, improve the judicial efficiency, recognize public interest litigation and rationalize the existing procedural rules. These critics noted that such amendments produced more shortcomings than innovations[19] and voiced their resentment that the minor revision should not be an excuse to further delay the comprehensive reform.[20]

Soon after, the Supreme People's Court promulgated its Third Reform Plan (2009–2013) in March 2009.[21] As compared with the first two reform plans, the new plan apparently places more emphases on the so-called adjudication for the people and the contradiction between the increasing demand of the public for judicial justice and the insufficient capability of the People's Courts. Moreover, among the seven guiding principles of the new plan, reform according to the law and objective law of the judicial work are placed at the end after the political principles, such as the CPC's leadership, the socialist direction and the mass line. Unlike the previous two reform plans, the third plan stresses the Chinese characteristics of a socialist country in its preliminary stage of development. The new reform plan further stated that while learning from external experience, foreign judicial systems and institutions should not be borrowed beyond the socialist reality of China.[22]

11.2. A new direction of the civil justice reform?

Despite the great efforts devoted to judicial reform, the practical effect of the reform seems not well appreciated in the society. In the National People's Congress, judicial justice has been a serious issue concerned. The Working Report of the Supreme People's Court is an important indicator of public satisfaction to the judicial work. This parameter has been sliding in recent years to a record low until 2010 when satisfaction slightly improved.[23] The Standing Committee of the National People's Congress on its examination report on the implementation of the *Law of Judges* and the *Law of Prosecutors*, openly pointed out that judicial incompetence and corruption were the major concerns of the people in China.[24] Such dissatisfaction and anger are reflected not only in the official reports, but also in some real tragedies. Since 2004, at least six fatal incidents have been reported in five different provinces with 10 deaths and 30 wounded when the losing parties in civil cases attacked the People's Courts with explosives or lethal weapons.[25]

Inside the People's Courts, the professionalization reform is apparently taking a reverse turn recently. When China acceded to the WTO in 2001, most of the presidents of the People's Courts at the provincial level, if not all, had a formal, systematic legal education. Yang Xiao as the Chief Justice and the President of the Supreme People's Court then was a veteran of legal profession with both university legal education and practical qualification. His successor, Mr Shengjun Wang, when transferred from the Political and Legal Committee of the CPC to head the Supreme People's Court in 2008, had neither a legal education background nor any judicial experience. As such, this appointment was highly controversial.[26] To follow suit, the newly appointed presidents of the High People's Courts in at least seven provinces took their offices without any formal legal education background or any judicial experience.[27] Most of such appointments were made to replace judicial veterans.[28]

This trend is also well reflected in some 'new thinking' as to judicial practice. At the central level, Mr Shengjun Wang made his well-known statement that judicial decisions should be made according to the feeling of the masses[29] and that the highest praise to the judiciary would be 'ordinary people judges' (*Pingmin faguan*). Such new ideology is echoed at the local level. For example, some comments made by Mr Liyong Zhang, newly appointed President of Henan High People's Court from a post as a CPC secretary, are also highly controversial. He openly criticized the judicial reform in the past years as blind acceptance of the Western judicial model so as to eventually desalinate, question and negate what the CPC had cultivated for a long time based on the Chinese traditional culture. According to him, a judge will distance himself from the masses once he wears his robe and judicial independence does not mean keeping distance from the CPC and the government.[30] Recently, in Henan Province a campaign involving 10,000 judges is being carried out to revisit parties in litigation within their jurisdictions and to make friends with them for the purpose of not only well settling their disputes, but also helping them for their living difficulties. According to the plan of the campaign, all the bold measures to stop parties to further petition their grievances to the upper level authorities after the normal judicial proceedings are completed may be tried as long as they do not violate the law and state policy and some 'defective decisions' of the courts may be dealt with by the measures 'outside the law'.[31]

In order to implement the policy of 'adjudication for the people' the Supreme People's Court promulgated a circular with 23 concrete measures in 2003, including improvement of the personal and letter petition handling, the reception conditions, mediation work and facilitating the parties' access to justice.[32] In recent years, various innovative measures have been developed by local courts to facilitate the implementation of the policy to a new level, such as establishment of 'holiday courts', 'lunch time courts', 'evening courts' and 'circuit courts',[33] 24-hour reception[34] and provision of stationary, cups and water, and explanation during and after the trial to the parties.[35] Some more inventive measures include adoption of an award and penalty scheme by using the rate of successful mediation of individual judges on a monthly basis as an assessment criterion,[36] court's own initiation to execute judgments before the parties' request,[37] the efforts to make the court a 'judicial supermarket' where consultancy for legal issues of people's daily life will be provided in the courtroom.[38] Some leaders of the People's Courts have openly professed the courts' readiness to share and relieve the worries of the government.[39]

The brief review of the civil justice reform in the past 30 years seems to suggest a recent change of tone. In order to better understand the new trend, attention may be directed to debates rising with the developments in the legal circle at the same period. These debates were over the so-called universal values, a reflection of the ideological struggle in the political transition. Although the rule of law was officially recognized by the Constitutional Amendment in 1999, some recent mainstream publications have openly challenged the ideology. For instance, some equate the so-called universal values with the Western value system of capitalism, including democracy, freedom, human rights, equality and rule of law. Promotion of this value system has the political purpose of changing the socialist direction of China.[40] Against this background, the recent sentencing of Dr Xiaobo Liu, the leading author of the Charter 2008 advocating universal values and further reform in China, for 11 years imprisonment clearly demonstrates the attitude of the leadership to the demands for ideological and political evolution.[41] As such, the setback of judicial reform may be just part of the resistance of the totalitarian political regime.

On 28 November 2008 the Politburo of the CPC issued 'The Opinions on Deepening the Reform of the Judicial System and its Working Mechanisms'. This document does not respond to the demands for major reforms at the system level, such as changing the way to fund the judiciary, appoint judges, provide the People's Court with more powers of judicial review and eliminate or restrict interference with judicial independence. Rather, this document puts its emphasis on the 'Chinese characteristics' and 'the national conditions' with 'popularization of law' and 'democratization of law' as its major themes. For this purpose, the tasks of the judicial reform set out by the CPC are optimizing the distribution of judicial functions and powers, balancing strict execution of criminal law with clemency in certain situations, ensuring a healthy budget for the People's Courts, stressing the function of judicial 'service' and flexibility while glossing over legal stability and predictability.[42] In a sense, this development has concretized the so-called Three Supremes theory, which was first raised by Jintao Hu in his speech at the National Conference of Political and Legal Affairs Committee of the CPC at the end of 2007. According to the theory, in their work judges should always regard as supreme the cause of the CPC, the people's interest, as well as the Constitution and law.[43]

Such a political environment has taken its expression in judicial practice. For example, the landmark reply of the Supreme People's Court to the Yuling Qi case in 2001, authorizing the local courts to decide cases by directly relying on the provision of the Constitution was repealed in 2008, without giving any reason.[44] Some commentators have linked the withdrawal to the CPC's new policy on judicial reform and the 'Three Supremes' theory; they believe such trend may not only delay the much-needed reform, but also weaken the entire judicial system.[45] For example, a recent message published by the People's Daily, the official newspaper of the CPC, is that the political and economic systems as well as the legal cultures of China and the Western countries are fundamentally different; as a result, there are two roads of the rule of law. The practice of promoting judicial reform by copying Western legal mechanisms is bound to be a dead end.[46]

The change of the reform direction has been noted by not only foreign scholars, but also domestic academia. In early 2010, the Annual Report of Judicial Reform in China (2009) was published by the South Western University of Political Science and Law, a leading law school in China. According to the Report, China's judicial reform has entered into a cross-roads where modernization, professionalism and normalization as the major themes in the early years have been replaced with the new directions to safeguard the social stability and to emphasize judicial popularity with mediation as the preferred means to solve civil disputes.[47]

11.3. Institutional alienation

In order to objectively assess the civil justice reform in China, the social reality in the transitional period should be taken into account. According to PRC official sources, 'public order disturbances' grew significantly in recent years from just more than 10,000 incidents in 2003, to 87,000 in 2005 and further to 127,000 in 2008.[48] The distinctive trends of the massive incidents in recent years have not only been a rapid increase in number, but also increasingly intensified and violent.[49] The Blue Paper on the Rule of Law Development published by the Social Science Academy of China in early 2010 has also confirmed that the financial crisis, high unemployment, polarization of the society and other social conflicts had led to a grave situation of political instability with an increasing large number of criminal cases and massive incidents.[50] The intensified social conflicts have been clearly reflected in the judicial practice. In 2009, the civil cases heard by the People's Courts at the first instance reached 5,797,000 as the new record high,[51] representing a steep rise from 3,517,000 in 1999.[52]

Against this background, it seems clear that the challenges facing the judiciary and civil justice reform in China include not only the intense conflicts in the full-scale transition, but also the unpredictable struggle of political ideology to deal with the pressing reality. Despite the bold advocacy and impressive progress made in the past 30 years, the judicial system still belongs more to the political regime than to the professional institution. In this context, leaving other factors such as biased rulings, judicial corruption and ineffective enforcement aside,[53] the entire civil justice system has been caught in between judicial justice, which is realized through impartial adjudication of disputes between the parties concerned, and the practical popularity as a means to provide the political regime with badly needed legitimate support. As a result, under the direction of the political policy some judicial mechanisms may have to be deployed to settle disputes that may not be suitable for their application at all. In this context, mediation in judicial proceedings may be a telling example of such institutional alienation.

Judicial mediation has been long recognized as a successful dispute resolution process representing the value of the traditional Confucianism in the modern society. However, the application of judicial mediation before the social transition towards a market economy was primarily limited to small-scale cases, such as family, neighbourhood and working-unit disputes. Moreover, lack of laws and underdevelopment of the judicial system in the early years of the reform also made mediation a preferable means for the courts to handle civil litigations. Thus, the importance of mediation may inevitably be reduced to give way to judicial efficiency and dispute settlement in strict accordance with the law when the legal infrastructure has significantly improved, with the rule of law being the goal of the national reorientation and professionalism as the direction of modernization of the judicial system. This development is explicitly recognized and reflected in the replacement of the old rule with the emphasis on the judicial mediation[54] by the new stipulation that judicial mediation may only be carried out on the basis of the law and the parties' voluntariness,[55] which apparently intends to strike a balance between promotion of judicial efficiency and preservation of the traditional Chinese legal culture.

The institutional modernization, however, was soon challenged by the escalation of social conflicts in the transitional period. Political stability became the top priority of the CPC and the government. In this situation, as the judiciary has been increasingly subject to the political control, the civil justice reform has been overtaken by the political agenda. As a result, despite the reform, mediation has been increasingly used in civil proceedings under the political policy to maintain social stability by way of reducing after-trial petitions, although the legislative framework has been constantly improved in recent years and the People's Courts are more capable of dealing with civil adjudication according to the law. The latest policy set out by the President of the Supreme People's Court Shenjun Wang in this regard is to make mediation a prevailing means by the People's Courts to handle civil litigation.[56] As such, it seems that the civil justice reform on judicial mediation has taken a full cycle in 30 years: from mediation first in 1980s, to mediation in accordance with the law and parties consent in 1990s, to deployment of mediation and judgment according to the nature of the disputes at the beginning of the new century, and finally returning to the prevalence of mediation with necessary adjudication in 2009. However, as compared with the application of judicial mediation in 1980s, the return of mediation is primarily guided by the Party-state policy as a tool for political purposes.

However, the political ideology apparently does not work well with judicial practice. In the first place, conflicts in the social transition to a large extent have taken away the basis of successful judicial mediation in the early reform years to settle small-scale and less confrontational disputes. As a result, judicial mediation as an institution has proved unable and inappropriate to deal with massive cases concerning environment pollution, transformation of state-owned enterprises, labour disputes and land appropriation. As some scholars pointed out, these may not be cases suitable for judicial solution and remedies in the transitional context of China.[57]

Moreover, the promotion of judicial mediation under the political policy has gone far beyond the legal provisions in practice. For example, some People's Courts have in effect made judicial mediation a compulsory procedure for the parties; an assessment criterion of judges' performance; a measure applicable to government–citizens disputes in violation of the law[58] and a means to force a party to compromise. Certain People's Courts have even developed their internal rigid rules to mandate parties to go through judicial mediation for certain times before a judgment can be rendered.[59]

On the other hand, in certain cases suitable for judicial solution under the legal rules, the political consideration may prevent the People's Courts from exercising its adjudicating powers. The examples in this regard may include the cases concerning fraud on the securities market and the recent dairy scandal.

Fraud and securities violations have been serious problems in China's market development. Despite the comprehensive amendments to the *Company Law* and the *Securities Law* in 2005, which have fuelled the significant increase of the civil claims against wrongdoers,[60] the People's Court has taken an inactive approach towards civil enforcement. For example, in the Certain Provisions on Hearing Civil Claims against False Statements on the Securities Market by the People's Courts adopted by the Supreme People's Court on 26 December 2002, a crucial condition for the People's Court to accept such claims was set out: in addition to other evidence the plaintiff must obtain either a punishment order issued by the administrative authority, or a criminal judgment against the defendant.[61] In effect, the People's Court gives up its own independent judicial power to find violations on the evidence presented by the plaintiffs independently. Although the amendment to the *Securities Law* in 2005 has widened the scope of the civil liabilities include to material omission of important information,[62] the Supreme People's Court has yet adopted any detailed rules to implement the reform in practice.

Investors' grievances have been, in fact, well known by the People's Courts, but the couts are more concerned over the political impact of mass litigation. Some judges, while being interviewed, have openly expressed their view that mass civil actions are too politically risky[63] and their biased position in favour of political stability over other market values.[64] As such, the characteristics of the People's Courts in dealing with civil claims against wrongdoings on the securities market have been identified as 'filings are not accepted, acceptance may not lead to trial, trial may not have any judgment, and the judgment, if any, may not be enforced'.[65] As a result, among a large number of civil lawsuits against various violations in the securities market during 1996–2006 only about 1,000 investors managed to receive some compensation. This represents less than 5 per cent of all the losses of the public investors.[66] The lax enforcement and sanctions have been long blamed for the extensive misappropriation and fraud on the market.[67]

Another example is the judicial handling of the mass product liability case of contaminated milk powders. The Sanlu scandal involved melamine contamination in dairy products which affected 300,000 children nationwide and the government cover-up. When the scandal became a public crisis in September 2008, the Central Government promised to provide all the children affected with free examination and treatment and some compensation on a one-off basis.

Soon, the government's settlement plan was challenged on the legal grounds for its lack of transparency and serious inadequateness. It is pointed out that the sum of compensation has not only proved insufficient to cover the medical bills in many cases, but also failed to compensate the losses suffered by many families, such as mental and physical suffering, loss of family income, costs of nursing and transportation.[68] After the confirmation of the milk contamination, claims against Sanlu started to be filed, but all the People's Courts refused to accept such actions for over six months until after Sanlu was declared bankrupt on 12 February 2009. In early March 2009, the Supreme People's Court told the public that 95 per cent of children affected by the poisoned milk products had accepted the settlement, although many forced settlements were reported.[69] As a matter of fact, by the end of February 2009, the lawyers nationwide had accepted at least 337 cases.[70]

In this context, some lawyers believe the bankruptcy of Sanlu to be an unlawful proceeding directed by the government with the intention to move the assets away from the claims of the victims. For instance, separation of some Sanlu's factories from the bankrupt company to continue their production in the bankruptcy proceedings, appointment of the administrator of

Sanlu bankruptcy and the liquidation group with the government control and settlement with some general creditors after the commencement of the bankruptcy proceeding are considered abnormal. Moreover, the takeover by Sanyuan, a Beijing-based dairy producer with the state controlling interest under 'the government instruction' is also controversial. In fact, the local Government openly stated in November 2008 that the government's goal was to restart Sanlu's production before the bankruptcy reorganization in order to continue the development of the enterprise and the local economy.[71] At the same time, the Supreme People's Court made it clear that the court would not support massive claims since administrative measures coordinated by the Government would be better suited to deal with the crisis.[72] Thus, the judicial refusal to hear all the cases and the Sanlu bankruptcy seem a well-orchestrated government scheme with the judicial assistance to block all the claims of the victims. Such joint efforts become even more evident when a father of a victim was put on a closed-door criminal trial for 'being an agitator that caused unrest'.[73]

As reflected in the aforementioned two examples, more and more policy pressure has been imposed on the People's Courts to engage in mediation or other means in all judicial proceedings as part of the construction of a 'harmonious society'. As a result, the legal principle that judicial mediation should be carried out in accordance with the law and the parties' voluntariness has been disregarded to a large extent under the political policy.[74] In these occasions, the judicial mediation is applied more likely for upholding the Party-state interest than the parties' dispute resolution.

The policy-guided practice, however, has met resistance in its application from many judges who are professionally trained and who are reform minded. This situation is well reflected in the national judicial statistics. According to a survey made by Professor Jianfeng Pan of Peking University, despite the forceful promotion, the settlement rate through judicial mediation has been on the wane from over 50 per cent in 1990s and stable at approximately 33 per cent among all civil cases heard by the People's Courts at the first instance during the last ten years and about 10 per cent at the appellate level.[75] The finding of an empirical study in three provinces has also confirmed this situation. While answering the question on their view and using of the judicial mediation, only 11 of 53 judges surveyed considered it was important and effective and would use it often. The others considered it either not important and did not use it often, or should not be generalized and its application should depend on specific circumstances.[76]

11.4. Transitional justice

In assessing the development of civil justice reform in China, two academic discourses at the international level on pragmatic adjudication may be considered for reference. The first one is the legal pragmatism movement. Although the famous dictum of Justice Holmes that 'the life of the law has not been logic: it has been experience'[77] has been well accepted as the slogan of legal pragmatism, the doctrine is further divided into philosophical pragmatism and the so-called everyday pragmatism. The former as a 'wet' approach puts great emphasis on the examination of claims to knowledge not only with regard for factual and theoretical assumptions, but equally for assumptions about the relationship between theory and practice; whereas the latter tends to be 'dry' with only the focus on what is at the stake in a practical sense in deciding a case and 'refuses to reify or sacralize' the virtues of the rule of law.[78] Despite the discrepancy, it is generally agreed that judges must not lose sight of the value of the rule of law and 'the courting of popularity by judges is rightly destructive of public confidence in the court'.[79] As Professor Dworkin pointed out, 'judges do and should rest their judgments on controversial cases on arguments of political principles, but not on the arguments of political policy'.[80]

Closely related with the pragmatic discourse is the debate between the realists and idealists on transitional justice, which is concerned with the rule of law development in the transitional political and economic regimes. As Professor Teitel observed, in this period:

> the law is caught between the past and the future, between backward-looking and forward-looking, between retrospective and prospective, between the individual and the collective. Accordingly, transitional justice is that justice associated with this context and political circumstances. ... Accordingly, in transition, the ordinary institution and predicates about the law simply do not apply.[81]

In a context of political flux, the legal adjudication may have to struggle between settled and unsettled rules and ideologies; as a result, adjudication's distinctive feature as reflected in the transitional economies is its mediating function.[82]

The arguments in the two dynamic discourses may provide China with valuable guidelines and references. However, in a sense neither of them may squarely apply to China. On the one hand, with the rule of law as a developing concept, the judiciary in China as part of the totalitarian regime cannot make their decisions without considering their political and social consequences. As such, the popularity of adjudication in the period with unsettled legal rules and political ideology may provide the CPC and the government with more pragmatic legitimacy. On the other hand, the transitional justice arguments may not be completely suitable to China, simply because the CPC is still not willing to give up socialism and totalitarianism in its governance. The persistence will inevitably render the transitional adjudication more in favour of the old or existing regime than making its contribution to shaping the new value and constitutionalism according to the rule of law.

Unlike other transitional countries where the judicial justice has been developed to facilitate the reform and political reorientation, in China the assignment of the primary importance on social stability to the judiciary is in effect to maintain social injustice in many cases. Despite the impressive economic achievement, the reform in China itself is entering a crucial stage where the confrontation caused by social polarization, distribution inequality, corruption, environment pollution, labour violations, deprivation of peasants through land requisition, socio-economic rifts including poverty, racism and exploitation is taking the country to the verge of revolution.[83]

In this context, any reform indeed should not go beyond the social reality and pragmatic compromise will be needed to skilfully deal with the complexity of the political transition.[84] In a huge developing country like China, insufficient resource, underdeveloped supporting institutions and the persistence of the legal culture are all serious concerns on the manner of civil justice reform and should be taken into account to decide the pace and ways of the reform.[85] However, the resistance of the Party-state since the Tiananmen Event has rendered the political reform long overdue and many social conflicts are actually the results of such intended delay for prolonging the political regime.[86] As Professor Jianrong Yu of the Social Science Academy of China correctly pointed out, deepening social conflicts were caused by the CPC's obsession with preserving its monopoly on power through 'state violence' and 'ideology', rather than justice.[87]

Many experts have argued that the Party-state should take more measures through political reform and democratic development to deal more effectively with the social conflicts in the transitional period.[88] The CPC and the government should give more recognition to public power rather than use administrative power to suppress social conflicts. However, thus far, only very limited progress has been made in developing such a resilient political system. As a result, 'the Chinese Party-state faces the pressure of maintaining both social order and regime legitimacy'. In this context, 'weak legal institution and the resulting limited institutionalization of dispute resolution are undermining the regime legitimacy'.[89]

As some scholars observed, in China once disputes are classified as politically sensitive cases including socio-economic cases and class action suits, the attention of the Party-state will be expected. Even after 30 years of reform, the Party-state influence will still determine, either directly or indirectly, the results of these cases.[90] As such the civil justice reform is bound to clash with the political agenda of the Party-state. With limited independence, the judiciary may only carry out its judicial justice within the totalitarian environment, which may not be measured by professional standards, but social popularity.

In fact, the change of direction in civil justice reform may raise many fundamental issues on a broader context concerning the development of the rules of law in China. For instance, the 'Three Supremes' theory itself may be illogical and directly contradictory with the Constitution, which explicitly stipulates that all the parties must abide by the Constitution and the law and shall not have any greater privilege.[91] On the 'adjudicating for the people' ideology, the challenge has been raised on the ground that 'adjudication for justice' is a legal principle well accepted by the whole world whereas 'adjudication for the people' is a political terminology. Adjudication will lose all its value if it deviates from safeguarding justice and dignity of the law.[92] Moreover, judicial justice, which is principally limited to the concrete cases and parties, and social justice, which to a large extent depend on the social environment and perception, are not the same and there is always difference in between. Thus, the judiciary may only earn its public trust with judicial justice; otherwise, neither judicial justice nor social justice can be realized.[93]

11.5. Conclusion

The brief examination of the developments in civil dispute resolution in the past 30 years demonstrates the difficulties and challenges facing civil justice reform as well as the development of the rule of law in China. The promotion of judicial professionalism, efficiency and authority has made its profound contribution to the institutional capacity building of the judiciary in the country's reorientation, although the pace of the reform may need to be adjusted according to the social conditions. However, after the 30-year evolution, the reform has apparently reached the stage where no further progress may be made without the corresponding political reform. From the Party-state perspective the potential implications the judicial reform carries is close to their tolerable limit. As a result, more political agendas have been inserted recently so as to provide the totalitarian regime with more legitimate and popular support in the reform at the cost of dignity of the law and the judiciary. In this context, the momentary change of the reform direction and focus may be unavoidable, but in the long run, the trend for more serious civil justice reform to support judicial professionalism, independence and efficiency is irreversible.

Notes

1 The Information Office of the State Council of the PRC, 'White Paper – China's Efforts and Achievements in Promoting the Rule of Law', 28 February 2008, sec. VI. An English version is available at http://news.xinhuanet.com/english/2008-02/28/content_7687418.htm (accessed 2 May 2009).

2 For some opinions on this debate, *see*, J. Cohen, 'The PRC Legal System at Sixty', *East Asia Forum*, 1 October 2009, available at http://www.eastasiaforum.org/209/10/01/the-prc-legal-system-at-sixty/ (accessed 19 December 2009); J. V. Feinerman, 'In China, Justice in Reverse', *The Washington Post*, (Washington, DC 18 December 2008), A25; and R. Peerenboom, 'Are China's Legal Reform Stalled?', Legal Studies Working Paper Series of La Trobe University School of Law 2008/13, available at http://ssrn.com/abstract=1283203 (accessed on 15 January 2010).

3 A. H. Y. Chen, *An Introduction to the Legal System of the People's Republic of China* (3rd edn), Hong Kong: LexisNexis-Butterworths, 2004: 44.

4 R. Peerenboom, *China Modernizes*, Oxford: Oxford University Press, 2007: 216; Dongsheng Zang, 'Shifting the Burden: Judicial Reform and the Political Economy of Evidence Law in China', paper presented at the annual meeting of the

Law and Society Association, Canada on 27 May 2008, available at http://www.allacademic.com/meta/p236328_index.html (accessed 15 December 2009).

5 Article 13 of the Constitutional Amendment of 1999, which reads that 'China shall practice ruling the country in accordance with the law and building a socialist country under the rule of law'.

6 For a brief review of the achievements of the reform, *see*, Liming Wang, 'The Achievements and Prospects of Court Reform in China', *Frontiers of Law in China,* 1, 2006: 1–13.

7 The two reform plans of the Supreme People's Court are available at http://www.dffy.com/faguixiazai/xf/200511/20051128111114.htm and http://www.dffy.com/faguixiazai/xf/200512/20051214221735.htm, respectively (accessed 12 March 2010).

8 The speech was made by Jintao Hu at the meeting to celebrate the 20th anniversary of the promulgation of the current Constitution on 5 December 2002; available at http://past.people.com.cn/GB/shizheng/252/9921/9922/20021204/881364.html (accessed 12 December 2009).

9 The case was published at *Zuigao Renmin Fayuan Gongbao* (The Bulletin of the Supreme People's Court of PRC), 5, 2001: 158–161. For a report of the case in English, *see* 'Qi Yuling v. Chen Xiaoqi et al', *Chinese Education & Society*, 39, 2006: 58–74.

10 5 U.S. 137 (1803). As a landmark case it set out the basis for the exercise of judicial review in the United States under Article III of the Constitution.

11 Songyou Huang, The Importance of Institutionalizing the Constitution in Judicial Process, *People's Court News*, 13 August 2001, available at http://lawprofessors.typepad.com/china_law_prof_blog/files/1109_huang_songyou_qi_yuling_case.pdf (accessed 12 December 2009).

12 Kui Shen, 'Is It the Beginning of the Era of the Rule of the Constitution? Reinterpreting China's First Constitutional Case' (translation), Pacific Rim Law & Policy Journal, 12, 2003: 199.

13 Protocol on the Accession of the People's Republic of China, WT/L/432, 23 November 2001: (01-5996), Part I.

14 Exiang Wan (Vice President of the Supreme People's Court), Accession to the WTO and the Judicial Reform in China, *Shanghai Duiwai Maoyi Xueyuan Xuebao* (Journal of Foreign Trade College of Shanghai), 7, 2001: 4–7.

15 The speech made at the Conference of the National High Court Presidents on 5 August 1999, printed in the Research Department of the Supreme People's Court (ed.), *Renmin Fayuan Wunian Gaige Gangyao* (Outlines of the Five-Year Reform of the People's Court), Beijing: People's Court Press, 2000: 227–228.

16 The speech made at the Conference of the National High Court Presidents on 14 December 1999, printed in the Research Department of the Supreme People's Court (ed.), *ibid.*, 222.

17 C. Lin, 'A Quiet Revolution: An Overview of China's Judicial Reform', *Asian-Pacific Law and Policy Journal*, 4(2), 2003: 255.

18 Wei Jiang and Bangqing Sun, Overhauling the Civil Procedure Law Is Expected, *Minshi Susong Luntan* (Civil Procedure Tribune), 2, 2008: 49–51.

19 Yong-an Liao and Hejun Deng, 'Comments on the Decision to Amend the Civil Procedure Law', *Xiandai Faxue* (Modern Law Science), 1, 2009: 150–160.

20 Liu Jialiang, 'It Is Necessary to Overhaul the Civil Procedure Law', *Jiancha Ribao* (The People's Procuracy Daily), 18 March 2008, 4.

21 The Third Reform Plan of the People's Courts (2009–2013) is available at http://www.court.gov.cn/html/article/200903/25/680.shtml (accessed 12 December 2009).

22 *Ibid.*, Sec. 1 (3).

23 The total votes against the Working Report and abstaining votes among the less than 3,000 national representatives presented at the annual meeting deputies were 470, 641, 711 and 607 in 2007, 2008, 2009 and 2010, respectively. The numbers are calculated by the author according to the media reports of the recent annual meetings of the National Congress.

24 Report of the Vice Chairwoman, Xiulian Gu of the Standing Committee of the National People's Congress dated 26 August 2006: 'The People's Concerns with Judicial Justice Caused by Minority Judges and Prosecutors', *Xinhua She* (Xinhua News Agency), available at http://news.xinhuanet.com/politics/2006-08/28/content_5016788.htm (accessed 20 July 2008).

25 The statistics made by the author based on the various media reports in this period.

26 J. Cohen, Body Blow for the Judiciary, *South China Morning Post*, 18 October 2008, 13; and R Peerenboom, 'Between Global Norms and Domestic Realities: Judicial Reforms in China', 8 May 2009, available at http://papers.ssrn.com/sol3/papers.cfm?abstract_id=1401232 (accessed 12 December 2009).

27 Based on the information of the introduction to the newly appointed presidents of High People's Courts, *Xinhua Wang* (Xinhua News Web site), 23 January 2008, available at http://news.xinhuanet.com/legal/2008-01/23/content_7479184.htm (accessed 5 January 2010) and the report, 'Half of the Presidents of the High People's Courts Coming from the Party or the Government', *Zaobao* (Morning Daily of Singapore), 21 July 2009, available at http://www.zaobao.com/special/china/cnpol/pages2/cnpol090721.shtml (accessed 24 July 2009).

28 Based on the author's own comparative study of the information available at the various Web sites.

29 *See*, *Xinhua Wang* (Xunhua News Web site), 11 April 2008, available at http://news.xinhuanet.com/legal/2008-04/11/content_7956313.htm (accessed 20 November 2009).

30 Yongtong Su, 'The High Court President Who Does Not Function According to the Legal Principles', *Nanfang Zhoumo* (Southern Weekend), 18 February 2009, available at http://www.infzm.com/content/24067/ (accessed 25 July 2009).

31 For more details of the campaign, *see*, *Zhongguo Fayuanwang* (The Web site of the China Courts), 8 January 2010, available at http://www.chinacourt.org/html/article/201001/08/389996.shtml (assessed 3 March 2010).

32 'The Guiding Opinion of the Supreme People's Court to Implement 23 Concrete Measures for Adjudication for the People', available at http://news.xinhuanet.com/legal/2003-12/03/content_1211777.htm (accessed 23 September 2009).

33 *See*, the report on the practice of the 'adjudication for the people' policy in Jiangsu Province, *Xinhua Ribao* (Xinhua Daily), 21 September 2009, available at http://jsnews.jschina.com.cn/a/200909/t186572.shtml (accessed 5 December 2009).

34 *See*, the report on the practice of the Haikuo Intermediate People's Court of Hainan Province of the 'adjudication for the people' policy, 26 October 2009, *Fazhi Ribao* (Legal Daily), available at http://jsnews.jschina.com.cn/a/200909/t186572.shtml (accessed 5 December 2009).

35 *See*, the report on the measures adopted by the Shijiazhuang Intermediate People's Court of Hebei Province to implement the 'adjudication for the people' policy,

10 April 2009, Shijiazhuang Government Web site, available at http://www.sjzzfw.gov.cn/art/2009/04/10/art_29317_307334.html (accessed 5 December 2009).

36 *See*, the report on the measures of Bazhou District People's Court of Sichuan Province to implement the 'adjudication for the people' policy, 11 June 2008, Bazhou District People's Court Web site, available at http://www.scbzrd.gov.cn/bzfayuan/dwjs/200806/885.html (accessed 5 December 2009).

37 *See*, 'Certain Provisions on Implementation of Court's Own Initiation of Execution' adopted by the Guangdong High People's Court (on a trial basis) on 29 July 2009.

38 *See*, the report on the measures of Wushe County of Henan Province to implement the 'adjudication for the people' policy, 2 November 2009, Jiaozuo People's Court Web site, available at http://jzzy.chinacourt.org/public/detail.php?id=1573 (accessed 5 December 2009).

39 Speech made by Mr Dianlong Luo, the President of the High People's Court of Guangxi Zhuang Autonomous Region on 7 January 2009, available at *Fazhi Kuaibao* (Legal Express), available at http://www.pagx.cn/html/2009/1-8/20090108101322 604.html (assessed 5 November 2009).

40 Yizhang Feng, 'How to Understand the So-Called "Universal Values"', *Renmin Ribao* (People's Daily), 10 September 2008; Tiancheng Zhou, 'Universal Values Promoted Are Actually Western Values', *Guangming Ribao* (Guangming Daily), 16 September 2008; and Study Center of Deng Xiaoping Theory and 'Three Representative Thoughts' of the Ministry of Education, 'Certain Issues Concerning the "Universal Values"', *Qiushi* (Truth Seeking), 22, 2008: 59–62.

41 Xun Jiang, '30 Years Reform – The Universal Values – Charter 2008', *Yazhou Zhoukan* (Asia Weekly), 25 December 2008, available at http://www.iasiaweekly.com/archives/1159 (accessed 20 November 2009).

42 For a detailed report of the Opinions of the CPC, *see*, Xudong Qin, 'Judicial Reform: A New Round', *Caijing* (Caijing Magazine), 24 January 2009, available at http://english.caijing.com.cn/ajax/ensprint.html (accessed 5 March 2009).

43 The speech of Jintao Hu is reported at the *Xinhua Wang* (Xinhua News Web site), 25 December 2007, available at http://news.xinhuanet.com/newscenter/2007-12/25/content_7312439.htm (accessed 5 December 2009).

44 Decision of the Supreme People's Court on Abolition of Certain Judicial Interpretations Promulgated before the End of 2007, dated 18 December 2008, item 26. Normally, a reason will be provided when an opinion of the Supreme People's Court is repealed, which may include 'circumstance change', 'replaced with the new rule', 'conflicting with other laws' or 'the amendment of the relevant law'; but in the Yuling Qi case the reason given is merely 'no longer applied'.

45 T. Kellogg, 'The Death of Constitutional Litigation in China?', *China Brief*, vol. 9 (7), 2009: 4–7.

46 'Comment: Let the People to Effectively Experience the Achievements of the Judicial Reform', *Renmin Ribao* (People's Daily), 22 February 2010: 1.

47 Ming Yang, 'The Judicial Reform in China Enters into a Crossroads', *Liaowang Dongfang Zhoukang* (Oriental Outlook), 24 February 2010, available at http://news.ifeng.com/society/5/201002/0224_2579_1554358.shtml (accessed 6 April 2010).

48 I. Johnson, 'China Protects Surge as Labor Makes Demands', *The Wall Street Journal (Asia)*, 10 July 2009, 3; and T. Lum, 'Social Unrest in China', Congressional Research Services – Library of Congress, 2005, available at http://www.fas.org/sgp/crs/row/RL33416.pdf (accessed 4 April 2010).

49 Guangnai Shan, 'A Full Analysis of Massive Incidents in 2009', *Nanfang Zhoumo* (Southern Weekend), 4 February 2010, available at http://www.chinaelections.org/newsinfo.asp?newsid=168508 (accessed 4 April 2010).
50 Lin Li (ed.), *Zhongguo Fazhi Fazhan Baogao (2010)* (The Rule of Law Development Report of 2010), Beijing: Social Science Publishing House, 2010. A brief on the report is available at *Shanghai Fazhi Bao* (Legal Daily of Shanghai), 1 March 2010, 1.
51 The Working Report of the Supreme People's Court of 2010, available at http://news.qq.com/a/20100311/003135.htm (accessed 8 April 2010).
52 The Working Report of the Supreme People's Court of 2000, *Zhonghua Renmin Gongheguo Zuigao Renmin Fayuan Gongbao* (The Bulletin of the Supreme People's Court of PRC), 2, 2000: 41.
53 For a discussion on these problems, *see*, Xin He, 'The Recent Decline in Economic Caseloads in Chinese Courts: Exploration of a Surprising Puzzle', *The China Quarterly*, 190, 2007: 352–374.
54 Article 6 of the *Civil Procedure Law* of 1982 (on trial), which stated that the People's Court in hearing civil disputes should put emphasis on mediation; the decision should be made in a timely manner if the meditative efforts failed.
55 Article of the *Civil Procedure Law* of 1991 as amended in 2007 provides that mediation should be carried out by the People's Court in hearing civil disputes in accordance with the law and the voluntariness of the parties; the decision should be made in a timely manner if the meditative efforts failed.
56 Speech of Mr Shengjun Wang made at the national conference on judicial mediation on 28 July 2009, published at *Renmin Fayuanwang* (Web site of the People's Courts), available at http://www.chinacourt.org/html/article/200907/29/367194.shtml (accessed 5 April 2010).
57 R Peerenboom, 'More Law, Less Courts: Legalized Governance, Judicialization and Retrenchment in China', in T. Ginsburg and A. H. Y. Chen (eds), *Administrative Law and Governance in Asia: Comparative Perspectives*, New York: Routledge, 2008: 190.
58 Article 50 of the *Procedure Law of Administrative Litigation* of 1989 explicitly provides that mediation shall not be applied to administrative cases.
59 Jianfeng Pan, 'Mediation Storm: A Landscape in Construction of a Harmonized Society', presentation made to the Conference on Constitutional Reform and Financial Regulation at the University of Hong Kong on 12 December 2009.
60 In terms of the compensation demanded, the figure for the year 2006 stood 20 times higher than the number in 2002. By June 2007, more than 250 civil actions had been filed with the People's Courts. Xiaoming Wang, 'Claims against Management Blowout', *21 Shiji Jingji Baodao* (21st Century Business Herald), 1 June 2007: 16.
61 Art. 6 of the Provisions.
62 Art. 69 of the *Securities Law* of 2005.
63 W. Hutchens, 'Private Securities Litigation in China: Material Disclosure about China's Legal System', *University of Pennsylvania Journal of International Economic Law* 24, 2003: 645.
64 N. Howson, 'Judicial Independence and the Company Law in Shanghai Courts', in R. Peerenboom (ed.), *Judicial Independence in China: Lessons for Global Rule of Law Promotion,* Cambridge: Cambridge University Press, 147.
65 Haitao Yu, 'Be Aware of Investors' Protection', *21 Shiji Jingji Baodao* (21st Century Business Herald), 1 January 2007: 9.

66 *Zhongguo Zhengquanbao* (China Securities), 24 July 2006, available at http://news.xinhuanet.com/stock/2006-07/24/content_4871138.htm (accessed 4 June 2008).
67 Zhong Zhang, 'Legal Deterrence: the Foundation of Corporate Governance – Evidence from China', 15 *Journal of Compliance*, 2007: 741–767.
68 'Report, Lawyers for the Affected Babies: Salu Compensation Is Not Sufficient and Transparent', *Sing Tao Web site* (Hong Kong), 9 December 2008, available at http://www.stnn.cc/china/200812/t20081229_950829.html (accessed 7 May 2009).
69 Report, 'No Free Treatment Will Be Given If the Parents Refuse to Sign the Settlement Agreement', *Ming Pao* (Hong Kong), 29 May 2009, A 20.
70 Ye Doudou and Chenzhong Xiaolu, 'Sanlu Civil Claims Are Expected to Be Accepted', *Caijing* (Caijing Journal), 5 March 2009, available at http://www.caijing.com.cn/2009-03-05/110113358.html (accessed 19 December 2009).
71 *China Law Net,* 7 November 2008, available at http://www.chinafalv.com/news/106/ 200811/07-14994.html (accessed 14 June 2009).
72 *Nanfang Daily* (Southern Daily), 12 March 2009, available at http://www1.nanfangdaily.com.cn/b5/www.nanfangdaily.com.cn/nfjx/200903120039.asp (accessed 6 June 2009).
73 'Milk Scandal: Closed Door Trial for Seeking Justice for Sick Children', Asia News, 31 March 2010, available at http://www.asianews.it/view4print.php?l=en&art=18028 (accessed 5 April 2010).
74 *See*, the report on the new concept of 'judicial harmony' of the Supreme People's Court, *Xinhua She* (Xinhua News Agency), 7 January 2007, available at http://news.163.com/07/0107/11/347SD32N000122EH.html (accessed 5 December 2009).
75 Pan, *supra note* 59.
76 Margaret Woo and Yaxin Wang, 'Civil Justice in China: An Empirical Study of Courts in Three Provinces', *American Journal of Comparative Law* 53, 2005: 936–937.
77 O. W. Holmes, Jr, The Common Law (1881), 1.
78 R. Posner, *Law, Pragmatism, and Democracy*, Cambridge: Harvard University Press, 2003: 11–12.
79 *Ibid.*, 334.
80 R. Dworkin, 'Political Judges and the Rule of Law', in A. Kavanagh and J. Oberdiek (eds), *Arguing about Law,* London/New York: Routledge, 2009: 193–194.
81 R. Teitel, *Transitional Justice,* Oxford: Oxford University Press, 2000: 1–6.
82 *Ibid.,* 220.
83 Jianrong Yu, 'Social Conflict in Rural China', *China Security* 3, 2007: 2–17, and Lum, *supra note* 48.
84 Peerenboom, *supra note* 26.
85 Woo and Wang, *supra note* 76, 911–940; and Hualing Fu, 'Access to Justice in China: Potentials, Limits, and Alternatives', 2009, available at http://ssrn.com/abstract=1474073 (accessed 5 January 2010).
86 'Hu Rejects China Political Reform', *BBC News*, 15 September 2004, available at http://news.bbc.co.uk/2/hi/asia-pacific/3657906.stm (accessed 23 February 2010).
87 J. Garnaut, 'China Insider Sees Revolution Brewing', *Sydney Morning Herald*, 27 February 2010, available at http://www.smh.com.au/world/china-insider-sees-revolution-brewing-20100226-p92d.html (accessed 12 April 2010).
88 Fu, *supra note* 85.

89 Yongshun Cai, 'Social Conflicts and Modes of Action in China', *The China Journal,* 59, 2008: 107–108.

90 Hualing Fu and R. Cullen, 'From Mediatory to Adjudicatory Justice: The Limits of Civil Justice Reform in China', 2007, available at http://papers.ssrn.com/sol3/papers.cfm?abstract_id=1306800 (accessed 15 January 2010); Yulin Fu and R. Peerenboom, 'A New Analytic Framework for Understanding and Promoting Judicial Independende in China', 2009, available at http://ssrn.com/abstract=1336069 (accessed 2 March 2010).

91 Article 5 of the Constitution of the PRC.

92 Zhong Chen, 'An Analysis of the Paradox of Adjudication for the People', *Sichuan Wenli Xueyuan Xuebao* (Sichuan University of Arts and Science Journal [Social Science Edition]), 3, 2008: 33–36.

93 Qimei Zhang, 'Thoughts on Judicial Justice and Social Justice', *Sifa Redian Wenti Diaocha* (Investigation of Pressing Issues in Judicial Practice), 1, 2004: 9.

12 China's arbitration
Restricted reform

Weixia Gu

12.1. Introduction

It has been noted that among various ways of settling business disputes in China, arbitration has become a preferred means for resolving trade and investment disputes between Chinese and foreign parties. Although promulgated as a milestone in China's arbitration history, after more than a decade of practice, the *China Arbitration Law* (AL) has been criticized as being much tainted by local standards and insufficient with respect to protection of party and tribunal autonomy. Recent years have seen many changes in the regulatory landscape of Chinese arbitration, particularly those led by the China International Economic Trade Arbitration Commission (CIETAC) and Supreme People's Court (SPC). This chapter probes into those most recent reforms and tests the extent to which they have actually improved the situation.

12.2. Arbitration with 'Chinese characteristics'

12.2.1. Regulatory framework

Arbitration in China is marked by a number of distinctive and even 'rigid' features which often catch seasoned practitioners unfamiliar with the system by surprise. For one, arbitrations in China must be conducted by and under the rules of definite 'arbitration commissions'.[1] As such, arbitral agreements with an innominate or unclear identity of the arbitration commission, particularly *ad hoc* arbitrations, are not permitted. Another principal weakness is that AL forbids the arbitral tribunal to determine the validity of arbitration agreements and therefore its own jurisdiction, which significantly departs from the international practice of *competence–competence*.[2] In addition, the Chinese arbitration system discriminates against the interest of parties to domestic disputes by adopting a 'dual-track difference' within the AL.[3] Parties whose disputes carry no foreign elements are not allowed to choose CIETAC or China Maritime Arbitration Commission (CMAC) due to their status as 'foreign-related arbitration commissions' under the AL[4] until the jurisdiction was later blurred.[5] It has been as well challenged that contrary to international practice, arbitration agreements without a foreign element are subject to substantive judicial review for award enforcement.[6] Moreover, most arbitral bodies in China require arbitrators be chosen by parties from a 'panel of arbitrators' established by each individual arbitration commission.[7] Prior to 1988, no foreigners appeared on the CIETAC panel.[8] Since then, foreign arbitrators have been appointed, although local commissions have been slower in including international panels. There are further concerns as to the scope of which parties can modify or deviate from the rules of arbitration commissions for designing dispute resolution process. Both AL and the rules of arbitration commissions have been silent on the point until very recently when CIETAC allowed parties to opt out of its rules.[9] This has subjected party and tribunal's procedural autonomy to 'powerful' arbitration commissions. In this regard, despite the critical role of commissions in formulating arbitration procedural rules in China, implementation schemes are lacking from the law to ensure their quality and integrity. It has been critically pointed out by several authors that AL has as its legislative intention of leading professional and independent arbitration commissions in China, but fails to lay down detailed rules in realizing them.[10]

12.2.2. Recent changes in the Chinese arbitration system

A number of significant developments have recently occurred as regards China's arbitration system. One of the most important is the recent revamp of CIETAC arbitration rules in 2005.[11] The rules introduced a series of important changes with respect to greater procedural management powers by parties and arbitral tribunals. Most noticeable of all, for the first time, CIETAC permits parties to appoint individuals not on its panel list, and the presiding arbitrator may now be chosen from the match found in the parties' list of preferential nominations.[12] This largely opens up the scope of choices, as CIETAC's panel predominantly consists of Chinese nationals, with a majority coming from its staff and government officials living in Beijing sharing acquaintance.[13] The widening of potential arbitrators will increase dramatically the pool of experts and foreigners available to serve on a CIETAC tribunal and hence has significant practical impact on increasing the parties' procedural autonomy. However, parties' selection of arbitrators does not enjoy full freedom, as the selection can only be done with confirmation by the chairman of CIETAC.[14] Yet, no implementation rules have been laid down to guide the chairman's discretion, the opaque practice of which may likely dim the early optimism. A further key change under the CIETAC reform is its fist-time introduction of jurisdiction autonomy to its arbitral tribunals through Article 6 of the newly amended rules. By virtue of that article, the commission may now delegate power to individual tribunals to decide jurisdictional challenges, which used to be monopolized by the commission's secretariat.[15] Nevertheless, the recently implemented rules seem to invite controversies as well. Similar to the lack of guidance on the chairman's discretion in handling appointment of non-listed arbitrators, the reform as to jurisdiction is also silent on necessary details under which jurisdiction power can be delegated. Given that AL only prescribes commissions to rule on arbitral jurisdiction, there are arguments that CIETAC's 'intentional' omission on implementation details is a 'cautious approach for self-protection and not offending the legislative mandate'.[16]

Another impressive aspect of the latest arbitration development is SPC's issuance of judicial interpretations in 2006 to liberalize defective arbitration agreements in China (SPC Interpretation).[17] Parties are accommodated with more drafting autonomy, where most of the drafting pathologies involving 'ambiguous and multiple arbitration commissions' would be deemed remediable and enforceable.[18] Specifically, parties' choice of any institutional arbitration rules will be considered as their selection of the arbitral institution which administers those rules.[19] As such, the new rules have significant support by the highest Chinese court to arbitration. It is noteworthy that, however, prior to the issuance of SPC Interpretation, some more liberal interpretative technique has been proposed in its draft provisions (SPC Draft Provisions) in 2004.[20] Most 'liberal' of all is Article 27 of the SPC Draft Provisions: *ad hoc* arbitration agreements may be allowed in China if both parties to the agreement are nationals of member states of the 1958 New York Convention, and neither country prohibits the practice of *ad hoc* arbitration.[21] The provision was considered restrictive in that *ad hoc* arbitral agreements between a Chinese party and a foreign party may still be excluded. However, the potential impact of the article would be far-reaching, that being the possible defrosting of *ad hoc* arbitral practice in China. The SPC Draft Provisions, particularly its Article 27, had high expectation of being formally endorsed with partial recognition of *ad hoc* arbitration agreements in China. This, however, did not occur, leaving the practice of *ad hoc* arbitration standing at the cross-roads of the SPC-led arbitration reform.

12.3. Reformed arbitration: why restricted?

This section of the discussion looks into the aforementioned reforms in an attempt to determine their actual effect in implementation.

12.3.1. Inherent defects of arbitration commissions

Are arbitration commissions in China professional and independent, and as such, capable of carrying out the reforms put forward by CIETAC in developing party and tribunal's procedural autonomy? Since AL came into force in 1995, more than 200 arbitration commissions have been founded, in addition to CIETAC and CMAC.[22] These new arbitration commissions are called local arbitration commissions (LACs), generally named after the administrative area in which they are registered. It seems that the new rules introduced by CIETAC in 2005 have not been followed by corresponding changes of rules in most LACs in China. Although there is no affiliation between CIETAC and

LACs, due to its premier leadership in Chinese arbitration practice, historically, CIETAC rules and practices have significant impact on LACs.[23] The following analysis tends to show the reasons why LACs have been reluctant to implement reforms. As most of the LACs rely greatly on local governments for survival and development, these commissions' lack of institutional professionalism and independence have thus made reforming steps much over-shadowed by local administrative influences.

In accordance with a State Council Notice in 1995, establishment and operation of local arbitration commissions in China shall be supervised by the local government's legislative affairs office where the commission is located and registered.[24] The local legislative affairs office, however, becomes the leading department, deciding upon the staffing and other important matters of development of the commission including remuneration of commission members.[25] Against this backdrop, whether a LAC can operate independently is largely an issue of the local administrative attitude towards arbitration. In other words, if the local government takes on arbitration as an independent means of dispute resolution, the particular LAC may enjoy more room for developing institutional independence. In this respect, the Beijing Arbitration Commission (BAC) benefits greatly from the 'non-interference' approach by the Beijing municipal government which puts forward BAC as a rising star on the Chinese arbitration forum.[26]

LACs under the category of 'institutions' (*shiye danwei*) are financially sponsored by the local treasury. In one situation, if a LAC makes profits from arbitral caseload and service charges, it may be justified as financially stable. These profits may nevertheless need to undergo administrative scrutiny, for example, the situation with BAC.[27] More problems rest with the other situation. Since the promulgation of AL, according to Article 10, LACs have been widespread in cities wherever the cities can be divided into districts. Such establishment has largely catered for administrative needs rather than market demand for dispute resolution. Local governments can use LACs for playing upon local protectionism, such as requiring the investing enterprises to include the LAC in the arbitration agreement.[28] The transitional economy in China and the vast territory leads to the unbalanced development of the regional economy with rapid progress in some areas and slow progress elsewhere. Many LACs still face the problem of 'looking for rice to cook', especially those in the vast hinterland, which largely rely on the local government for survival, both in funding and arbitration caseload.[29] This has further increased LACs' reliance on the local administrative power.

The AL reflects the fact that administrative influences remain strong on the operation of Chinese arbitration commissions. This implies the administrative undermining of arbitral powers as well. First, by analogy to the hierarchical relationship, the arbitral tribunal is also deemed as structurally inferior and functionally subordinate to the commission. Thus, the ruling of arbitral jurisdiction as one of the key functions of an arbitral tribunal is interpreted as executing 'administrative hierarchical commands' from the arbitration commission.[30]

Second, owing to the governmental control permeating the institutional infrastructure, LACs are prone to administrative interferences. The conclusion could be drawn that the administratively dominated commissions may in turn administratively overshadow the jurisdictional competence and arbitral autonomy of its lower-level tribunals. Because *ad hoc* arbitration practice is still not recognized in China, no individual tribunal could be lucky enough to escape the administrative impact.

The CIETAC-led, off-panel appointment reform shares the similar problem with its reform of tribunal's *competence–competence*. Due to the administrative infrastructure, discretionary approval from the commission chairman may actually defeat the parties' original intention of selecting arbitrators not included on the panel list. The conditional permission on parties' wider choices thus could become an awkward compromise on party autonomy within the context of institutional control, and it clearly gives the institution leverage over the parties' procedural interests. However, the institutional control derives from many intertwined political and administrative pressures, which makes the CIETAC-led arbitral reform appear competent yet hesitant. Indeed, the reform has been viewed sceptically by LACs; moreover, such an off-panel appointment has rarely been reported within CIETAC since its promulgation of the new rules.[31] Parties are still very cautious and even reluctant to exercise their rights to make an off-panel appointment. There are reasonable concerns that the subsequent enforcement of the award might be problematic owing to uncertainty over the proper 'qualifications' of outside arbitrators.

The discussions may provide further insights into the reform hurdles of the arbitration institutions and in addition, one of the key challenges facing the Chinese arbitration system, i.e. the way in which arbitration commissions work. In this regard, it might be more understandable why reforming tribunal's *competence–competence* and off-panel appointment have been such difficult issues, as they depend much upon the political environment to allow further independence of arbitration commissions in China, particularly large numbers of LACs, which should provide strong institutional support for tribunal's independence and integrity. The infrastructure deficiency has thwarted party and tribunal autonomy where parties should have complete freedom to choose any arbitrators which shall have full power to rule on its own jurisdiction. The CIETAC-reform is, therefore, subject to the institutional deficiency of most Chinese arbitration commissions (large numbers of LACs), which mirrors political and administrative embeddedness on legal institutions in China during transitions.

12.3.2. Denial of Ad Hoc arbitration

Although almost all countries permit *ad hoc* arbitration in their national arbitration legislation, in the history of commercial arbitration in China, *ad hoc* arbitration has never been admitted by the legislation, nor has it been protected in practice. The regulatory discouragement may be reflected, most recently, in SPC's omission of the issue in its 2006 interpretation on arbitration, plus an earlier case in 2003 where the SPC struck down an arbitration clause providing for *ad hoc* arbitration in China.[32] In the absence of a legitimate basis, the following case may be one of the few exceptional ones where *ad hoc* arbitration is actually practised without changing the current legal framework:

> Sinotrans Dalian Company ('Sinotrans') as charterer, entered into a time charter with the ship owner Hainan Dongda Shipping Company ('Dongda') on 20 October 1998. The arbitration clause in the contract provided that, 'All disputes arising out of the contract shall be arbitrated in Beijing'. Both companies are located in Dalian. The disputes arose and Dongda asked Mr. Hu Zhengliang, a law professor at the Dalian Maritime University and a Beijing CMAC panel-arbitrator to assist them in resolving the dispute. Subsequently, Sinotrans also requested Mr. Hu to arbitrate the dispute. On 18 May 1999, the parties agreed for the dispute to be arbitrated by Mr. Hu. Mr. Hu asked for both parties' submissions. He then requested Mr. Wang Jianping, also a professor at the Dalian Maritime University but with a specialty in navigation technology, to give an expert report of the navigation database provided by the parties. On 10 July 1999, Mr. Hu drafted and delivered to the parties his decision by way of a document entitled 'An Opinion on Mediation'. Both parties honoured the decision.[33]

Although it was entitled 'An Opinion on Mediation', in essence, the document was not only an arbitral award, but also an *ad hoc* arbitral award due to the following reasons. First, there was an intention to arbitrate rather than mediate. Moreover, neither party considered the resolution as 'mediation' at any stage. It is important to note that 'arbitration' rather than 'mediation' was requested in writing by both parties in their correspondence. Most notable of all, Mr Hu made no attempt to mediate such as to persuade the parties to reach an agreed compromise. Rather, he relied on his professional knowledge of maritime law, expert's opinion and relevant legal provisions and shipping customs to deal with the dispute by following arbitral procedures. The 'Opinion' was made independently of the parties and contained orders rather than suggestions.[34] The question is then posed with respect to why the term 'Opinion on Mediation' was used. As Kang Ming, the then Deputy Secretary General of CIETAC analysed the case, although it was expected that the parties would honour Mr Hu's decisions, a risk remained that the losing party might not do so due to the lack of enforcement mechanism of *ad hoc* arbitration in China. In case this should happen, the winning party would not have been able to enforce the award, for it being the outcome of *ad hoc* arbitration. The word 'mediation' was, therefore, used as a technicality to avoid the risk of non-enforcement of the *ad hoc* arbitral award.

Despite the encouraging result of the foregoing case report, it is worth noting that such success of *ad hoc* practice – under the 'pretence' of mediation – is just a technical device to circumvent legal requirements; or more accurately, a kind of 'fashioning of practical remedies without violating the current legal framework'.[35] Given the fact that *ad hoc* arbitration has not yet been liberalized in China, such practice of 'formal mediation, actual arbitration' might be arguably acceptable before the amendment of AL. However, in the long run, and indeed to align the Chinese arbitration system with international norms, legislative recognition is required for *ad hoc* arbitration to be practised in China. Likewise, it is highly advocated that foreign arbitration be allowed in China and be written into the amendment of AL. The merits for legalizing *ad hoc* and foreign arbitrations in China are evident. Parties are expected to enjoy more choices of arbitration that can be facilitated by both institutional and *ad hoc* arbitrations and conducted by both Chinese and foreign arbitral bodies. Additionally, given the current bureaucratic practice of most LACs, the introduction of *ad hoc* arbitration seems particularly necessary in China, which would either provide an alternative to the administratively tainted institutional arbitrations in China, thus providing parties with a way to avoid administrative interference; or pressure LACs to be better qualified and more transparent in catering to market demand rather than administrative needs.

However, even when legalization has been acknowledged to benefit the Chinese arbitration regime, one has to realize that the political problem of state control remains a much more serious challenge to the inclusion in the revised AL. Politicians tend to object to the inclusion by blaming Chinese economic conditions. Because in *ad hoc* arbitration, the burden is placed on the parties to organize and administer the arbitral proceeding; and if problems arise, such as intentional delays by the parties or arbitrators, the assistance of an arbitration institution or an independent appointing authority will not be available,[36] it thus requires the highest degree of good faith in conducting an *ad hoc* arbitration agreement, i.e. the duty to participate in the arbitral proceeding and carry it forward.[37] Hence, arguments have been made that the fledging level of fiduciary duties in the socialist market transition in China is still unable to assure the high degree of good faith in *ad hoc* arbitration. Likewise, arguments have been put forward that outcome of *ad hoc* dispute resolution will be hard to predict; it will thus be detrimental to socio-economic stability and hence be detrimental to the immature market system in China.[38]

A similar perspective has been raised by one Chinese top legislative official responsible for AL legislation. Mr Liu Maoliang, Deputy Head of Legislative Affairs Office of the State Council, expressed that 'implementation of *ad hoc* arbitration in China should be slow without a developed and mature market economy'.[39] Such argument is superficial, as the Chinese leadership has made it clear very recently that China will remain over a rather long term in the initial period of a developing country.[40] As such, there is more political than economic resistance in allowing *ad hoc* arbitration and foreign arbitration in China. The resistance is political in the sense that China still wants to significantly 'oversee' the final result of arbitration through its institutional and administrative influence, thereby exercising 'control' over economic matters such as its domestic market and foreign trade and investment.

12.3.3. Judicial restrictions

At the enforcement side, arbitration enforcement is one aspect reflecting the general enforcement problems faced by the Chinese judiciary; and hence, a couple of defects are evident. In the first place, during the transition from a planned to a market economy and in the process of developing rule of law in China, most local people's courts suffer institutional deficiency in terms of finance and function. As such, within the current Chinese context where local protectionism and corruption are still rampant, local courts may not be able to refrain from local Party and governmental pressures which seriously influence their decision-making process, such as arbitral enforcement. Lately, the Baotao Intermediate People's Court declared an arbitration agreement invalid and the award accordingly revoked, as the enforcement may lead to the losing party (a key domestic enterprise with the local government support) becoming bankrupt.[41] The striking ruling in the *Baotou* case indicates that, until very recently, some local courts still tend to intervene into arbitration where local businesses are involved, particularly where the business is important to the local economy.

Indeed, caution against local protectionism over arbitral enforcement has been noted as early as 1996 where SPC adopted a series of 'pre-reporting' mechanisms. By virtue of the 'pre-reporting', any denial of enforcement of foreign-related arbitral agreements and awards must be reported to SPC for approval.[42] However, the scheme has serious shortcomings. Most obviously, it is only applicable to the foreign-related regime. Thus far, in the most recent arbitral reform led by SPC in late 2006, the dual-track practice has not been picked up. The degree of judicial caution varies substantially between the two tracks and more preferential treatment has been reserved for the foreign-related track. The *Baotao* case echoes a previous study done by Professor Randall Peerenboom. In that study, among the sixty-three domestic awards handled by one court in a large city in Jiangsu province, two were refused and thirty-five listed as pending.[43] Hence, domestic parties may worry about their autonomy and interest in arbitration being denied without the procedural remedy such as the 'pre-reporting' system available to their foreign-related counterpart. It must be pointed out, however, that local protectionism attacks not only foreign parties but also domestic parties from outside the region of enforcement parties. Therefore, it remains uncertain how to protect the lawful arbitral interests of large numbers of domestic 'alien' parties. The dual-track system and the foreign-party-favoured treatment have been warmly welcomed by foreign investors as centralized review will prompt better enforcement results.[44] Nevertheless, it may not be welcomed by domestic investors and this practice has been criticized for having overlooked domestic interests. Moreover, it has been increasingly challenged that, by hierarchical reporting, the higher-level judiciary can interfere into jurisdictional rulings of the lower-level, which patently violates due process and independent judicial decision-making.

Apart from local influence concerns, there is as well inadequate qualification of local judges with respect to knowledge and practice of arbitration which leads to arbitrary interpretation of arbitration agreements and awards. For example, in a pair of recent cases in Wuhan and Tsingdao Intermediate Courts, there is a common judicial ignorance of the applicable law rules in reviewing foreign-related arbitration agreements by the judiciary.[45] The general application of AL could easily find a foreign-related arbitration agreement without a clearly specified arbitral institution to be invalid.[46] Besides, the perception that rapid development of arbitration may unfairly disadvantage the court's caseload has fostered a judicial hostility towards arbitration in some less developed parts of China. Such judicial hostility tends to make local people's courts compete with local arbitration commissions where local judges use their review power to turn down arbitration agreements in order to 'win' jurisdiction.[47]

Therefore, while SPC has been working hard to pay more judicial respect to parties' autonomy and interest in arbitration by issuing a long list of liberal guidelines, the efforts are found to have been dissipated down stream. It is observed that the Chinese lower-level courts are not sufficiently equipped, both infrastructurally and professionally, to keep up with the pro-arbitration reforms initiated by SPC. Thus, lack of cooperation by the local judiciary has been shown to be a frequent occurrence in the enforcement of arbitration agreements and awards, thereby possibly negating advantages promoted by SPC's pro-validity and pro-enforcement initiatives. As previously mentioned, arbitration has been one of the areas reflecting the general enforcement problems encountered in the Chinese judiciary; in particular, the uncertain scope of enforcement by the Chinese local courts. In view of such uncertainty, foreign investors, suspicious about the biased local judges and to avoid the unpredictable and sometimes corrupt Chinese court system, often add an arbitration clause for pursuing a more impartial outcome of commercial disputes. However, given that both arbitration agreements and arbitral awards must undergo the review by local Chinese courts for enforcement, foreign parties may yet find themselves falling again into the trap that they initially sought to avoid. It is advocated that the sooner local people's courts can realize their institutional independence and improve their quality, the better China's enforcement records, including enforcement records in the area of arbitration, can develop.

It is important to note that, in order to redress the enforcement difficulties pervasive among the lower-level judiciary (especially in the less developed vast hinterland), SPC has introduced directives towards the independence and integrity of the judiciary, including three rounds of Five-Year reform outlines,[48] and has attempted to provide education opportunities for lower-level judges.[49] The improved independence and education is expected to bring along, generally, the increased judicial respect to the parties' autonomy in arbitration. Although an optimistic view has been taken towards the implementation of the ambitious Second Five-Year Outline, thus far, except for Shanghai, neither the practice of 'guaranteed financing' nor 'uniform recruitment of lower-level judges' has been reported in other places of China.[50] As such, the real extent to which these reforms are actually implemented are yet to be seen. Based on the analysis of Professor Jerome Cohen, the political status quo in China does not allow the rapid expansion of its judicial power as the Party government may not wish to make quick changes, especially those that might threaten the primacy of administrative power.[51] This, from another perspective, explains the chequered development of the Chinese judiciary and the associated development of arbitration enforcement, which is largely subject to state control such as political and administrative powers. Therefore, more breakthrough changes need to take place to *empower* the courts and individual judges in decision-making process, which will be proposed in the next section.

12.4. The way forward

This section examines the practical constraints of the Chinese arbitration system and its development. Following this discussion will be some proposals for prospective arbitration reforms in China. Specific reforms for tackling the practical constraints will be featured in this section, particularly with respect to the restructuring of large numbers of LACs and empowering people's courts for effective judicial review over arbitration.

12.4.1. Practical constraints

As the major argument of this article, the fundamental problem of the Chinese arbitration system is that state control over arbitration is still very pervasive. Formally, AL is overly rigid. Empirically, state control has been expressed in the way of controlling the *outcome* of arbitration, by way of political and administrative powers intervening with respect to the formation of the arbitral tribunal, and infrastructure of both arbitration commissions and people's courts. Hence, the state continues to affect significantly decision-making processes of arbitral tribunals, arbitration commissions and people's courts.

'State control' has constituted a hidden but serious obstacle to the *functioning* of the entire Chinese arbitration system. If we put the Chinese arbitration system into a triangular relationship with three legs, and each leg represents one of its key role-players, it is observed that, in China, however, the leg of 'arbitration commission' has been too long. The arbitration commission has controlled almost all the arbitral matters covering jurisdiction, arbitrator qualification, tribunal formation, procedural details and, probably, final outcome of arbitration. As has been explained, doing so is consistent with the interest of Chinese administrative governance whereby most arbitration commissions in China are indeed administrative institutions under the shadow of local people's governments. It therefore curbs the functioning and development of the second leg, the 'arbitral tribunal', which should be the core leg in the modern arbitration system ensuring party autonomy and exercising arbitral power. The third leg, the 'people's court', although claimed to be very powerful for deciding upon arbitration enforcement, is practically very weak in decision-making of individual cases under the current Chinese political and administrative framework. This triangular relationship thus shows an unstable and even 'dangerous' chair of Chinese arbitration system which is subject to the threat of political and administrative interventions.

Likewise, the argument can be made that 'state control' has handicapped the *development* of Chinese arbitration generally. Support for this argument can be derived from the finding of insufficient protection of party and tribunal autonomy despite the vigorous progress of arbitral regulations issued by CIETAC and SPC over the past couple of years. First, the new rules introduced by CIETAC in 2005 have not been followed by corresponding changes in most LACs. As has been demonstrated, the reluctance of the reform of LACs is because many of them suffer distorting reliance on the local people's governments for survival and development which have left the institutional endeavours many political challenges. Second, while there is validity in the argument that SPC has been working hard to pay more judicial respect to parties' autonomy and interest in arbitration, one can see people's courts at the lower level may not be. Due to uncertainty at the local level (local protectionism, lack of competence in handling arbitration cases, etc.), the level of cooperation by the local judiciary has not been encouraging. Their institutional incapacity (including incapacity of judicial personnel) has thus subjected the enforcement, i.e. outcome of arbitration, to political and administrative interference. The Chinese *guanxi* culture influence only aggravates political and administrative interventions from a 'software' perspective, because the Party, government, judiciary and finally arbitration commissions, all belong to the same family under the top-down administrative governance, exerting cross-impacts with intertwining relationships.

The Chinese system of 'state control', however, contrasts drastically with that of the modern Western arbitration model. The Western model first recognizes the effective and efficient arbitral tribunal as the core of modern arbitration. The Western government supports the authority of arbitral tribunal by providing a liberal modern arbitration law. Then, the Western government maintains its influence over arbitration through effective judicial review as exercised by the powerful judiciary if the arbitral process fails to follow the law.[52] As such, the Western style of 'state control' on arbitration works in a legal system whereby the court takes final checks and balances.

It might thus be arguable that the Chinese system, although attempts to walk a legal path, has been restricted with administrative minds and eyes. The study on the practical constraints of Chinese arbitration hence reflects systematic problems in China. However, the problem seriously affects the quality of Chinese arbitration as a whole and has negatively impacted on China's business reputation. Moreover, China will very much lose the competition in the international arbitration market to its regional competitors such as Hong Kong and Singapore which have been aligned with international arbitration standards. It is thus significantly argued that the unstable and dangerous 'chair' of Chinese arbitration system should be mended right away. The power of an arbitral tribunal should be essentially *increased* while that of the arbitration commission be significantly *decreased*. Meanwhile, the power of the people's court should be *maintained*, but its quality needs to be *improved* to exercise real checks and balances over arbitration. It is further argued that the Chinese state control should be *decoupled* from the arbitration system for any future reform. Detailed proposals are to be introduced as follows.

12.4.2. AL revision

As an apparent obstacle to the Chinese arbitration system and its development, the current AL (1994 AL) has been proved unable to cope with the practical needs. Revisions are therefore required to remedy the regulatory defects.[53] It is notable that although the appeal to reform has been strong, no definite timetable has been set in the national legislative agenda thus far for revision.[54] It seems that now the conditions are ready for the AL revision to take place in the near future. First, after more than a decade of practice, both positive and negative lessons have been drawn from the accumulation of experience of CIETAC and other experienced local arbitration commissions such as BAC. Second, the SPC interpretations on arbitration and its reforms of the judiciary over the past decade have prepared the courts to embrace a more pro-arbitration approach. Last but not least, academic studies and research provide the legislative reform with a solid theoretical ground.

The Chinese legislature should take advantage of the best experience of international arbitration norms, including *UNCITRAL Model Law on International Commercial Arbitration*, *English Arbitration Act* and *ICC Arbitration Rules*, in its legislative reform. Indeed, replacing the out-dated and rigid 1994 AL with an up-to-date and liberal *Arbitration Law* reflecting international standards will benefit the Chinese market economy and be conducive to its integration with the global economy as well. Reasons are straightforward. The adoption of international arbitration norms and practices would significantly increase party and tribunal autonomy, thus making arbitration in China more commercially oriented and user-friendly. Evidently, this serves the interests of the entire commercial sector, especially the commercial interests of foreign-related parties who prefer using arbitration in resolving their trade and investment disputes. It thus serves China's trade and investment interests and hence, will be beneficial to China's integration into the global economy.

At the same time, in conducting the legislative revision, the Chinese legislature also need to pay attention to its consistency with other types of arbitral regulations, whose uncertain and even conflicting interactions with the 1994 AL have been at least partly blamed for distorting Chinese arbitral practices. In this regard, the revised *Arbitration Law* should confirm the initiatives of the most recent SPC interpretations on arbitration in 2006 so as to prevent any future inconsistencies. Another point worth noting is that, the concept of 'foreign-related arbitration commission' should be discarded, which has caused practical confusion concerning arbitral jurisdiction. Indeed, all arbitration commissions in China are now able to receive both domestic and foreign-related disputes as a result of the State Council Notice in 1996 and subsequent revisions to the CIETAC Rules in 1998. There are no longer any jurisdictional divisions predicated on the characterization of arbitration commissions. As such, only the concept of 'foreign-related dispute' may be retained (as in accordance with the judicial interpretations of both *General Principles of Civil Law* and *Civil Procedure Law*). Bifurcations should only be maintained to the extent of different treatment of judicial review over arbitral awards resulting from the two types of disputes; and grounds for reviewing domestic awards should be narrowed only to procedural aspects.

12.4.3. Restructuring arbitration commissions and emphasis on CAA

This section argues for independent and professional arbitration commissions to be developed in China drawing institutional experience from advanced arbitral institutions such as the International Chamber of Commerce (ICC) Court of Arbitration and Hong Kong International Arbitration Center (HKIAC). Two aspects should be achieved in reforming arbitration commissions.

One is that, structurally, arbitration commissions must be *decoupled* from the local governments and thus achieve independence and self-sufficiency. This purports to eliminate the external intervention by political and administrative powers into arbitration commissions. For this purpose, arbitration commissions should be independent in both aspects of personnel and finance. The personnel composition within a commission, particularly that of its leadership, should be selected from the legal professionals rather than from representatives of administrative departments. On financial matters, arbitration commissions should rely on its arbitration fees for operation and development instead of being under the 'shelter' of local governments.

This will push arbitration commissions in China to strive for quality development under market competition, because whether or not an arbitration commission can attract caseload ultimately depends on its quality and market competitiveness; and the local government should be prohibited from forcing local enterprises to use local arbitration commissions playing upon local sentiment. In this regard, it is good to see that BAC has successfully restructured itself in terms of both integrity and quality; and BAC has further won itself rising fame in resolving commercial and technology disputes in the arbitration field.[55] The success of BAC tests the feasibility of structural reform of large numbers of locally based arbitration commissions in China. In the meantime, one has to realize that the restructuring might lead to survival problems for many local arbitration commissions. It is the current arbitration system that fails to rationally allocate the resources to some qualified arbitration commissions whereby the qualified commissions have been outnumbered throughout the country by other commissions catering to local administrative needs rather than real market demands. This section of the chapter thus advocates that those less developed commissions which have no or very little caseload to support its operation should be eliminated from the market.

The other aspect is to reform the power division within the arbitration commission and hence their *functions*, which aims at reducing any possible influences from practical constraints within the commission. Indeed, arbitral powers should be transferred from the commission back to the arbitration tribunal. Fundamentally, commissions should be denied powers in both merit adjudication and jurisdictional determination so that tribunals could play the key role in arbitration and the arbitral tribunal's autonomy and power should be strengthened. Drawing experience from the ICC Court of Arbitration, a Chinese arbitration commission should mainly be responsible for managing daily institutional operations. The commission should also provide liberal arbitration rules for facilitating dispute resolution and helping to ensure compliance with the rules. In addition, the commissions may exercise power to administer either arbitral procedures or make appointment of arbitrators when parties default in their choices. However, the purpose of their administrative power is to secure the procedural efficiency of the arbitration rather than to interfere or control the decision-making of arbitral tribunals. Moreover, the role of the staff of Chinese arbitration commissions should change. Commission staff should refrain from acting as arbitrators in the cases submitted to their commissions; in addition, the commission secretariat should not play any role in deciding procedural or substantive issues in individual cases. Finally, the remuneration of arbitrators should be duly raised, although it may take time to align the amount to international levels.

The closed-panel system in tribunal formation should be abolished as it is very likely that party autonomy and interest would be endangered. This is partly explained by the closing of the panels; and partly by the defective commission-controlled arbitrator qualifying scheme by each individual commission under the political, administrative and institutional influence. This leads to the conclusion that if the open-panel has been adopted, but the power of accrediting outside arbitrators remains with the government, it would remain difficult to eliminate political and administrative influence. A change in the accreditation scheme of arbitrators will therefore be necessary.

It is advocated that accreditation should be managed by a self-regulatory body rather than controlled by arbitration commissions. The self-regulation of arbitrators would be a major improvement, because it can eliminate the institutional as well as political and administrative impacts on the screening process and thus help *delink* state involvement in arbitration. Previous studies have illustrated that the institutional panel system has been used in the days when Chinese arbitration was immature and there were only a few experts to handle commercial and trade disputes. However, over the past fourteen years, arbitration intellectuals have developed dramatically. There is no shortage of experts today and conditions are now ripe for *self-regulation*. In this respect, the China Arbitration Association (CAA) should be the most appropriate authority for qualifying and overseeing arbitrators given its legal status to coordinate and supervise all Chinese arbitration commissions.[56] Indeed, the establishment of CAA should be settled as soon as possible, which has been a lingering issue[57] for more than a decade since the promulgation of AL.[58]

It is further advocated that the power of CAA should develop to cover all areas of regulations of arbitrators, from qualifying/training to disciplining, so that powers can be transferred from the government to the self-regulatory body. One point which is worth noting, however, is who should establish CAA? An ideal solution would be that CAA would be set up by all the non-governmental Chinese arbitration commissions, which is conditional upon these commissions first fulfilling their restructuring. CAA should be independent from any Party and governmental bodies to prevent any potential danger of administrative influence and it must be self-financing by collecting fees from its members as practiced by, e.g. the Chartered Institute of Arbitrators (CIArb) in London.[59] Since China has not had a tradition of arbitrator professionalism, further experience can be drawn from CIArb with respect to organizing standardized exams and training for Chinese and foreign citizens to become accredited and remain competent.[60] Moreover, preparing ethical and disciplinary codes for the conduct of arbitrators should also be within the ambit of CAA. By doing so, CAA would provide its users, i.e. arbitral parties, with the confidence that its members have an assured level of training and experience in arbitration in China. The *detachment* of arbitrator accreditation from the commission will help implement the open-panel proposal whereby parties can enjoy the freedom of appointing competent arbitrators both inside and outside the panels. Further, it will facilitate the introduction of *ad hoc* arbitration practice in China.

12.4.4. Empowering people's courts

As argued previously, Chinese government influence should pursue itself in a way of 'legal control' as modern arbitration systems do – with ante-control by a modern *Arbitration Law*; and if the arbitral process fails to abide by the Law, then the people's court will step in providing effective judicial review as post-control.

This will first rely on the clear power division between arbitration commissions and people's courts to live up to the international standard that 'courts cannot intervene into arbitral proceedings unless otherwise clearly provided'.[61] More importantly, significant improvement of judicial *integrity* as well as *quality* of people's courts should be achieved in order to provide checks and balances to arbitration under a 'legal system'. It is encouragingly noted that the retarded Chinese court system has been seriously addressed in the past decade, especially the two rounds of SPC reforms of the people's courts in response to rising international pressures to establish an independent judiciary in China.

Local protectionism and corruption may be mitigated by the SPC directives. The second SPC Five-Year Reform Outline (2004–2008) appears particularly bold in exploring a number of goals for upgrading the Chinese judicial system. It is fair to say that China is still struggling for its optimal judicial framework where the Party leadership is in a dilemma with respect to the role of the judiciary in Chinese society and governance. Although it has been strenuously argued that people's courts should be empowered to play a more active role from which enforcement of arbitration could benefit, fundamentally reforming Chinese courts will be a very difficult and complex task which needs an entire rule-of-law system to be established. The rule-of-law is increasingly pushed by the more civilized Chinese society for achieving effective prohibition of all kinds of external interferences in the adjudication and enforcement processes from the Party, government or other sources.

Laws and policies from the Central Government are needed to officially support SPC reforms with the expanding progress of the nation's rule-of-law, under which the court should develop into an independent organ or branch of the state. This would suggest the judiciary gradually manage its own *financial* and *personnel* affairs. For example, the budget of each people's court would be determined and administered by SPC to prevent local governments from using budgetary powers to influence adjudication and enforcement. This would further suggest that, the appointment and removal of judges would be centralized in SPC, whereby impacts of Party committee or local government on personnel affairs could be minimized. Specifically, to improve the quality of enforcement over arbitration (both arbitration agreements and arbitral awards), the overall quality of Chinese judges in terms of knowledge of and practical experience in arbitration should be enhanced. Judges at lower levels should understand properly SPC's liberal interpretations on arbitration, as well as international arbitration norms and the worldwide pro-arbitration judicial trend. The education arrangement organized by SPC should persist, and more international legal education programs should be promoted to the lower-level people's courts.

12.5. Concluding remarks

While this chapter has argued that there are practical constraints to the Chinese arbitration system and its development, and as such, the most recent reforms led by CIETAC and SPC have been restricted in effect, one has to admit that these practical constraints are rooted in Chinese systematic problems. To thoroughly wipe out the practical fungus will be dependent on reforming the entire Chinese governance system or rule of law in general, but this would go beyond the scope of this chapter. This chapter is therefore not suggesting revolution to the Chinese arbitration regime. However, it suggests *evolution* from an academic point of view, by providing a package of proposals on both legislative and practical aspects that can be adopted step by step by the Chinese government.

On the one hand, the *legislative revisions* have been paying attention to the experience of most advanced international arbitration norms. The very reason for taking advantage of these best practices is that the author firmly believes that Chinese arbitration legislation will finally develop to the international level as has already taken place in the regime of intellectual property laws.[62] This is because arbitration is important to the commercial sector. Arbitration serves the nation's trade and investment interests. Indeed, this article has explained that it is very likely legislative changes will take place in the not too distant future.

On the other hand, the *specific proposals* suggested, such as restructuring of arbitration commissions, emphasis on CAA in arbitrator regulation and empowering people's courts in providing effective judicial review over arbitration, are not only urgent for redressing the practical constraints but also plausible for implementation in the near future. This is because a very positive scene has been observed in the development of modern Chinese local arbitration commissions such as BAC; moreover, there has been vigorous growth in arbitral talents and increasing recognition of the importance of judicial power in China over the past decade.

In conclusion, this is an academic piece which provides academic insights into the reform of the arbitration system in China. It identifies the major problems of the Chinese arbitration system. For tackling them, legislative and specific proposals are raised. The proposals are indeed forward-looking, as the author is confident and optimistic about the future of Chinese arbitration, that China will finally be aligned with international norms and standards.

Notes

1 Articles 16 and 18, AL.
2 Articles 19 and 20, AL.
3 Chapter VII, AL.
4 Articles 66–70, AL.
5 CIETAC and CMAC were established as to cater for resolving foreign-related business and trade disputes under AL. The jurisdiction is blurred by both the State Council Notice in 1996 and subsequent CIETAC and CMAC Rules revision in 1998.
6 Articles 63 and 71, AL.
7 Articles 11 and 13, AL.
8 Figures provided by CIETAC (on file with the author).
9 Article 4, Section 2, CIETAC Rules (2005).
10 Weixia Gu and R. Morgan, 'Improving Commercial Dispute Resolution in China', *Asian Dispute Review,* 1, 2005: 6; Lianbin Song, 'From Ideology to Rules: Several Issues Worthy of Attention for the Revision of PRC Arbitration Law', *Arbitration in Beijing*, 4, 2005: 6.
11 The CIETAC rules were revised and adopted in January 2005 and became effective on 1 May 2005.
12 Article 21, Section 2, and Article 22, Section 3, CIETAC Rules (2005).

13 Weixia Gu, 'The China-Style Closed Panel System in Arbitral Tribunal Formation: Analysis of Chinese Adaptation to Globalization', *Journal of International Arbitration*, 1, 2008: 140–144.
14 Article 21, Section 2, CIETAC Rules (2005).
15 Article 6, CIETAC Rules (2005).
16 This view is expressed by the current CIETAC Secretary General, Mr Yu Jianlong, in his talk on the conference 'Managing Business Disputes in China', held at Harvard Club, New York, 26 March 2007.
17 *Interpretation on Certain Issues Relating to Application of China Arbitration Law*, issued by SPC in August 2006, and with the effect from 8 August 2006.
18 Articles 1–9, SPC Interpretation (2006).
19 Article 4, SPC Interpretation (2006).
20 *Interpretations to Several Issues on the Application of the China Arbitration Law (Draft Provisions for Opinion Solicitation)*, issued by SPC on 22 July 2004.
21 Article 27, SPC Draft Provisions (2004).
22 Figures by CIETAC (on file with the author).
23 Shengchang Wang, 'Towards a Higher Degree of Party Autonomy and Transparency: CIETAC Introduces New Rules', *International Arbitration Law Review*, 6, 2005: 118.
24 *Notice on Further the Work of Restructuring the Arbitration Institutions*, issued by the General Office of the State Council, 22 May 1995.
25 Hongsong Wang, 'Existing Problems of the Arbitration Law and Its Reform Suggestions', *Arbitration in Beijing*, 2, 2005: 21.
26 Secretary General Wang Hongsong, 'Decade Review of Beijing Arbitration Commission', available at the BAC Web site, http://www.bjac.com.cn/introduce/2007.htm (accessed 22 February 2010).
27 *Ibid.*
28 *See, generally,* Lianbin Song, 'From Ideologies to Rules – Several Issues of Attention for Amending the Arbitration Law', *Arbitration in Beijing*, 6, 2005: 1–17. Song, *supra note* 10.
29 According to the CIETAC survey, more than three-fourths of LACs are facing 'grim' difficulties in balancing their budgets. (Source: Interview with Dr Wang Wenying, Director of CIETAC Arbitration Research Institute, 22 December 2008).
30 S. Lubman, *Bird in a Cage: Legal Reform in China after Mao*, Stanford: Stanford University Press, 1999: 94.
31 According to the statistics of the CIETAC Research Institute, since the promulgation of the updated CIETAC Rules, only three cases have adopted the arbitrators chosen from beyond the panel list. (Source: E-mail interview with Dr Wang Wenying, Head of the CIETAC Research Institute, 28 February 2008).
32 *People's Insurance Company of China, Guangzhou v. Guanghope Power et al.*, [Min Si Zhong Zi] No. 29 of 2003, Civil Division, SPC.
33 Ming Kang, 'Ad Hoc Arbitration's Status Quo and Future in China', in Baoshu Wang (ed.), *Collective Essays on Commercial Law,* Beijing: China Law Press, 3, 2001: 168.
34 One of the major differences between arbitration and mediation is that the procedure of the former is independent from both parties leading to an award of final resolution as order of enforcement. However, the latter requires both parties' involvement and cooperation with the mediator assisting in reaching the final

compromise and suggestions. *See*, Shengchang Wang, 'The Relation between Arbitration and Mediation', *China Law,* 49, 2004: 28.

35 Liu Xiaohong, *Jurisprudence and Empirical Research on International Commercial Arbitration Agreement,* Beijing: Commercial Publishing House, 2005: 88.

36 Professor W. Tetley, 'Good Faith in Contract: Particularly in the Contracts of Arbitration', *Journal of Maritime Law and Commerce,* 35, 2004: 561.

37 These duties are derived from the application of good-faith principle in general contract performance where the parties should observe various ancillary duties including the duty to cooperate with and assist each other in the performance of the contract. *See*, Liming Wang and Chuanxi Xu, 'Fundamental Principles of China's Contract Law', *Columbia Journal of Asian Law*, 13, 1999: 12.

38 Maoliang Liu, Vice Chief of the Legislative Affairs Office of the State Council, 'Ad Hoc Arbitration Should Be Slow for Implementation in China', *Arbitration in Beijing*, 54, 2005: 8–12.

39 *Ibid.*

40 Chinese Premier Wen Jiabao mentioned in his 2008 New Year address that 'China will remain in a rather long period of time in the status of the initial period of socialist market economy (*Shehuizhuyi Chujijieduan*)', *Xinhua News Net*, Beijing, 26 January 2008.

41 Baotou Intermediate Court Civil Adjudication (2006) No. 024. For a full picture of the case, *see* Weixia Gu, 'Judicial Review over Arbitration in China: Assessing the Extent of Latest Pro-arbitration Move by the SPC', *Wisconsin International Law Journal*, 2, 2009: 246–248.

42 *SPC Notice on Some Issues Concerning Foreign Arbitration and Arbitration in Foreign Countries*, Fa Fa (1995) No. 18; *SPC Notice on Some Issues Concerning Setting Aside Arbitration Awards Related to Foreign Elements by the People's Court*, Fa Fa (1998) No. 40.

43 R. Peerenboom, 'Seek Truth from Facts: An Empirical Study of Enforcement of Arbitral Awards in the PRC', *American Journal of Comparative Law*, 4, 2001: 249.

44 Hu Li, 'Setting Aside an Arbitral Award in the People's Republic of China', *American Review of International Arbitration*, 12, 2001: 43.

45 Nanshen Sun, 'Jurisdictional Conflict in the Judicial Review of the Foreign-related Arbitration', in CIETAC South China Sub-commission (ed.), *Judicial Review of Foreign-Related Arbitration,* Beijing: China Law Press, 2006: 24.

46 *Ibid.*

47 Weixia Gu, 'Recourse against Arbitral Awards: How Far Can a Court Go?', *Chinese Journal of International Law*, 2, 2005: 497.

48 *Five-Year People's Courts Reform Plan* (1999–2003); *Outline of the Second Five-Year People's Court Reform Plan* (2004–2008); *Outline of the Second Five-Year People's Court Reform Plan* (2009–2013). All documents are available at SPC's homepage, http://www.court.gov.cn/ (accessed 22 February 2010).

49 Since 1999, more than 240 provincial- and intermediate-court-level judges have graduated from the Tsinghua-Temple International Business Law LLM program sponsored by SPC in which an intensive course on 'International Commercial Arbitration' is involved.

50 Mei Ying Gechlik, 'Judicial Reform in China: Lessons from Shanghai', *Columbia Journal of Asian Law*, 2, 2006: 87.

51 J. A. Cohen, 'China's Legal Reform at the Crossroads', *Far Eastern Economic Review*, 2, 2006: 26.

52 For example, the United Kingdom and Hong Kong.

53 *See*, previous discussions on the regulatory defects of AL.

54 The AL revision has not been included in the 2009 NPC legislative agenda.

55 Fuyong Chen, 'Striving for Independence, Competence, and Fairness: A Case Study of the Beijing Arbitration Commission', *American Review of International Arbitration*, 3, 2007: 313.

56 Article 15, paragraph 2 of AL.

57 There have been concerns and worries that once arbitration commissions broke off from the supervision of local administrative bodies, they would be out of control. This to some extent might help explain why the establishment of CAA has been such a lingering issue. *See* Wen Ge, 'On the Lingering Establishment of China Arbitration Association: Worries by Arbitration Academics and Practitioners', available at http://www.china-arbitration.com (accessed 22 February 2010).

58 It has been highly urged that CAA should be established before the revision to 1994 AL. *See* Lianbin Song, 'Seven Years' Critical Awaiting: Several Suggestions to the Draft Judicial Interpretations on Foreign-related Arbitration', in CIETAC South-China Sub-Commission (ed.), *Judicial Review of the Foreign-Related Arbitration*, Beijing: China Law Press, 2006: 166.

59 CIArb is a world recognized self-regulatory institutional leader in providing accreditation and training to arbitrators and mediators. The institute is accessible at http://www.arbitrators.org/ (accessed 22 February 2010).

60 For example, *see* the 'Catalogue of Courses' offered to the different categories of CIArb members (Association, Member and Fellow), accessible at http://www.arbitrators.org/Courses/QualIntro.asp?pd=1 (accessed 22 February 2010).

61 For example, Article 5 of the UNCITRAL *Model Law on International Commercial Arbitration* states that, 'In matters governed by this Law, no court shall intervene except where so provided by this Law'.

62 For example, the most recently revised *China Patent Law* (2007) has been a very advanced piece of legislation which has been aligned with various international conventions in the field.

Part VI

Law and regulation with international implications

13 Environmental law and policy in China

Responding to climate change

*Jolene Lin**

Climate change has been described as the most challenging environmental issue of our time. It is an environmental issue that cuts across almost every area of human activity, forcing social actors from governments to businesses to reconsider the way we live, work and produce goods and services. Responses to climate change include both mitigation (reducing the emission of greenhouse gases [GHG]) and adaptation to the impacts of climate change that are already underway or anticipated.[1] This chapter examines the legal and regulatory developments in China that have emerged in response to climate change. In this regard, many of these developments are on the mitigation front and driven by the central government. China's mitigation strategy is principally centred on energy policy, particularly energy efficiency and conservation, and renewable energy, and the Kyoto Protocol's Clean Development Mechanism (CDM).[2] The urgency of adaptation has been recognized, but given the highly localized nature of adaptation measures, the central government has sought to devolve responsibility to local government to develop and implement adaptation programmes.

Part 1 of this chapter provides some background to China's response to climate change on both the international and domestic levels. Part 2 examines the regulatory framework governing the CDM in China and argues that the CDM has the potential to play a more significant role in promoting sustainable development in China. The chapter then examines developments in the renewable energy area which bear implications for climate change mitigation. The case study on Shanghai's Green Electricity Scheme demonstrates effort to promote renewable energy at the local level but also highlights the need for regulatory innovation to advance demand-side energy policies in China. Part 3 considers some of the measures that have been taken to build the country's adaptive capacity to respond to the impacts of climate change. Part 4 concludes the chapter.

13.1. International and domestic influences on China's response to climate change

Both international law and domestic pressure exert influence on China's legal and policy responses to climate change. The climate change multilateral treaty framework provides an important platform for China and the international community to address climate change which has a global nature and complex interfaces with global trade, economics and development.[3] China's position on legally binding emissions reduction targets has drawn much international attention which arguably has had the effect of encouraging China to do more at home to deflect criticisms that it is not doing enough to tackle climate change. More directly, China's treaty obligations constitute a legal platform for the introduction of legal and administrative measures for climate change mitigation and adaptation. Domestic factors that press for action on climate change have more to do with the co-benefits that can be gained from tackling conventional pollution of the air, water and land and with the concern on the government's part that environmental problems pose a threat to political stability.

13.1.1. International law

The United Nations Framework Convention on Climate Change (UNFCCC) and the Kyoto Protocol constitute the main international legal framework addressing climate change. China ratified the UNFCCC on 5 January 1993.[4] The PRC approved the Kyoto Protocol in 2002 and the protocol entered into force on 16 February 2005.[5] As negotiations for the post-2012 international climate change agreement are underway, international attention has been particularly focused on the United States and China, two of the world's largest GHG emitters. In its 2007 World Energy Outlook, the International Energy Agency predicted that China was likely to have overtaken the United States to become the world's largest emitter of energy-related carbon dioxide in 2007 and, by around 2010, China would overtake the United States to become the world's largest consumer of energy.[6]

China's refusal to take on legally binding emission reduction targets under the Kyoto Protocol (and the post-2012 treaty) is based on the country's adherence to the principle of common but differentiated responsibility (CDR principle) which is enshrined in the UNFCCC. Article 3(1) of the UNFCCC states

> [t]he Parties should protect the climate system for the benefit of present and future generations of humankind, on the basis of equity and in accordance with their common but differentiated responsibilities and respective capabilities. Accordingly, the developed country Parties should take the lead in combating climate change and the adverse effects thereof.

Further, sub-section (2) states

> [t]he specific needs and special circumstances of developing country Parties, especially those that are particularly vulnerable to the adverse effects of climate change, and of those Parties, especially developing country Parties, that would have to bear a disproportionate or abnormal burden under the Convention, should be given full consideration.

China has argued that, according to the CDR principle, developed countries are obliged to take the lead on reducing GHG emissions and provide financial assistance and technological transfer to developing countries which will utilize these resources to take adaptation and mitigation measures to fulfil their part of the common responsibility of tackling climate change.[7] The United States had refused to ratify the Kyoto Protocol because of the lack of legally binding targets on rapidly growing developing-country economies like China and continues to hinge its ratification of any climate change multilateral agreement on whether China takes on such targets or their equivalence.[8] China's negotiating position on the climate change issue is therefore of twofold importance. First, the US position on climate change hinges upon the Chinese position. Second, it is widely recognized that the post-2012 climate change arrangements will be of limited environmental effectiveness without some form of restrictions on China's GHG emissions.

China recognizes that it can no longer say that tackling climate change is purely a developed country issue now that its total GHG emissions surpasses that of other major economies, including the United States, and the Chinese leadership is keenly aware of the country's vulnerability to the impacts of climate change.[9] At a UN climate change summit in September 2009, China announced that it was willing to take on a carbon intensity target by 2020 from 2005 levels. The PRC will also increase forest coverage by 40 million hectares by 2020 from 2005 levels out of a sense of responsibility to the international community.[10] At the UNFCCC Conference of the Parties held in Copenhagen in December 2009, China maintained its traditional position on legally binding emission reduction targets.[11] In the final hours of the conference negotiations, the Copenhagen Accord was drawn up by a number of Member States including China, and Paragraph 5 of the Accord sets out the 'bottom-up mitigation approach' that will be taken by non-Annex I countries such as China.[12] Summarily, Paragraph 5 proposes that non-Annex I countries will take the initiative to undertake mitigation actions that '...will be subject to their domestic measurement, reporting and verification the result of which will be reported through their national communications every two years'. There will be provisions for '...international consultations and analysis under clearly defined guidelines that will ensure that national sovereignty is respected'. In addition, those measures seeking international financial support '...will be subject to international measurement, reporting and verification in accordance with guidelines adopted by the Conference of the Parties'.

In addition to the multilateral framework, China has also established bilateral arrangements with the United States and the European Union to promote research and development in climate change technologies such as carbon capture and storage (CCS). On 28 July 2009, in Washington DC, the United States and China signed a Memorandum of Understanding to Enhance Cooperation on Climate Change, Energy and the Environment.[13] In the same month, the European Commission announced that 50 million euros of EU funds will be spent on a CCS plant in China as part of a bilateral agreement to develop CCS in China and Europe by 2020.[14] Chinese cities are also involved in global projects that promote climate action by municipalities and other sub-state actors. On 3 October 2009, at the sidelines of the Governors' Global Climate Summit in Los Angeles, Governor Arnold Schwarzenegger announced that California and Jiangsu Province will form a partnership to collaborate on addressing climate change through research and development, information sharing and personnel training programmes.[15] Collectively, these various examples of China's involvement in global climate change governance constitute the external aspect of China's response to climate change. These external obligations provide an impetus for domestic action as Chinese policy-makers will have to introduce legal and regulatory programmes to fulfil China's international commitments. The bilateral treaties also constitute an important source of financial support, technical assistance and knowledge transfer.

13.1.2. Domestic factors

The Chinese leadership now recognize that climate change will have dire impacts on the country, and it is no longer tenable to adopt a wait-and-see attitude. The National Climate Change Programme, which is the Chinese blueprint for climate change action, contains a comprehensive documentation of the various impacts of climate change on the country. They include 'increased instability in agricultural production' and decreased yields in wheat, rice and maize; a nearly 30 per cent reduction by 2050 in the size of the glaciers in Western China that are an important source of drinking water; threats to biodiversity, including a conclusion that 'the giant panda [and other native creatures] are likely to be greatly affected'; substantial droughts in the already-arid northern provinces; a sea level rise along the coast; more frequent typhoons and storm surges and more frequent and intense heat waves.[16]

Secondly, there is a link between addressing climate change and conventional pollution within China. The extremely high levels of pollution that affects China's air, water and land is well known. The high levels of conventional air pollutants such as sulphur dioxide, nitrogen oxide and particulate matter in many Chinese cities bear significant public health costs and, as Wiener has suggested, the co-benefits of tackling both climate change and local air pollution act as an incentive for domestic action.[17] The need to address local pollution is also linked with the Chinese government's desire to maintain social and political stability. Environmental disasters in recent times have led to violent protests by Chinese citizens, and Chinese policy-makers, steeped in their knowledge of Chinese history, would be keenly sensitive to the fact that such uprisings have led to the downfall of dynasties and must be addressed promptly.[18]

13.1.3. National climate change programme

The combination of external and domestic forces, as discussed in the preceding section, has resulted in the top echelon of the Chinese government prioritizing climate change on its policy agenda. Climate change policy has been placed within the jurisdiction of the National Development and Reform Commission (NDRC), one of the most powerful Chinese government agencies.[19] In June 2007, the NRDC published China's official climate change strategy. The National Climate Change Programme (NCCP) is a comprehensive document that sets out China's position on the UNFCCC regime (specifically, its adherence to the CDR principle), the impacts of climate change on China, mitigation and adaptation measures and an institutional framework to implement the policies outlined in the Programme.[20]

Given the traditional emphasis on mitigation over adaptation, it is noteworthy that the NCCP places equal emphasis on both mitigation and adaptation as one of the guiding principles of China's climate change strategy.[21] In this regard, mitigation measures will focus on energy conservation and 'energy structure optimization' while adaptation will focus on projects aimed at ecosystem protection, disaster prevention and reduction and infrastructure development.[22] Given the significant opportunities for energy efficiency gains in Chinese industries, particularly those using obsolete technology, it is not surprising that the low-hanging fruit represented by energy saving and efficiency is targeted for GHG mitigation.[23] However, mitigation measures are driven primarily by economic instead of environmental considerations. For example, the NCCP elaborates that 'optimizing the energy consumption structure' will include measures such as rapid development of renewable energy (the target is to raise the proportion of renewable energy (including large-scale hydropower) in China's primary energy supply to 10 per cent by 2010), nuclear power and increasing extraction of coal bed methane (up to 10 billion cubic meters).[24] These measures are not entirely compatible with mitigation goals, and the concept of 'optimizing the energy consumption structure' is arguably more about energy security, costs, and diversification of the country's energy sources than concerns about climate change.

With regard to adaptation, the NCCP sets out four main issue areas.[25] First, efforts will be put into 'adaptation-proofing' agricultural infrastructure and practices such as selecting and breeding stress-resistant crop varieties, adjusting cropping systems and improving the efficiency of irrigation practices. Secondly, nature conservation and protecting key ecological systems and areas will be part of the adaptation strategy. The third aspect of the adaptation programme is concerned with water resources as many areas are expected to face greater water scarcity and drought conditions. The proposed measures include the use of market-based mechanisms to rationalize the allocation of water resources, public education to reduce water wastage and developing anti-flood and drought-relief systems. The fourth aspect is concerned with coastal adaptation and measures include increasing mangrove coverage, better protection of marine areas and constructing shelter belts along coastlines. Yang has pointed out that these adaptation policies, not unlike the mitigation ones, are designed to coincide with existing agricultural policies and resource management programs.[26] He further argues that this menu of policy options merely contain 'no regrets' responses to climate change. It does not address salient issues such as integrating adaptation requirements into existing planning and environmental laws. The issue of resource allocation for adaptation initiatives at the local level is also not addressed.

Finally, the promulgation of the *Energy Law* (still not in force) and the implementation of existing laws such as the *Renewable Energy Law* is viewed as being important for rationalizing energy production and consumption. Such rationalization will reduce GHG emissions.[27] Part 2 below will address these issues in greater detail after analysing the implementation of the CDM in China.

13.2. Examining the CDM and developments in renewable energy

The CDM is a scheme created under the Kyoto Protocol to promote GHG-reduction projects (including renewable energy) in developing countries.[28] The allocation of competences in the overall CDM approval process between the relevant United Nations bodies and Member States gives the latter significant room to structure the regulatory field to meet domestic policy objectives such as promoting certain types of renewable energy over others. This sort of policy intervention is evident in the Chinese context. However, the absence of coordination between the CDM and the *Renewable Energy Law* is notable and the CDM could be optimized to drive the development of renewable energy. The discussion below of the controversy over Chinese wind farms demonstrates the close links between the CDM and renewable energy policy and the appropriateness of more policy coordination between the two concerns.

The discussion in this section begins with a brief overview of the CDM and the performance of the CDM in China so far. The discussion then turns to an examination of the development of renewable energy and uses a case study on Shanghai's Green Electricity Scheme to illustrate the difficulties of deploying demand-side measures in China.

13.2.1. Brief introduction of the CDM

The Kyoto Protocol establishes three market mechanisms (also known as the Flexible Mechanisms) to help industrialized countries (Annex I countries)[29] meet their emission reduction commitments in a cost-effective manner. Joint Implementation, the Clean Development Mechanism and Emissions Trading are established under Articles 6, 12 and 17 of the Kyoto Protocol, respectively. Article 12 states '[t]he purpose of the clean development mechanism shall be to assist Parties not included in Annex I in achieving sustainable development... and to assist Parties included in Annex I in achieving compliance with their quantified emission limitation and reduction commitments...' The CDM allows an Annex I country to carry out a GHG-reduction project in a non-Annex I country (i.e. a developing country that does not have any legally binding emission reduction targets under the Kyoto Protocol) and use the resulting Certified Emission Reductions (CERs) to meet its own commitment under the Kyoto Protocol. One of the most innovative features of the CDM is the direct involvement of private entities in the compliance framework of the Kyoto Protocol. The CDM allows countries to authorize private-sector entities to sell and acquire CERs from projects in developing countries.[30] These CERs can be transacted on international carbon markets.

13.2.2. The CDM regulatory framework in China

The Interim Measures for the Administration of Operation of Clean Development Mechanism Projects (Interim Measures), which came into force on 30 June 2004, was the first step towards creating a regulatory framework governing the CDM in China. The Interim Measures were replaced by the current Measures for Operation and Management of Clean Development Mechanism Projects in China (CDM Measures) on 12 October 2005.

As reflected in Article 1 of the CDM Measures, these Measures aim to facilitate the implementation of CDM projects in China in accordance with the UNFCCC and the Kyoto Protocol. They also provide a specific legal basis for such projects in China. Article 4 sets out the priority areas for CDM projects in China, which are energy efficiency improvement, development and utilization of renewable energy, and, methane recovery and utilization. Articles 6–12 contain the conditions for the approval of a CDM project. Articles 13–17 establish the organizational structure responsible for regulating and approving CDM projects in China. The National CDM Board, which is responsible for keeping the CDM under review and making necessary recommendations, consists of the NDRC and Ministry of Science and Technology (MOST) as co-chairs and the Ministry of Foreign Affairs (MFA) as the vice chair. The other board members are the Ministry of Environmental Protection, China Meteorological Administration, Ministry of Finance and Ministry of Agriculture.[31] The final authority for accepting applications and giving the requisite approvals before a CDM project can be carried out lies with the NRDC.[32]

While the regulatory framework provides certainty and creates a relatively favourable investment climate, China is unique amongst non-Annex I countries in imposing a number of conditions and restrictions on CDM projects.[33] They include a minimum price for CERs, restrictions on the sale of CERs that will accrue after 2012, a levy of 2–65 per cent on the revenue from the sale of CERs, a cap on the number of CERs that may be transferred to the purchaser in a transaction, and a requirement that the CDM project entity be under Chinese control.[34] From the perspective of promoting environmental activities and projects in China, the levy imposed on CDM projects is noteworthy. The levies collected are earmarked for environmental projects (transferred to a dedicated CDM Fund which is intended to provide loans and other forms of financial aid for climate change projects) and therefore provide a significant revenue stream for sustainable development initiatives. The highest levy of 65 per cent is imposed on projects that are regarded as contributing least to sustainable development, and therefore acts as a disincentive. At present, the

CDM Fund has seen limited activity, as detailed rules on the collection of the levy and the use of the funds have not been finalized.[35]

13.2.3. *Optimizing the CDM as a vehicle for sustainable development*

China has emerged as the world's largest producer of CERs. As of 1 December 2009, its average annual reductions amount to 192,857,865 units which is 59 per cent of the global aggregate amount of CERS produced and the country is host to 675 registered CDM projects which is about 35 per cent of the number of registered projects worldwide. However, while these figures are indicative of the phenomenal success of the CDM in China, there is greater scope for the CDM to promote environmentally progressive sustainable development. In the early stages of the implementation of the CDM in China, the type of projects that was enjoying CDM accreditation was controversial because of their questionable environmental merit.[36] Presently, the United Nations body responsible for approving and registering CDM projects at the international level, the CDM Executive Board, has halted approval for a number of Chinese projects because of the additionality requirement. These issues are discussed in turn in the following section.

13.2.3.1. HFC-23 projects

China's lead position in the CDM market was established by HFC-23 destruction projects. HFC-23 is generated as a by-product of HCFC-22 manufacture, which is used as a refrigerant or as a feedstock, for example, in Teflon manufacture.[37] The 100-year Global Warming Potential (GWP) of HFC-23 is 11,700. This means that, under the rules of the CDM which converts the other six Kyoto Protocol regulated gases to carbon dioxide and hence CERs based on their GWPs, a ton of HFC-23 abated is considered equivalent to 11,700 tons of carbon dioxide.[38] This was a controversial issue, because these projects can hardly be described as contributing to sustainable development, which is one of the two goals of the CDM, and the CDM was, in effect, turned into a mechanism providing costly subsidies for the destruction of high-GWP gases. Wara has argued that this is a poor use of Annex I party resources because to abate all developing world HFC-23 emissions would cost approximately US$31 million per year. Instead, through participation in the CDM, the Annex I nations have paid between US$250 and US$750 million to abate 67 per cent of Non-Annex I HFC-23 emissions.[39]

HFC-23 opportunities are numbered, and we have seen a much wider variety of Chinese projects registered under the CDM. However, the restriction on the sale of post-2012 CERs has had the effect of encouraging investment in projects that produce CERs quickly (at least before 2012) and such projects tend to be in the industrial sector rather than rural renewable energy initiatives. Strengthening the sustainable development criteria that the NRDC applies in the CDM project approval process is essential if the CDM is to fulfil its potential of achieving sustainable development and climate change mitigation in China.

13.2.3.2. State aid and additionality

One of the requirements for qualifying under the CDM is that a project must demonstrate additionality. Therefore, under the CDM Rules, a project proponent is required to undertake an investment analysis to demonstrate that the project 'is unlikely to be the most financially attractive or is unlikely to be financially attractive'.[40] The idea is that the project should receive CDM financing only if it is economically unviable but is environmentally beneficial. The aim of the CDM is to promote new projects that face insurmountable barriers of some sort (for example, that the particular type of technology is not available in the region, or capital from international and domestic markets is difficult to raise because of the perceived risks of investing in the proposed CDM destination), not on projects that would have been built anyway.[41]

On 1 December 2009, the international media reported that the CDM Executive Board halted approval of a number of Chinese wind farms as the Board was not convinced that these projects met the 'additionality' criterion.[42] The CDM Executive Board expressed concerns that Beijing's new wind-power rates and subsidies were set low precisely to enable wind-farm projects to demonstrate lack of financial viability and therefore be eligible for CDM funding. Some Chinese CDM consultants disagree, arguing that subsidies have been reduced to meet other objectives such as preventing over-capacity in the wind turbine industry.

If this is the case, this controversy presents an example of China's industrial policy having significant impact on its climate change agenda. It is unusual for a government to be criticized for reducing, rather than increasing, subsidies. In light of the CDM's objective to promote renewable energy projects in developing countries and preferably through private capital, it is interesting to note that the debate is cast in language about 'international aid' and whether China still needs a 'crutch' to attain its wind energy targets.[43] There are currently no rules on anti-competitive conduct in the CDM and unless substantial evidence surfaces, it is hard to prove that the Chinese government, in lowering its wind power rates and reducing subsidies to the industry, was motivated by CDM considerations.

13.2.4. ***Renewable energy***

The *Renewable Energy Law* was promulgated on 28 February 2005 and entered into force on 1 January 2006.[44] Article 1 stipulates that the objectives of this Law are '...to promote the development and utilization of renewable energy, improve the energy structure, diversify energy supplies, safeguard energy security, protect the environment, and realize the sustainable development of the economy and society...'.

The *Renewable Energy Law* was the legal basis upon which Shanghai launched its Green Electricity Scheme, the first scheme in the country to offer consumers the option to purchase electricity produced from renewable sources.[45] The focus of governmental efforts to promote renewable energy has been on the supply side. The Shanghai Green Electricity Scheme is unique because of its focus on consumer demand for renewable energy. The scheme has not been successful. The case study presented in the next section highlights the need for regulatory innovation to advance demand-side energy policies in China.

13.2.5. The Shanghai green electricity scheme

This scheme provides consumers the option to purchase electricity produced from renewable sources such as solar and wind (defined as 'green electricity' in Article 2 of the Implementation Guidelines). The target audience of the scheme is large, non-household consumers, but the scheme is available to households and commercial customers as well.[46] The municipal government guarantees that the additional payment that consumers make when purchasing green electricity will be directed towards development of renewable energy projects in the Shanghai Municipality, and an independent supervisory body ensures the integrity of the scheme.[47] While most policy efforts to promote renewable energy in China are focused on providing incentives for production such as feed-in tariffs and preferential low-interest loans, the Shanghai Green Electricity Scheme is unique because of its focus on creating and promoting consumer demand for renewable energy.

The Implementation Guidelines stipulate incentives that have been created to encourage take-up. First, a list of green electricity purchasers will be publicized and these purchasers will receive 'honorary certificates'.[48] Second, those users who have signed up for a contract of two-year duration or longer and subscribe for a certain quantity (the quantity is significant, which means that the measure is directed at large industrial users) and whose use of green electricity account for 10 per cent or more of the total amount of electricity used for manufacturing their products will be issued with an emblem.[49] Finally, medals will be awarded to major purchasers.[50] Unsurprisingly, these measures have not had notable effect in encouraging businesses to turn to green electricity. From June 2005 when the scheme was launched till the end of 2006, only twenty-two industries and about seven thousand households purchased green electricity amounting to a total of 15.82 GWh (gigawatts per hour). In 2006, the total amount of green electricity purchased was about 8.5 GWh while the total amount of green electricity generated amounted to more than 20 GWh.

There are a number of reasons for the lacklustre results of the scheme. Renewable energy is decidedly more expensive than conventional energy, and consumers are reluctant to pay more. For domestic users, the reluctance to pay more for renewable energy is likely to stem from a lack of understanding about the environmental merits of renewable energy. The measures are targeted at large manufacturing industries which may not be sensitive to consumer preferences. Yet, the idea of using labels is premised on the anticipation of using marketing and brand recognition to promote the use of renewable energy. Finally, it should be noted that the price support provided by the Guidelines can only be a temporary measure. It is anti-competitive, does not reflect the real costs of energy production and has the perverse effect of dampening consumer demand, because the price is too high. Other measures to support the development of renewable energy such as feed-in tariffs and promoting innovation to bring down the costs of domestic production of renewable energy equipment should be given more consideration. This takes the scheme away from its demand-side focus, but these suggestions highlight the importance of addressing both demand and supply factors.

13.3. Adapting to climate change

Developing and implementing successful climate change adaptive strategies requires the participation of local governments, who are likely to have the requisite information and knowledge of local conditions and needs. This approach is in line with that of environmental governance and sustainable development in general. As stated in Agenda 21:

> '[l]ocal authorities construct, operate and maintain economic, social and environmental infrastructure, oversee planning processes, establish local environmental policies and regulations, and assist in implementing national and subnational environmental policies. As the level of governance closest to the people, they play a vital role in educating, mobilizing and responding to the public to promote sustainable development'.[51]

China is one of the few developing countries which have clear arrangements for local government involvement in its climate change programmes. Local governments have been tasked with enhancing the organization and leadership on local responses to climate change, and to formulate and implement local climate change programmes as a matter of priority.[52] There have been proposals to set up a regional administration system to coordinate climate-related work, build up local expertise, initiate proper climate change policy and measures according to local conditions such as geographical environment, climatic conditions and levels of economic development, and strengthen coordination between national and local governments to ensure the smooth implementation of policies and measures.[53] Nonetheless, challenges remain as to how such a regional system will work in tandem with the existing environmental protection bureaucracy which itself has difficulties achieving policy coordination between bureaux at different levels of government.[54]

There is less scope in China for citizens and civil society actors to use the courts and legal processes to assert pressure on the local government to take adequate measures to prepare communities for the impacts of climate change such as increased flood risks in coastal areas. An emerging trend in jurisdictions such as Australia and the United Kingdom is the mainstreaming of climate change adaptation measures in environmental and planning law. In these jurisdictions, the plaintiffs resort to the courts to press for responses to climate change concerns by utilizing general principles of judicial review or broad-standing provisions within specific environmental legislation that give interested parties the ability to seek judicial review of administrative decisions. The role of Environmental Impact Assessment (EIA) is quite significant in this trend. The Australian cases, for example, generally involve judicial or merits review, usually challenging governmental decision-making on the basis that the EIA has not adequately considered climate change impacts and is therefore invalid.[55] China has an EIA law, and while the resort to litigation is an unlikely prospect, the process of conducting the mandatory EIA for most development projects can be one pathway for introducing adaptation policies and measures into the overall planning framework.[56]

13.4. Conclusion

This chapter has sought to give an overview of the contemporaneous developments in China as the country responds to international and domestic pressures to address climate change. The discussion has focused on regulatory and legal measures that have been introduced to facilitate climate change mitigation and adaptation. It is impossible to canvass all the relevant issues, but this chapter has sought to provide discussion of what, in the author's view, are interesting and topical aspects. As China and the rest of the international community continue on the quest to meet the challenges posed by climate change, law and regulation in this field will witness the unfolding of interesting developments.

Notes

* I would like to thank Ms Gao Li for superb and dedicated research assistance. The usual disclaimers apply.

1 In general, the term 'adaptation' is applied in the climate change literature to describe any action taken to adjust to changing climatic conditions, whether in natural or socio-economic systems; R. J. T. Klein and R. S. J. Tol, 'Adaptation to Climate Change: Options and Technologies', (Document Number: FCCC/TP/1997/3), UNFCCC, 1997. The Intergovernmental Panel on Climate Change (IPCC) defines adaptation as '...the adjustment in natural or human systems in response to actual or expected climatic stimuli or their effects, which moderates harm or exploits beneficial opportunities'; M. L. Parry, *et al.* (eds), *Climate Change 2007: Impacts, Adaptation and Vulnerability. Contribution of Working Group II to the Fourth Assessment Report of the Intergovernmental Panel on Climate Change*, Cambridge, United Kingdom, Cambridge University Press, 2007.

2 Tseming Yang, 'The Implementation Challenge of Mitigating China's Greenhouse Gas Emissions', *Georgetown International Environmental Law Review*, 20, 2008: 681, 684.

3 For discussion on the trade-climate change interface, *see*, *Trade and Climate Change: A Report by the United Nations Environment Programme and the World Trade Organization* (United Nations, 2009), online: www.unep.org/Documents.Multilingual/Default.asp?DocumentID=589&ArticleID=6235&l=en (accessed 1 March 2010).

4 UNFCCC, Status of Ratification, online: unfccc.int/essential_background/convention/status_of_ratification/items/2631.php (accessed 1 March 2010).

5 Kyoto Protocol, Status of Ratification, online: unfccc.int/files/kyoto_protocol/status_of_ratification/application/pdf/kp_ratification_20091203.pdf (accessed 1 March 2010).

6 *World Energy Outlook 2007: India and China Insights* (Organisation for Economic Cooperation and Development (OECD)/International Energy Agency, 2007).

7 This is frequently articulated. *See*, e.g. Section 3.2 of China's National Climate Change Programme, prepared under the auspices of the National Development and Reform Commission, June 2007, available online at: www.ccchina.gov.cn/WebSite/CCChina/UpFile/File188.pdf (accessed 1 March 2010) (hereinafter, NCCP).

8 As a result of the Byrd-Hagle Resolution (105th Congress, S. Res. 98), the US Congress has tied the country's acceptance of binding emission reduction targets, *inter alia*, to developing countries like China accepting such targets too.

9 'China Overtakes U.S. in Greenhouse Gas Emissions', *New York Times*, 20 June 2007, online: www.nytimes.com/2007/06/20/business/worldbusiness/20iht-emit.1. 6227564.html (accessed 1 March 2010). *See also*, Tao Wang and Jim Watson 'China's Energy Transition: Pathways for Low Carbon Development', Sussex Energy Group (University of Sussex, United Kingdom) and Tyndall Centre for Climate Change Research, 2009: 14–15.

10 Text of Hu Jintao's speech at UN climate summit, 23 September 2009. Such language about being a responsible state indicates China's self-perception as an emerging great power, but more to the point, also harks back to its adherence to the CDR principle in international environmental law.

11 For China's negotiating position at the Copenhagen conference, *see*, 'Implementation of the Bali Roadmap – China's Position on the Copenhagen Climate Change Conference', 20 May 2009, online: Permanent Mission of the People's Republic of China to the United Nations Office at Geneva and other International Organizations in Switzerland, www.china-un.ch/eng/bjzl/t564324.htm (accessed 2 March 2010).

12 Copenhagen Accord, Draft decision -/CP.15, Conference of the Parties, Fifteenth Session, Copenhagen, 7–18 December 2009.

13 More information available on the EPA China Environmental Law Initiative Web site: www.epa.gov/ogc/china/initiative_home.htm.

14 'Carbon Capture and Geological Storage (CCS) in emerging developing countries: financing the EU–China Near Zero Emissions Coal Plant project', EUROPA press release, Brussels, 25 June 2009.

15 'California to Partner with China's Jiangsu to Advance Climate Policies', 3 October 2009, BBC Monitoring Asia Pacific – Political.

16 NCCP, pp. 16–17.

17 J. B. Wiener, 'Climate Change Policy and Policy Change in China', *UCLA Law Review*, 55, 2008: 1805, 1817. *See also*, P. R. McCubbin, 'China and Climate Change: Domestic Environmental Needs, Differentiated International Responsibilities, and Rule of Law Weaknesses', *Environmental & Energy Law & Policy Journal*,

3, 2008: 200, 215–216: 'Thus, because the Chinese leadership's ultimate goal is to maintain the social stability or "harmonious development" necessary to stay in power, the citizen protests are pushing environmental issues to the forefront of the leadership's agenda'.

18 E. C. Economy, 'The Great Leap Backward?', *Foreign Affairs*, September–October 2007: 38, 47, in which the author noted that in 2006, the Chinese government reported 1,000 environmental protests per week, and in May 2007 there were major protests involving 7,000–20,000 marchers against a proposed petrochemical facility in Xiamen. *See also*, M. Magnier, 'As China Spews Pollution, Villagers Rise Up', *Los Angeles Times*, 3 September 2006, online: http://articles.latimes.com/2006/sep/03/world/fg-enviro3 (accessed on 2 March 2010).

19 However, Yang has pointed out that, given the NDRC's primary focus on economic reform, the fact that climate change has been placed within its mandate suggests that 'climate change policies are first and foremost seen as economic development policies'. Yang further argues that many of the measures such as those promoting energy efficiency and conservation are taken primarily with the view towards energy security and costs, and only secondarily with a view towards reducing environmental impacts, especially climate change. Yang, *supra note* 2, p. 688.

20 *See*, NCCP, p. 29 for institutional framework.

21 NCCP, p. 24. For discussion of the historic emphasis on mitigation over adaptation in the climate change discourse, *see*, E. L. F. Schipper, 'Conceptual History of Adaptation in the UNFCCC Process', *Review of European Community and International Environmental Law*, 15, 2006: 82; M. Parry, N. Arnell, M. Hulme, R. Nicholls and M. Livermore, 'Adapting to the Inevitable', *Nature*, 395, 1998: 741–742.

22 *Ibid.*

23 *See*, page 20 of the NCCP where it is noted that one 'of the main reasons for China's low energy efficiency and high GHG-emission intensity is the backward technologies of energy production and utilization in China … [where] out-of-date processes and technologies still occupy a relatively high proportion of China's key industries'.

24 *Ibid.*, p. 26.

25 This paragraph contains information extracted from pages 27–28 of the NCCP.

26 Yang, *supra note* 2, p. 688.

27 NCCP, pp. 30–31.

28 Renewable energies such as hydropower, solar energy, wind power and geothermal energy form a significant focus of climate change mitigation strategies because they are alternatives to conventional fossil fuel options such as coal and oil which are major sources of GHGs when used to produce energy. The production of renewable energy usually does not emit GHGs directly.

29 Annex I refers to the Annex to the United Nations Framework Convention on Climate Change and the Kyoto Protocol which lists the countries which agreed to assume binding emission limitation and reduction targets. Such targets are set in Annex B of the Kyoto Protocol.

30 Articles 6(3) and 12(9) of the Kyoto Protocol provide the Parties to the Kyoto Protocol the legal basis to authorize the participation of private entities in the generation and transfer of carbon rights.

31 Article 15 of the CDM Measures.

32 Article 16 states that the NRDC is China's National Designated Authority for the CDM.

33 *See*, C. Tung, 'Carbon Law and Practice in China', in D. Freestone and C. Streck, *Legal Aspects of Carbon Trading: Kyoto, Copenhagen and Beyond*, Oxford, United Kingdom, Oxford University Press, 2009: 498–500. *See*, M. Schroeder, 'Varieties of Carbon Governance: Utilizing the Clean Development Mechanism for Chinese Priorities', *Journal of Environment and Development*, 18, 2009: 371, 377ff for discussion of the success of the Chinese government in creating a favourable investment climate through effective governance.

34 Article 24 sets out the levies imposed on various types of CDM projects. These restrictions and conditions that are unique to the Chinese CDM regulatory framework can be viewed as attempts by the Chinese government to steer CDM investments into their priority areas that are not prioritized by the international CDM rules. Schroeder, *supra note* 33, p. 379.

35 Tung, *supra note* 33, p. 500.

36 For discussion of early CDM projects in China, *see*, J. Nygard, A. Murray and C. Streck, 'Clean Development Mechanism in China: Taking a Proactive and Sustainable Approach', *Sinosphere Journal,* 8, 2005: 5.

37 J. Ellis and S. Kamel, 'Overcoming Barriers to Clean Development Mechanism Projects', Organisation for Economic Cooperation and Development (OECD)/ International Energy Agency, May 2007: 10, footnote 4.

38 M. Wara, 'Measuring the Clean Development Mechanism's Performance and Potential', Working Paper No. 56, July 2006, Program on Energy and Sustainable Development at the Centre for Environmental Science and Policy, Stanford University, p. 26.

39 *Ibid.*

40 'Methodological Tool, "Tool for the demonstration and assessment of additionality" (Version 05.2)', EB39 Report/Annex 10, online: cdm.unfccc.int/methodologies/ PAmethodologies/tools/am-tool-01-v5.2.pdf (accessed 1 March 2010), p. 1.

41 *Ibid.*, pp. 8–9.

42 'UN Halts Funds to China Wind Farms', *Financial Times*, 1 December 2009, online: www.ft.com/cms/s/0/128a52de-deaf-11de-adff-00144feab49a.html (accessed 1 March 2010).

43 K. Johnson, 'Fickle Breezes: China's Wind Power Growth Collides with the UN', Environmental Capital, *The Wall Street Journal*, 2 December 2009, online: blogs. wsj.com/environmentalcapital/2009/12/02/fickle-breezes-chinas-wind-power-growth-collides-with-the-un/ (accessed 4 December 2009).

44 For discussion on the barriers to developing renewable energy in China, *see*, J. A. Cherni and J. Kentish, 'Renewable Energy Policy and Electricity Market Reforms in China', *Energy Policy,* 35, 2007: 3616.

45 Article 1, Trial Implementation Procedures of Shanghai Municipality on the Subscription to and Marketing of Green Electricity (hereinafter 'Implementation Guidelines').

46 World Bank, Asia Sustainable and Alternative Energy Program, 'China: Jade Electricity', online: siteresources.worldbank.org/EXTEAPASTAE/Resources/ China_Green_Electricity.pdf (accessed on 1 March 2010).

47 Article 14 stipulates that the price for a unit of green electricity is determined by the difference between the annual average on-grid price of green electricity and the model on-grid price of coal-generated electricity.

48 Article 16 of the Implementation Guidelines.

49 Article 17 of the Implementation Guidelines.

50 Article 18 of the Implementation Guidelines.

51 *See*, Agenda 21, Chapter 28 'Local Authorities' Initiatives in support of Agenda 21', online: www.un.org/esa/sustdev/documents/agenda21/english/agenda21chapter28.htm (accessed 1 March 2010).

52 *See*, State Council Document (2006) No. 28, 'Decision on Strengthening Energy Conservation Work', p. 56. *See also*, M. A. Schreurs, 'From the Bottom Up: Local and Subnational Climate Change Politics', *Journal of Environment and Development*, 2008: 343, 352.

53 *Ibid.*

54 *See*, K. Lieberthal, 'China's Governing System and Its Impact on Environmental Policy', *China Environment Series*, 1, 1997, 3; J. Lin, 'Assessing the Dragon's Choice: The Use of Market-Based Instruments in Chinese Environmental Policy', *Georgetown International Environmental Law Review*, 16, 2004: 617–653, Part II for discussion of the institutional and legal framework of China's environmental management regime.

55 Some of the leading cases include *Minister for Planning v. Walker* [2008] NSWCA 224, *Gippsland Coastal Board v. South Gippsland Shire Council* [2008] VCAT 1545, *Gray v. Minister for Planning* [2006] 152 LGERA 258. For discussion, *see*, J. Peel, 'The Role of Climate Change Litigation in Australia's Response to Global Warming, Melbourne Law School, Legal Studies Research Paper No. 269.

56 For discussion about EIA in China, *see*, L. Gu and W. Sheat, 'Environmental Assessment – Institutional Challenges for EIA Implementation in China: A Case Study of Development versus Environmental Protection', *Environmental Management*, 36, 2005: 121.

14 WTO and developing countries

The case for liberalization of telecommunications services in China

*Yun Zhao**

14.1. Introduction

As developing countries have grown in terms of membership numbers, they have increasingly played an important role in the WTO arena. Encouraging the participation and strengthening the capacity of developing countries in the WTO system has become one of the vital issues since the establishment of the WTO in 1995. The WTO membership in 2001 proves to be a double-edged sword for China. This chapter takes liberalizing telecommunications as an example to elaborate the influence of the WTO membership on China, the biggest developing country.

The telecommunications industry is developing rapidly in China with many improvements underway and plenty of plans in the pipeline. For example, China had 40 million cell phone users in a population of 1.4 billion – something must be done about this pathetic 3 per cent market penetration after 2001. It is generally believed that telecom use, both land-based and wireless, will grow at a rate of 50 per cent or more in the coming years.[1] This rapid rate of growth of course requires appropriate regulation and thorough planning.

Telecommunications services were considered as a monopolized branch due to its sensitiveness to national security.[2] China's telecommunications industry has long been listed as an area prohibiting foreign investment by the previous Ministry of Foreign Trade and Economic Cooperation (MOFTEC).[3] Following the ongoing trend of liberalization in the world, this idea is finally facing evolution. Chinese government acknowledged this trend as inevitable and so had begun the reform as early as the 1980s. However, this process was decided upon whilst still under the illusion that the State played a strong role in telecommunications.

In the negotiations concerning China's entry, the WTO Members had successfully obtained a formal promise from the Chinese government to liberalize telecommunications services.[4] Substantial commitments on telecommunications services were made: 50 per cent ownership was permitted in some sectors within two years of entry (this is a huge advancement from a complete absence of foreign ownership previously).[5] Even though such achievements were obtained only after a series of intensive negotiations and heated discussions, we should be careful not to simply accept the general perception that China has a reluctant and stubborn attitude towards foreign entry. In fact, the Chinese government has, to a certain extent, voluntarily agreed to open its telecommunications market while witnessing the benefits entailed in liberalization that joining the WTO brings.[6]

Once China had formally entered the WTO, it naturally began to carry out its obligations immediately, i.e. from 12 December 2001. It is important to take note of China's efforts to comply with the WTO and offer an analysis on its performance in the up-coming phase where we will witness several substantial implementations.

So far, there are no national laws on telecommunications services in China. However, several regulations have been made by the State Council and relevant ministries. Regulations of the People's Republic of China on Telecommunications (Telecommunications Regulations) is the most important one promulgated by the State Council in September 2000 and since then, provides the most important guidelines for telecommunications services in China. However, with China's accession to the WTO, several new regulations have been made to meet China's commitments under the WTO framework.

Accordingly, this chapter is a timely work in offering tentative evaluation of China's performance and showing the influence of WTO membership on China. The purpose of the chapter is to focus on the Chinese government in producing a pro-competitive market, establishing an independent regulator and realizing other regulatory principles provided in the WTO Reference Paper on Telecommunications Services (Reference Paper).[7] Thus, after a short description of the opening of the telecommunications market, Part 2 elaborates on China's commitments as required by the Reference Paper. We can already see that the Chinese government is on the right track, but there is still much room for improvement.

14.2. Telecommunications liberalization in China: evaluation and comments

14.2.1. General observation

China's entry into the WTO and its impact on the telecommunication industry has brought with it opportunities as well as challenges. In the political economic context, WTO accession has accelerated the transition of China's telecom industry from a planned economy to a market economy. This is characterized by a pattern of competition among multiple players, diversified investment, more rational and effective distribution of telecom resources and the introduction of legal and economic measure to regulate the telecommunication market.[8]

For China's telecom enterprises, entry into the WTO has also created opportunities for reform and development from the introduction of advanced management experience from abroad and participation in international economic and technical cooperation to seeking new financing channels and exploring the international telecom market. Overall, entry into the WTO has pushed China to improve its telecom regulatory standard in line with its commitments. This means opportunities to maintain stable and predictable commercial relationships with China's trading partners.[9]

It is for the first time that telecommunications liberalization is set to a multilateral arena. The positive results achieved so far show the way forward. With this background, it would be sensible for the Chinese government to follow this trend where in endeavouring to protect national interests, the government also tries to absorb the benefits of the liberalization.

The General Agreement on Trade in Services (GATS) has no direct effect on the Members *per se*. The specific and additional commitments attached to the GATS are the direct obligations for the Members and China has made substantial commitments on value-added and basic services. Specific commitments, as shown by the terminology, have been made very specific by the clear definition of the applicable geographical location, percentage and period of time. The geographical scope of the commitments is in accordance with the longstanding preference of China for testing liberalization strategies in individual provinces before applying them to the country as a whole.

China's promising history of compliance with international obligations means that we should have no doubt that China will proceed as it has promised[10] especially since the Chinese government has pledged to do so on various occasions.[11] China even opened up some areas earlier than under the agreement[12] and this was revealed in the annual evaluation made by the WTO, which was rather impressed with China's performance in the first year. The clear wording in the specific commitments leaves no room or grey area for evasion. Nevertheless, the geographical restrictions of the specific commitments are disputed to negate the benefits accorded to foreign value-added service providers. The Ministry of Information Industry (MII) prohibits inter-regional service, i.e. being based in one city but serving customers in another.[13] This practice will be examined to decide on its legality.

China has accepted the Reference Paper as additional commitments, but as discussed earlier, it has been disputed as being too ambiguous. Such ambiguity has led to various considerations during the implementation period, including national conditions, stage of national development and liberalization and the understanding of certain terms. Whether China's performance is in compliance with the Reference Paper is difficult to determine, so an in-depth analysis of the document is required.

To start, we must settle the basis for interpreting the Reference Paper. With no other documents for further clarification, we shall turn to the Vienna Convention on the Law of Treaties. Article 31(1) provides that a treaty shall be interpreted in good faith in accordance with the ordinary meaning to be given to the terms of the treaty in their context, and in light of its object and purpose. Accordingly, when we try to give an appropriate understanding to the Reference Paper, we should resort to the object and purpose of this document and further to the goal of the WTO: trade liberalization – developing an integrated, more viable and durable multilateral trade system.[14]

We shall now look at how China has performed in honouring the Reference Paper. There are three particular points which will be discussed: establishing an independent regulator; procuring a pro-competitive market; and, formulating regulations on foreign investment and licensing practices. The principles of interconnection, universal services, transparency, allocation and use of scarce resources can be achieved with the successful establishment of a fair market and an independent regulator. Since China has only been in the WTO for some years, it is perfectly reasonable to expect strict conformity with all the principles, provided that a reasonable regulatory structure is established. However, measures to achieve a healthy market and regulator are big steps for China to take in its few years of entry.

14.2.2. Establishing an independent regulator

The transformation of telecommunications services regulation is normally targeting the following three aspects: the independence of telecommunications regulation; the separation of regulation and service provision; and the diversification of telecommunications services. The telecommunications regulation policy in China has largely fallen behind the demands of market and technical development, which has become one of the bottlenecks restricting the development of the whole industry.

Since 1998, when the State Council reorganized the administrative structure, there has been much effort to alter this situation.[15] This effort continued when the Ministry of Industry and Information Technology (MIIT) was set up to replace the former Ministry of Information Industry (MII) in 2008. The purpose was simple: to establish a regulatory body in accordance with the international standard. Nevertheless, this reform also aimed at boosting the growth of national carriers in order to meet the competition ahead.

According to the Reference Paper, the regulatory body should be separated from service providers where the regulator should not have any interest in the telecommunications industry.[16] While market forces will play the fundamental role in the regulation of services, the regulatory body will undertake the task of preventing anti-competitive practices. Only when the regulator is separated from providing services, will fair and even-handed regulation be procured. This can build trust from actual service providers and further promote professional operations.

Formerly, the ministry was not simply a regulator; it also owned the telecommunications corporation exclusively with its own investment.[17] Understandable enough, it is difficult for the ministry to take an objective stance with business at stake. This move to separate the Ministry from business shows that the government is heading in the right direction. The Ministry cannot directly involve itself in the network operation and telecommunications corporations are detached from the Ministry with their own management strategy.

The regulatory and operational function was thus nominally split for the first time in nearly fifty years. This ministerial reorganization has formally paved the way for complete separation of the regulatory function from the service provider function.

The Ministry began to perform its task from the date of establishment and one of its most important tasks is to make regulations. Fortunately, an increasing amount of regulations are being placed on the Web, aiming at establishing the rules of market competition. This is a bright start and this task will be enhanced with further liberalization.

We should note that such a separation between the regulatory and operational functions is only a prerequisite, rather than an ambitious strategy to create a fair, transparent, pro-competitive and independent regulatory institution in accordance with the Reference Paper. The Ministry is able to evolve into the independent regulator, though at the present stage, the benefactor of this role is yet unclear.[18] When we analyze further the management of the corporations, we can see that the connection between the Ministry and the corporations still exists.[19]

Historically, the Ministry has a deep-rooted and complicated relationship with China Telecom and other regulated carriers. The Ministry enjoys the power to appoint, promote and dismiss key officials of postal, telephone and telegraph branches, including China Telecom, China Mobile and Unicom. For instance, the former Vice Minister of the Ministry of Posts and Telecommunications (MPT) was transferred to the position of Chairman of Board of China Telecom.[20] As a result, there is still doubt concerning the real independency of the regulator. The event of raising international interconnection fee unilaterally in November 2002 has further aroused doubts concerning the independence of the services and the functions of the regulator.

Considering the present political and economic situation in China, this phenomenon is unavoidable and since it is difficult to make drastic change within such a short period, we ought to accept the progress that has been made and recognize the correct direction we ought to be taking. We should maintain optimistic expectations and hopefully, with further implementation of the WTO commitments, a truly independent regulator will not be just a dream, but a reality.

14.2.3. Producing a pro-competitive market

The WTO is an organization promoting liberalization of trade. This can be realized through different means – an important way has been constructing a competitive environment. In certain situations, competition and liberalization have been used interchangeably and in the present context, competition is believed to be a way to realize total liberalization.

In the WTO Reference Paper, principles have been laid down to promote competition. Direct reference can be made to the first principle where the competitive safeguards exert less direct or indirect effects in establishing a competitive environment for telecommunications. Since China has formally committed to this Paper, measures should be undertaken to stay within the obligations. As the Minister of the MII stated, China would not only continue to reinforce regulatory efforts in the telecommunications industry by carefully examining the qualifications of all foreign investors, but would facilitate orderly competition according to the relevant regulations.[21]

The process began even before China's formal entry into the WTO; several structural modifications were carried out in February 1999 when the State Council passed the plan to restrict China Telecom;[22] three corporations – China Mobile, China Telecom and ChinaSat – were organized, respectively, in December 1999, January 2000 and June 2000. Meanwhile, Unicom was also reconstructed to include Paging Corporation. A competitive structure came into being with two or more corporations involved in each type of basic services.

It is obvious that this reform has substantially reformulated the competitive structure for basic services in China. Competition in the real sense has been introduced in the Chinese market, though such competition is carried out among the Chinese service providers themselves only. In order for extension to foreign providers to occur, it is necessary to formulate coherent telecommunications policy to safeguard competition, which will avoid cross-subsidy, distorted tariffs and highly concentrated markets.

Furthermore, competition should exist in at least three areas of the telecommunications services: competition between telecommunications expenses and other expenses for ultimate users (consumers); competition among service providers and competition among interconnection providers. Only when these three platforms are totally open for competition can the telecommunications market experience full and true liberalization. The restriction on liberalization on any one platform will distort the logic of market economy. Thus, full liberalization of the telecommunications market will be the ultimate goal. With further liberalization, as shown in the agenda, foreign service providers can gain more and more access. The period in between creates a golden opportunity for Chinese providers to gain experience and prepare for the fierce international competition, not only in the Chinese market, but also in the foreign markets.

14.2.4. Formulating regulations on foreign investment in telecommunications services and licensing practices

While the rest of the world retrenches, China continues to gear up for investing in the telecommunications infrastructure. In the past years, total investment in telecommunications infrastructure has registered an impressive annual increase of 62 per cent.[23] During this period, some of the largest telecom companies entrenched in the Chinese market through various means. China's WTO membership has no doubt led to upsurge in investment.

For foreign providers, joint venture (referred to as 'localization' in the telecommunications industry) has been considered as one of the best ways to invest.

They can take advantage of China's considerable low labour costs and bypass the tariff and non-tariff barriers. Formerly, to evade the prohibition of direct involvement of foreign providers in this field, the so-called foreign–Chinese–Chinese joint venture has been constructed.[24] Foreigner providers seeking to invest must negotiate a pre-determined rate of return with Unicom and then link with a local partner in a joint venture, which then funds Unicom.[25] However, after a drastic change in the attitudes of the Chinese government, this practice was considered in breach.[26] A statement was released stating that such contracts executed between Unicom and foreign investment enterprises were contrary to State policy and regulation.[27]

With WTO's commitments allowing for foreign investment, joint ventures could revive again in a more direct form: foreign–Chinese. Closely related with this development are the two regulations preventing foreign investment in telecommunications that were repealed on 11 December 2001. On the same date, the State Council promulgated the Provisions on the Administration of Foreign-Invested Telecommunications, permitting foreign investment in the telecoms sector in the form of a Chinese–foreign structure.[28]

Moreover, anticipating foreign direct investment, the MII has introduced several regulations.[29] For example, the Regulation on the Administration of Foreign-Funded Telecommunications Enterprises tightens the management strings to licensed joint-ventures carriers, acknowledging the legality of foreign direct investment.[30] It stipulated rules for joint ventures set up by basic telecom operators and other domestic State-owned firms. If the licensed carrier holds less than 51 per cent of the shares, the joint venture should apply to the MII for a license before engaging in telecom business. If the licensed carrier holds more than 51 per cent of the shares, the joint venture should register with the MII if it wishes to operate a telecom business.[31] It is clear from this regulation that investors are limited to high-profit foreign firms and high-profit Chinese firms, so this will narrow the pool of foreign firms qualified to enjoy China's market access commitments.[32]

Some may argue such a regulation restricts the threshold requirements for qualified foreign firms. However, as long as all the foreign firms are treated under the same process, there should be no violation of Most-Favoured-Nation (MFN) obligations.[33] Moreover, such restrictions are in line with international practice and thus cause no violation of national treatment obligations.[34]

Another change is that more and more telecommunications companies are publicly listed in the foreign stock markets.[35] This has been one efficient way of absorbing capital from international channels and benefiting from the experience of modern enterprise management. For foreign investors, public listing also presents a unique means to invest in China's telecommunications.[36] The amount of possible foreign investment shall comply with the progressive process of China's commitments.

A new regulation has been adopted regarding foreign capital in the profitable sector.[37] This regulation was issued after China's formal entry and reiterated its commitments in the WTO. According to Article 6, the limit for foreign investment in basic and value-added telecommunications services is, respectively, 49 and 50 per cent. Applications should be made to responsible departments in the MII, which are required to examine and make decisions within 180 and 90 days for basic and value-added services, respectively.[38] The provision of time limits for making decisions can successfully avoid former strategies of delay, to prevent the entry of foreign competitors.

Other new regulations include the Administrative Regulations on Operational Licenses for Telecom Business,[39] and the MII Rule on Management of Telecom Business Operating Licenses.[40] All the new regulations[41] have closely aligned foreign investment requirements with China's WTO commitments and allowed the MII to gradually lift equity and geographic restrictions in accordance with China's WTO telecommunications commitments.[42]

14.2.5. Miscellaneous

To promote a competitive environment, the government is required to take more measures than those listed in the foregoing section. As shown in the Reference Paper, interconnection, universal service, licensing criteria, etc. shall be available to all the existing and potential providers.

First of all, the obligation of transparency is very important.[43] Chinese law is generally believed to be highly generalized and lacking in procedural guidelines.[44] Formerly there were quite a lot of internal regulations which were unknown or difficult to trace for providers thereof. Such a vague legal framework reflects a tension between encouraging foreign investment and maintaining State control over the economy.[45] The WTO requires a single access point for Chinese law and regulations, so China needs to streamline the multilayered complexity that plagues its present-day legal system.[46] Now, with the assistance of electronic facilities, the government can make the access to all those regulations easier and more systematic for the public. With the Web site of the Ministry, the purpose of transparency can be easily achieved. However, continuous efforts will be maintained to provide updated information, guidance and efficient response.

Nevertheless, as described by one practitioner, the present regulatory structure is an odd mix of detailed regulations in certain areas but lacking in a comprehensive national telecoms law and governing regulations which address industry concerns.[47] The current absence of a telecommunications law has subjected telecommunications policy to the discretion of officials.[48] This means that it is even more important to pass a telecommunications law, which can work as the constitutional document for telecommunications services in China, covering regulatory aspects of the telecommunications services.[49] Such a law will define the government's role in the industry, allow deregulation of tariffs, outline rules for new entrants and foster orderly competition.[50] This legislation is an urgent task for the government and it is to be noted that China must take into account the rules-of-law of the WTO while making economic policies for telecommunications.[51]

Secondly, efficient interconnection will be vital to the entry of foreign providers. Formerly, China has been reluctant to mandate the interconnection[52] and various obstacles were created to delay or deny the interconnection of other providers. In this era of liberalization, we ought to try to figure out the crux of the problem – the reallocation of economic benefits. 'Temporary Regulation on Telecommunications Network Interconnection' has been issued earlier by the MII. However, this Regulation is considered as insufficient compared with the requirements of the Reference Paper. For example, the problem of sufficient unbundling requirement is missing; nothing in the Regulation touched on the issue of number portability.[53] Thus, it is necessary to obtain opinions from existing service providers and offer a complete legal framework for interconnection, meeting the requirement stated in the Reference Paper that competitors are permitted to interconnect with public telecommunications networks at any technically feasible point, under non-discriminatory terms.[54] The interconnection rates must be non-discriminatory, cost-oriented, transparent, reasonable, economically feasible and sufficiently unbundled. Furthermore, the interconnection procedures and agreements must be made publicly available.[55]

Thirdly, universal service is of paramount importance to China. These policies are not regarded as anti-competitive *per se* if they are administered in a transparent, non-discriminatory and competitively neutral manner and are not more burdensome than necessary.[56] Deciding on how to provide services to the Western part of China is a tough issue for the Chinese government.[57] The harsh natural conditions and sparse population has directly led to costly services. The 'Grand Exploitation of Western Areas' Movement mobilized by the Chinese government can serve as an impetus to achieve this goal. Favourable policies are provided for investment in Western areas, but it is important in this regard to prevent 'cream-skimming' and fairly allocate the universal service obligation among the targeted telecommunications service providers in accordance with the requirements of the Reference Paper.

Fourthly, technical considerations should be put in place to realize the real convergence of telecommunications in China. The resolution of all the issues concerning the entrance of foreign providers shall be based on technical consideration. This would mean that, implementing regulations will be well in place offering a clear guidance on technical factors. For example, the former administrative-oriented allocation of frequency system should be substituted by an objective, pro-competitive one.

Lastly, national security concerns for telecommunications are equally shared by Members. Luckily, Article XIV *bis* of the GATS provides the possibility of actions for the protection of essential security interests in time of war or other emergencies in international relations.[58] Relevant provision can also be found in Article XIV where measures can be adopted or enforced to protect public morals or to maintain public order.[59] Thus, the loose wordings of 'emergency' and 'public order' offer the possibility of adopting measures out of national security considerations. These two terms are fully within the discretion of the

Members.[60] The 1993 National Security Law of China has defined five classes of acts that endanger national security.[61] With the WTO entry, China should reconsider the list and clarify the application of the provision in telecommunications services. While striving to observe the WTO obligations, China should provide the justified legal framework for possible deviation.

14.3. Conclusion

The WTO Membership has had a tremendously positive impact on Members' national liberalization agenda, but such effects shall vary and mainly depend on the specific institutional endowments and regulatory stances of Members.[62] When studying the WTO's effects on a specific Member, it is necessary to note the institutions' objective within that specific Member.

The process of China's liberalization of telecommunications services has been accelerated by its entry into the WTO, and it is believed that it has posed substantial influence on China's political and economic reforms. The World Bank predicts that China will be the world's second largest trader by 2020.[63] The growth of the Chinese economy combined with the development currently taking place in Chinese telecommunications will no doubt contribute to further increase of foreign investment.

Within a short period, great achievements have already been made and this has been recognized internationally. These developments have brought benefits not only to the WTO Members in gaining profits through entering the enormous Chinese market, but also to the Chinese residents who can directly benefit from the lower service fee and better service quality. With the 'win-win' situation, the accession itself has even brought further gains to the world as a whole: since the potential influence of telecommunications on national economic development is so great, the chances of this positive impact extending worldwide is extremely high, providing that the WTO commitments are further implemented by the Chinese government. This chapter can thus conclude in a positive way to view the WTO memberships for developing countries in general. As long as the special situations of developing countries are well taken into account and various interests are well balanced, the WTO memberships will offer developing countries ample opportunities to interact with other countries and achieve further healthy development not only economically, but also politically.

Notes

* An earlier version of the paper was published in *Journal of Chinese and Comparative Law*, 6, 2003: 169–187. The work described in this paper was fully supported by a Grant from the Research Grants Council of the Hong Kong Special Administrative Region, China (Project No. 755109).

1 The Impact of WTO on China's Telecommunications, available at www.es123.com (accessed 9 April 2010).

2 Foreign investment has been shielded in basic services since the very beginning. Limited competition in wireless sector was introduced only with the entry of Unicom in 1994. *See*, H. Chang and Lian Tong, 'A Quantum Leap in the Reform of China's Telecommunications', *Telecommunications Policy*, 18, 1994: 206–210.

3 *See*, Catalogue for the Guidance of Foreign Investment Industries which was promulgated by the former State Development Planning Commission, the former State Economy and Trade Commission and the former Ministry of Foreign Trade and Economic Cooperation on 11 March 2002. This was amended by the Ministry of Commerce in 2004 and came into force on 1 January 2005. Prior to 1994, China's telecommunications industry was a monopoly market dominated by the State run China Telecom.

4 *See*, e.g. Historic US–China Trade Agreement, available at http://www.sinomania.com (accessed 9 April 2010); The US–China WTO Accession Deal: A Clear Win for U.S. High Technology, Greater Openness and U.S. Interests, 1 March 2000, available at http://clinton6.nara.gov/2000/03/2000-03-01-fact-sheet-on-us-china-wto-accession-deal.html (accessed 9 April 2010)

5 C. Chandler, 'China Clears Barrier to WTO', *Washington Post*, 15 September 2001, D1. *See also*, European Commission, EU–China WTO Accession Negotiations, Highlights of the EU–China Agreement on WTO, available at http://trade.ec.europa.eu/ (accessed 9 April 2010).

6 *See*, X. Fan, 'China's WTO Accession and Its Telecom Liberalization', International Communications Study Program, Center for Strategic and International Studies, Washington D.C., 8.

7 Available at www.wto.org/english/tratop_e/serv_e/telecom_e/telecom_e.htm (accessed 9 April 2010).

8 J. Su, Director General, Ministry of Information Industry, China, WTO: Opportunities and Challenges, Address at the ITU Telecom Asia, December 2002, available at www.itu.int/TELECOM/ast2002/cfp/pap_5613.pdf (accessed 9 April 2010).

9 *Ibid.*

10 China's record, though mixed, is better than most detractors think. *See*, D. H. Rosen, 'China and the World Trade Organization: An Economic Balance Sheet', *Institute for International Economics, International Economics Policy Briefs*, June 1999 available at www.iie.com/publications/pb/pb.cfm?researchid=93 (accessed 9 April 2010).

11 The Ministry of Information Industry (MII) stated that administrative statutes, including the regulations on Computer Networks and Information Safety Management, would be adopted to facilitate China's entry into the WTO.

12 For example, China will open up mobile phone markets two years sooner than under the agreement, *see*, www.interlinkchina.com/wto.htm (accessed 9 April 2010).

13 *See*, G. Blue, China WTO Written Comments by Trade Policy Staff Committee, Office of the U.S. Trade Representative, 10 September 2002, available at www.uscib.org (accessed 9 April 2010).

14 Final Act Embodying Results of the Uruguay Round of Multilateral Trade Negotiations, 15 April 1994, Legal Instruments – Results of the Uruguay Round Vol. 1, (1994): 33 I.L.M. 1125, 1144. *See also*, J. H. Jackson, 'GATT and Recent International Trade Problems', *Maryland Journal of International Law & Trade*, 11, 1987: 8.

15 Morrison & Foerster LLP, *China's Telecommunications Industry: The New Ministry of Information Industry (MII) and Foreign Investment Opportunities*, 1 March 1998, available at http://mofo.com (accessed 9 April 2010).
16 B. Zhang and M. W. Peng, 'Telecom Competition, Post-WTO Style', *China Business Review*, 1 May 2000, 5.
17 It is described as the mode of 'twin status as both referee and player'. *See*, Y. Xu and D. Pitt, 'One Country, Two Systems: Contrasting Approaches to Telecommunications Deregulation in Hong Kong and China', *Telecommunications Policy* 23, 1999: 248.
18 M. Forney, 'China Gives Foreign Firms Telecom Access: New Rules May Open Sector, Maintain Regulatory Ties', *Asian Wall Street Journal*, June 2000: 7.
19 J. Leahy, 'China: Foreigners Eye the China Pie', *Financial Times*, 13 November 2000.
20 J. Wang, 'Breakup of China Telecom', U.S. & Foreign Commercial Service, May 2000.
21 *See*, 'China's Net Czar Downplays WTO Effect on High Tech Industry', *China Online*, 19 November 1999.
22 C. B. Chuan *et al.*, 'Telecommunications and Information Technology' in J. J. Williams, *et al.* (eds), *Business Opportunities in Northeastern China*, Singapore, New York: Prentice Hall, 1999: 244.
23 'Telecommunications Industry in China', available at www.interliance.com (accessed 9 April 2010).
24 M. O'Neill, 'Beijing May Scrap Unicom Foreign-Investment Formula', *South China Morning Post-Business Post*, 23 September 1998: 4.
25 R. Janda, 'Benchmarking a Chinese Offer on Telecommunications: Context and Comparisons', *International Journal of Communications Law & Policy*, 3, Summer 1999: 5.
26 For further discussion, *see*, L. D. Chuang, 'Investing in China's Telecommunications Market: Reflections on the Rule of Law and Foreign Investment in China', *Journal of International Law & Business*, 20, Spring 2000: 516–522; M. Forney and S. Webb, 'China Phone Firm Remains Ensnared by Bureaucracy', *Wall Street Journal*, 13 June 2000.
27 'China: Telecoms Firm Told to Abandon Foreign-Funded Joint Ventures', BBC Monitoring Asia Pacific – Political, BBC Worldwide Monitoring, 4 February 1999.
28 *Decree No. 333* of the State Council of the People's Republic of China, available at www.chinaitlaw.org/?p1=print&p2=041001004415 (accessed 9 April 2010).
29 One set of rules, entitled Framework Regulations on Liberalizing Last Mile Broadband Access, targets the growing number of unlicensed broadband operators, who must reapply for a license. Another Regulation bans companies from extending their licenses to their joint-venture units without approval.
30 This Regulation was passed at the 49th executive meeting of the State Council on 11 December 2001 and promulgated for implementation as of 1 January 2002. This Regulation has been revised on 10 September 2008.
31 The Regulation on the Management of Foreign-Funded Telecommunications Enterprises, Article 6. 'China's Telecom Market, Legislation Undergoing Changes as Country Readies for Global Trade', *Pulse Online*, Vol. 2 Issue 12, October 2001, available at http://pulse.tiaonline.org/pulse_archive/pulse.tiaonline.org/article-591--.html?id=591 (accessed 9 April 2010).

32 As provided, the select group of foreign firms must have telecom revenues greater than US$10 billion during the last two years prior to applying to operate in China; Chinese partner should be appointed as chairperson of the joint venture. *See*, Telecommunications Regulations of the People's Republic of China (Guowuling No. 291), 25 September 2000; M. Forney, 'Chinese Investors Offer Static on Telecom Rules: Smaller Foreign Investors May Get Shut Out', *Asian Wall Street Journal*, 26 September 2000.

33 L. B. Sherman, 'China after the WTO, What You Need to Know Now: The Impact of China's WTO Entry on the Telecommunications and IT Sectors', PLI Order No. A0-0095, at 230–231 (February 2001).

34 *See*, R. Abramson, 'Catching Flies with Chopsticks: China's Strategic Leap into Wireless Telecommunications', *Minnesota Journal of Global Trade*, 11, Winter 2002: 31.

35 For example, China Unicom sold more than a 20 per cent share on the New York and Hong Kong stock exchanges, raising US$5.65 billion. *See*, P. Wonacott, 'China Maps IPO to Gird for Foreign Telecom Invasion', *Wall Street Journal*, 6 December 2000.

36 *See*, e.g. 'China Unicom's IPO Rings up $4.92 Billion', *Asian Wall Street Journal*, 19 June 2000, 14; R. Lachica, 'China Unicom Gets Strong Welcome in First Session', *Asian Wall Street Journal*, 22 June 2000, 2.

37 The Regulation on the Management of Foreign Investment in Telecommunications Enterprises was promulgated on 11 December 2001 and came into force on 1 January 2002.

38 Article 11 of the Regulation.

39 Issued by the MII on 26 December 2001 and took effect on 1 January 2002.

40 *See*, MII Order No. 19.

41 One exception is the Administrative Measures for International Gateway Facilities, which was issued on 26 June 2002 and took effect on 1 October 2002. This regulation restricts operation of gateway facilities to wholly State-owned telecommunications providers, thus was claimed not to be in accordance with the market access commitments.

42 G. Blue, China's WTO Written Comments by Trade Policy Staff Committee, Office of the U.S. Trade Representative, 10 September 2002, available at http://www.uscib.org (accessed 9 April 2010).

43 S. Ostry, 'China and the WTO: The Transparency Issues', *UCLA Journal of International Law & Foreign Affairs*, 3, 1998: 11.

44 C. D. Lee, 'Legal Reform in China: A Role for Nongovernmental Organizations', *Yale Journal of International Law*, 25, 2000: 368.

45 P. B. Potter, 'Foreign Investment in the People's Republic of China Dilemmas of State Control' in S. Lubman (ed.), *China's Legal Reforms*, Oxford, New York: Oxford University Press, 1996: 155.

46 Ostry, *supra notes* 43, 13; B. Bacon, 'The People's Republic of China and the World Trade Organization: Anticipating a United States Congressional Dilemma', *Minnesota Journal of Global Trade*, 9, 2000: 387.

47 J. P. L. Teoh, 'Sector Seeks Level Pathway between the Legal Potholes', *South China Morning Post*, 11 June 1998.

48 N. Ingelbrecht, 'The China Syndrome', *Communications Week International*, 1 June 1998.

49 In September 2000, China released the Telecommunications Administration Regulations as a preview of the anticipated comprehensive Telecommunications Law.

50 C. Chan, 'Unicom Document Reveals New Law's Intent', *South China Morning Post*, 18 May 2000.

51 The most important characteristic of the WTO is that it is a rules-oriented organization. For discussion, *see*, G. Winham, 'The World Trade Organization: Institution-Building in the Multilateral Trade System', *The World Economy*, 21, 1998: 362.

52 R. B. Chong and W. Chow, 'Financing Telecommunications Project in Asia: A Promising Regulatory Perspective', *Federal Communications Law Journal*, 52, 1999: 14.

53 For discussion on number portability, *see*, B. Petrazzini, *Global Telecom Talks: A Trillion Dollar Deal*, Washington D.C.: Institute for International Economics, 1996: 64.

54 *See* Reference Paper to the Fourth Protocol to the General Agreement on Trade in Services, 30 April 1996: 36 I.L.M., at 2. Interconnection.

55 *Ibid.*, at 2.2 (a) and (b); 2.3 and 2.4.

56 FCC Memo, Connecting the Globe: A Regulator's Guide to Building a Global Information Community, Universal Service, Part VI, 16 June 1999, available at www.fcc.gov/connectglobe/ (accessed 9 April 2010).

57 J. Ure, 'China's Telecommunications: Options and Opportunities', in P. S. N. Lee (ed.), *Telecommunications and Development in China*, Cresskill, NJ: Hampton Press, 1997, 248; L. Ladany, *Law and Legality in China: The Testament of a China-Watcher*, [London]: University of Hawaii Press, 1992: 17; Z. He, A History of Telecommunications in China, Development and Policy Implications, in P. S. N. Lee (ed.), *Telecommunications and Development in China*, Cresskill: Hampton Press, 1997: 84.

58 It provides that nothing in this Agreement shall be construed to: (b) to prevent any Member from taking any action which it considers necessary for the protection of its essential security interests…(iii) taken in time of war or other emergency in international relations …

59 It provides:

> subject to the requirement that such measures are not applied in a manner which would constitute a means of arbitrary or unjustifiable discrimination between countries where like conditions prevail, or a disguised restriction on trade in services, nothing in this Agreement shall be construed to prevent the adoption or enforcement by any Member of measures: (a) necessary to protect public moral or to maintain public order …

60 D. Shapiro, 'Be Careful What You Wish for: U.S. Politics and the Future of the National Security Exception to the GATT', *George Washington Journal of International Law & Economics*, 31, 1997: 97; M. Hahn, 'Vital Interests and the Law of GATT: An Analysis of GATT's Security Exception', *Michigan Journal of International Law*, 12, 1991: 558.

61 Article 4 identifies the following five acts: plotting to subvert the government, dismember the State or overthrow the socialist system participating in foreign intelligence organizations or accepting missions from such organizations or their agents; stealing, probing, purchasing or unlawfully providing State secrets; instigating, bribing or luring State personnel to defect; and any other sabotage endangering State security. For a complete analysis of this legislation, *see*, H. Fu and R. Cullen, 'National Security Law in China', *Columbia Journal of Transnational Law*, 34, 1996: 449.

62 *See*, *generally*, D. North, *Institutions*, *Institutional Change*, *and Economic Performance*, Cambridge: Cambridge University Press, 1990: 101.

63 Y. Huang, Director, World Bank China Program, Realizing China's Potential, Address at the Asian Investment Conference, March 2000, available at www.worldbank.org.cn/English/content/529z6146591.shtml (accessed 9 April 2010). *See also*, W. Martin and C. Bach, 'The Importance of State Trading in China's Trade Regime', in F. M. Abbott (ed.), *China in the World Trading System*, Cambridge: Kluwer Law International, 1998: 155.

Index